THE WORLD OF ARCHAEOLOGY
General Editor: GLYN DANIEL

The Neolithic of the Near East

JAMES MELLAART

The Neolithic of the Near East.

with 164 illustrations

CHARLES SCRIBNER'S SONS · NEW YORK

To my parents-in-law,
Ülviye and Kadri Cenani

Contents

The purpose of this book is to bring together in a coherent account the fragmented and often little known material that forms the basis of our knowledge of the development of the Neolithic of the Near East. This material, most of which is only partly published, is rather like a roughly cemented breccia at the bottom, that grades into a more tightly knit conglomerate of facts nearer the top of the chronological sequence. The geological parallel is useful, for it emphasizes how uneven is our evidence, very rough and ready for the early periods, less so in the later, yet varying in weight and volume. The matrix which holds together these snippets of information about man's cultural development is coarse and patchy at first but becomes more fine-grained as time goes on – it is the continuity of human life and endeavour. Cultures and civilizations rise and fall, some disappear altogether, blotted out from the face of the earth, but man, who made and unmade them, remains; man does not disappear and although he may change his way of life, culture, religion, language, habits, etc., he cannot change his ancestors. All of us are descendants of Upper Palaeo-lithic *Homo sapiens*, or as it was put in a simpler age, the sons of Adam. Beyond a certain point every genealogical line fails, yet these ancestral figures had ancestors also, of whom nothing is remembered. The bulk of a population is almost certainly autochthonous, whatever accretions were made by time and place, but it is usually the last important accretion that ultimately sets the tone. This process has been going on since time immemorial yet people still do the same things as their remote ancestors did and it is this underlying continuity that lends to the study of prehistoric archaeology a particular charm of its own.

I have tried to preserve this continuity by describing events within an area or tradition until some important break occurs. Hence we start with the Epipalaeolithic groups in the Levant (chapter 1) and the Zagros (chapter 2); the Anatolian development (chapter 3) that overlaps aceramic and ceramic cultures, usually split by a gap in the record elsewhere, for example in Mesopotamia (chapter 4) and Iran (chapter 5), is described next. From Iran it is a natural step to both its northern and eastern neighbours on the margins of the Near East: Transcaucasia (chapter 6) and Trans-caspia (chapter 7). In chapter 8, the ceramic Neolithic of Syria and Palestine is dealt with; it can be read after chapter 1 in chrono-logical order, or after chapter 3 on Anatolia and 4 on Mesopotamia to clarify the interaction and influences exerted by these two areas successively. Likewise, chapter 9, on Greece and the Balkans, logically comes after Anatolia (chapter 3), from which the cultural impetus came. There follows, by way of contrast, a short account of developments in Egypt and the Sahara (chapter 10) which rounds off our description of the Neolithic cultures of the Near East, but in a final chapter (11) some of the evidence is summarized and a few lines of investigation usually ignored by the archaeologist are briefly pursued. For reasons of space, footnotes have had to be dispensed with but a bibliography, divided into chapters, is provided, stating the sources from which the information is extracted.

Chronological and agricultural tables as well as a list of C14 dates complete the text. In the choice of illustrations I have been guided by two considerations: to provide a certain number of familiar ones because they are essential, while at the same time trying to introduce material that is new or not easily accessible. Some pottery from Iraq and Iran has been tentatively restored on paper to show both shape and decoration, but no accuracy is claimed.

The author acknowledges the help given by many colleagues throughout the world who have contributed photographs, personal information or offprints of their work, thus stimulating research. To all of them, too numerous to mention here, I tender my thanks.

London. January 1975

Introduction

*Pour bien savoir les choses, il en faut savoir le détail; et comme il est
presque infini, nos connaissances sont toujours superficielles et imparfaites.*
La Rochefoucauld

The subject of this book is the cultural development of man in the
Near East over a period of some ten thousand years, from *c.* 15000
to 5000 B C. The story begins with Epipalaeolithic hunters developing a new awareness of their environment and its food resources,
both plant and animal, and the ways in which this influenced his
equipment and way of life. Even before the beginning of the
Holocene, *c.* 8000 B C, some of these groups had started to experiment with the planting of crops – the first steps towards agriculture,
and the domestication of some animals. The Neolithic, i.e. the
period of early farming, had begun. Over the next millennium
the new techniques spread far and wide along new trade routes,
and by *c.* 7000 B C (6000 B C in radiocarbon terms) Neolithic
communities were established from southeastern Europe to the
desert edge of Central Asia, and from the Caucasus to southern
Palestine. The next two millennia saw the consolidation of the
Neolithic, further expansion into Europe and the rise of metallurgy
in the highland areas of the Near East, but its most characteristic
product was painted pottery, in which was expressed a sense of
individuality, artistry and abstraction lacking among many of the
earlier, purely artifactual household assemblages. This mature
Neolithic phase of the Early Painted Pottery cultures has frequently
been referred to as Early Chalcolithic in Anatolia, a term that has
lost its meaning now we know that metal objects were in use in
certain parts of the Near East as early as the eighth millennium.

A date of *c.* 5200 B C has been chosen to end our account of the
Neolithic (exceeded only in chapter 10). In Mesopotamia and
Iran it is marked by many innovations: cast copper tools and
weapons, wheel-made pottery (Iran). In Syria also metal now
appears and in the Balkans a new phase, the Middle Neolithic,
begins. In Anatolia and Greece changes had appeared earlier so
that the date of 5200 B C is here an arbitrary division, but in Egypt
it marks the beginning of the local Neolithic.

This account is concerned with cultural developments over a
long span of time and within a vast area, which extends from the
Hungarian plain to Central Asia and the Sahara. Since Herodotus
it has been customary to separate Europe from Asia; I prefer to
ignore this artificial division. Southeastern Europe was not a
backwater that received civilization from the Fertile Crescent
over the Anatolian bridge. On the contrary, it formed as much a
part of the Near East as did Turkmenia, Transcaucasia, the Persian
Gulf regions, or Sinai – to cite some other neglected areas. Over the
last 2500 years southeastern Europe has played an important role
in the history of successive empires, from the Persian to the

Ottoman, only one of which, the Roman, was neither exclusively East Mediterranean nor Near Eastern.

In the period with which this book is concerned neither Egypt nor Mesopotamia had yet reached a position of cultural dominance over its neighbours. There were farming villages on the Rhine before there were any in Egypt, and urban civilization, long thought to be a Mesopotamian invention, now has predecessors at sites like Jericho or Çatal Hüyük, in Palestine and Anatolia, long regarded as backwaters. In recent years it has become abundantly clear that there was no area in the Near East during the Neolithic period that can claim an uninterrupted cultural development; cultures rise and fall and the bits are picked up by others in their turn. In Egypt and Sumer in dynastic times, as prehistory faded into dim history in the third millennium B C, new factors were at work: stronger political and economic control which ensured a stability of culture that could and did outlast political strife, foreign invasion, floods and disasters with greater success than had earlier cultures. Egyptian, Mesopotamian and Elamite civilizations each lasted nearly three thousand years, or about three times as long as the longest Neolithic or Chalcolithic culture. However, Egypt and Mesopotamia happen to be the exceptions, neither being typical of its time. Minoan, Mycenaean, Hittite, Hurrian or Indus civilizations, splendid and short-lived, were probably more normal and closer to earlier cultures in their time spans.

With only a fraction of the findings adequately published – most of the material on which this book is based comes from preliminary reports and notices – all one can hope to achieve is a compilation of the evidence, while suggesting some lines of development. A great deal more hard work will have to be done in archaeology before one can hope to answer the many questions of why and how early farming started. I am suspicious of theoretical short cuts, especially when they come from outside the discipline.

Archaeology is concerned with human beings in the past and therefore such a study is clearly part of the humanities. Rigid, dogmatic and pseudo-scientific approaches to archaeology are unlikely to contribute much in the positive sense. Archaeology has been called many things by many scholars, yet all agree that it is not an exact science. One can measure, weigh, classify, etc. man's relics and artifacts, and this all archaeologists do; but we cannot classify man's behaviour patterns and predict what he will do even now, far less deduce how he should have reacted in the past. A study of history shows at once that it is the exceptions – the élite – who are the bearers of culture, not the masses. Even today, in spite of greatly improved living conditions and ample opportunity, culture is still a veneer. The study of cultural development in the prehistoric past – the subject of archaeology – is almost confined to tracing changes and progress, whereas anthropology when studying 'primitive cultures' is more often concerned with those communities which for one reason or another got left behind. In the prehistory of the Near East also there were cultural backwaters, peripheral villages, nomads, hunters and fishermen, and these same conditions still obtain today. The reasons are not always only economic or geographical, they can be political, racial, or social, also. It is perfectly possible to find cave occupation, temporary camp sites of nomads and essentially Neolithic villages in the twentieth century A D. Study of this kind should be made by anthropologists, anxious to formulate theories about prehistoric man in the Near East, for in this field there is a good chance that the present groups may have inherited cultural traits and behaviour patterns from prehistoric and historical people in this same area. One can compare 'like with like', but it is dangerous to introduce concepts derived from a study of the 'present-day Neolithic' of, say, the highlands of New Guinea to that of the Near East or for that matter any other unrelated area. Near Eastern archaeologists, then, make a habit of studying the progressive aspects of culture, the pioneering efforts of an élite. Hence the choice of large sites, palaces and temples, royal tombs and graves in general, and towns rather than villages for excavation in the historical periods.

For earlier periods, poorer in monuments, the same choice of richer and more promising sites prevails whether in the Neolithic or the Palaeolithic. As archaeology is a quest for knowledge one naturally selects sites which one hopes – for one cannot be certain before excavation – will yield the best possible return for the money invested. The picture of cultural progress is based on the best material that can be found, but this search for the products of an 'aristocratic' élite never rules out the existence of less civilized communities. They inevitably existed – as they exist today – but they are less likely to satisfy research and no discriminating archaeologist will dig a poor site if he knows of, and has the opportunity to dig a rich one. Whereas it is impossible from the remains of a village to assess the potential wealth of a town site of the period, the reverse process is fairly simple. In many cultures, for example the Palestinian Pre-Pottery Neolithic B culture, evidence from both town and village is available, but in many others it is not. Ideally, then, several sites of a culture should be excavated, in order to establish at least the upper and medium cultural levels.

As archaeology in the Near East is thus mainly concerned with the 'aristocratic' aspects of culture, it is essential not to underestimate the role of the individual in the community. Throughout recorded history the arts and crafts, spiritual and temporal achievements have been linked with named individuals. Exceptional men are unlikely to have developed only since prehistory ended, otherwise there would have been no cultural development. The tendency to draw a veil of anonymity over prehistoric cultures is clearly misplaced; communities do not invent, initiate, or formulate ideas; individuals do, and then persuade or compel others to adopt the invention or the idea. Certain to us seemingly essential inventions such as pottery were not adopted by neighbouring groups, or tried and discarded. Possible reasons for this are not hard to find: the force of tradition 'what the peasant does not know he does not eat' – inadequate craftsmanship, learning or resources (bad clay, poor kilns) even an inherent suspicion of what a neighbour was doing and making. The presence or absence of certain categories of tools or utensils in cultures which are clearly in contact with each other are often striking and inexplicable. They show that man could be no less irrational than he is now. All this indicates that one can predict man's behaviour neither as an individual nor as a group. Marked individualism of culture is an extraordinarily strong feature of the Neolithic cultures of the Near East. It is impossible to say within certain technological limits of course, what was beyond their capabilities and this is clearly demonstrated by the number of surprising things each new site reveals. It is for this reason that one should keep an open mind and study the evidence rather than advance premature theories about how things should have developed and where and then manipulate the evidence to suit. Such methods, while they may save money and effort, would seem to be neither 'new' nor 'scientific' – a fashionable word that has acquired arrogant overtones; on the contrary, they would seem to continue the ignorant approach of the eighteenth century. In archaeology we cannot afford to formulate global theory until we have the evidence, and data are far too thin on the ground to warrant philosophical tracts on the development of agriculture, etc. What we need is more, not less excavation of a sustained and balanced kind, and not a random sampling of numerous sites; just as one should no longer be digging for treasure, art objects or tablets *per se*, but in order to acquire general information, so one should not reverse the process and ignore art, architecture and religion and only concentrate on economic details, however fascinating these may be.

The development of new methods and machinery to recover material where other methods fail can only be welcomed, but they must be put to intelligent use. An inventor of a technique can hardly blame his predecessors for not having used it. What is useful at one site may be superfluous or useless at another, and what should be avoided at all costs is a single and dogmatically rigid approach.

Being human, I suggest that we look at archaeology in a human way and try to discover the men and women who made what we excavate. We find his mortal remains, his food and drink, both plant and animal, his environment, the land with flora and fauna and other resources. From the bones his state of health may be deduced. Then there are the tools he made to get his food and prepare it – those needed in building houses and shelters, those used for the manufacture of clothing and his articles of adornment. One can find the camps, dwelling places, cattle pens, and the storage facilities he provided for his food and that of his animals. There should be evidence for contact with other groups, raw materials and finished products exchanged through tribute, barter and trade, some obtained from groups not on the same cultural level as himself. There may be evidence for settled farmers, transhumant groups of pastoralists, nomads, hunters and fishermen. Evidence of this sort can be gained from most settlements, but there are other things one wants to know about. What evidence is there for man's spiritual needs, his beliefs, magic, religion and burial practices? What about art, statuettes, figurines and shrines, without which no Near Eastern culture existed? In exceptional cases, as at Çatal Hüyük with its wall paintings, it may be possible to form some opinion of man's thoughts enshrined in religious symbolism. This sort of evidence may be much less rare than is generally assumed; if archaeologists dug settlements and not just trenches and soundings, the results might well be different.

Were we to excavate entire villages and towns we should be better able to offer an opinion about the sort of life the people led there, but such information is not afforded by mound-hopping and random digging of soundings. As things are, we can deduce relatively little about social structure, the nature of authority, laws, customs, etc. Nevertheless we should not overlook any available archaeological evidence concerning the rites and rituals and the various forms of sport and entertainment that may have played a part in the life of early man.

In dealing with cultures two very important points must be settled: their geographical distribution and their chronology. The first can usually be done satisfactorily through field surveys, but it is essential that these are properly published, which is rarely the case. A bare map is not enough; one also wants to see the illustrated evidence on which the attribution of sites to various periods is based.

Without a chronological framework the archaeologist is lost. A relative chronology based on the stratigraphy of excavated sites is the basis of all the work, and an absolute chronology in calendar years B C can be provided by C14 dating. The old method of guessing at dates is now superseded, but radiocarbon dating is not yet infallible. Radiocarbon laboratories usually quote dates with the Libby or lower half-life of 5568 years in years B P (before present) and B C. Subsequent research suggested that the true half-life was 5730 years and dates were recalculated by 3 per cent to the B P date. As dates thus calculated came nearer to known historical dates many Near Eastern archaeologists, including myself, adopted radiocarbon dates with the higher half-life. Important discrepancies still remained and in the last few years it has become clear through dendrochronological studies on Bristlecone pine that all C14 dates need significant upward adjustments to obtain the true age in calendar years. This calibration, as it is called, now provides for a better absolute chronology (though there are still variations) but only up to 5200 B C. Work is now going on to establish it up to Palaeolithic times. A date of 4133 (lower half-life) equals 4322 (higher half-life) and both correspond to a calibrated date of 5072. This is one of the dates for the beginning of the Late Ubaid period at which we end our survey in this book, except in chapter 10. It is therefore not yet possible to suggest a true calibrated time-scale for the events to be described and, in order to prevent confusion, radiocarbon dates are quoted with the *lower half-life* only. As both systems are in need of calibration there seems little need for retaining the dates calculated with higher half-life. Recent studies tentatively suggest that carbon dates in the range of 7000–4500 B C will give dates about 1000 years earlier when calibrated,[86] but as far as I am aware no suggestions have yet been made for the calibration of earlier dates on either side of the Pleistocene-Holocene boundary, plausibly fixed at *c.* 10000 B P (8050 B C).

Calibrated date BC	C14 (5568 half-life) BC	Egypt	Iron gates Lepenski Vir	Bulgaria Karanovo	Yugoslavia Serbia Macedonia	Greek Macedonia	Thessaly	Franchthi cave	Knossos	Cyclades
						Late				
4000		Faiyum 'A' Neolithic		v (Maritsa)	Vinca Early	Sitagroi III (Maritsa)	Arapi	Late Neolithic	EN II	Saliagos
5200	4200			iv (Kalojano Vetz) III Veselinovo	Anza IV	II	Tsangli (matt- painted phase)			
						I Veselinovo				
4500			III Starčevo	II	Azmak I Starčevo Late	III	Sesklo	?		
			II	I	Middle	II				
5000		Atlantic	'Mesolithic'					Middle Neolithic	EN I	
			I		Early B A I	II Nea Nikomedeia	N S Pre- Sesklo			
5500		Faiyum Epipalae- olithic				I	Proto- Sesklo	Early Neolithic		
									Skyros	
6000		Boreal				A C E R A M I C				
								Knossos x		
		El Kab								
6500			Epipalaeolithic				Mesolithic			
							?	Mesolithic	Melian obsidian	
7000							Boibe		seafaring	
		Pre-Boreal								
7500										
8000			Holocene Pleistocene boundary							
8500		Younger Dryas	Epi-Gravettian							
9000			Late Palaeolithic							
9500		Allerød						Late Palaeolithic		
		El Kilh								
10000		Complex 'G'								
		Older Dryas								

14

Table I Chronological table

	S. and W. coast Anatolia	S.W. Anatolian plateau	Konya plain	Cilicia: Mersin	Cyprus	N. Syria Amuq plain	N. Syria Ras Shamra	Lebanon and S. Syria	Palestine North	Palestine South
		Beycesultan	Çatal Hüyük	Can Hasan I		T. es-Sheikh I–X 'E'	IIIB 'Ubaid'			
		Late Chalcolithic			?					
4000	3	3	Late Chalcolithic	XV				Byblos Late		Proto-Ghassulian
4200			surface finds	XVB					Kabri	
4500	2	2		XVIA / XVI / XVIZ	Troulli	IIIC		Neolithic	Wadi Rabah	
	1?	I	Çatal West surface (2A)	2A 5–1 / XVII / XVIII / XIX	Philia	D	IVA 3/2/1	Byblos		Jericho PNB
	Ayio Gala	I d–a Hacılar	Late Çatal West	2B 3/2/1 XX/XXI/XXII	IV / III		IVB 4–1	Ard Tlaïli M upper		upper Ghrubba
5000	'Lydian Neolithic'	II b Hacılar / II a Hacılar	Early Çatal Hüyük	3 XXIII/XXIV	II	C	IVC 3/2/1	lower	Munhata phase	lower
	Ayio Gala	III / IV Hacılar / V	0/I/II	4/5/6/7 XXV/XXVI/XXVII	I	B	VA 3/2/1	Byblos Early Neolithic	Yarmukian =	Jericho PNA
5500		VI–VII / VIII–IX	III/IV/V	? XXVIII/XXIX	?				Hagoshrim	
		Kızılkaya and Erbaba (ceramic)	VIA/VIB/VII/VIII	XXX/XXXI/XXXII/XXXIII	Khirokitia Aceramic	A	VB 3/2/1	T. Ramad III / Labwe II	Beisamoun (Aceramic)	Abu Ghosh
6000		Suberde II upper	IX/X/XI/XII	Can Hasan III Aceramic	? Kataliondas Aceramic ?	VC 2/1 (Aceramic)		Labwe I / T. Ramad II / T. Ramad I	Munhata 3/4/5/6 late	Beidha II / Jericho III
6500		II lower		?					? PPNB	IV
		Aceramic Hacılar I–VII				Slenfé (PPNB)	Saaide (PPNB)	W. Fallah I (PPNB)	6650 / early PPNB	V / VI / VII / VIII
	?		Aşıklı Hüyük							IX
7000	Ceramics / top level					?	?		gap	
		B I							7350 Jericho	
7500	Beldibi B								late PPNA 7650	
8000		B 2							early PPNA	
								Wadi Fallah II	8350	
8500			Central Anatolian Çiftlik obsidian						Jericho	
9000	?	?				Jabrud			'Proto-Neolithic'	
		C 1				Jebel Saaide	Ain Mallaha		9250 Jericho Natufian	
	Beldibi C				Amuq Natufian?	Natufian				
9500								W. Fallah I / El Wad / Kebara	Beidha 'early Natufian'	
10000		C 2 Kara'In, Öküzlü'In, Çark'In and Beldibi engravings, art mobilier (not dated)								
	Belbası							Geometric Kebaran 'A'		

15

C14 BC	Sakçagözü	T. Turlu	Yunus	T. Halaf	Chagar Bazar	Arpachiyah	Nineveh	Hassuna	T. Shemshara	Matarrah	Baghouz	T. es-Sawwan	Chogha Mami	Eridu	Deh Luran	Susiana
4000	IV			Late Ubaid (rare)	4		3							6 Late		Susa 'A' Jaffarabad 1–3
4200														7 Ubaid	Bayat	
4500							Ubaid ?						Mehmeh	8 Early / 9 / 10 Ubaid / 11 / 12	Mehmeh	Susiana 'C'
	5	6		bichrome+ incised	6 / 7 / 8	5 / 6	2c	X / IX / VIII					TT 6 / Chogha / Mami ware	13 Hajji / 14 Muhammed	Khazineh	Susiana 'B'
	III 6	5	4 (M)	developed Halaf	9 / 10 / 11	7		VII / VI			poly-chrome	V	Hajji Muhammed / Late Samarra	15	Sabz	Jaffarabad
5000	7 / 8	4	3 (J–K)		12	8	2b	V / IV	9–	upper	mono-chrome	IV phase I / IIIB 2 3		16 / 17 Eridu	Chogha Sefid	
	II 9 / 10	3 / 2 / 1	2b (H) / 2a (A–D) / 1 (kilns)		13 / 14	9 / 10		III	13	lower		IIIA 4		18 / 19		
	I 11 / 12 / 13			Early Halaf	15	Syrian grey ware	pre-TT 10 / Early Halaf 2a / 1	II / IC / IB	14– / 16		(Ac.)	II / I				
5500				'altmono-chrome'	Umm 1–4 / Daba-ghiyah 5–12			IA			basal			Tamerkhan = Ceramic Jarmo	1 Ceramic 2 / 3 Jarmo 4 / 5	A1 Muhammed Jafar A2
6000	El Kowm / upper / PPNB	Bouqras III 7 6 / II 5 4 / I 3 2 1	?											6– Aceramic / 16 Jarmo	Alikosh	B1 / A2
6500	lower PPNB		Mureybet 5 / IV (PPNB) 4 / Çayönü 3											M'Lefaat	Bus Mordeh	C1
7000			2 / 1											Karim Shahir		
7500			XVII / XVI / III (PPNA) / II (PPNA)					Nemrut Dağ obsidian								C2
8000			II / I													
8500			I (Natufian)											Zawi Chemi and Shanidar cave, Layer B1		
9000																
9500			Söğüt Tarlası Biriş Mezarliği ?													
10000														Layer B2, Zarzian		

4 (5568 half-life)	Central Zagros	Azerbaijan	Transcaucasia	N. Iranian plateau and Gurgan	S.W. Turkmenia Kopet Dagh piedmont	Geoksyur oasis	N. Afghanistan and Aral Sea	S. Iranian plateau Fars	Kerman
4000	—Giyan —VC, I	= Seh Gabi – – – – – – – –			Siyalk III, 4–5	Hisar IB	Namazga	Geoksyur			Yahya
4200		Dalma					II (late)			Bakun AI	Iblis I	VIA VIB
	—VB —Dalma	Seh Gabi Dalma			III, 1–3	IA	II (early)	Yalangach		Gap IA Bakun II	Iblis 0	VI C D E
4500	—VA — —	Bog-i-No		Shulaveri	3 II 2 1	Hotu cave Siyalk II	Namazga I (=Anau IB)	Dashliji		T. Musłki
5000	—Chia —Zargaran —Chia Siyah — —	1 2 3 .Hajji 4 Firuz 5 6	Yaniktepe 'late Neo-lithic'	Shomu Tepe Armenian aceramic	5 4 I 3 2 1	Tureng and Yarim Tepe (=Jeitun)	Anau IA Chakmakli Jeitun late middle early		Aq Köprük Ghar-i-Mar ceramic Neolithic	T. Jarri B
5500	—D Tepe — Guran upper Tepe Sarab —H	– – – –		Zaghe aceramic			Caves		
6000	— lower —				Hotu 2 Belt 7–9	Jebel 6–5 Nishapur-Maden turquoise			
6500	V Aceramic —Ganjdareh —A —		Epipalaeolithic Kobystan art style 2	Anarak copper				Aq Köprük Ghar-i-Mar	
7000	—B —C — —D —			art style 1		Hotu 3–4		aceramic Neolithic	
7500	— —Tepe —Asiab								
8000	— — —							Aq Köprük	Holocene	Pleistocene
8500	—Ganjdareh —E —							Ghar-i-Asp	
9000	—Ghar-i- —Khar —				Ali Tappeh cave V				
9500	— — —				IVB IVA				
10000	— — —								
	—Pa Sangar —Zarzian —				III II				

17

Chapter One

The Levant from the Epipalaeolithic
to the End of the Aceramic Period

Distinctive Upper Palaeolithic stone industries of blade and burin type used by *Homo sapiens* for the manufacture of weapons as well as for various household objects in stone, bone, antler, wood and other perishable materials have been recognized in caves or open sites in various regions of the Near East, but they are still relatively little known in many parts of southeastern Europe and the Anatolian-Caucasian area.

The two best known groups are the Levanto-Aurignacian of Palestine[7] and the Lebanon, which extends into southern Turkey and may have its equivalent in the Kemerian of the Antalya region,[101] and the Baradostian of the Zagros Mountains of western Iran. There is possible contact with the Transcaucasian group in Georgia and Soviet Armenia to the north of the Baradostian,[220] but only in Transcaucasia was obsidian used for the manufacture of tools, which were made of flint or chert in all other regions.

The Baradostian is roughly dated between 34000 and 20000, the Levanto-Aurignacian between 25000 and 18000 BC.[74] Sites of this period can be divided into base camps, butchering places and intermediate camp sites of hunting bands where numbers were probably limited. Most of the large cave sites served as base camps; smaller shelters may have been used as intermediate sites, but butchering places are often out in the open, though the use of such sites may have varied from season to season. Of permanent occupation there is no trace, and these hunters were evidently migratory throughout the territories they occupied; each group may well have had several sets of caves at their disposal.

Osteological studies suggest that during this Upper Palaeolithic period man was interested in only a few species of large game, and paid little or no attention to the many other varieties of food, such as small mammals, birds, fish, snails, etc., which nature provided.[92] In the Baradostian of the Zagros the principal game was onager, aurochs, red deer, wild goat and gazelle,[74] whereas at Ksar Akil in the Levanto-Aurignacian the main food animals were fallow deer, goat and roe deer, with some red deer, aurochs, bear, fox and wild cat. It seems likely, though, that man did not live on meat alone, and nuts, berries, fruit, green vegetables, roots, etc. were probably collected, though there is no actual evidence to prove this.

Apart from similarities in tool types, there is little evidence to show contact and trade between the various groups at this period. The total number of individuals was probably limited, and indeed burials are rare. No evidence for art has yet been discovered.

Some time between 20000 and 16000 BC the Upper Palaeolithic gave rise to new cultures, collectively named Epipalaeolithic; Kebaran in the Levant, Belbası in the Antalya region, and Zarzian in the Zagros. The Epipalaeolithic period is of great importance and sees marked improvements in every archaeologically recognizable aspect of the cultures. The chief technological invention is that of the composite tool, equipped with microlithic flint, chert or obsidian elements set in rows in wooden shafts or mounted singly at the top of an arrow. Intact weapons have not survived but one can picture barbed spears and javelins, bows and arrows with pointed, transverse or lunate-shaped tips, as well as straight reaping knives with several bladelets set end to end in a groove and cemented into the slot with resin or bitumen. Such reaping knives may well have been devised for cutting reeds and tough grasses, to be woven into mats for shelters or into baskets for collecting. Such usage would produce a silica sheen on the tool's cutting edge as would the reaping of wheat and barley. Silica sheen is, however, not by itself an indication of reaping crops.

The presence of some microliths in the Baradostian[74] and a tendency towards smaller tools in the late Levanto-Aurignacian[22] strongly suggests, among other features in the tool typology, that the Epipalaeolithic cultures were not the result of the arrival of newcomers but represent regional developments from the preceding Upper Palaeolithic. Do these tendencies, which may be observed also in Egypt, North Africa and Europe, indicate an increase in cultural contact and the breakdown of the previous isolation? This is a question to which no satisfactory answer can be given, but on the basis of a few radiocarbon dates it would appear that the Baradostian microliths are the earliest. If the Epipalaeolithic Zarzian culture began as early as 20000 BC the east was well ahead of the Epipalacolithic Kebaran in the Levant or the more or less contemporary use of microliths in Upper Egypt.

It is not only in the use of more developed tools and weapons that the Epipalaeolithic marks a definite advance, for they are only a manifestation of new needs.[7] In the Levant, there are far more sites of the Kebaran culture than there were in the previous period and the same is the case in Upper Egypt. In the Zagros the evidence is less conclusive; Zarzian sites seem more common than Baradostian ones, but their numbers remain small.[74] Did the new technology result in a greater efficiency in hunting thus causing better and more stable conditions leading to an increase in population, or did Kebaran man start to exploit new food supplies, using bow and arrow to kill fleeter animals which had hitherto eluded him? In the sand dunes and oak forests of the Palestinian coastal plain, Kebaran sites abound;[6] does this indicate a population increase or had Kebaran man become more mobile, camping repeatedly in these favourite hunting grounds?

A study of the animal bones from Epipalaeolithic sites shows a general change towards a greater exploitation of available food resources, perhaps the result of the new weapons.[92] No longer are the larger animals – as in the Upper Palaeolithic – the only source of meat, although they continued to supply the bulk of it. The hunt becomes gradually more intensified and more species find

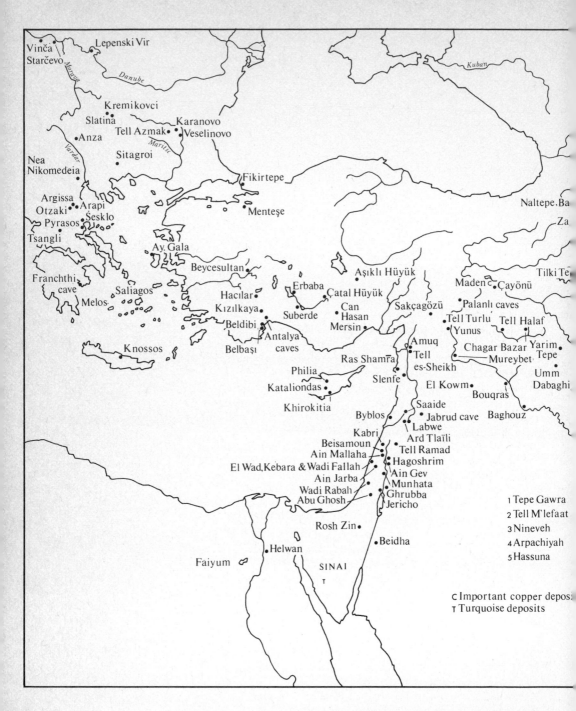

Vinča
Starčevo

Lepenski Vir

Morava

Danube

Kuban

Kremikovci

Slatina

Tell Azmak Karanovo
Veselinovo

Anza

Maritza

Sitagroi

Nea
Nikomedeia

Vardar

Fikirtepe

Naltepe.Ba

Argissa

Za

Otzaki Arapi
Sesklo

Pyrasos

Mentese

Tsangli

Ay. Gala

Franchthi
cave

Beycesultan

Aşıklı Hüyük

Tilki Te

Maden Çayönü

Melos

Saliagos

Erbaba

Hacılar

Çatal Hüyük

Palanlı caves

Kızılkaya

Suberde

Can
Hasan

Sakçagözü

Tell Turlu Tell Halaf
Yunus

Beldibi

Mersin

Knossos

Antalya
caves

Belbaşı

Ras Shamra

Amuq

Chagar Bazar Yarim
Mureybet Tepe

Tell
es-Sheikh

Philia

Slenfe

Umm
Dabaghi

Kataliondas

El Kowm

Bouqras

Khirokitia

Saaide

Byblos

Jabrud cave Baghouz

Kabri

Labwe

Beisamoun

Ard Tlaïli

Ain Mallaha

Tell Ramad

El Wad,Kebara &Wadi Fallah

Hagoshrim

Ain Jarba

Ain Gev

Wadi Rabah

Munhata

Abu Ghosh

Ghrubba

Jericho

Rosh Zin

Beidha

Helwan

Faiyum

SINAI

1 Tepe Gawra
2 Tell M'lefaat
3 Nineveh
4 Arpachiyah
5 Hassuna

c Important copper depos
т Turquoise deposits

their way into man's diet, although it must not be assumed that all
animals whose bones we find were necessarily consumed by man.
Certain creatures, such as small mammals, rodents, snakes,
tortoises and birds, may have been killed for their skins, feathers
and the like, rather than for their meat. This new interest in additional food supplies is marked in the Levant (Kebara: fallow deer,

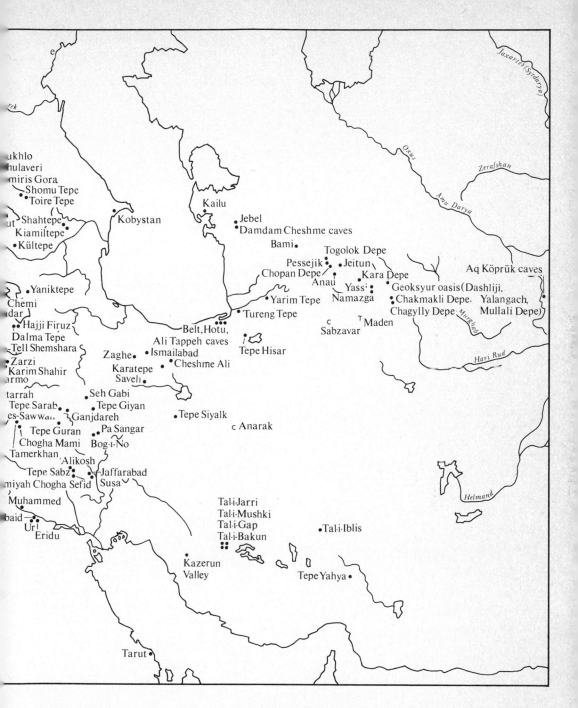

e

ukhlo
hulaveri
miris Gora
Shomu Tepe
Toire Tepe
ut Shahtepe
Kiamiltepe
Kültepe
Yaniktepe
Chemi
dar
Hajji Firuz
Dalma Tepe
Tell Shemshara
Zarzi
Karim Shahir
armo
tarrah
Tepe Sarab
es-Sawwan
Tepe Guran
Chogha Mami
Tamerkhan
Tepe Sabz
miyah Chogha Sefid
Muhammed
baid
Ur
Eridu

Kobystan

Kailu

Jebel
Damdam Cheshme caves
Bami

Pessejik
Chopan Depe
Anau
Yarim Tepe

Seh Gabi
Tepe Giyan
Ganjdareh
Pa Sangar
Bog-i-No
Alikosh
Jaffarabad
Susa

Zaghe
Karatepe
Saveh
Ismailabad
Cheshme Ali

Tepe Siyalk

Tepe Hisar

c Anarak

Belt, Hotu,
Ali Tappeh caves

Togolok Depe
Jeitun
Kara Depe
Yass
Namazga

Sabzavar

T Maden

Geoksyur oasis (Dashliji,
Chakmakli Depe
Chagylly Depe

Aq Köprük caves

Yalangach,
Mullali Depe)

Jaxartes (Syrdarya)

Oxus

Amu Darya

Zerafshan

Murghab

Hari Rud

Helmand

Tal-i-Jarri
Tal-i-Mushki
Tal-i-Gap
Tal-i-Bakun

Tal-i-Iblis

Kazerun
Valley

Tepe Yahya

Tarut

gazelle, onager, aurochs, pigs, birds), the Zagros and Upper Egypt, and may have been general. It is reasonable to assume that, as the sources of meat became more diversified, the search for new plant foods kept pace, yet there is still no direct evidence for this. In the Zagros, snails and freshwater mussels became part of the diet during the Zarzian. Although the enlargement of the diet during

1 Map of the Near East showing Epipalaeolithic and Neolithic sites

the Epipalaeolithic is a clearly recognizable fact, one can only speculate on what caused it. Did the invention of composite tools enable man to catch many creatures previously beyond his reach, thus leading to a firm economic basis and a gradual expansion of population? Or did population pressure force man to invent new tools in order to get more food to satisfy the increased demand?[71] Cause and effect are always hard to distinguish in the remote past, and the evidence is open to several interpretations. In my opinion it is the invention of more efficient tools that led to this cultural advance; the increase of population I see as the result, not the cause, of the new technology and economy.

The Kebaran

During the Kebaran there is evidence for some remarkable concentration of certain animals on a few sites, which appears to be in contrast to the wider exploitation of food resources.[56] At Wadi Madamagh near Petra, bones of goat amount to 82 per cent and at Wadi Fallah (Nahal Oren) on Mt Carmel those of gazelle reach 74 per cent (with fallow deer 18·5 per cent and aurochs 3·5 per cent).[53] Although rather specialized hunting cannot be excluded, a far more plausible explanation for this phenomenon has been offered. Wild goat and gazelle are fairly easily tamed and it is possible (if not probable) that at these two sites Kebaran man had learned to herd goat or gazelle.[56] The main disadvantage of hunting must always have been the availability of game, but this could be surmounted by herding, which ensured a steady and reliable food supply, stored on the hoof. Consciously or unconsciously the Kebarans of Wadi Madamagh and Wadi Fallah may have taken the first steps towards animal domestication. This of course suggests that herds of these animals were available near by and we have no reason to doubt this. Thus, instead of killing whenever food was needed, man rounded up the whole herd (or as many of the animals as he could catch, especially females and the young) and started herding them. In the course of this process, which must have been fairly tricky and may have taken some time, he must have learned to observe what goat and gazelle fed on. It would not have been long before the herdsman tried to eat some of these herbs and grasses himself, and he may have found that though many plants were unpalatable, others such as wild wheat and barley grains could be eaten after separation from their husks, which could be done by pounding between two stones. This too would be a long process, but a herdsman has plenty of time to spare.

It is perhaps not surprising that at Ain Gev I on the eastern shore of Lake Tiberias there is evidence for a Late Kebaran site with round huts, plenty of grinding slabs and a large mortar of the type that becomes typical in the Natufian culture.[7] Blades with silica sheen were also found, as well as the burial of a young woman. The equipment suggests the preparation of plant food. On typological grounds, never very convincing at such an early date, this site was placed at the very end of the Kebaran, but a recent radiocarbon date (*GRN–5576*) places it at 13750±415 B C.[5]

Herding had the further advantage of keeping the animals from cropping the native wild ancestors of wheat and barley – a potential

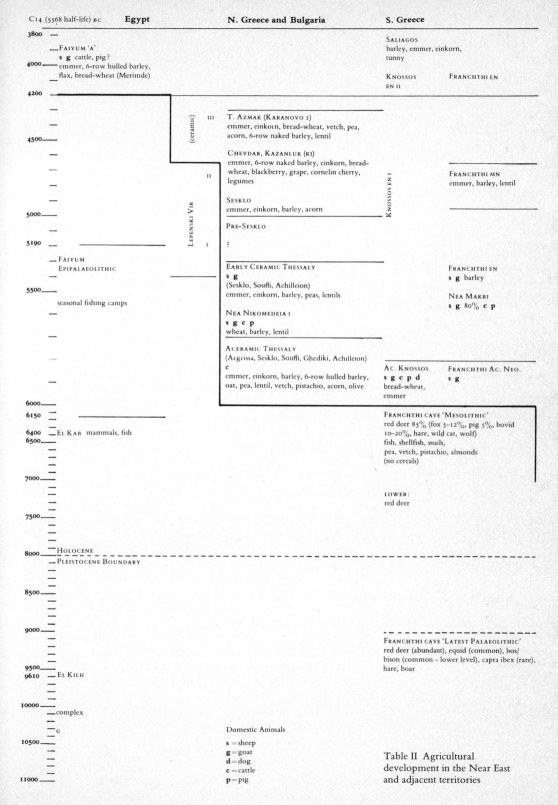

C14 (5568 half-life) BC | **Egypt** | **N. Greece and Bulgaria** | **S. Greece**

C14 BC	Egypt	N. Greece and Bulgaria	S. Greece
3800			SALIAGOS barley, emmer, einkorn, tunny
	FAIYUM 'A' **s g** cattle, pig?		
4000	emmer, 6-row hulled barley, flax, bread-wheat (Merimde)		
			KNOSSOS EN II — FRANCHTHI LN
4200			
		(ceramic) III — T. AZMAK (KARANOVO I) emmer, einkorn, bread-wheat, vetch, pea, acorn, 6-row naked barley, lentil	
4500			
		CHEVDAR, KAZANLUK (KI) emmer, 6-row naked barley, einkorn, bread-wheat, blackberry, grape, cornelin cherry, legumes	
		II —	KNOSSOS EN I — FRANCHTHI MN emmer, barley, lentil
		LEPENSKI VIR — SESKLO emmer, einkorn, barley, acorn	
5000			
		PRE-SESKLO	
5190		I — ?	
	FAIYUM EPIPALAEOLITHIC	EARLY CERAMIC THESSALY **s g** (Sesklo, Soufli, Achilleion) emmer, einkorn, barley, peas, lentils	FRANCHTHI EN **s g** barley
5500	seasonal fishing camps		NEA MAKRI **s g** 80% **c p**
		NEA NIKOMEDEIA I **s g c p** wheat, barley, lentil	
		ACERAMIC THESSALY (Argissa, Sesklo, Soufli, Ghediki, Achilleion) **c** emmer, einkorn, barley, 6-row hulled barley, oat, pea, lentil, vetch, pistachio, acorn, olive	AC. KNOSSOS **s g c p d** bread-wheat, emmer — FRANCHTHI AC. NEO. **s g**
6000			
6150			FRANCHTHI CAVE 'MESOLITHIC' red deer 85% (fox 5–12%, pig 5%, bovid 10–20%, hare, wild cat, wolf) fish, shellfish, snails, pea, vetch, pistachio, almonds (no cereals)
6400	EL KAB mammals, fish		
6500			
7000			
			LOWER: red deer
7500			
8000	HOLOCENE / PLEISTOCENE BOUNDARY		
8500			
9000			
			FRANCHTHI CAVE 'LATEST PALAEOLITHIC' red deer (abundant), equid (common), bos/bison (common – lower level), capra ibex (rare), hare, boar
9500			
9610	EL KILH		
10000	complex		
	G		
10500		Domestic Animals	
		s = sheep	
		g = goat	
		d = dog	Table II Agricultural development in the Near East and adjacent territories
11000		**c** = cattle	
		p = pig	

S.W. Anatolia   Konya plain   Mediterranean Syria

3800 — BEYCESULTAN   CAN HASAN   RAS SHAMRA IIIB   AMUQ

4000 — L. CHALCOLITHIC   3   I   E

4200 —

     2   RAS SHAMRA IIIC   **c**

4500 —

     I   RAS SHAMRA IVA'   **p**
UPPER ARD TLAÏLI
    2A   RAS SHAMRA IVB   **s d**   D
CAN HASAN 2B   **s g c p**   ARD TLAÏLI
bread-wheat, 6-row barley

— HACILAR I–VII   MERSIN XXII–I

5000 — emmer, einkorn, bread-wheat, 6-row naked   emmer, 6-row erect barley   RAS SHAMRA IVC   C
barley, Hacılar pea, vetch, lentil, bitter vetch,   RAS SHAMRA VA   **c**   B
chick pea, acorn, pistachio, caper, hackberry   AMUQ B   **s**
— **d** (sheep/goat, cattle, pig?, red deer)

     II   ÇATAL HÜYÜK   **c d**
       wild sheep, onager, red deer

5500 —   emmer, einkorn, bread-wheat, 6-row
       naked barley, pea, Hacılar pea, bitter   RAS SHAMRA VB   A
— HACILAR VIII–IX   vetch, crucifers, almond, apple,   **c s p**
       pistachio, hackberry, juniper, acorn,   AMUQ A   emmer, barley
— ERBABA **s g g**   caper   **g P**
(crops – no details yet)   X   (fish, birds, eggs)

6000 —   XII   CAN HASAN III   RAS SHAMRA VC
— SUBERBE   wild cattle, sheep/goat, pig, onager?   **c**
— II UPPER: red and roe deer, canid   goat?, pig?, boar
       d red deer, wild sheep,   emmer, bread-wheat, club-wheat,
— II LOWER: cattle, boar   hulled and naked 2-row barley,
       (no botanical details)   einkorn, lentil, vetch, bitter vetch,

6500 — - - - - - - -   walnut, hackberry, grape, prunus,
— AC. HACILAR V   hawthorn
— **d**
— barley, emmer, w. einkorn, naked barley,   AŞIKLI HÜYÜK
— lentil   hackberry
— red deer, cattle, sheep/goat, boar   red deer, cattle, onager?, sheep/goat, hare

7000 —

— BI

7500 —

— BELDIBI B
   deer, cattle, ibex/goat

— B2

8000 — -

8500 —

9000 — - - - - - - - - - - - -

— CI

9500 — BELDIBI C
   deer, cattle, ibex/goat

— C2

10000 —

— BELBAŞI

10500 —

11000 —

24

	Lebanon Syria	Palestine	Euphrates–Tigris Drainage and	Zagros Zone

```
.00  —
.00  — Byblos                                                              LATE UBAID
            L
.00  —
     — N
.00  —                                    Girikihaciyan        Halaf      EARLY UBAID
                                          s g p wild cattle
     — Byblos            W. Rabah phase   Banahilk                        Ras el-Amiyah
     — MN                Munhata 2A       s g c                           (Hajji Muhammed)
                         Jericho PNB (VIII) Arpachiyah (level 7)          s g g (45%)
.00  —                   s g             emmer, barley, flax
     —                   Munhata phase    Yarim Tepe I (Hassuna)          Chogha Mami
     —                   Munhata 2B       s g c p                         s g c
                         Jericho PNA (IX) emmer, einkorn, barley          emmer, bread-wheat, einkorn, 6-row hulled
     —                   Ghrubba                                          barley, flax
.00  — Byblos en                                                          T. es-Sawwan
     — emmer, grape      Hagoshrim                                        s g c fish (III)
                         c 60% d p?                                       emmer, 6-row naked and hulled barley,
                                                                          einkorn, bread-wheat, flax, caper, prosopis,
     — T. Ramad III      Beisamoun        Umm Dabaghiyah                  thistle
     — s g p c           wild sheep/goat  emmer, einkorn, barley          Ceramic Jarmo (1–5)
.00  —                                                                    s g d p
ATE    T. Ramad II c p   Munhata 3–6      Bouqras III                     Aceramic Jarmo (6–16)
NB   — emmer, barley, lentil, wild: caprids, gazelle, s c ?              s g d snail
     — pea, almond, pistachio, boar, cattle, cervids                     emmer, einkorn, barley, lentil, pea, vetchling,
       hawthorn, gazelle                   Bouqras I–II                   acorn, pistachio
       T. Ramad I                          wild sheep/goat, cattle, wild cereals?
     — emmer, barley, pea,                 El Kowm
.00  — lentil, gazelle, deer, cat          wheat, barley, wild sheep/goat, onager, cattle,
RLY    — II                                gazelle                        M'Lefaat
NB     VI    Beidha g 86%
     —       emmer, cultivated, wild barley (naked             Karim Shahir
             barley, wild oat), pistachio, acorn,              wild: sheep, goat, cattle, gazelle, boar, deer,
             pea, vetch                                        fox, marten, turtle, birds, snail
.00  —       Jericho PPNB                  Çayönü 4–5
     —       g  cat (gazelle 17·86%)       g s p d (not cattle)
             emmer, einkorn, barley, pea, vetch, lentil, emmer, barley, pea, lentil, vetch, pistachio,
     —       caper?, oat?                  almond, acorn
     —  ------------------------------     Çayönü 1–2  d
     —                                     wild animals, wild emmer, einkorn, vetch,
                                           pistachio, almond
.00  — Jericho PPNA                        Mureybet II–III
ATE  — gazelle (36·9%), cattle, goat, boar wild: gazelle, cattle, Palestinian ass, 33% each,
PNA  — emmer, barley, lentil, fig          fallow deer, boar
     —                                     cultivated 'wild' einkorn, barley, lentil, bitter
     — W. Fallah (N. Oren)                 vetch
     — gazelle 89%
.00  —
RLY    — El Khiam (3–4)
PNA  — goat 83%, gazelle 14%
```

```
.00  — Jericho                   Mureybet I (Natufian)                Zawi Chemi (upper)
     — Proto-Neolithic           Palestinian ass, aurochs, gazelle    s wild goat
       gazelle, cattle, boar, fox fish, shellfish              8650  B1 hackberry, cerealia pollen
     —
```

```
.00  — W. Fallah (N. Oren) Natufian                             8920  Shanidar Cave B1
     — gazelle 76·5%, cattle 12·8%, fallow deer 4·1%,                 wild goat, boar, red deer, fallow deer,
       roe deer 0·3%                                                  wolf, jackal, tawny fox, Syrian
                                                                      brown bear, marten, beaver, tortoise,
     — Jericho 'Natufian'                                             gerbils, river clams (fish), snails (helix)

     — NATUFIAN                  NATUFIAN
.00  — Beidha Natufian goat 76%, gazelle 30%
       Ain Mallaha (Eynan)                                           Palegawra 'Zarzian'
     — gazelle 44%, roe deer 15%, fallow deer 15%,                   wild cattle, goat, sheep?, onager?, red deer,
     — boar 15%, cattle, goat, hyena, fox, hare, small   Söğüt Tarlasi and Biriş Mezarligi  roe deer, boar, fox, lynx, wolf, hedgehog,
     — carnivores, rodents, birds, fish, crustaceans,                tortoise, toad, birds, crab, clam, snail (helix)
.00  — tortoise, snails, snake                          ?           10050 B2
     — KEBARAN
                                                                     Shanidar B2
.00  — W. Fallah (N. Oren)
     — gazelle 74%, fallow deer 18·5%, cattle 3·5%                   ZARZIAN
     — W. Madamagh
.00  — goat 82%
```

Date	Khuzistan	W. Iranian plateau	Caspian. S.W. Turkmenia	N. Afghanistan
4000	BAYAT		SIYALK III 4,5	
4200				
	MEHMEH **s g c** bread-wheat, 2-, 6-row naked and hulled barley, lentils, vetch, vetchling, flax		YALANGACH (Namazga II) **c** 41–54%, **s g** 25–49%, **p** 2–22%, bread-wheat, 2- and 6-row barley III 1–3	
4500	KHAZINEH **s g c** bread-wheat, 2-, 6-row naked and hulled barley, lentils, vetch, vetchling, flax	BOG-I-NO? emmer, bread-wheat, 2-, 6-row barley, pistachio, jujube	DASHLIJI (late Namazga I) **s g c p** barley II **d p**? NAMAZGA I **c**	
5000	T. SABZ **g s c d** emmer, bread-wheat, einkorn, 6-row naked barley, flax, peas, lentils	HAJJI FIRUZ **s g p d**	ANAU IA (MONJUKLI) **s g c** 60% I 1,2 **g** LATE JEITUN barley **s g c**	AQ KÖPRÜK CAVE 1 (CERAMIC NEOLITHIC) **s g** wild horse
5500	JAFFARABAD **g s c**	SARAB **s g** emmer, barley, wild barley, pistachio, snails	PRE-SIYALK EARLY JEITUN **s c** 16% gazelle, wild sheep, goat 65%, barley, emmer	
	M. JAFAR **g s** prosopis agricultural decline	UPPER GURAN **g** wild cattle emmer, barley, wild barley, pistachio		
6000			HOTU 2, BELT 7–9, JEBEL 6–5 sheep/goat 53%, 84%, majority cattle 14%, deer 19%	
	ALIKOSH **g s** (wild cattle, onager) emmer, einkorn, 6-row hulled and naked barley	LOWER GURAN (N–V) wild barley goat herding hunting: gazelle, birds		
6500	BUS MORDEH **g** 73% **s** (hornless) emmer, barley, wild legumes aquatic resources hunting: gazelle, onager, cattle, boar	A B C		AQ KÖPRÜK CAVE 1 (ACERAMIC NEOLITHIC) **s g** poss. cattle (plant remains)
7000		c. 7000 GANJDAREH D **g** wild sheep (no botanical details yet)	HOTU CAVE 3 sheep/goat 72%, pig 5%, cattle 13%, deer 3%, 4 sheep/goat 50%, pig 17%, cattle 17%, canids 17%, wild grain collection?	
7500				
		ASIAB? **g**? freshwater clams		
8000				AQ KÖPRÜK CAVE 2 **s g**
8500		GANJDAREH E		
9000			ALI TAPPEH CAVE V gazelle 30%, peak – sheep/goat	
			IVB rise in gazelle	
9500			IVA seal 30%, gazelle 71%, sheep/goat 15%	
10000			III gazelle, cattle, pig, few sheep/goat	
			II gazelle down to 40%	
10500			I gazelle 60%, goat/sheep 20%, cattle 5%	
11000				

source of food for man – and diverting them from these wild crops to graze on other herbs, not edible by humans. In this way man may have learned not only to eliminate rival consumers, but to conserve food, for goat and gazelle were stored on the hoof, leaving the wild cereals protected. With goat and gazelle eliminated, few serious competitors remained – occasional aurochs, deer, pig and onager, though there were still the birds. Kebaran man may have started keeping an eye on the grain crops as they were ripening, building a few stone huts or reed shelters for the purpose, and so taken another first step towards settlement near a food supply.

The discovery of an alternate food supply to meat may thus have taken place some time during the Kebaran period throughout the Near East, wherever wild wheat and barley grew on the hills. No single region has as yet any definite priority, and full exploitation was to come much later, once man had learnt that in the right circumstances he could move the wild plants at his will.

The material remains of these Epipalaeolithic cultures – the Kebaran of the Levant,[7] the Belbaşı culture of the Antalya region of Turkey,[103] the Zarzian of the Zagros Mountains of Iran and Iraq[75] and the Zarzian-like Epipalaeolithic of Ali Tappeh cave on the Caspian in Gurgan[230] – while fascinating to the specialist are of minor importance compared to the dimly emerging picture of an increasing awareness of the potentialities of the environment, the first steps towards food conservation through herding, wild grain collecting and its preparation as food, and a trend, however limited, to sedentary life. Such features did not appear everywhere at the same time, they were as yet isolated and experimental, yet they constituted the embryo stage of plant and animal domestication which was ultimately to carry man from a hunting existence to that of the farmer and trader.

Habitation during this period was still in caves and camps, without any indication of permanence;[8] groups were still small – most sites cover only 200 sq. m, but they are more numerous than before. Distributed over some six or ten thousand years (Kebaran or Zarzian) they hardly suggest overpopulation, and all one can infer is that there were probably more people in the Epipalaeolithic than in the Upper Palaeolithic. To use statistics on such flimsy evidence seems wholly unwarranted and to use such statistics in order to explain culture changes is, in my opinion, foolhardy.

The Kebaran is now divided into two phases: an Early Kebaran with microliths but no geometrics, and characterized by obliquely truncated bladelets and narrow micropoints, and a later Geometric Kebaran A with geometric microliths (trapezes and rectangles) and fewer burins. A still later Geometric Kebaran B, characterized by triangles and lunates, is contemporary with the ensuing Natufian culture; it is a sort of desert Natufian of Kebaran tradition, representing the tool-kit of hunters in the marginal areas, whereas the real Natufian is the culture with the many innovations. The important point of the new classification is, however, that it strongly suggests that the Natufian grew out of the Kebaran and was not an introduction from the north as some scholars were inclined to think.[25] Such precision cannot yet be applied to the Zarzian culture, which may show several variants, as for example at Shanidar cave in Iraq[79] or at Pa Sangar in Luristan.[75] Temporal divisions have not yet been worked out and radiocarbon dates are few. Belbaşı looks most like Geometric Kebaran A, while Ali Tappeh cave is carbon-dated to the eleventh–tenth millennia B C, i.e. late in comparison with Pa Sangar.

The diminution in the size of flint tools and weapons is not confined to the manufacture of small elements for composite tools; it also extends to scrapers – perhaps used for preparing the skin of small mammals, which would then be sewn together with bone needles to make garments – and to microburins for more minute and precise cutting tools. Except for needles, bone tools remain rare. Microliths then made several refinements possible in all sorts of home industries, but surprisingly art is still not encountered, though it may have been expressed in perishable materials, such as stitched leatherwork, composite fur garments, painted skins, basketry or carved wood. In archaeology one should never forget that the absence of certain categories of objects on a site does not necessarily mean that they did not originally exist.

Most of the structures of this period were of a perishable nature; small round stone circles for huts, about 2 m in diameter, some containing a hearth, occurred in the sands of the Palestinian coastal plain at Poleg 18M.[6] More substantial huts, partly sunk into the ground occurred at Ain Gev I, one of which was excavated.[45] It contained two pestles, a basalt mortar, several flat stones, animal bones and horn cores, sickle blades with lustre and the skeleton of a young woman of gracile build buried below the floor. The only other (late) Kebaran burial is from the shelter of Abri Bergy in Lebanon.[22] Neither skeleton has yet been described.

Elementary trade in the form of Mediterranean shells, including dentalium, is attested at inland sites; at Ain Gev, and at Nahal Zin in the Negev.[38] Dentalium shells also occur at Pa Sangar, but these may have come from the Persian Gulf,[74] for there is no evidence whatsoever for contact between the Kebaran and the Zarzian. No obsidian is known in the Kebaran or in the ensuing Natufian culture, but evidence of the beginning of contact with the north is found at Shanidar cave in layer C (Baradostian)[84] where obsidian from Kars-Erevan (type 1e, 1f) and from Nemrut Dağ on Lake Van (type 4c) occurs in minute quantities.[85] Two pieces of obsidian were also found in layer B at Zarzi (Zarzian). In Anatolia, central Anatolian obsidian, type 2b from Çiftlik, found its way into the caves of Kara'In and Öküzlü'In during 'Aurignacian IV', but whether this is Upper or Epipalaeolithic is by no means clear. Obsidian has not been reported from near-by Belbaşı. This evidence is admittedly slender, but against that stands the spread of the use of microliths, the hall-mark of the Epipalaeolithic. Contact, however rare, must have been established for the new ideas to have spread.

The Natufian

The Natufian culture, which at a number of sites succeeds Geometric Kebaran A from which it is probably descended, is much better known from numerous excavations. It is still Epipalaeolithic and is conventionally dated between *c.* 10000 and *c.* 8000 B C,

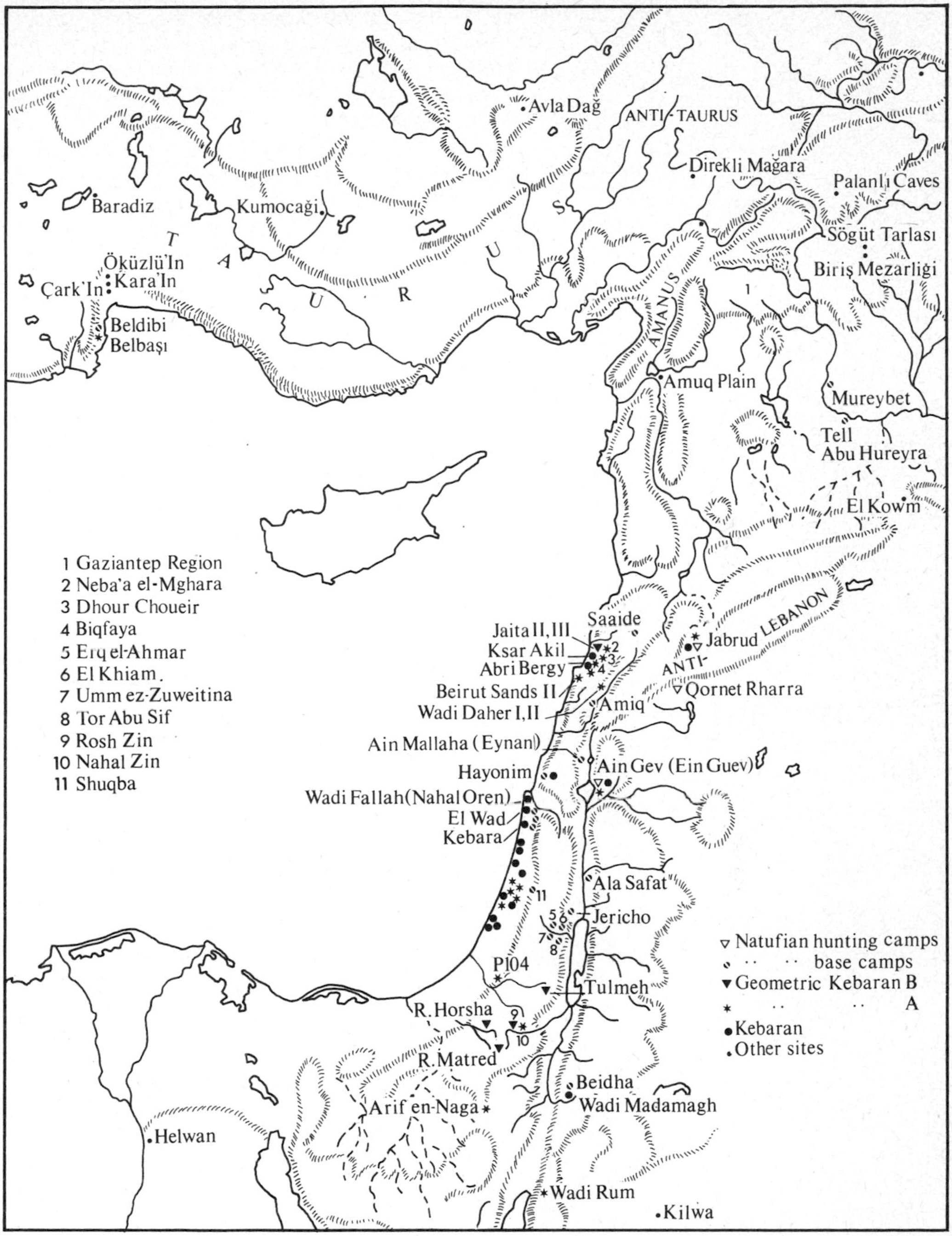
Avla Dağ
ANTI-TAURUS
Direkli Mağara
Palanlı Caves
Baradiz
Kumocaği
T A U R U S
Sögüt Tarlası
Biriş Mezarliği
Öküzlü'In
Kara'In
Çark'In
Beldibi
Belbaşı
AMANUS
Amuq Plain
Mureybet
Tell Abu Hureyra
El Kowm
1 Gaziantep Region
2 Neba'a el-Mghara
3 Dhour Choueir
4 Biqfaya
5 Erq el-Ahmar
6 El Khiam
7 Umm ez-Zuweitina
8 Tor Abu Sif
9 Rosh Zin
10 Nahal Zin
11 Shuqba
Saaide
Jaita II, III
Ksar Akil
Abri Bergy
Beirut Sands II
Wadi Daher I, II
Jabrud
ANTI-LEBANON
Qornet Rharra
Amiq
Ain Mallaha (Eynan)
Hayonim
Ain Gev (Ein Guev)
Wadi Fallah (Nahal Oren)
El Wad
Kebara
Ala Safat
Jericho
P104
Tulmeh
R. Horsha
R. Matred
Arif en-Naga
Beidha
Wadi Madamagh
Helwan
Wadi Rum
Kilwa
Natufian hunting camps
base camps
Geometric Kebaran B
A
Kebaran
Other sites

2 Map of Epipalaeolithic sites in the Levant and southern Anatolia

in other words it belongs to the very end of the Pleistocene period. Two recent radiocarbon dates[43] suggest a range from 10300 ± 65 to 8640 ± 140 B.C.[27]

The distribution of the main Natufian sites, the base camps, shows a deliberate change of settlement pattern compared to that of the previous culture.[7] Instead of concentrating on the open forest and sand dunes of the coastal plain of Palestine,[8] the Natufians preferred the *terra rossa* limestone uplands. This region, with a rainfall even higher than today, enjoyed the most favourable climate; it was covered at that time by Mediterranean *Pistacieto-quercetum*,[93] a belt of oak and pistachio woodlands among which grew the wild ancestors of emmer wheat and two-row barley. This main area of Natufian occupation, seemingly chosen for its environment,[47] was bordered by the Mediterranean coast to the west, and to the east by the arid zones in which a number of Natufian seasonal camps were situated. The latter are marked by the absence of permanent structures, by implements for the preparation of plant food (querns, mortars, bone sickles, sickle blades) and art objects.[19] Their equipment is that of hunters and gatherers and is predominantly microlithic. In size these Natufian hunting camps do not materially differ from the earlier Kebaran camps, covering on the average *c*. 200 sq. m. In certain areas the Natufians shared the land's resources with other less advanced groups of hunters of the Kebaran tradition, the so-called desert Natufian or Geometric Kebaran B. The latter continued to live in the marginal areas, especially in the Negev, Transjordan and the Lebanon.[7]

This dichotomy is very marked and evidently has an economic basis. The hunters and food gatherers of the Kebaran culture were being outstripped by their more advanced cousins the Natufians, who organized themselves better and thus exploited their well-chosen environment with greater success. As a result they made corresponding economic and cultural advances which at certain sites enabled them to establish and maintain more or less permanent settlements.

As the Natufians chose the zone in which wild cereals were available for their base camps, it is hardly a coincidence that agricultural tools such as sickles and querns, mortars, pounders, pestles, etc. should occupy such a prominent place in the Natufian economy. We have already seen the first appearance of such an equipment at Ain Gev I in the Late Kebaran in the fourteenth millennium B C, but now it is widespread. The large size of the mortars, fixed in the floors of huts or cut into the rock terraces in front of caves (El Wad,[25] Rosh Zin,[27] etc.), the use of old mortars, perforated through too much pounding as marking stones over Natufian burials (Wadi Fallah)[46] or as building material (in the so-called shrine) at Jericho,[29] all testify to the importance attached by the Natufians to this new tool-kit designed beyond much doubt for the preparation of plant foods, in this case almost certainly wild wheat and barley. People do not normally invent new tools and implements until the need is there and as the preparation of these large mortars, fashioned with flint picks out of hard limestone and even harder basalt, involved a considerable amount of labour, the processing of cereal food must be presumed to have reached paramount importance within the economy. No actual deposits of charred grain have yet been found – none of the excavated sites was conveniently burnt – and clay-lined storage pits, which now occur for the first time were all found empty. Both barley and wheat grow wild in the uplands of the Levant and they ripen around April to May. As ripe wild grain scatters easily, baskets or other containers would be needed to catch it before it fell to the ground; alternatively the ears could be plucked by hand or they could be cut with sickles before they had fully ripened. Although wild grain is eminently edible and contains more nutrients than domestic grain, the kernels are enclosed in a tough glume which must be removed either by roasting or by pounding in a mortar.[75] Once pounded, the husks can easily be separated from the grain and the latter can be ground on a saddle quern. Bone spatulae may have been used to scrape the flour off the quern. More likely than not the flour was mixed with water and eaten as porridge, since cooking pots had not yet been invented. Acorns, another possible food, would not need such elaborate treatment; they could be eaten roasted or ground into flour. The grinding of vegetable foods inevitably produces a certain amount of grit from the quern mixed with the flour; excess consumption of such food wears down the teeth and it is highly characteristic that a number of skeletons from Ain Mallaha (Eynan) show excessive dental wear.[87] All this circumstantial evidence points very clearly to a new approach in the exploitation of wild plant foods, probably wheat and barley, acorns from the hills, perhaps already seeds of legumes from grassland and steppe as well as the old gathered items, fruit, berries and nuts. One day someone may be fortunate enough to find the actual remains.

As in the Kebaran, some sites show extremely high percentages of a specific animal, suggesting that it was herded. At Beidha near Petra, in rocky country, the goat accounted for 76 per cent (gazelle 20 per cent) of the remains;[35] at Wadi Fallah the figure for gazelle was 76·5 per cent.[53] Yet elsewhere, for example at Ain Mallaha, while gazelle reached 44 per cent, roe deer, fallow deer and boar accounted for 15 per cent each.[53] Some gazelle herding may have been practised here, but it is also possible that all animals were hunted, gazelle being the favoured quarry. The full exploitation of natural resources is well illustrated at this famous site;[42] situated near a spring not far from the northwest shore of Lake Huleh, it occupies a basin surrounded by hills on all sides, a natural trap for game. Besides the animals already mentioned there is evidence for wild cattle, goat, hyaena, fox, hare, small carnivores, rodents, birds, fish, freshwater mussels, tortoise, snake and snail. Fish-hooks, gorgets and net-weights attest fishing with hook and line as well as with nets. Bone tools, including awls, needles, sickles, etc., are characteristic of the Natufian and the by-product of the hunt.

Hunting of course varied from area to area: gazelle and fallow deer on Mt Carmel,[47] fallow deer, ibex and ostrich in the Negev (Rosh Zin, Rosh Horsha).[38] At Ain Gev IV, a seasonal Natufian camp on the eastern shore of Lake Tiberias, there is evidence for equid, cattle, pig, roe deer, fallow deer, wolf, wild cat, hare, birds, tortoise, snake, snail, fish and molluscs.

We cannot yet estimate to what extent herding, hunting, wild food gathering, fishing, snail and mollusc collection individually contributed to the food resources of the Natufian. No doubt it varied from place to place, but it is very important to note that there is no evidence whatsoever for the domestication of any plant or animal, so that the term 'Proto-Neolithic' once bestowed on this culture is inappropriate.

There is some evidence from the size of the base camps or settlements that in the Natufian we are dealing with larger and better organized groups than were found in the Kebaran.[8] This is based on the size of living floors in cave terraces, and that of open sites, but as the Natufian period is estimated to have lasted some two thousand years and no clear stratigraphic subdivisions have been fully and convincingly established, these conclusions may be founded on too general a basis. Was the increase in size the result of the economic success of the Natufian culture, or did it start off with larger groupings? The hypothesis that it was demographic pressure which forced the Natufians to look for new foodstuffs has not been scientifically verified by the few facts at our disposal.[71] It may well be that Natufian groups learned to band together to form larger, more effective units, but there is no proof that at the beginning of the period they were more numerous than their Kebaran ancestors. There can be little doubt, however, that by the end of the period their numbers would have increased as the result of a greatly improved economy.

Climatic fluctuations do not appear to have seriously affected the Levant until the end of the Natufian period.[10] The dry cold climate of the Upper Palaeolithic, and the less cold conditions during the Kebaran (when it was wetter than today) were followed by a gradual increase in dryness during the Natufian, although it was not until the end of the Natufian towards *c.* 8000 B C, that the Mediterranean forest retreated northwards. The sudden changes at the beginning of the Natufian cannot therefore be ascribed to climatic deterioration and resulting demographic pressure. On the contrary, they seem to be due to man's awareness of new opportunities of food conservation and exploitation, already tentatively explored during the preceding Kebaran.

The network of Natufian base camps, whether cave terraces or open-built settlements at favourable sites near springs, lakes or rivers, and seasonal hunting camps must inevitably have led to increased contact not only between them but also with the hunting groups of the older Kebaran tradition. Seasonal occupations such as hunting, fishing, fowling, and the gathering of wild grain, berries, nuts and snails, imply greater mobility. To this day, permanent settlement in the Near East tends to be tempered by the change of seasons and transhumance is generally practised for one reason or another. Animals need food that is to be found in midsummer only on higher ground; fish and birds migrate, while many humans flee oppressive heat, humidity or vermin-infested villages for part of the year. In this period we have not yet reached a continuous and permanent occupation of sites, otherwise tells containing a much larger number of successive occupation floors than the maximum of three building levels at Ain Mallaha would have formed.[42] The situation is exactly the same in the Zagros zone, where long periods are represented by only a small number of living floors or building levels at Alikosh in the Bus Mordeh phase.[75] Sites such as the Natufian ones or Bus Mordeh should be compared to Kostienki, Gagarino and Avdeevo in the Ukraine, rather than with the typical Near Eastern tells that begin to appear only after the end of the Natufian period in places like Jericho, Mureybet, El Kowm and Asıklı, where permanency of occupation leads to a massive accumulation of debris.

Fortunately there is plenty of evidence for small-scale trade and barter within the Natufian period in the form of simple luxury objects, such as dentalium and other shells.[25] This continued a trend that had already begun in the Kebaran. There is scarcely a Natufian site where no Mediterranean dentalium occurs and in the Negev, at places such as Rosh Zin, *dentalium giganticum* and other Red Sea shells are also found.[38] This trade in Mediterranean and Red Sea shells, like the somewhat later obsidian trade, undoubtedly facilitated contacts and led to exchange of information, knowledge and ideas, without which cultural advance is impossible. Many other items, foodstuffs, skins, and salt – a new necessity when cereals were being consumed – were presumedly traded. Luxury objects such as bone and stone carvings, or engraved ostrich shell (Rosh Zin) would be likely objects of exchange. Obsidian was not yet imported, but the Natufians had a plentiful supply of excellent flint in the Levant. A study of flint sources might throw light on trade routes and possibly support the contention that nomadism was a feature of certain Natufian sites on Mt Carmel, where some of these sources are located.

The stone industry of the Natufians[22] consists of chipped flint tools and pecked and ground (and sometimes polished) limestone and basalt implements.[63] The latter class of tools represents an innovation, the beginnings of which go back to the Late Kebaran at Ain Gev I; from the Natufian onwards they become standard equipment of all later cultures. Characteristic of the Natufian are abundant microliths, but as in the Kebaran, tools of larger size also occur. Backed bladelets (some with double-edged 'Helwan' retouch) and lunates, probably used as arrow tips or barbs, are the most typical. A systematic microburin technique is used for the manufacture of lunates and triangles. Among the larger tools sickle blades with lustre are prominent and distinctive, as well as notched and denticulated pieces, presumably used for woodwork, and awls and borers related to bone-working. New are large heavy-duty tools – scrapers for cleaning hides, picks for pecking mortars from limestone and basalt blocks, choppers for butchering and breaking bones to extract the marrow. A few sites such as Ain Mallaha and Hayonim show certain deviations; they have few microliths but an abundance of burins, probably used in stone- and bone-working. This may represent a specialization within the Natufian, but the heavy tools occur in both groups.

Among the ground stone implements the large mortars stand out.[42] They are roughly pecked or, in the smaller examples, occasionally decorated with relief patterns along the rim showing meander and curvilinear designs. Pestles sometimes end in a naturalistic rendering of an animal hoof.[25] Vessels are made of limestone, marble and less frequently basalt. Some are polished dishes with a pecked centre which in one case contained traces of red ochre in the depression;[42] others form cups or beakers. There are also polishing stones and pounders, querns and rubbers, hammer-stones, grooved whetstones for polishing bone, notched net-weights, stones with cup-marks etc. Figurines, both human and animal, were also carved from pebbles of varying hardness; they are the earliest figurines in the Near East and are small in size. One figure (headless) from Ain Mallaha was coated with red ochre.[42] From the same site came two rather crude heads; a third was found at El Wad. An erotic group of an embracing couple was found at Ain Sakhri, but all these are outshone by the exquisite carving of a gazelle from Umm ez-Zuweitina, which unfortunately has lost its head.[25]

Art also appears on the bone-work[9] in which the Natufian culture is very rich.[46] There are awls and needles, straight-sided reaping knives with a V-shaped groove to take the flint blades and a handle frequently carved to represent an animal head or even a whole figure of a fawn. There are in addition fish-hooks, gorgets, so-called harpoons (probably used in hunting, not fishing), various decorated pieces of indeterminate use, spatulae, beads made of the phalanges (toe bones) of gazelle, beads, combs, etc. Many of these objects are decorated either with carving in relief or with incised and often hatched patterns.

In their broader context, the art forms of the Natufian fall clearly in the final Upper Palaeolithic phase of European art with its double tradition of naturalistic and geometric styles. The Natufian material is *art mobilier*, rock carvings or paintings have not yet been discovered. Art of this kind may of course have existed but, with a single exception, left no trace if it was practised

3

3 Tools, weapons and ornaments of the Natufian culture of Palestine. Complete reaping knife from Kebara, reaping knife handle with fawn from El Wad and limestone ruminant from Umm ez-Zuweitina. The arrowheads, bottom left, are now thought to be intrusive and belong to the Pre-Pottery Neolithic A period (after Braidwood)

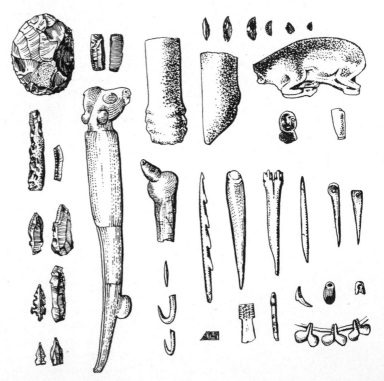

in the open.[50] In recent years examples of cave art have been found (accompanied by *art mobilier*) in the caves and rock-shelters of the Antalya region in Anatolia;[98] in two caves at Palanlı near Adiyaman in the Upper Euphrates valley, and in the open-air rock sanctuaries of Kobystan near Baku on the Caspian. The Antalya and Palanlı material could well be of Epipalaeolithic date, and at Kobystan the earliest scenes with bulls and large human figures may be of comparable age.[221] It is proverbially difficult to date rock art in the absence of excavations and many fantastic claims as to its age have been made. At present there is no evidence to date any Near Eastern rock art earlier than the Natufian, or possibly the Late Kebaran, on the assumption that the roots of Natufian art may go back a few millennia earlier. This would put its beginning somewhere around 12000–10000 BC, but this is pure surmise.

In the Natufian there is no evidence for the use of clay, either baked or unbaked and the use of pisé or mud brick is likewise unknown. Nor is there any definite evidence for spinning or weaving, basketry or matting, although the latter may well have existed. Clothing presumably was still of animal skin and hides.

Until recently little was known of Natufian habitations, which fall into two groups: occupation of terraces in front of caves (Mt Carmel,[26] Judaean desert) or stone-built round or oval huts in open settlements (Ain Mallaha, 2000 sq. m or more;[42] Rosh Zin, 70 sq. m). Stone walls and pavements occur at several cave terraces, but they have not yielded a coherent plan; the structures themselves may have been flimsy shelters supported by posts with

4 Plan of part of the Natufian settlement of Ain Mallaha (Eynan), level III, with round houses and storage pits, some re-used for burials: (a) the 'chieftain's' tomb inside a house; (b) hearth with mortar to the right, fixed in the floor (after Perrot)

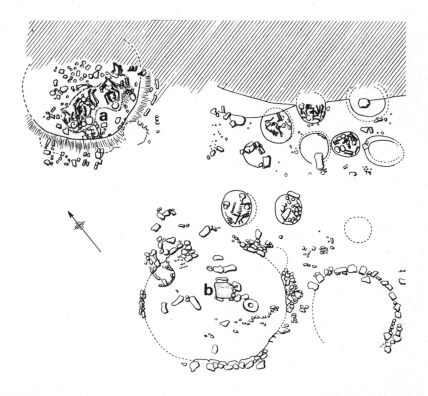

5 Ain Mallaha, level III: round house with plastered and red painted parapet, re-used as a tomb, covered with a stone pavement with hearth

mats or brushwood wind-breaks, such as one still sees throughout the Mediterranean. Five oval structures, one with a stone pavement, were recently discovered at Rosh Zin in the Negev,[28] but the principal type site is Ain Mallaha (Eynan), where the settlement (only partly excavated) is thought to have consisted of about fifty round houses in each of the three successive building levels.[42] It had an established population of 200–300.

4   The round houses, with diameters varying from 7 to 9 m in the lower level (III) to 3 to 4 m were sunk into the soil to a depth of 1·3 m with a lining of rubble; the superstructure was probably made of reeds or matting, possibly supported by posts standing on flat bases. The entrance is usually on the lower side of the slope into which the houses are built, near the spring.

Each hut has, usually near the centre, a stone-built hearth of square or oval shape bordered by stones (often large mortar fragments).[5] Sometimes the hearth is surrounded by a stone pavement of flat slabs (as at Wadi Fallah,[46] Ala Safat, Beidha[35]). In one case a large mortar was placed in the floor near the hearth. Round storage pits 80 cm deep, covered with thick white plaster, are usually found outside the huts, and sometimes inside. The third and lowest level contained cradle-shaped stone constructions which served an unknown purpose. One house, no. 1 in the lowest level, is unusual in that it has a paved stone floor whilst its wall is covered with calcined wall plaster still bearing traces of red paint. The plaster formed a 60 cm-wide parapet over the top of the wall. At a later date tomb 3 was sunk into the fill of the house. This is the earliest known instance of the use of lime (?) plaster stained with red ochre in the Near East, a fashion that was to remain in vogue for a very long time. Another special building was found on virgin soil at Jericho.[29] It was oval with a clean natural clay floor, and was constructed of rubble and previously used mortars. It had been kept scrupulously clean, but was surrounded by rubbish deposits on the rock around. Destroyed by fire, it was dated by C14 to 9250 BC, one of the few Natufian radiocarbon dates. Unfortunately its position within the Natufian

6 Jericho: 'Natufian' oval structure on bedrock, 9250 BC

culture is not clear and the excavators' 'Early Natufian' date has been challenged.

Natufian burials amounting to some two hundred individuals in all have been found;[60] while these evidently represent only a minute proportion of the Natufian population, they are a distinct improvement on the two Late Kebaran skeletons.[61] Natufian burials have been found in caves (Kebara, Shuqba, Erq el-Ahmar), on terraces (El Wad, Wadi Fallah) and outside the houses (Ain Mallaha). There is evidence for both primary and secondary burial. Among the primary burials, usually individual, no definite orientation can be observed. In some instances bodies lay extended on their back (El Wad); others were tightly flexed with knees drawn up to the chin (Wadi Fallah), others again, loosely contracted with hands placed in front of the face (El Wad, Ain Mallaha). Possibly they had been tied up or sewn into skins. At Ain Mallaha there were also seated burials while others resting on their back had their head placed between stones and all joints covered with stones, a measure to ensure that the deceased would not rise from his grave.[42] Occasionally several burials occured in one grave – two adults placed face to face at Erq el-Ahmar, an adult with two children at Shuqba, and an adult with child at Wadi Fallah; but such cases are rare.

There is good evidence for secondary burial in the Natufian[26] with incomplete burials in shallow graves or piles of bones in disused storage pits (Ain Mallaha, Erq el-Ahmar, El Wad, Kebara). Red ochre occurs on the bones in numerous instances at Ain Mallaha and Wadi Fallah.

Graves were frequently covered with stone pavements (El Wad, Erq el-Ahmar). At Ain Mallaha tomb 3 containing two burials, a male and a female, lay beneath a circle of stone 2·5 m in diameter, bordered by a little wall and covered with three large stones. 7 Vertical grave-markers occur at Ain Mallaha, whereas at Wadi Fallah old mortars were placed over individual graves.[46] J. Perrot explains the occurrence within the Natufian of both primary and secondary burial as the result of a semi-nomadic existence;[42] the

7 The 'chieftain's' burial at Ain Mallaha. An extended Natufian burial with the head supported by stones and others covering the joints

secondary burials, he believes, are made up of those who died while away from the base camp. After temporary burial they were exhumed and brought home at the end of the seasonal migration. Such a process may well explain the incompleteness of many of the skeletons.

Natufian funerary gifts are rare;[26] the cores of gazelle horns were found with skulls at Ain Mallaha,[42] and each of the seven skulls at Erq el-Ahmar was accompanied by an equid's tooth. Personal jewellery, on the other hand, is common and mostly made of rows of dentalium shells sewn together in the form of chaplets, diadems or frontlets, bonnets, bracelets and anklets. Necklaces of gazelle phalanges or bone ornaments, which when painted red resemble male organs, are also common, as well as strings of bone beads and shells. Stone vessels, figurines, bone sickles or art objects did not yet accompany the dead into the grave.

The Natufians have been studied by several eminent physical anthropologists.[60] Natufian man, best known from the skeletons from Erq el-Ahmar and Ain Mallaha, appears to be a descendant from an Upper Palaeolithic Combe Capelle-like ancestor. They were of rugged Eurafrican (Robust Mediterranean, Linear Basic White) stock with a dolichocephalic skull and of rather short stature. At El Wad (87 individuals) and Shuqba (45 individuals) the majority of the males were 160 (a few 165) cm tall and females averaged 152 cm. At Ain Mallaha (82 individuals) males measured about 165, females 160 cm. A fine Eurafrican type, also dolichocephalic and probably ancestral to the Proto-Mediterranean type is first seen at or after the end of the Natufian at Wadi Fallah II. Moreover, there are traces of a tendency towards an Alpine brachycephalic development in the Natufian. More work remains to be done on the Ain Mallaha material.

Cultures of Natufian Tradition

There is evidence for a gradual onset of drier conditions during the Natufian[8] and the Mediterranean forest cover is thought to have retreated northwards from Palestine by the end of the period.[10] Its gradual disappearance may well have precipitated a crisis which affected Natufian man and his livelihood. Many Natufian sites were deserted (Ain Mallaha, Hayonim, Wadi Fallah, Kebara, El Wad). Perhaps numbers of Natufians gradually followed the game northwards in its migration to Lebanon and Syria. Natufian sites are now known in the Beqa'a (Jebel Sadiyeh) and at Mureybet on the east bank of the Euphrates, east of Aleppo. Some sites, however, were reoccupied by Natufians or their descendants, namely Wadi Fallah II, El Khiam 3–4 and Jericho, 'the Proto-Neolithic nucleus tell'.

These various communities, small in numbers, continued Natufian traditions in their stone industry. Flint picks, lunates (rarer than before), borers, knife blades, sickle blades, burins, end- and core-scrapers are in the old tradition. Composite elements on the other hand are in decline, blades and sickle blades now predominate and new elements, hitherto unknown, are added to the

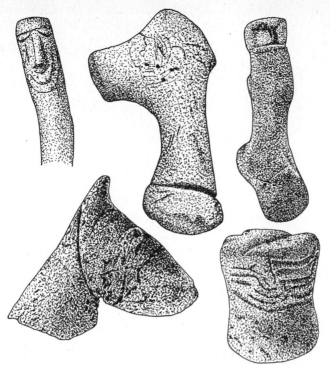

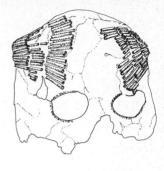

tool-kit. Among these are the highly distinctive tranchet axes, characterized by a cutting edge wider than the depth of the blade, and double-notched and often hollow-based triangular arrow-heads. Only at El Khiam, far south in the Judaean desert, are picks and tranchets absent. The more spectacular aspect of the Natufian culture, its art, had, however, disappeared, though at Wadi Fallah some clumsy female figurines were made from pebbles. Yet the most remarkable feature of this immediately post-Natufian period is the establishment of trading contacts with central Anatolia[84] from which Çiftlik (type 2b) obsidian was obtained in small quantities at both Wadi Fallah II and Jericho.[85] It did not, however, reach El Khiam.

WADI FALLAH

At Wadi Fallah II fourteen small round huts with walls still standing to a height of 1 m were found arranged on four terraces with massive retaining walls.[46] The huts are of the same type as those found in the top layer at Ain Mallaha. They had a hearth, often in the centre of the room, surrounded by flat stones or slabs with cup-marks. Specialization of labour is suggested by finds from some of the huts. It is possible that the graves with skeletons of fine Eurafrican type mentioned above come from this settlement. If not they must just precede its construction.

PROTO-NEOLITHIC JERICHO

At Jericho, to the southwest of the Natufian oval structure, a small mound arose as innumerable floors and humps of eroded clay walls followed each other in repeated succession.[29] The plans of

8 Natufian art objects from the cemetery of Wadi Fallah (Nahal Oren), including a gazelle head in bone and a bifacial figure (after Stekelis)

9 Natufian burial from El Wad: skull with cap of dentalium beads and necklace of gazelle phalanges (after Garrod)

12

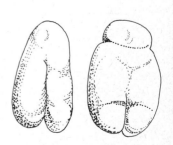

10 Figurines of soft limestone from Wadi Fallah (after Stekelis)

39

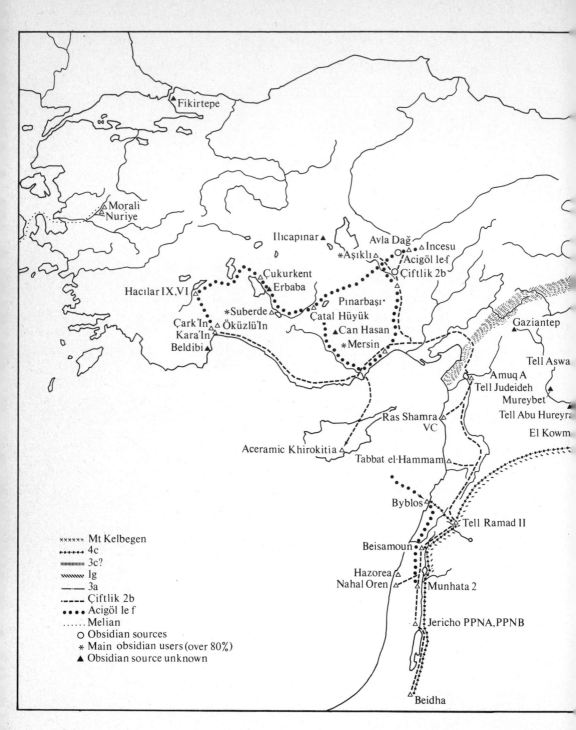

Fikirtepe

Morali
Nuriye

Ilıcapınar ▲   Avla Dağ
              *Aşıklı ▲ △ Incesu
                         △ Acigöl le·f
                      ○ Çiftlik 2b
          △ Çukurkent
          ▲ Erbaba
Hacılar IX,VI ▲
                    Pınarbaşı·
     *Suberde △   Çatal Hüyük
Çark'In △ Öküzlü'In
Kara'In   ▲ Can Hasan
Beldibi ▲   *Mersin
                                        Gaziantep
                                          ▲

                              Amuq A
                            △ Tell Judeideh ▲   Tell Aswa
                              Mureybet
                      Ras Shamra △   Tell Abu Hureyra
                           VC   El Kowm

Aceramic Khirokitia △
              Tabbat el·Hammam △

         Byblos

                   ▲ Tell Ramad II

Beisamoun △

Hazorea △
Nahal Oren △   Munhata 2

                △ Jericho PPNA,PPNB

              △ Beidha

×××××× Mt Kelbegen
•·•·•·• 4c
ıιιιιιιι 3c?
ᵕᵕᵕᵕᵕ lg
—— 3a
-·-·- Çiftlik 2b
•••• Acigöl le f
...... Melian
○ Obsidian sources
* Main obsidian users (over 80%)
▲ Obsidian source unknown

these could no longer be made out, but the depth of deposit, amounting to some 4 m, suggests frequent occupation near the spring, though the 'settlement' may have been no more permanent than in the Natufian. There is no evidence that any of these sites were occupied all the year round. The term 'Proto-Neolithic'

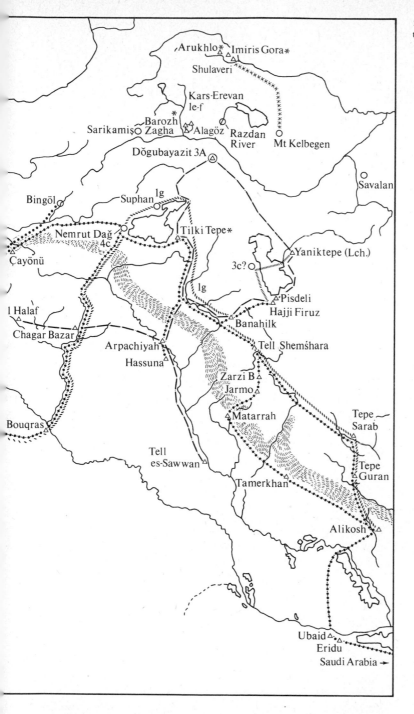

Arukhlo
Imiris Gora
Shulaveri
Kars-Erevan le-f
Barozh Zagha
Sarikamiş
Alagöz
Razdan River
Mt Kelbegen
Dŏgubayazit 3A
Savalan
Bingöl
Suphan
1g
Nemrut Dağ 4c
Tilki Tepe
Çayönü
Yaniktepe (Lch.)
3c?
1g
Pisdeli
Hajji Firuz
Banahilk
l Halaf
Chagar Bazar
Arpachiyah
Tell Shemśhara
Hassuna
Zarzi B
Jarmo
Matarrah
Tepe Sarab
Bouqras
Tell es-Sawwan
Tepe Guran
Tamerkhan
Alikosh
Ubaid
Eridu
Saudi Arabia →

certainly seems rather premature for Jericho, for no grain, querns or mortars were found in these deposits (which may, however, have been grouped in domestic courtyards outside the limits of the excavation) and the animal bones consisted of gazelle, cattle, boar and especially fox, the remains of hunting.[52] At El Khiam 3–4, on

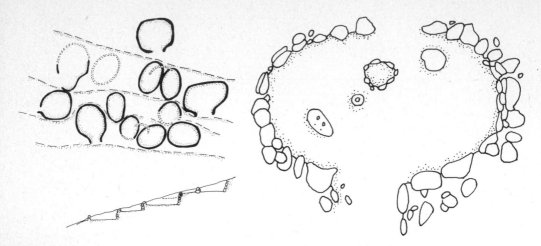

12 Plan of the post-Natufian
settlement of Wadi Fallah with
small round houses of Ain
Mallaha I–II type on terraces
(after Stekelis)

the other hand, goat (with 83 per cent of all the bones, and these
mostly of kids) was probably herded. Gazelle (with 14 per cent)
was relatively unimportant.[53] At Wadi Fallah II, where gazelle
herding was probably practised since the Kebaran, a climax is
reached with 88 per cent of all animal bones belonging to this
species.[56]

On the basis of the evidence at present available it does not seem
that any significant changes were as yet taking place in the economy
of Palestine. A few new tool types are introduced, tranchet axe and
arrowhead, and firm contact is established with the north.[22] This
is significant, but the real impact cannot be gauged until sites along
the trade route in Cilicia, Syria and Lebanon yield their secrets.
Similarities in chipped-stone tradition between the Antalya region
on the south coast of Turkey and the Lebanon–Palestinian stretch
of the Levant have been noted since the Kebaran.[105] The Belbaşı
culture gave way to the Beldibi culture,[107] the earlier form of
which (layer C) shows affinities with the Natufian.[7] Such affinities
suggest the presence of other groups of hunters and gatherers in
the territories that lie along the shores of Cilicia and north Syria.
Support is given to this idea by a number of sporadic finds:
lunates and backed blades at Direkli cave near Göksun in the
Anti-Taurus, a 'Natufian' lunate from the Amuq plain,[244]
microliths of undetermined type from the Gaziantep area, and a
laconic report on two sites, Söğüt Tarlası and Biriş Mezarligi near
Bozova just across the Euphrates, tentatively dated to *c.* 10000 or
a little later.[12]

MUREYBET

The main site of this period in north Syria is the mound of
Mureybet,[13] situated on the east bank of the Euphrates at the
traditional crossing-point some 80 km southeast of Aleppo.[14]
Recent excavations on the river bank by J. Cauvin have yielded the
remains of a Natufian settlement of fishermen and hunters
(Mureybet I) with four successive occupation levels, suggesting
some permanency.[14] In the three upper levels, floors of stamped
clay with hearths, some surrounded with clay horseshoe kerbs, and
pits filled with burnt pebbles and ashes, were found. The latter

13 Mureybet: (a, b) lunates and
adze in flint from the Natufian
period (Mureybet I); (c–e) carved
bone combs from Mureybet II;
(f) limestone figurine from
Mureybet II; (g) bone container,
levels VIII–X; (h) stone bowl with
incised decoration near the rim
(cf. Ain Mallaha and Çayönü);
(i) bone needles from level VII;
(j) greenstone ring, levels II–V;
(k) limestone flags with incised
snakes (?), level VII; (l) mortar,
level VII; (m) marble plate with
pecked centre (cf. Ain Mallaha),
level XVII; (n) limestone plate,
level VII; (o) quern, level VII
(after Cauvin and van Loon)

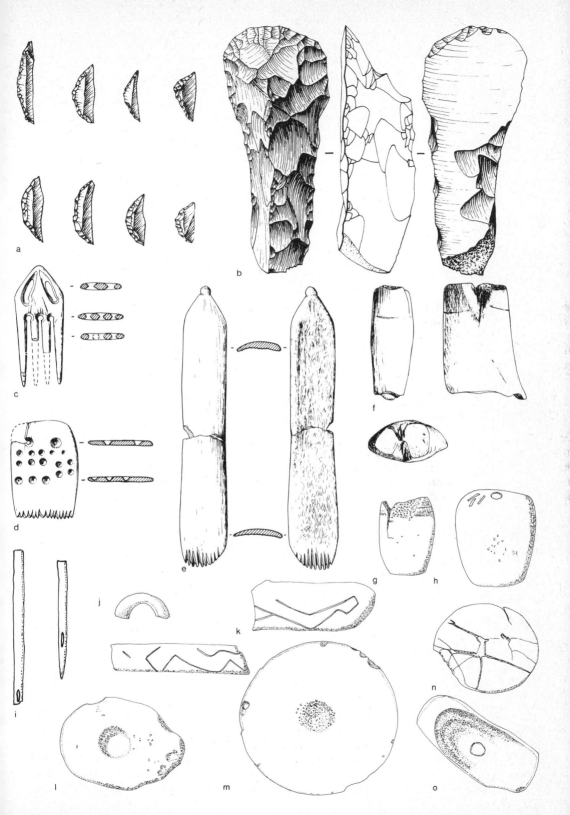

occur in all levels of the site, including the lowest, which yielded the remains on virgin soil of a round hut with a thin clay 'wall' still standing to a height of 50 cm and bearing the imprint on the outside of decayed vertical wooden posts with diameters of 7–12 cm. The 10 cm-thick clay plaster was smoothed on the inside. Near by a bucranium as well as two shoulder blades of equids had been intentionally covered by a clay bench. The chipped-stone industry of this northern Natufian site is entirely in flint, obsidian being not yet known. Microliths, mainly lunates but including some triangles and trapezes, form 7–17 per cent of the total of the tools in these levels of Mureybet I, and there are many micro-piercers and some backed blades. Most of the tools are piercers and 'mèches de forêt'; there are some scrapers, burins, retouched and denticulated pieces, but sickle blades hardly appear. Arrowheads, though primitive and very rare, are nevertheless present from the very beginning and so are picks and adzes, tools typical of Mureybet. The polished-bone industry contains awls and cylindrical beads. The site was destroyed by fire *c.* 8640±140 B C.[27]

The Natufian faunal remains are mainly those of the Palestinian wild ass, together with aurochs and gazelle.[14] Bird bones, fish bones and freshwater mussels occur in abundance, showing that Natufian man fully exploited the aquatic resources of the site. Plant remains include among others wild barley, and the pits filled with pebbles and ashes *could* already have been used for roasting wild grain as well as meat or fish, as in the overlying building levels of Mureybet II and III.

The extent of the Natufian settlement is not known, but the next stage in the development of the site, Mureybet II, was partly founded on its remains and partly on virgin soil. This is the 'round house phase' of M. van Loon, in which he found eight superposed building levels (I–VIII) on virgin soil,[37] whereas in the new excavations some five building levels have been found on top of the Natufian settlement.

The round or oval huts vary in diameter from 2·7 to 4 m, as in the upper levels of Ain Mallaha or Wadi Fallah II. They were no longer built of wood, but had walls of pisé or red clay with rubble or disused querns and mortars as a foundation. These were limited in height and the upper part of the structures are thought to have consisted of light materials. Stone floors set in red clay reinforced with pebbles are typical. Gravelled paths are sometimes found outside the huts, a necessity for the rainy Syrian winters. Fire-pits lined with stone and clay continue from the previous phase, serving as outdoor hearths and roasting-pits for grain. In levels VII–XIII they occur grouped together.

The chipped-stone industry, mainly in local chert and flint found in the river gravels but with some rare pieces of obsidian (source not yet analysed), now lacks the geometric microliths of the previous Natufian phase, but there are still some microlithic tools. Micro-piercers, large piercers and 'mèches de forêt' form a group which characterizes Mureybet II and which in some levels accounts for more than half the number of tools. Scrapers and burins, on the other hand, are few, and the same can be said of the sickle blades. Of the fairly numerous arrowheads most are of the

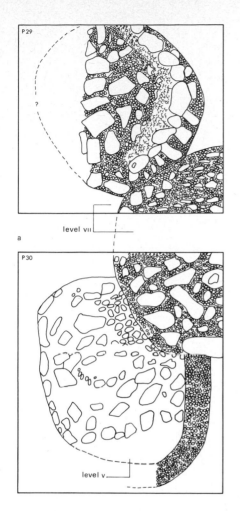

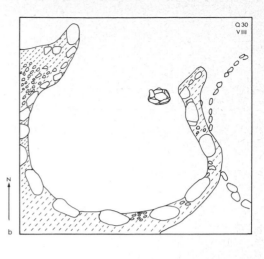

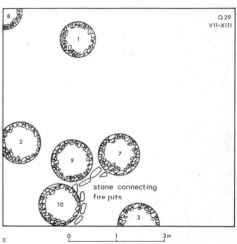

notched type, but others have simple tangs and all have an abrupt marginal retouch. Among the heavy tools, picks, large scrapers and adzes continue in use. In the ground-stone category there are the familiar querns, mortars and pestles, as well as stone bowls and dishes, some with zigzag moulding, still reminiscent of Ain Mallaha. A Natufian ancestry is equally obvious in the fine bone industry with carved combs from early Mureybet II deposits, and the ubiquitous awls and needles. A fragment of a limestone figurine, which may be compared with similar figures from Wadi Fallah II, was also found.

Radiocarbon tests date the end of the first round-hut level of Mureybet II to 8142±118 BC, that is, not far removed from the beginning of Pre-Pottery Neolithic A of Jericho, c. 8350±200 BC.

The economy of Mureybet II shows – like the rest of the culture – much continuity; aquatic resources were still exploited and the same animals were hunted: Palestinian wild ass, gazelle and aurochs, but apparently now in equal proportions with the wild ass no longer predominating.[54] Some fallow deer, boar, hare and

14 Mureybet: plan of round huts (Mureybet II); (a) level V and VII; (b) level VIII; (c) roasting pits, levels VII–XIII (after van Loon)

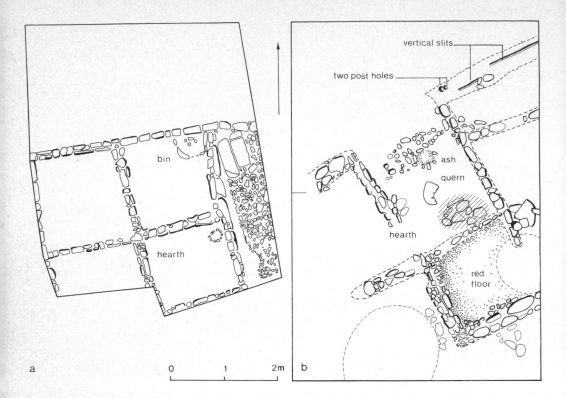

vertical slits

two post holes

bin

ash

quern

hearth

hearth

red
floor

a   0   1   2m   b

15 Mureybet: plan of rectangular structures (Mureybet III); (a) structure 16, level XIV; (b) structure 19, level XVI (after van Loon)

wolf are also found, but their remains amount to only 1 per cent, compared to 33 per cent for each of the three main game animals. Such proportions do not suggest a preference for one animal that might be herded, and there are indeed no traces of domestication. On the other hand, Mureybet II continues to yield some of the earliest charred grains and seeds found in the Near East.[57] They consist of wild einkorn of the large two-seeded variety *thaoudar*, wild barley, lentils and bitter vetch, accompanied by pistachio, a possible pea, astragalus, milk-vetch seeds and toad-rush.[59] Whereas the legumes and weeds may have grown locally among the grasses of the surrounding steppe, and the pistachio is still found in the neighbouring hills, wild einkorn or wild barley were not at home in such a low-lying environment, less than 300 m above sea-level. The nearest area where they would have had their natural habitat lies in the rocky basalt hills of the Gaziantep region, some 100–150 km to the northwest. The size of the site, with perhaps as many as two hundred round houses, militates against the idea of wild grain collecting on such a scale – even by boat, for which there is no evidence – and Hans Helbaek suggests that we have here the first attested case of the cultivation by man of wild cereals, carefully transported from their natural habitat in the hills into a foreign and man-made environment. At this stage the mutation leading to the development of a tough stem (rachis) had not yet occurred and morphologically the grain, although cultivated, is still wild. This find at Mureybet is of extraordinary importance in that it shows not merely the reaping of wild grain in its natural environment – as may have begun in the Late Kebaran and was probably normal practice during the Natufian period – but the next step in which man no longer merely reaps, but begins to plant certain crops outside their natural habitat. This process of planting, weeding and nurturing the young shoots and keeping them safe from predators, both animals and birds, would have encouraged if not necessitated all-the-year-round occupation of the settlement. The size of the site and the long occupation, estimated to cover most of the eighth millennium B C, strongly suggests that at Mureybet we are witnessing a first successful attempt at early farming in what for the first time might be regarded as an early village. The alternative suggestion that Mureybet was merely a camp of game hunters who each year collected seeds of einkorn, barley, etc. up to a distance of *c.*100–150 km and bore the loads back to the site,[2] carries little conviction as it contradicts both common sense and human nature. They could have settled nearer to their grain supplies without losing the benefits of hunting and fishing, and avoided laborious transport.

Mureybet III, the third phase, is marked by the appearance of the first rectangular structures,[13] building levels X–XVII of the first excavations.[37] Yet the change is not as decisive as was then thought, for round houses persisted side by side with them, as recent discoveries have shown. Both are built from loaf-shaped pieces of soft limestone, easily cut with flint tools, laid horizontally like bricks in clay mortar often mixed with broken pebbles. Floors, as before, were paved with stones or pebbles and covered with a layer of clay mixed with straw. The red clay of the floors had an upward curve where they joined the walls, but when the floors were relaid, as happened seven times in one structure, the floor was first levelled with a layer of fine sand. Walls too were replastered. A square structure in level XIV, measuring 3·5 m a side, had no doorway and must have been entered from the roof. It was divided into four rooms, each 1·5 m square; one of these contained a sunken hearth, another was provided with a storage bin. In one of the walls was a peephole and the jaw of a large carnivore was embedded in another. In other houses bulls' horns were used in a similar way. Outside the house was a paved courtyard with a doorway and a pivot stone for a door.

The top levels XVI and XVII contained multiple-roomed houses destroyed by fire. They had walls of clay with both vertical and horizontal wooden supports. Again horn cores of cattle were found in the walls and in three instances detached human skulls had been placed in corners of rooms and covered with debris and red clay. These houses were paved with pebbles or had red clay floors. Groups of human bones were found below floors in these two levels only, suggesting secondary burials. Another secondary burial, consisting of the skull and some long bones, was found immediately below the hearth in a round house which is still partly unexcavated. A geometric wall painting, the earliest yet found on a man-made wall, decorated the interior of this building, with several rows of horizontally placed zigzags in black on a buff ground.[13] Also found were a small obsidian dagger and a stylized human head, carved in limestone. It is possible that this structure served a cult purpose.

16 Anthropomorphic limestone figure, from Mureybet III: top, side view; bottom, front view

47

17 Jericho Pre-Pottery Neolithic A: view of the superimposed walls

The stone industry of Mureybet III continues the local tradition, but certain changes take place; micro-piercers and retouched bladelets are the last microliths.[13] Arrowheads increase in number, together with scrapers and burins, and a flat retouch appears. Obsidian becomes more common, and the bone industry now has many tools like paper-knives, as well as awls and beads. No changes are yet apparent in the economy during phase III.

The two radiocarbon dates of 7542 ± 122 (XVI) and 7954 ± 114 for Mureybet III seem a little too high,[37] and phases II and III may be contemporary on the whole with Jericho Pre-Pottery Neolithic A, which ends *c.* 7350 BC. Like Jericho, Mureybet seems to have been deserted before reoccupation took place in the Pre-Pottery Neolithic B period, represented at the latter site by stray finds outside the area of the old tell of pressure-flaked tanged arrowheads and boat-shaped cores (Mureybet IV).

Tell Abu Hureyra

Some 40 km downstream from Mureybet, but on the opposite bank of the Euphrates lies Tell Abu Hureyra, the largest Neolithic site known in Syria, covering 500×300 m with a deposit about 5 m thick. Excavations during 1972 and 1973 have revealed that the site was occupied in the Natufian period and after a stratigraphic break in the Pre-Pottery Neolithic B period, *c.* 7000–5800 BC, when it was burnt and deserted.[48]

The Natufian settlement on virgin soil was small and was characterized by a microlithic Natufian industry with lunates, backed bladelets and borers as well as large tools such as flake- and core-scrapers. Earth floors, pits, fire hollows, etc. form the earliest occupation as at Mureybet I. Many animal bones and seeds were found as well as fish bones and freshwater mussels, but details are not yet available.

Pre-Pottery Neolithic A Jericho, *c.* 8350–7350 BC

An even more remarkable development took place in the Jericho oasis where a vast agglomeration of round houses spreading over some 10 acres engulfed the small 'Proto-Neolithic' tell in up to twenty-five building levels.[29] Over a period of a thousand years, fixed by radiocarbon dating, this would mean an average of forty years per building level or about two generations, which seems feasible enough. The dwellings are round or oval with diameters of 5 m or more, partly sunk into the soil and entered through a small passage with a few timber steps and a socket for a doorpost. Occasionally there is a second room. In the absence of stone, the walls are built of 'hog-backed' bricks, loaf-shaped like the similar limestone blocks used at Mureybet. This is an intermediate form between shapeless pisé pads and moulded mud brick. The upper part of the walls was of sticks and branches smeared with clay.

At Jericho these well-constructed round houses are a definite improvement on the simpler shelters of the 'Proto-Neolithic' tell, but the virtual identity of the stone industry and the continued import of Çiftlik obsidian from central Anatolia links the two periods very closely, suggesting that at Jericho the one developed locally out of the other.

The earliest phase(s) of PPNA Jericho did not apparently need a defensive wall and remains of a round house were found below the first stone wall and tower. Later a stone wall, 3 m thick and 4 m high or more, was built with an apsidal tower inside. The tower, 10 m in diameter and 8·5 m high, was solid except for a staircase of twenty-two steps. It was entered by a door 1·7 m high on its eastern side. This structure was encountered on the west side of the mound and the wall was subsequently picked up near the north and south limits of the tell. It is thought to have encircled the whole 10-acre area, and which would give it a length of at least 700 m. The population of PPNA Jericho is estimated at two thousand or more. J. Perrot has suggested that there was perhaps no great circuit wall, but a series of fortified enclosures separated by more open spaces. This would have made the site less impressive, while involving even more work, and I regard it as a rather unlikely supposition.

At a somewhat later date curved enclosures, thickly plastered and with no visible entrance (and therefore probably entered from the top) were built up against the tower, thereby blocking the original entrance, now only accessible through a trap door. One of the storage rooms of this second phase contained charred grain and others have sedimentary deposits and a water channel. There were five such structures reaching a height of over 3 m, but eventually they, and the passage in the tower, fell into disuse and were used as a burial ground. A skin wall, approximately 1 m thick, was subsequently built around the now solid tower, above the level of the filled storage chambers, and a new town wall was built on top of two earlier ones, of which the second was associated with a rock-cut ditch. In this third phase the tower stood unencumbered by other structures, but once again storage rooms (for grain?) were built up against it; one of them had a low opening near the base.

As time went on these storage rooms in turn went out of use and the area was given over to normal round dwellings; six phases of these could be distinguished, but there may originally have been

18

18 Jericho Pre-Pottery Neolithic A: plan of the round tower (after Kenyon)

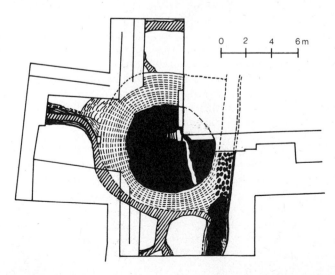

more as the top of the deserted town was exposed to erosion for an unknown length of time. This complex sequence of events could be repeated for other parts of the tell; the town-like occupation, the numerous rebuildings – up to twenty-five times – all show stability and permanent occupation. The massive fortifications, the lookout tower (or towers?), the cutting of the ditch in the second phase and the rebuilding of the walls, all make it appear that Jericho had considerable resources of man-power, a social structure with a ruler or rulers who could organize such public works and an economy that could support early town life in this remote age. Jericho deserves to be called 'the earliest town in the world' and the legend of the walls of Jericho may have originated long before the days of Joshua! It is a pity that so little of Jericho could be excavated, for a site of this importance must have contained shrines. Burials occur below house floors as well as in disused plots. Isolated adult skulls as well as groups of infant skulls were found on several occasions. Burials are usually contracted and unaccompanied by funeral gifts. Anthropological studies show that these people were of the same stock as the Natufians, the same rugged Eurafricans we have already met at Ain Mallaha and Erq el-Ahmar. They must therefore be regarded as descendants of the Natufians. Among them there are also some brachycephalic Alpines, but gracile Proto-Mediterraneans have not yet been reported. Skull deformation seems to have been practised.

Very little is yet known about the material culture of this people; the stone industry continues the 'Proto-Neolithic' tradition and contains microliths together with axes, adzes, picks and chisels which suggest woodworking.[64] A fine bone industry is present, but there are no characteristic stone bowls as later; figurines do not occur and indeed art of all kinds is lacking, and there is no evidence of cult places.

As regards the economy, there were still no domestic animals. Gazelle (36·9 per cent), either hunted or herded, was the chief source of meat; cattle, goat and boar were hunted.[52] The great achievement of PPNA Jericho lies elsewhere, in the domestication of two-row hulled barley and emmer wheat.[55] Deposits no longer show the wild forms as at contemporary Mureybet, but the domestic forms; these, through mutation, had developed a tough rachis which made reaping easier, as the grains no longer scattered. Among the carbonized seeds lentil and fig are also present. So we can now answer the question of how such a large and permanent settlement as Jericho could maintain itself for over a millennium: it was through growing domestic wheat, barley and legumes in the well-watered lands of the Jericho oasis.

As wild barley and grain, being medium-altitude plants and denizens of the oak and pistachio belt, would not have grown wild in the Jericho oasis – though they are still to be found in the uplands (Wadi Kelt, Wadi Auja, Salt plateau) on either side of the Jordan valley – one must postulate an intermediate period of cultivation of wild forms brought down from their natural habitat, which preceded the 'domesticated' forms. If the 'Proto-Neolithic' Jerichoans were in fact thus occupied around the spring, and the venture was a success, this would account for the phenomenal advance during the PPNA period. Their newly found wealth in food, perhaps unique in the Jordan valley, may have been the reason for the construction of the great walls and the watch-tower (or watch-towers) from which the arable land in the oasis could be carefully guarded against marauding bands of hunters and gatherers.

Since the development of its PPNA culture[5] came at a time which climatologists tell us was one of gradually increasing aridity,[10] Jericho, unlike many other settlements, may have been saved by the domestication of wheat and barley. The town's large population might have been the result, not just of 'population explosion' that invariably accompanies successful agriculture, but of an influx of other groups into the oasis to join these first food producers. The building of the walls at the beginning of the period was obviously intended not only to guard their wealth, but to deny it to others, and the repairs of the fortifications over such a long period may well reflect demographic pressure as desiccation made itself felt outside the oasis. PPNA settlements are in fact extremely rare in Palestine.

It has been suggested that trading was to some extent responsible for Jericho's status,[1] but this has been ridiculed by others on the grounds that the material found in Jericho does not show great wealth,[5] let alone the presence of manufactured goods which could have served as barter.

Asphalt, sulphur and salt, products of the Dead Sea, may have played a moderate role in the barter and exchange of the time, but these commodities are fairly widespread in Palestine. Çiftlik obsidian continued to reach Jericho in small quantities throughout the period,[83−5] but the chief source of Jericho's wealth – at a time of population pressure and desiccation – must have been barley and wheat, lentils, etc. Surplus food, seed-corn, as well as the instructions on how to grow it, would have been far more valuable than gold. As H. Helbaek has put it, 'grain is man's most precious artefact'. The invention of domestic grain easily explains Jericho's pre-eminence, but the desertion of this great site *c.* 7350 BC without any trace of violence has not been explained.[287] Could it be that early agricultural methods had overtaxed and exhausted the soil?

Recent excavations at Tell Aswad, east of Damascus, have brought to light a site, apparently without permanent architecture but with numerous clay figurines, dated by C14 to a period which may be contemporary or just after the PPNA of Jericho. [20, 20a]

With the end of PPNA the Palestine Natufian tradition had run its full course, and when Jericho was reoccupied, perhaps *c.* 7000 BC but possibly somewhat earlier, it was by people with a different tradition, arriving with a fully fledged culture. It would now appear that the PPNB culture of Jericho and other sites in Palestine, south Syria and the Lebanon, bore the imprint – stronger at Jericho perhaps than elsewhere – of north Syrian developments on a Natufian basis, the beginnings of which we have already sketched at Mureybet. It is to these further developments in the north that we must now turn in order to understand the nature of the PPNB culture in Palestine.

North Syrian Developments in the Late Eighth and Early Seventh Millennia

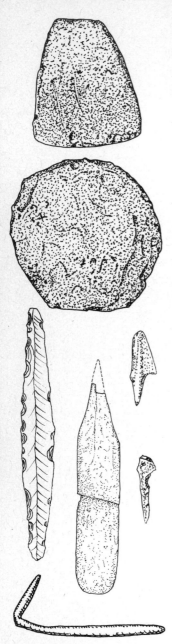

19 Çayönü: polished stone celt and scraper, flint projectile point, bone awl, bone piercers and hammered copper pin (after Çambel and Braidwood)

ÇAYÖNÜ

At Mureybet[37] the top levels seem to show the transition from PPNA to PPNB,[13] which may be further clarified in the future by more excavations, both here and at El Kowm, northeast of Palmyra.[23] For the moment the best example of a north Syrian PPNB site is undoubtedly Çayönü,[12] an oval mound with a maximum width of 250 m and some 4–5 m in height.[51] It lies on a tributary of the Tigris, north-northwest of Diyarbakir in Turkey and just south of the Taurus Mountains which form the northern limit of the Syrian plains. A number of radiocarbon dates suggest occupation, in five building levels, between c. 7500 and 6800(?) BC, a period roughly contemporary with early PPNB in the Levant. It would appear that here we have another site where it is possible to demonstrate local processes of domestication of both plants and animals. Conclusions are still preliminary, but it appears that in the earliest two building levels (I and II) only the dog was domesticated, the rest of the animals – aurochs, pig, red deer, fallow deer, sheep, goat and some smaller animals – being hunted as wild game. At the same time emmer wheat, still wild, was most common, but einkorn which included some wild forms, was also in cultivation.[58] Wild barley and wild twin-grained einkorn were virtually absent, which suggests that these forms of wild grain, native to the area, were unimportant in the economy of Çayönü. Pistachio, almond and wild vetch were gathered. Flax occurs in the lowest levels only, which suggests that it was collected as a wild crop or that attempts at growing flax were early abandoned.

In the top levels of the site (IV and V) there is a greater dependence on domestic animals, sheep, goat and pig(?), but aurochs and deer were still hunted in considerable numbers.[90] Domestic emmer and einkorn were grown, together with large quantities of peas, lentils, bitter vetch and wild vetch; pistachio, almond, acorn and hackberry were collected.

Compared to Mureybet or Jericho this is a late development; nevertheless it is of considerable interest as it illustrates the nature in which such developments took place throughout the Near East, wherever the wild ancestors of wheat and barley and those of the domestic animals were to be found. Spontaneous in one area, or set off by contact stimulus from another, the techniques of early farming were invented or diffused throughout the Near East in the course of a few millennia.

Other features of considerable interest at Çayönü are the stone buildings, the earliest use of hammered native copper, the first use of clay bricks, baked figurines, etc., and even some timid attempts at making pottery, thereafter abandoned.

Çayönü has five building levels, somewhat confusingly numbered from the bottom up. In the earliest of these there were only remains of pit ovens, but level II contained a number of rectangular stone buildings, measuring up to 5 × 10 m. One of these – there is a succession of at least three superimposed structures – had its plaster floors preserved as well as interior partitions. The grid-like arrangement of the walls may have served to raise the floor above the damp ground and the floors may have been supported on beams or planks. The result was a multi-roomed house with a hall, a square room, and two rows of three subsidiary cubicles alongside. In level III stone-paved rectangular areas appear with two vertical free-standing stones and internal buttresses. It is still not clear whether these are houses or open courtyards. There is also a structure measuring 9 × 10 m, tentatively interpreted as a 'shrine'. It had internally buttressed walls and a bench at the rear. Its elaborate floor was made up of two layers, a thick lower one with stones set in cement-like mortar and an upper one with a terrazzo 'mosaic' of salmon-coloured pebbles, 1–3 cm wide, set in red mortar. On either side of the room, running transversely, white marble pebbles had been arranged in two strips 5 cm wide and over 4 m long. After the mortar had set the whole of this floor was ground smooth and polished. In level IV, which was burnt, there was a workshop measuring approximately 5 × 8 m with six to seven small rooms, each with its own yield of tools. In this level we first encounter square or rectangular mud-brick buildings and the continued use of this material is evidenced in level V, the top aceramic level, which yielded a single room structure measuring 5 × 9 m. A model from level IV shows such a house; it has a door-way with curved jambs at the narrow end, a flat roof and a low curb round the base. Sunken hearths and clay bins are found inside the houses.

Baked clay was used for a few cups and a dish found in level III, but it first appears in level II in the form of female figurines, animal figurines (horned caprids and bovids) and geometric objects (cones, spheres, discs, cylinders) and a few beads. Female figurines do not yet approach naturalistic forms but look like the Upper Palaeolithic or Kobystan females – faceless, armless and breastless, but with a strongly curved back line, a rounded belly on a square base with two legs and a stalk-like head. The more stylized versions have stumpy legs or are turned into a cylinder with a groove to indicate the legs. T-shaped figures also appear and a few fragments show loin cloths or a necklace of pellets. These small figurines, 2·5–5 cm high, have later parallels at Jarmo, at Çatal Hüyük and even as far west as Aceramic Sesklo. Burials have not yet been reported.

Little is known of the stone industry in which flint predominates in the form of unretouched blades, some sickle blades with silica sheen, and a few retouched scrapers, knives, piercing tools and well-shaped arrowheads. In level IV there were several caches of large-sized obsidian implements, blades, points and specialized tools as much as 20 cm long. In this phase obsidian is as common as flint, whereas in the lower levels flint predominated. Analysis shows the obsidian to have come from a number of East Anatolian sources: Bingöl, Suphan (grey type 1g) and Nemrut Dağ on Lake Van (green type 4c).

Ground stone tools include polished celts, querns, hand-stones, hammers, as well as beads, pendants and bracelets. There are fragments of stone bowls with excised triangles leaving a zigzag pattern in relief as at Mureybet. The level IV workshop yielded

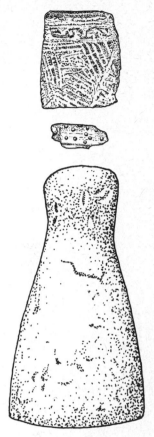

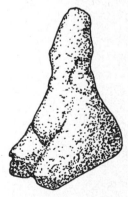

20 Çayönü: fragment of decorated stone bowl, bone object, clay object and clay figure (after Çambel and Braidwood)

many ground stone and bone implements, including two nearly complete sickle hafts of deer antler; there were also a dozen marine shells. Bone objects and Mediterranean whelks are decorated with drilled holes.

Çayönü is only 20 km from Ergani Maden, a well-known source of native copper and malachite ores. In levels I and II drilled beads, straight pins and a square-sectional reamer were found, neatly hammered from native copper and, in the case of the pins, ground to a point. This is the first attested use of native copper in the Near East and precedes the use of hammered and, later, smelted copper at Çatal Hüyük by perhaps a thousand years. It is characteristic that this should have happened at the nearest known site to Maden where the heavy shining red malleable material must have attracted man's attention as much as the bright green malachite which occurs in the later levels at Çayönü.

The origins of the Çayönü culture are obscure, nor is it known what followed it. Evidence of a few links with Mureybet perhaps suggests that it developed out of a similar culture, but this is by no means certain. At present Çayönü stands alone, though as the site is under excavation there may be more surprises in store.

TELL ABU HUREYRA

In the PPNB period a huge settlement, *c.* 500 × 300 m, grew up on the south bank of the Euphrates, completely covering the long-since-abandoned Natufian site and spreading far beyond it, with its massive deposits of numerous building levels with rectangular houses. Pisé, or tauf, as it is called in Iraq, was the usual building material, mud brick appears later. Floors were of stamped earth or red or black burnished plaster and fragments of white plaster with painted red lines shows the use of wall painting for decoration. At Tell Abu Hureyra there appears to be a continuous development from (PPNB) later aceramic into an early ceramic with dark burnished wares and projectile points, of a type familiar from Bouqras, Amuq A and Early Neolithic Byblos.

Apart from house remains which are frequently rebuilt, there is good evidence in this aceramic period for specialized activities, such as the manufacture of flint, obsidian, polished stone and bone tools, and areas for cooking and butchering.

The dead were buried below the floors of buildings or in the yards outside. Most of them were in the contracted position, and at least one was wrapped in fibrous material. Red-ochre burials were more common, with both primary and secondary burial attested. Pits filled with bones and groups of skulls were found, one containing sixteen skeletons with only three skulls attached.

Clay figurines, both human and animal, were rare. Stone vessels do not occur in the earliest levels, but become quite common in the upper ones, marble and gypsum small polished hemispherical bowls as well as a 'white ware' cup being found. There is evidence for reeds in building, for rush mats and containers, which left their impressions on bitumen. Bone needles were used for sewing cloth and there are spatulae, borers and a fish-hook. Sling-stones in the form of small pecked stone balls were found, and numerous arrowheads, mostly in local flint, rarely in Anatolian obsidian.

The flint tools are made from bipolar boat-shaped cores. Tanged arrowheads and some spearheads prevail with abrupt retouch at tang and tip, whereas pressure-flaked examples occur only in the upper levels of this period. There are awls and burins and end-scrapers on blades and a wide variety of flake- and core-scrapers made from pebbles. Sickle blades, parts of composite tools fixed with bitumen into a wooden (?) haft, are relatively rare and have a light retouch on the cutting edge. Then there are pebbles with bitumen used as palettes, a pecked stone spoon, pecked and polished axes, and many querns and rubbing stones. Winged beads and triangular pendants made of thin flat serpentine pebbles that must have been imported from the north or west, were also found.

As at Mureybet there is evidence that these people were agriculturists living in an environment that was evidently more favoured than it is today. The fauna includes sheep or goat, gazelle, cow, *Bos primigenius*, equid, birds and rodents. Details about possible domestication are not yet available. Fish and freshwater mussels were collected. Domestic wheats, including emmer, domestic barley and cultivated chick-pea have so far been identified from the upper aceramic levels.

The Pre-Pottery Neolithic B Culture

Unlike the preceding PPNA culture, settlements of the PPNB are widespread in Palestine[5] and in recent years they have also been discovered in southern Syria, the Lebanon and northern Syria. At most of these sites the PPNB occupation lies on virgin soil; only at Jericho and Wadi Fallah II is it superimposed on earlier material, though separated by a stratigraphical hiatus. Continuity between PPNA and PPNB can be demonstrated only in northern Syria, at Mureybet. On the basis of the Jericho material alone there has been a tendency to see the PPNB culture as utterly different from PPNA, suggesting a sharp break between them. At the time this seemed quite justified, but the excavations at Beidha, Tell Ramad and Mureybet now shed a different light on this problem, and the old view of an invasion of northerners from northern Syria may have to be considerably modified. It may well be that at Jericho there was indeed such a settlement of newcomers, but at other places, like Beidha or Tell Ramad, many PPNA features survived, suggesting perhaps local developments and continuity fertilized by new ideas from the north. Technological improvements such as more efficient querns, larger reaping knives and more efficient arrowheads, rectangular structures and decorative features such as red plaster floors and dadoes, could easily be adopted without significant changes in the population.

The chronology of the period raises some problems, although it is clear that the PPNB spans the seventh millennium (in radiocarbon dates). It could have begun in the late eighth millennium and may – on certain sites – run into the sixth. C14 dates suggest that early PPNB (Beidha VI) ended *c.* 6650 B C.[287] Beidha V–I, together with all the Syrian PPNB sites as well as Munhata 6–3, may fall into a *late* PPNB. Jericho, with over twenty building levels, probably covers both early and late PPNB, but if any cultural changes occurred there, they have yet to be established.

21

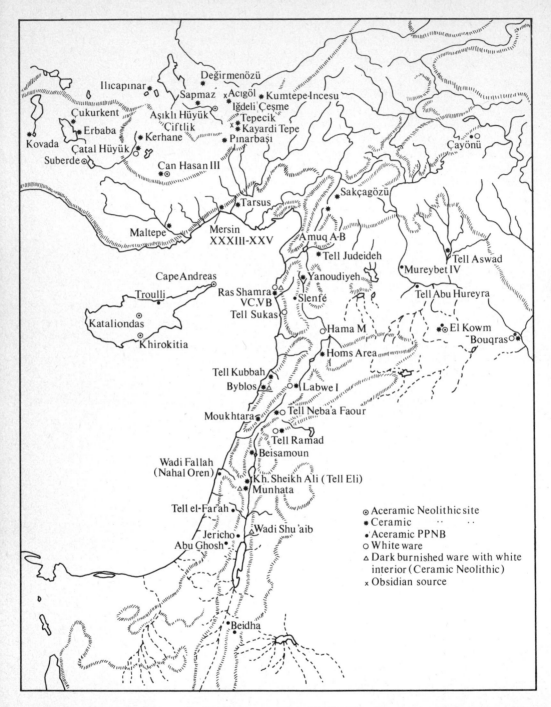

21 Map of Pre-Pottery Neolithic B settlements in the Levant and adjacent cultures in Anatolia

The map contains the following labels:

Ilıcapınar
Değirmenözü
Sapmaz
Acıgöl
Kumtepe·Incesu
Çukurkent
Aşıklı Hüyük
Iğdeli Çeşme
Çiftlik
Tepecik
Çayönü
Erbaba
Kerhane
Kayardi Tepe
Kovada
Çatal Hüyük
Pınarbaşı
Suberde
Can Hasan III
Sakçagözü
Tarsus
Maltepe
Mersin
XXXIII-XXV
Amuq A-B
Tell Aswad
Tell Judeideh
Mureybet IV
Cape Andreas
Yanoudiyeh
Tell Abu Hureyra
Troulli
Ras Shamra
VC,VB
Slenfé
Tell Sukas
El Kowm
Kataliondas
Hama M
Bouqras
Khirokitia
Homs Area
Tell Kubbah
Byblos
Labwe I
Moukhtara
Tell Neba'a Faour
Tell Ramad
Beisamoun
Wadi Fallah
(Nahal Oren)
Kh. Sheikh Ali (Tell Eli)
Munhata
Tell el-Far'ah
Wadi Shu'aib
Jericho
Abu Ghosh
Beidha

⊙ Aceramic Neolithic site
✱ Ceramic
• Aceramic PPNB
○ White ware
△ Dark burnished ware with white interior (Ceramic Neolithic)
x Obsidian source

At Beidha, near Petra,[32] the Natufian open-air site covered by 2 m of sterile sand was reoccupied early in the seventh millennium.[35] Three supcrimposed living floors with post holes and sunken hearths (levels IX–VII) suggest some sort of temporary or seasonal settlement and finds are few. In level VI substantial semi-subterranean round houses up to 4 m in diameter were built with

stone walls surrounding an inner skeleton of wooden posts, not
visible, but plastered over. These together with a central post,
supported an intricate roof of wooden beams, reed and clay. These
round houses, clearly of Natufian and PPNA ancestry, were
arranged in clusters, each comprising a few houses and storerooms
within a walled court. The village, entered by a few stone steps,
was surrounded by a terrace wall to retain the sand dune on which
it was built. It was destroyed by fire *c.* 6650 B C. When rebuilt in
level V, the post-house tradition was continued, but some of the
houses were now free-standing, and though many were round,
some had become more polygonal with rounded corners. In
level IV the latter predominate and the centre of the village is now
occupied by a group of large rectangular houses, measuring
5×6 m, with plaster floors painted red and brown.

A further change takes place in levels III and II. There are rooms, *23b*
all of rectangular plan, grouped together to form a large house
and several corridor houses. The large house, measuring 7×9 m,
has on floor and walls white burnished plaster painted with a red
band along the bottom of the latter, and contains a hearth and a
seat. Outside is a courtyard with room for storage. The corridor
houses are some 8 m long with a set of three rooms leading off a
central corridor. Heavy buttresses separating the cubicles probably
supported an upper living floor. These corridor houses, sunk into
the ground and approached by a few steps like the traditional large
house, appear to have been workshops for the manufacture of
bone tools (horn and antler), polished stone, beads, etc. Each house *22*
seems to have been associated with several of the corridor houses
and the plan gives the impression of a busy manufacturing (and
trading) community. The final village (I) is of smaller size than its
predecessors and its houses resemble those of level IV, but they are
poorly preserved.

The importance of this sequence of buildings at Beidha lies in
its unbroken development from round hut to round house and
from there through a polygonal phase into proper rectangular
structures; all except the first were built of stone and all were
associated with a cultural inventory of the PPNB type.

The buildings of Jericho PPNB, on the other hand, are all built
of long cigar-shaped bricks with rows of thumb impressions on
top to facilitate the application of mortar.[29] Stone foundations are
not always present. We can regard as the hall-mark of the period
the fine lime-plastered floors, often laid on a gravel bed. They are
stained red, orange, pink or left unpainted, and are polished
smooth. This plaster curves up walls and covers rounded door
jambs. Painted patterns, such as a few simple herring-bones, are
extremely rare. The red paint certainly formed dadoes, but it is
not known how high it was carried up the walls. At Jericho there
is no evidence for alleys or passages as at Beidha, and houses (no
complete plan of which was recovered) seem to connect with each
other through screen walls pierced by three doorways – a large
central one, flanked by two smaller ones – courtyards and open
spaces. Hearths are rectangular and let into the floor. Subsidiary
rooms, some with curvilinear walls are found, and one small
structure has a niche in the wall, like many houses at contemporary.

22 Beidha VI: view of workshop with horn cores

Munhata. In PPNB Jericho rectangular plans prevail from the very beginning and no architectural development has been recorded – the culture appeared fully fledged and saw no local development. It is interesting that round mats covered the floors of rectangular buildings; one would imagine such a shape more suitable to round houses, but perhaps this shows the strength of an old tradition.

At Munhata, farther up the Jordan valley, the architecture resembles that at Jericho, but larger areas of building are exposed.[40] In level 5 a vast complex covers more than 300 sq. m, with a platform at the centre composed of large basalt blocks carved with water channels. Surrounding this are carefully paved basins and open spaces, plaster floors and numerous hearths. In level 3, an almost continuous area of plaster floors and screen walls extends over more than 2000 sq. m and there are large, more or less circular

23a   structures consisting of a pebbled central space surrounded by a series of rooms.[41]

At Tell Ramad, southwest of Damascus, the earliest level (I)

24   contains a series of small semi-subterranean huts, either round or oval, made of pisé.[15–18] They have lime-plastered floors and the plaster curves up where it joins the wall. Some are stained red. They were found to contain hearths, large storage bins and wooden basins.

In level II the structures had become rectangular and were built

25   of rectangular bricks on stone foundations. Single-roomed houses with plaster floors are often separated by narrow alleys (also with plaster floors) and courtyards. Outside the room, which often has thin screen-like walls, there are sunk areas, storage pits, hearths, ovens and grinding floors. Similar rectangular rooms, sometimes with a portico and with courtyards attached, were found at Labwe in the Beqa'a,[242] again with red and white plaster floors; at

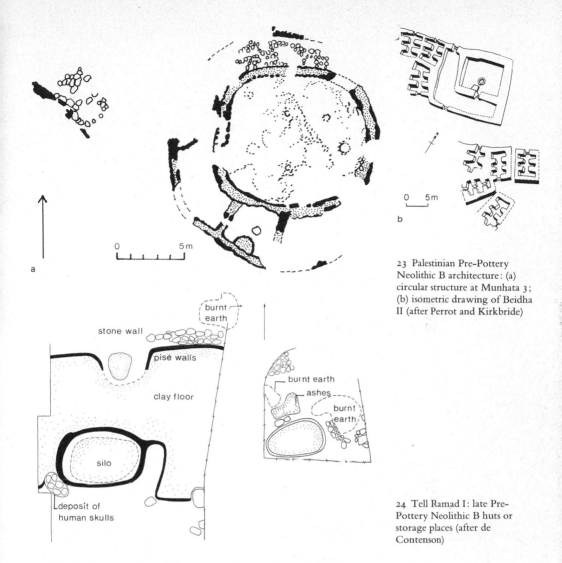

a

b

23 Palestinian Pre-Pottery Neolithic B architecture: (a) circular structure at Munhata 3; (b) isometric drawing of Beidha II (after Perrot and Kirkbride)

stone wall

burnt earth

pisé walls

clay floor

burnt earth

ashes

burnt earth

silo

deposit of human skulls

24 Tell Ramad I: late Pre-Pottery Neolithic B huts or storage places (after de Contenson)

Saaide, likewise in the Beqa'a; at El Kowm, where there is even a plastered mud-brick staircase winding round a central block;[23] and earlier at Mureybet (XVI–XVII). Developed mud-brick architecture is also a feature at Bouqras on the middle Euphrates.[21] Here limited soundings prevented the excavation of complete house plans, but there are such interesting features as mud-brick pillars, benches, etc. A fragment of stone walling at Jericho has sometimes been taken as an indication of fortifications, but it may well have been a retaining wall. As far as we know, none of these PPNB settlements was enclosed in circuit walls. What is perhaps more surprising is that no clear instance of cult rooms or shrines has yet been found, with the possible exception of some curious structures at Beidha to be described later. The small room with a standing stone in a niche at Jericho could be a modest cult room, but the large 'shrine' with the curvilinear storerooms contained no evidence of cult practices.[29] Neither the painted skulls, nor the

15b

59

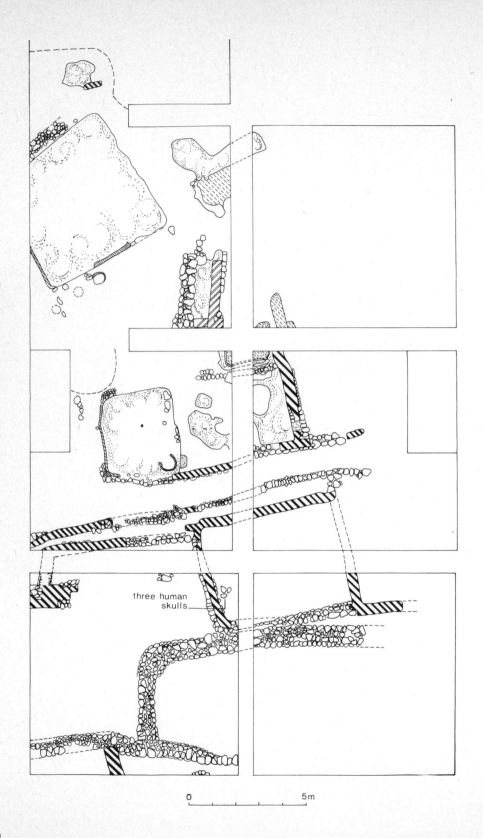

three human
skulls

0   5m

life-size figures found by J. Garstang were associated with specific buildings that could be interpreted as shrines.[5] The Ramad skulls and supports also came from a pit.[18] More extensive excavations will no doubt one day throw light on this.

At Beidha a group of three structures, 45 m outside the settlement, is neatly stratified but their characteristics are not those of normal dwellings.[34] They are approached by a paved path leading from the settlement. The earliest of the three is round with a door at the east side, and has a clean floor of large flag-stones. Outside the south wall lies a large, flat slab of white sandstone. This building was filled with dark clay, mixed with boulders and containing flint waste flakes. Half-way up the fill is a burnt patch with bone fragments, probably the remains of a meal, above which the fill continues up to the top of the wall. The latest of the buildings is floored with clean gravel and with an iron deposit lying between it and soft sand. It was filled with burnt clay and carbonized remains of burnt beams, probably the roof of the structure. The middle structure is oval, measuring $6 \times 3 \cdot 5$ m, and has a floor paved with angular broken pieces of stone. In the centre stood a large flat block of sandstone, set on edge. Against the south wall lay a very large slab with a parapet built around the edge. Outside the northwest corner lay another of these slabs with a parapet; also, south of the wall, was a huge roughly subtriangular basin made from a slab measuring $3 \cdot 8 \times 2 \cdot 65 \times 0 \cdot 25$ m; this too had a parapet. The fill was the same as in the first building, with a burnt patch and remains of a half-eaten meal. Below the floor was found a similar layer of ironstone deposited between the pavement and the sand below.

The purpose of these buildings, which are clearly linked to the round-house phases of the Beidha settlement, is unknown. There are indications here of deliberate ritual and it is possible that these structures cover tombs – the stone pavements at El Wad, Erq el-Ahmar and Ain Mallaha spring to mind. Burials are found only rarely – they occur in disused houses at Beidha – so that the discovery of an extramural burial would cause no surprise. Only further excavations can throw light on these curious structures and the rites associated with them.

The PPNB disposal of the dead shows many analogies with the practices of the previous periods. There is no special orientation and the corpse lies loosely contracted on its side. Single burial is the rule, usually without any gifts. Infant burials are frequent and are usually intact, but in adult burials the cranium, but not the lower jaw, is often removed. Such 'headless' burials have been found at Jericho,[29] Beidha (upper levels)[35] and Tell Eli (Khirbet Sheikh Ali).[6] Sometimes the skull is placed near the body, often it is buried separately or is kept in a room. At Jericho, forty incomplete skeletons, mostly headless, were found below one room. There and at Ramad I and II groups of skulls were found that had the facial features restored in plaster and paint, both red and black. Shells, either bivalves or cowries, were set in the empty eye-sockets. Many of these skulls lack the lower jaw, but in the finest example from Jericho and at least two from Ramad it was not removed, and at the latter site some of the neck vertebrae were

25 Tell Ramad II: plan of part of the settlement (after de Contenson)

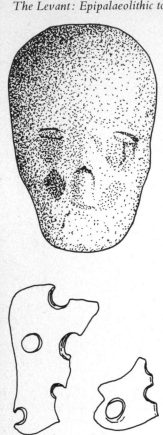

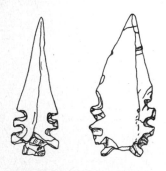

26 Tell Ramad: plastered human skull of a young woman, level I; flint arrowheads and carvings in bone and mother of pearl, level II (after de Contenson)

also included. The two finest Ramad I skulls belong to young women of Proto-Mediterranean type, like the rest of the Ramad population.[62] They were between eighteen and twenty years old. Male skulls were treated in a similar way, and one from Jericho has a painted black moustache. At Ramad, headless seated clay female figures, approximately 25 cm high, made of clay coated with plaster and with traces of red paint, served as skull supports. 'Skull cults' are usually regarded as an indication of ancestor worship, but at Jericho (in the later PPNB) near life-size plaster figures were made without the benefit of human skulls. Fragments of a group, comprising a male, female and child, modelled in clay on a base of reeds, were found in one room. Later still we have highly schematic busts made in the same fashion. Whether these represent ancestors or deities is a moot point; revered ancestors may well have been transformed into deities and it is often difficult to draw a sharp dividing line.

More or less naturalistic figurines are commoner than before in this period; Ramad I, Tell Aswad, Beidha VI and Jericho have all produced small female figurines of baked clay, and at Munhata appear crude cone-shaped male and female figurines with bulging round eyes, breasts and other indications of sex. Figures in stone are very rare, but Jericho has yielded a little stone head. Small animal figures of baked clay, perhaps used in magic rites to increase the fertility of the herd or the hunted quarry, are not uncommon – there are goat and ibex in rocky Beidha, horned animals at Jericho and Munhata, and bovids, ovids, equids and boar at Ramad I. While baked clay was in common use for the manufacture of figurines, there was still no pottery though one or two chance survivals in burnt levels such as those of Beidha VI suggest that occasionally small sun-baked clay pots were made. Most containers were made of perishable materials, such as basketry and wood. At Beidha VI there are baskets with lids, frequently coated with asphalt or gypsum plaster to make them impervious. Then there are wooden bins (Ramad, Beidha) and rectangular and oval boxes (Beidha VI). Various materials were also used for stone wares: marl plates at Beidha, plates and thin-rimmed shallow bowls of limestone and basalt at Jericho and Munhata, and alabaster from the Euphrates region at Bouqras and Ramad, where it may be an import.

Yet the most characteristic product of the PPNB of Syria is 'white ware', a composite of lime (as used in the lime plaster) and salty grey ashes. Vessels, often of large size, were built up in coils round a basket, which left a plaited or ropelike impression on base and sides. When dried and fired this 'white ware' turns into a hard white material resembling white limestone. The surface was smoothed or even burnished and was sometimes ornamented with wide stripes of red ochre or even polychrome painting in red and brown (import into Çatal Hüyük VIB). Not pottery in the ordinary sense, this ware seems to have been invented in the gypsum areas of southern Syria, where it occurs in the later part of the seventh millennium in Ramad II, Labwe I and other Beqa'a sites, at Hama, El Kowm and Bouqras (and somewhat later at Ras Shamra VB, Byblos Early Neolithic, Tell Sukas 84–82). It has

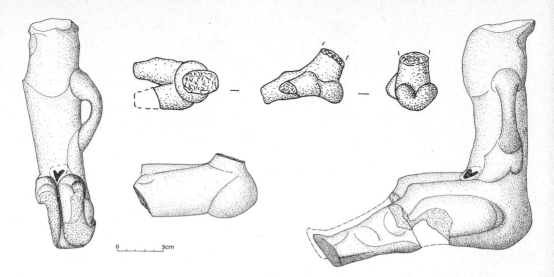

27 Tell Ramad I: clay and plaster female figures, apparently serving as supports for plastered human skulls. A small figurine of the same type is also shown (after de Contenson)

turned up at Çayönü and Çatal VIB in the north, and at Munhata 3,[40] the last PPNB level in the south. As far as I know it was not encountered at Jericho, but it was found again at Wadi Shu'aib. These 'artificial stone' vessels are of great interest, now that a new centre for very early pottery has been discovered at Umm Dabaghiyah south of Jebel Sinjar in northern Iraq. Here also we have large vessels of rather clumsy shapes moulded perhaps on baskets. Without the benefit of more radiocarbon dates it is not at present possible to say which came first, 'white ware' or Umm Dabaghiyah coarse ware.[160-62] With the introduction of hard-baked, coiled, dark burnished ware, typical of northern Syria from Amuq A onwards but also found in lighter colours in the early levels of Umm Dabaghiyah and hence possibly of even earlier date, the 'white ware' disappears after a short coexistence (El Kowm, Byblos Early Neolithic, etc.).

The ground-stone industry includes a new type of quern open on one side and with a double depression; it is often made of basalt. Beidha VI has produced local granite troughs, while mortars, pestles, grindstones and polishers, often in attractively coloured stone, are found everywhere. Stones with cup-marks still appear, but their purpose remains unknown. There is evidence for weaving in the form of stone spindle whorls from Tell Ramad I, which also has incised pebbles of more problematical use.[18] Polished stone axes occur too, but most are chipped out of flint and have only polished bits. Tranchets, chisels and picks are a heritage of the PPNA tradition.

An important new advance is the use of a boat-shaped flint core from which long blades or points were struck from both sides.[64] Another innovation is a fine flat retouch (pressure flaking). Burins on blades are common, and were used for the production of tangs on projectile points – arrow and javelin heads made at some sites like Beidha in an astonishing variety of as many as twenty different types.[65] Long blades used as reaping knives, finely denticulated and made in once piece, take the place of the earlier ones where the cutting edge was made of several small blades set edge to edge.

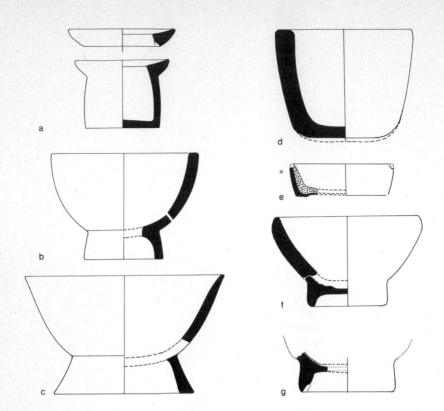

28 Late Pre-Pottery Neolithic B 'white ware' vessels: (a–d) from Labwe; (e, g) from Tell Neba'a Faour; (f) from Tell Ramad (after Kirkbride, Copeland and de Contenson)

Microliths virtually disappear except at Tell Ramad I.[18] Here Palestinian types include long sickle blades, notched arrowheads, burins and borers in the PPNA tradition, in mauve to white flint with abrupt retouch. Syrian types in dark brown flint, rectangular sickle blades and tanged arrowheads have a flat pressure retouch. In Palestine the arrowheads (and reaping knives) are often made of spectacular varieties of flint: mauve, pink, salmon- or honey-coloured, the sources of many of which remain to be determined.

26   The earliest type of PPNB arrowhead is notched (like those of the Proto-Neolithic and PPNA) with concave-based sections, but gradually tanged leaf-shaped types appear, some of them still notched. Typical of Jericho and Munhata are rhomboid points with pressure-flaked tangs (Amuq type) or laurel leaves flaked all over. Long barbed arrowheads also occur there, but are missing at Beidha. Firestones for the striking of fire were recognized at Beidha.

Bone and shell objects include awls and spatulae (Ramad I) but were much richer in Ramad II with awls, spatulae, needles, sheaths, zoomorphic pendants of bone, beads of obsidian, and pendants of mother-of-pearl.[18] Bone beads, some dentalium, little pierced shells and cowries were found in Beidha VI. Some of these objects had been obtained by trade. At Jericho the trade in Çiftlik obsidian with central Anatolia continued, but there is less than in the PPNA.[64] Ninety per cent of the obsidian in Ramad I–II also came from Çiftlik,[18] but 10 per cent is green obsidian from Nemrut Dağ on Lake Van, which is also the source of one piece found in

Beidha V (the obsidian of Beidha II–III is of Çiftlik type).[65] At
Bouqras, on the other hand, *all* the obsidian came from Nemrut
Dağ;[84] the material from El Kowm has not yet been analysed, and
may well be the same. It is probably through Bouqras and Tell
Ramad that Vannic obsidian reached Beidha. The presence of
alabaster at Bouqras and Ramad strengthens the case for such a
trade route through the Syrian desert. Other materials were also
traded; greenstone/jadeite was used for the manufacture of small
axes, spatulae and beads at Ramad II,[18] the nearest source being the
greenstone beds of Jebel Akra, north of Ras Shamra, or those of
the Amanus Mountains across the Orontes to the north. This is the
first known occurrence of this material in southern Syria, but it
was already used at Mureybet. At Jericho turquoise matrix from
southwestern Sinai was found, and PPNB sites which could have
engaged in such trade are known in the Negev at Divshon and
near Timna, west of Petra, and Jebel el-Anrar in north Sinai.[38]
Ochres, malachite and haematite occur in roughly shaped blocks
in Beidha VI together with Red Sea cowries and other shells. A
native copper bead was found at Tell Ramad, the one example so
far of metal in the PPNB of Syria.[24] But the main raw material
traded in the PPNB period was flint, which by virtue of its various
colours was much prized.[237] The brown flint was Syrian, the
honey-coloured was found in the Hauran,[254] while the salmon-
coloured flint is said to come from the Mt Carmel area.[46] A close
study of the flint resources of the Levant would greatly increase
our knowledge of early trade.

There can be little doubt that the PPNB period was one of
widespread economic and cultural advance expressed in a number
of different ways at various sites. There is a refreshing display of
individuality in this culture and a widening of horizons through
trade and interaction. The variety of environment exploited in this
period is interesting and many sites now lie outside the old Mediterranean belt of oak and pistachio which had deteriorated as the
forest moved north with the onset of a postglacial climate.[10] The
aridity of PPNA times was followed by a wetter phase during
PPNB, and sites spread throughout the Levant.[7] Their greatest
concentration lies in the great Rift valley and the adjacent plateau,
and there is an interesting spread into the Syrian steppe (El Kowm,
Bouqras), the Negev (Divshon, Timna area), the Transjordanian
desert (Kilwa, site 19) and the lush Mediterranean coast in Lebanon
(Tell aux Scies, Beirut, Dik el-Mehdi)[237] and Syria (Tell Sukas,
Ras Shamra, Slenfé). Cave-terrace habitations are now rare (Wadi
Fallah I),[46] and though the marginal regions of the south may have
seen hunting and trading stations of a transient nature, in the more
central and northern areas tells are now the rule, an indication of
permanent occupation. Of these, the PPNB Jericho with over
twenty building levels is still the largest known, the obvious
centre for the Jordan valley.

Characteristic of the PPNB economy is the continued importance of hunting, and the first definitely domestic goats with
twisted horn cores are reported only from Jericho and Beidha
(where they amount to 86 per cent of the animal bones).[35] The
remaining 14 per cent comprise aurochs, ibex, bezoar, gazelle,

11

wild boar, hare, jackal, hyrax and an equid. At Jericho, gazelle –
long the dominant food animal – becomes unimportant (only
14 per cent) and yields its first place to domestic goat.[52] Wild pigs
are commonly hunted and the wild cat is reported. Farther along
the Jordan valley, at Munhata 5–6, gazelle still predominates
(44·6 per cent), then pig (14·2 per cent), goats (11·6 per cent) and
finally aurochs (3·31 per cent).[53] At the foot of Mt Hermon, in
the Huleh basin, the rainiest part of Palestine, the end of the PPNB
sees at the site of Beisamoun a great concentration of aurochs
(35·9 per cent), goat (29·4 per cent), pig (24·1 per cent), besides
gazelle (7·2 per cent) and cervids (1·7 per cent). At Tell Ramad I–II,
where hills and steppe meet, gazelle and deer were the principal
game, together with an equid and wild cat.[18] In the Syrian steppe
at El Kowm, gazelle and wild ass, large cattle and sheep (or goat)
are reported[23] and the same fauna, minus gazelle, was found at
Bouqras on the Euphrates.[21] In the Negev hills fallow deer and
ibex were hunted at Divshon, an indication that forest cover had
not altogether vanished (remains of it still exist at Jebel Alliq in
northern Sinai). In the far north, at Ras Shamra VC, domestic
cattle has been provisionally identified, and possibly domestic goat
and pig.[251] Wild pig was hunted.

As the PPNB record for animal domestication (goat) is not
particularly impressive compared to, say, Çayönü with sheep,
goat, pig(?) and dog,[51] it may be pertinent to ask why this should
be. One strongly suspects that the old habit of herding goat and
gazelle had accustomed the inhabitants to an easy supply of meat,
demanding no further efforts, especially as the diet could always
be varied with a little beef or venison. The ferocious wild cattle
and dangerous wild pigs were more than a match for them, and
sheep, a possible alternative for goat and gazelle, was not native to
south Syria or Palestine. A further consideration is that gazelle and
goat, being small, have just enough meat on them to feed a family;
as it must have been difficult to keep meat fresh in hot countries
they were the ideal solution. When in the Late Chalcolithic period
cattle and sheep are kept, it is for their milk and dairy produce,
wool and skin, and not as a meat supply.[53] The aims of domestication were not always the same.

The growing of crops, on the other hand, is well established. In
the burnt houses at Beidha VI there were thousands of imprints in
the plaster as well as buckets full of carbonized plant material.[35]
They cultivated wheat and especially barley, which was still the
wild *Hordeum spontaneum* native to the area. The wheat showed a
series of intermediate types between the wild and the domestic
emmer, and is thought to have been brought from the north, as it
is not a local plant. There were also traces of naked barley and wild
oat on the site. Some five gallons of pistachio nuts were found as
well as acorns. Field pea, two kinds of wild lentil, vetch, medick,
cock's-comb and various other leguminous plants were eaten.

At Jericho in the PPNB layers, there were only domestic forms
of two-row hulled barley, emmer and einkorn,[55] the latter
introduced from the north, as it is not native to Palestine. Among
the legumes were field pea, lentil and vetch. There have also been
reports of caper and oat.

At Tell Ramad I, domestic barley, emmer, einkorn and club-wheat were grown as well as lentils, and wild vetch and brome were collected (as at Mureybet).[18] Wild fruits supplemented the diet along with pistachio, almond and hawthorn. The floral remains of level II are the same.

The material from El Kowm has not yet been studied, but wheat and barley were found.[23] No plant material was recovered from either Munhata or Bouqras, sites with plenty of agricultural implements used for the preparation of plant food, so that the non-agricultural character of these sites, stressed by the excavators, fails to carry conviction. Presumed sites of hunting camps, such as Divshon in the Negev, appear to lack sickle blades and a ground stone industry.[38]

There seems little doubt, then, that the PPNB culture was based economically on a combination of hunting and agriculture, maintaining a balanced diet of cereal starch, vegetable fats (pistachios, acorns), vegetable protein (leguminous seeds) and animal protein and fat from domestic goat, herded gazelle or other game. Birds and fish are conspicuous by their absence and so are snails and freshwater mussels, which had previously been of some importance in the Epipalaeolithic.

On the physical characteristics of the people of this period little has yet been published. At Tell Ramad, forty-five skeletons were studied;[62] with one exception, a Eurafrican, all were of gracile Proto-Mediterranean stock, descended, it is thought, from the fine Natufian type, known from late Natufian or Proto-Neolithic Wadi Fallah II. The forty-three skeletons from Beidha have not yet been examined, but a study of those from Jericho is under way. Here, side by side with the fine Natufian types of Wadi Fallah stock, there is a new strain from the north, the Proto-Mediterranean. Definite Alpine types have not yet been recognized.

The End of the Pre-Pottery Neolithic B and the Transition to the Pottery Neolithic Period

Around 6000 BC the PPNB culture disappears[5] and there is a widespread desertion of sites in Palestine as well as in the Syrian steppe.[261] Nowhere is this accompanied by destruction or violence; the people evidently decided it was time to leave. Only in the very north of Palestine, in the Huleh basin, or the adjacent regions of the Beqa'a and the Damascus area, does life continue. New sites also appear, sites such as Abu Ghosh near Jerusalem in the uplands, and Ascalon and Givat ha-Parsa in the coastal plain. The coastal sites in northern Syria, Tell Sukas and Ras Shamra, are apparently unaffected.

Supported by the study of pollen from Lakes Huleh and Tiberias and the Dead Sea, which all show a decrease in tree pollen culminating *c.* 6000 BC, J. Perrot has postulated desiccation in the arid Irano-Turanian vegetational zone as the cause for the decline and disappearance of the PPNB culture. It may be pointed out that there are at this time similar signs of stress in the Mesopotamian steppe, for example at Alikosh in the Muhammed Jafar phase, which shows a decline in agriculture,[75] while in northern Mesopotamia, the Umm Dabaghiyah culture, settled on marginal territories south of Jebel Sinjar, may be that of refugees from the more northwesterly area.[160–62]

What does desiccation mean in human terms? Shortage of water forces animals to migrate and plants find difficulty in growing. Faced by diminishing food supplies, man moves elsewhere. The desertion of the PPNB sites is widespread in Palestine (Beidha, Jericho, Munhata, Tell el-Farah, Wadi Shu'aib, Khirbet Sheikh Ali) and in the Syrian desert (El Kowm, Bouqras, Mureybet IV). Only the more favoured Mediterranean littoral and the Huleh-Hermon area would have continued to offer viable conditions; Labwe[242] and Tell Ramad survived.[18] They were soon to be joined by refugees from the southern lands affected by drought. In the Huleh basin to the west of the lake, Beisamoun was founded, a site nearly as large as Jericho and clearly PPNB in its original layout.[5] Other settlements were established on the humid Mediterranean coast of the Lebanon, to join the few scattered PPNB outposts like Tell aux Scies and Dik el-Mehdi.[237] A new culture arose, the Early Neolithic of Byblos, which embraced all the Lebanon,[243] the coast and Beqa'a[240] as well as the Damascus basin (Tell Ramad III). At Byblos classic PPNB features were retained: rectangular houses with plaster floors, sometimes stained red, intramural burials, 'white ware' in the lowest layers, and a chipped-stone industry which is clearly based on that of the earlier culture. To this were added new features such as dark burnished pottery, showing a technique and forms that came from northern Syria but which in the Lebanon was decorated with combing and incisions in local taste. Notable also is the establishment in the forested zone of the Lebanon of a people who designed new heavy tools in local flint to deal with the forest cover.[239] These forms, nicknamed 'gigantoliths', are typical of southern Lebanon from the coast at Adlun to the gorges of the upper Jordan valley. Does this imply signs of overpopulation as more and more land-hungry people arrived from the south?

At Tell Ramad III, we see a new emphasis on the herding of domestic animals, goat, sheep and cattle, in which they are assisted by dogs.[18] Some grain cultivation, however, continues. Yet the new preoccupation with stockbreeding coincides with a complete lack of architecture and it looks as if semi-nomadic herding, leaving only seasonal pit dwellings, has taken the place of long-established farming. In Labwe II (upper levels) large pits, perhaps the substructures of round huts of semi-nomads, follow settled occupation.[242] Nevertheless, these semi-nomads make pottery in the Early Neolithic Byblos tradition, though the stone and bone industries show signs of decay.

It certainly looks as if a climatic oscillation affected the drier parts of the Levant, inland Syria and Mesopotamia *c.* 6000 BC destroying the previous pattern of agricultural settlements. The response of the population was twofold: emigration both northward and westward into the Mediterranean forest zone, which gradually led to the opening-up of this previously shunned area. Others adjusted by turning to semi-nomadic pastoralism and stockbreeding, occasionally visiting the ancestral sites, and setting up their seasonal camps on the ruins of the villages of their fathers. For perhaps half a millennium or so these conditions prevailed until at last, enriched by new ideas and technological achievements – pottery, plain and painted, spindle whorls, new types of figurines, etc. – picked up in the north and east during their wanderings, they gradually filtered back into Palestine, conditions permitting, to found the various cultures of the 'Pottery Neolithic' period with their strong semi-sedentary overtones. As the result of this cultural break, Palestine had lost its erstwhile pre-eminence and from *c*. 6000 BC onwards it was destined to become an appendix to Syria. The balance was not redressed, and then only partially, until the Ghassulians arrived in Chalcolithic times.

The end of the PPNB in the Levant marks a convenient point to break our narrative of the cultural development there and consider parallel developments elsewhere in the Near East. Up to the beginning of the sixth millennium the Levant had developed along local lines in two parallel traditions, a Palestinian and a Syrian one, both rooted in variants of the Natufian. With the Pottery Neolithic, Anatolian and Mesopotamian influences were to increase.

Chapter Two

The Zagros Zone: the Development from the Epipalaeolithic to the Neolithic

Around 10000 BC the Epipalaeolithic Zarzian culture, the rough equivalent of the Kebaran of the Levant, came to an end according to a radiocarbon date from Shanidar cave.[79] There is as yet no single site in the Zagros zone that offers a full stratigraphic record of the development from Zarzian to the ceramic Neolithic. Instead there are several shorter sequences at sites such as Zawi Chemi, Alikosh, Ganjdareh, Tepe Guran and Jarmo, some of which are of great potential. Yet for this same reason and the lack of overlaps the record may still be incomplete.

    The period that follows the Zarzian, the two millennia or so that are approximately equivalent to the Natufian of the Levant, has not yet a generally accepted name. It might be preferable to call it the Zawi Chemi-Shanidar phase after the most important site, rather than the Karim Shahirian, as others call it after an ephemeral, unstratified, undated and unpublished site, which may be somewhat later in date.

The Zawi Chemi-Shanidar Phase

Zawi Chemi is an open-air site,[82] situated some 425 m above sea-level 4 km south of Shanidar cave (822 m),[79] a large base camp of some 1000 sq. m in the valley of the Upper Zab in northernmost Iraq.[80] The cave lies at the entrance to a box canyon surrounded by high mountains within the oak-pistachio belt that covered the foot-hills and lower slopes of the Zagros Mountains at this period. There are two radiocarbon dates: 8920± 300 BC for the beginning of occupation at Zawi Chemi and 8650± 400 BC for the end of contemporary layer BI in Shanidar cave. A cemetery containing twenty-six individuals in Shanidar cave is thought to belong to the people of the open-air site. Were they put there after occupation of the cave had ceased or was only part of the cave used for burial and the rest occupied by the living? Zawi Chemi has many occupation levels and is thought to have been inhabited for a long time, perhaps as much as a millennium, but the nature of the occupation may well have been seasonal, with summer encampment at the open site and winter refuge being sought in the warm cave.

    The animal bones from Shanidar cave show that the preferred game was wild goat which must have abounded on the rocky cliffs all around, but there is also evidence for wild pig, red deer, fallow deer, wolf, jackal and tawny fox, Syrian brown bear, marten, gerbil and beaver.[89-90] Some of the animals may have been hunted for their skins. The inhabitants further collected

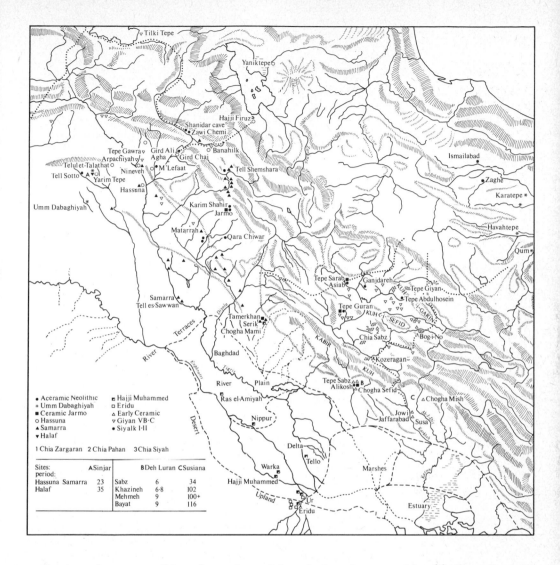

The map shows various archaeological site locations including:

Tilki Tepe, Yaniktepe, Hajji Firuz, Shanidar cave, Zawi Chemi, Tepe Gawra, Gird Ali, Agha, Banahilk, Arpachiyah, Gird Chai, Ismailabad, Telulet-Talathat, M'Lefaat, Nineveh, Zaghe, Tell Sotto, Yarim Tepe, Tell Shemshara, Karatepe, Hassuna, Karim Shahir, Jarmo, Umm Dabaghiyah, Havahtepe, Matarrah, Qara Chiwar, Qum, Tepe Sarab, Ganjdareh, Tepe Giyan, Asiab, Tepe Abdulhosein, Samarra, Tell es-Sawwan, Tepe Guran, KUH-I-SEFID, KUH-I-CARIN, Tamerkhan, Serik, Chogha Mami, KABIR KUH, Chia Sabz, Bog-i-No, Baghdad, Kozeragan, River Plain, Tepe Sabz, Alikosh, Chogha Sefid, Ras el-Amiyah, Nippur, Chogha Mish, Jowi, Jaffarabad, Susa, Delta, Warka, Tello, Marshes, Hajji Muhammed, Upland, Ur, Eridu, Estuary

Legend:

Symbol	Description	Symbol	Description
• Aceramic Neolithic		□ Hajji Muhammed	
∗ Umm Dabaghiyah		▫ Eridu	
■ Ceramic Jarmo		△ Early Ceramic	
○ Hassuna		▽ Giyan VB-C	
▲ Samarra		● Siyalk I-II	
▼ Halaf			

1 Chia Zargaran 2 Chia Pahan 3 Chia Siyah

Sites: period:	A Sinjar	B Deh Luran	C Susiana
Hassuna Samarra	23	Sabz 6	34
Halaf	35	Khazineh 6·8	102
		Mehmeh 9	100+
		Bayat 9	116

snails, river clams, some fish and tortoise and though there is no direct evidence for plant food, except hackberry, a wealth of agricultural implements was found at both sites. From Zawi Chemi there is evidence especially for red deer, wild sheep and wild goat, but in the top layers of the site – alas, not closely datable, though possibly as late as 8000 B C – there is dramatic evidence, in the form of a very high ratio of young animals, that sheep herding had become the prevailing occupation. It should be pointed out that at Ghar-i-Asp (Horse cave) near Aq-Köprük in northern Afghanistan domestic sheep and goat are also reported in a layer dated to 8260±235 B C.[72-3] Moreover, morphologically domestic hornless female sheep occur in the lowest level at Alikosh (Bus Mordeh phase) for which there is a doubtful(?) radiocarbon date of 7950±200 B C.[75] The cumulative evidence points to herding followed by domestication of sheep at a very early date along the edges of the Iranian plateau.

29 Map of the Zagros Mountain zone and the adjacent Mesopotamian lowlands showing aceramic and ceramic sites

The occupation layers in Shanidar cave contained storage pits, querns, mortars, grinding slabs and chipped stone tools, as well as basket impressions.[89-90] There was a total of twenty-eight burials, all but two grouped in the cemetery. Several platforms of stones, some arranged in an arc, were associated with them. One burial of a young woman was accompanied by a quern and a lump of red ochre; another was buried with a bone reaping knife with a single flint blade fixed into a slot with asphalt, the nearest source of which would be found in the Kirkuk area. Nemrut Dağ obsidian occurs here, as at Zawi Chemi, in minute quantity. The bodies from this cemetery have not yet been studied.

Zawi Chemi covers an area of 275 × 215 m and the deposit is 2 m thick.[82] Large refuse pits occurred at the base of the occupation as at so many other early sites. A circular area, built of stone, and approximately 4 m in diameter, may be the remains of a hut. Successive rebuildings took place and three building levels were distinguished. Walls are made of river boulders, whole or broken artifacts such as querns, grindstones, etc. Hearths were not associated with these structures.

Burials also occur at this site and some eight individuals were each interred with a very young child, suggesting rites of a possibly gruesome nature. Physically these people were of Eurafrican type like their Natufian contemporaries, of medium stature, but more modern in development.[96] Some features of the skulls suggest a close-knit community with in-breeding and not less than three of the five well-preserved skulls show the practice of incomplete trepanation, surprisingly without signs of any infection. Health left much to be desired; three individuals showed signs of strong anaemia, leading to a thickening of the skull, another suffered from tuberculosis of the bone, syphilis or cancer, and three out of seven had dental troubles and jaw infection, perhaps the result of eating too many grits in ground plant food.

The heavy stone industry, unknown in the Zarzian, consists of pecked and ground artifacts; large trough querns with V- and U-shaped hollows, grindstones, together with pestles and combined querns and mortars. Hammer-stones are common, including a ball-shaped type of green chert. Bevelled and cigar-shaped pebbles were used as smoothers, while grooved steatite whetstones appear, sometimes incised with cross-hatching, which probably served for polishing bone. Axes and celts with polish occur only towards the very top of the deposit.

Among the flaked stone tools there are – as in the Natufian – heavy-duty tools, possible adzes, picks and numerous choppers. Small tools, ovate in shape and made of quartzite are common, and these were perhaps used for dressing skins.

The chipped-stone industry has implements of various sizes, but looks technically impoverished compared to that of the Zarzian. Microliths are still common, especially backed blades, as well as lunates, subtriangular points, burins, triangles and scrapers. Serrated and notched blades and flakes (woodworking?) are also found. Borers and side- but not end-scrapers are characteristic and there are knives, angle burins and crude pebble cores, but no sickle blades with silica sheen are present.

Bone tools are abundant, and many are decorated with carvings, notches and incised designs. These generally take the form of curved lines, herring-bone and linear patterns or cross-hatching, though a few possibly naturalistic designs also occur. A fine sickle haft was found as well as many awls, points with rounded ends and bevelled antler flakers.

Ornaments are not rare; there are bone tubular beads, flat beads, beads of steatite, greenstone and bluestone or marble and one native copper bead;[81] also deer teeth, pendants of bone and stone, sometimes incised. Red ochre and haematite were used, but there is no evidence for pottery or clay objects.

30

The distribution of the Zawi Chemi-Shanidar culture is quite unknown and the position of the type site and its northern (obsidian) and northeastern links (sheep are thought to be natives of the rolling uplands southwest of the Caspian) suggest possible connections with the Transcaucasian area (Odishi, Kobystan). The presence, however faint, of geometric and naturalistic (?) art immediately draws attention to the rock sanctuaries of Kobystan with their naturalistic pictures of animals and men.[221-2] It may well be that the rock art of the northern zone from southwestern Anatolia to the Caspian was not only reflected in the art of the Natufian, but also influenced that of the Zagros in this early phase.

30 Zawi Chemi settlement and Shanidar cave: flint microliths, bone reaping knife with flint blade, curved bone sickle handle, whetstones, incised bone-work, stone palettes and beads (after Solecki)

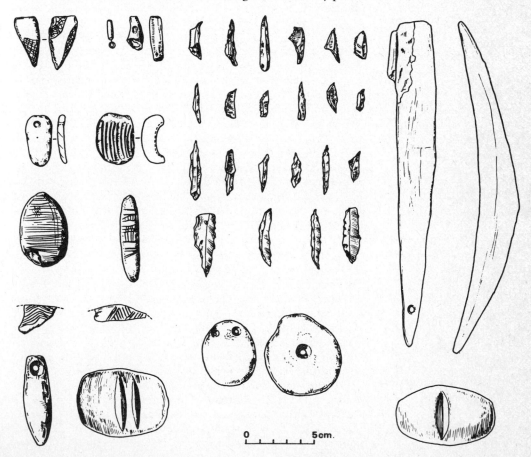

The material from Karim Shahir, a seasonal (?) hill-top site with a scatter of fire-cracked stones and pits in a single shallow occupation deposit,[67] shows a greater dependence on chipped stone tools, including celts, than on ground stone tools, whereas the reverse was the case at Zawi Chemi. The manufacture is less rough, microlithic lunates are absent, some sickle blades with silica sheen and two small clay figurines, lightly baked, were among the finds. One was found in a red-ochre deposit in a pit. Marble rings and bracelets were also made, and there are simple bone tools and beads of bone and shell. All these features might suggest a somewhat later date than the Zawi Chemi-Shanidar culture, and the innovations are matched in the roughly contemporary Bus Mordeh phase of the site of Alikosh, and later at Jarmo. The most characteristic tool types are mortars, querns and pestles and notched and serrated blades and flakes; obsidian is said to be 'virtually absent'. Animal bones from Karim Shahir all belong to wild animals: sheep or goat, aurochs, gazelle, boar, deer, fox and marten. Snails were collected and there are many turtle bones and remains of birds. No grain was found and there are no radiocarbon dates for this site. The material from Gird Chai, where no buildings or pits were found, is similar to that from Karim Shahir, with chipped celts, but virtually no grinding artifacts.[67]

Some obsidian was found and this also occurred at Tell M'lefaat.[67] There was some evidence here for round (diameter 4 m) or oval sunken structures measuring $3·55 \times 2·7$ m, later enlarged to 4×3 m as the huts were rebuilt. They had a stone floor and the vertical walls were sunk to a depth of 1·2 m. In one, a hearth depression was found. Fire-cracked stones, boulder mortars and querns occurred in quantity as well as ground and fully polished celts. The chipped-stone industry was like that of Karim Shahir. Then there were lightly baked schematic figurines, rods and balls of clay, clay beads, a mat impression on a lump of red ochre and fragments of shallow stone bowls. Animal bones have not so far been studied, no grain was found and C14 dates are not yet available. Typologically M'lefaat may be somewhat later or more developed than Karim Shahir and the unexcavated site of Qara Chiwar may be even later still and form a hypothetical link between the Karim Shahir phase and Jarmo.[67]

Fortunately one now has the fully published material from the Bus Mordeh phase at Alikosh (c. 8000?–6500 B C)[75] to supplement this meagre information from the Karim Shahir phase, with more substantial and all-important economic details. The mound of Alikosh (diameter 135 m) is situated on the semi-arid steppe, the winter grassland of the north Khuzistan plain, approximately 200 m above sea-level. It lies well outside the oak and pistachio woodlands on the hilly flanks of the Zagros Mountains.

It would seem that c. 8000 B C herdsmen of domestic sheep and herded but osteologically still wild goat descended from the Luristan uplands to the east to take advantage of the lush winter grazing offered by the plain, and settled at Alikosh. In this new environment they hunted gazelle in huge numbers, as well as onagers, some aurochs and wild pig. They also exploited the aquatic resources of the region along the River Mehmeh and the marshes, where they caught carp and catfish, turtles and fresh-water mussels and occasionally some seasonal winter water-fowl. Not only the goat and the much less numerous sheep thrived on the flora of the steppe; at Alikosh man collected for protein innumerable seeds of wild small legumes which formed 94·6 per cent of the total bulk of the plant material of more than thirty species (trigonella, milk-vetch, medick, vetch, vetchling, etc. as well as capers, goosefoot, canary grass, oat grass). In addition, the Bus Mordeh people planted already domestic two-row hulled barley and emmer wheat (3·4 per cent) introduced from the mountain zone together with certain weed grasses: wild einkorn, rye grass, goat-face grass. Grains and seeds were present from the very beginning of the site. Pistachio was brought from the mountains, less than half a day's walk away, but most of the fat in the diet of these people must have come from animal sources. The grainfields were near the marsh (club-rush seeds were found mixed up with cereals); the grain was harvested with flint sickles and was roasted or parched before threshing on flat or saddle querns of limestone. Mortars were unknown. The absence of summer products in the settlement strongly suggests transhumance during the torrid summer heat of Khuzistan. Alikosh probably only saw seasonal occupation.

Small houses or huts of rectangular plan were built of cut slabs *31a* of local red clay (25 × 15 × 10 cm) used as bricks. The rooms were small, up to 2·25 m long, walls were thin and supported a single storey. Entrances 1·5 m wide, probably had no doors, but were covered with matting. There were no hearths or other features on the floor, which was made of stamped mud and covered with mats. There seem to have been some five to six building levels in the trench cut into the mound.

Local flint nodules were used for toolmaking and microliths abound. Some of these, diagonally ended and backed, may have been used in offensive weapons. End-scrapers for cleaning hides are found, drills are abundant and there are reamers, burins and retouched blades, some used in sickles. Ground stone tools are few and unvaried: limestone and sandstone querns and pounders, smoothers and picks. Bone awls occur, but they show no traces of artistic expression. Mats are found, and blankets may have been woven. There are a few stone bowls, polished flat pebbles, tubular stone beads; red, white and black disc beads; pendants and buttons of mussel shell, mother-of-pearl, and boar-tusk; cowrie shells probably from the Persian Gulf. Trade and contact with other regions is hesitantly attested; sea-shells, foodstuffs obtained during the annual migration to the Zagros hills and obsidian (196 pieces or roughly 1 per cent) from Nemrut Dağ on Lake Van, about 800 km to the north.[84] Among local exports, asphalt may have figured. Crude unbaked-clay figurines of goats, possibly used in fertility magic, occur but no female figurines as yet. No burials of this phase have so far been found, which would suggest that one day in the future cemeteries may be found outside the settle-ment area.

To this same period belong the sites of Ganjdareh and Asiab, in the Kermanshah area of western Iran. Ganjdareh lies near Harsin at an elevation of 1350 m, and Asiab lies on the Karasu, 6 km east of Kermanshah, at a height of 1400 m. Both are now outside the oak-pistachio belt. A third unexcavated site, Tepe Abdulhosein, lies somewhat farther east in Luristan.

The earliest occupation at Ganjdareh (level E),[78] a mound about 60 m in diameter and 8 m high, consists of shallow pits and hollows of circular or oval plan scooped out of virgin soil, containing ashes and burnt stones.[69] One is partially surrounded by an arc of stone slabs set on edge. They may have been used for heating or roasting, like the fire-pits of roughly contemporary Mureybet. A C14 date gave 8450± 150 B C. There is as yet no sign of solid architecture and the occupation probably was of seasonal type with light shelters. A few clay animal figures were found and flint tools of the same types as in the succeeding levels. Ganjdareh E has yielded animal bones which remain to be studied, and further pointers to the economy will, it is hoped, emerge from the excavation work still in progress there.

Tepe Asiab – a flat flint-knapping site – yielded an industry contemporary but not identical with that of Karim Shahir.[66] Radiocarbon dates range from 7100–6750 B C, i.e., considerably later than Braidwood's guess of c. 8000 B C. Some kind of semi-subterranean structure with an estimated diameter of 10 m suggests seasonal occupation between February and April and occasionally between August and April, to judge from the animal bones.[86] Goats may have been domesticated, but further details of

31 Architectural remains in the Zagros zone and southern Mesopotamia: (a) Alikosh: Bus Mordeh phase; (b) Alikosh: Alikosh phase; (c) Eridu IX, Early Ubaid temple on platform; (d) Jarmo; (e) Eridu XV–XVIII; (f) house at Tepe Ashrafabad, Deh Luran (Mehmeh phase); (g) Ras el-Amiyah (=Hajji Muhammed phase) (after Hole, Flannery and Neely)

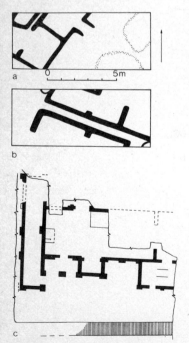

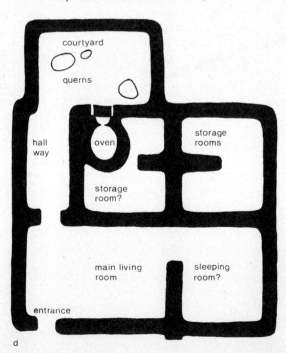

courtyard

querns

hall way

oven

storage rooms

storage room?

main living room

sleeping room?

entrance

the fauna have not yet been published. Freshwater mussels occur in great quantities but virtually no land snails. Coprolites found within the living area suggest a human origin, but they show that small amphibians or reptiles as well as unspecified plant foods were part of the diet. Two burials were found stained with red ochre. Numerous clay objects – cones, balls, and a few enigmatic figurines – were found, as well as ground stone artifacts, beads, pendants and fragments of marble bracelets. A few pieces of obsidian also occur (source unknown) among about a million flint and chert tools, which still await publication.

In contrast to Ganjdareh F, Ganjdareh D is a small village settlement with solid mud-brick architecture, showing signs of repairs and rebuildings and possibly more than one destruction by fire.[78] Radiocarbon dates range from 7289±196 through 7018 ±100 and 6960±170 to 6938±98, suggesting that level D belonged to the second half of the eighth millennium and was finally destroyed by fire c. 7000 BC. Some 144 sq. m of the village have been excavated without reaching the edge. Small rectangular rooms have walls constructed of plano-convex bricks up to 1 m in length and heavily tempered with straw. Strips and lumps of pisé or plaster-faced rubble were also employed for the walls. The structures, often mere cubicles 1 m or so square, cluster tightly together and there is no evidence for alleys, courtyards or large open spaces, nor are there any doorways. Port-holes, circular or oval, occur in some walls, and these are often sealed with clay cones or discs. Mud plaster was used on floors and walls.

Some at least of the structures in the centre of the village may have been two-storeyed buildings, with a lightly built living floor supported on wooden beams overlying the small cubicles and

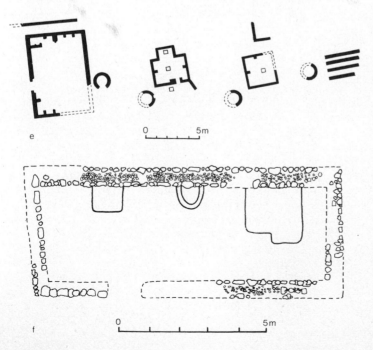

32 Ganjdareh, level D: the earliest known pottery vessels

alcoves that made up the basement warren of storerooms. Roofs were made of beams and reeds overlaid with clay. The absence of hearths suggests that the many cubicles were used for storage and some contained large and small pots, lightly fired; these unfortunately were found empty. Inside one of the cubicles was found not only pottery, but sun-baked vertical slabs of clay with *34* bevelled edges joined together to form very small compartments or boxes.

The most interesting discovery in the centre of the site was a *33* cubicle containing a niche into which were fixed two skulls one above the other. Probably belonging to wild sheep, they lack the mandible (lower jaw), but are otherwise intact. The use of animal skulls in the decoration of buildings, presumably of religious significance, has already been referred to when Mureybet was discussed; it reached its climax at Çatal Hüyük at a later date.

Built-in 'furniture' includes large boulder mortars, packed in mud and pebble foundations. They are provided with clay rims which are baked onto them. These mortars, pestles, sickle blades with sheen, and the clay domed bins, containers and large storage pots up to 80 cm in height, provide much indirect evidence for the use of plant food. Yet, in spite of flotation, few actual floral remains have so far been found and their nature has not yet been disclosed. Animal bones are common and include those of sheep, cattle, deer and pig, but of these only the goat appears to have reached domestic status. Incidentally, hoofprints are common on brick. Although the actual details still escape us, it would appear from the careful storage facilities, the use of straw for bricks and pottery, and the fact that domestic barley and emmer wheat were brought down from these areas to Alikosh by *c.* 8000 BC[75] that Ganjdareh D possibly was a permanent agricultural village.

32 Ganjdareh D has yielded the earliest dated pottery in the Near East – though that from Beldibi B may be contemporary.[105] It is a lightly fired chaff-tempered coarse ware with large vessels up to 80 cm, as well as smaller and miniature vessels, 5 cm in height. Smaller pottery continued to be made at Ganjdareh and occurs

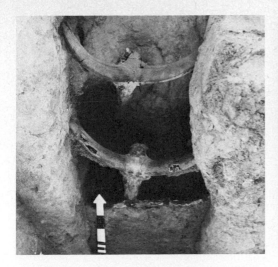

33 Ganjdareh, level D: niche with skulls of wild rams

34 Rectangular boxes of clay in the agricultural village of Ganjdareh, level D, mid-eighth millennium

again in the top levels B and A. Other baked clay objects include human figurines with tall stalk-like heads and pointed breasts of 'Tepe Sarab' type, animal figurines including those of bearded goats and sheep and quantities of 'counters', spheres, discs, cones and small seal-like pieces so characteristic of all the Zagros sites. Some of the female figurines bear nail impressions. Among bone tools there are grooved sickle fragments, awls and wrist guards with four corner holes. A notched cane fragment may be the butt of an arrow.

Flint artifacts (no obsidian was found) abound at all levels, but show little change from top to bottom. There are very few microliths such as trapezes and lunates. Most of the tools are backed and truncated blades and bladelets, struck from conical or cylindrical cores. There are many retouched pieces, end- and side-scrapers, while sickle blades are not uncommon except in the bottom level where they are absent. There are no ground stone axes or celts, and none of the marble rings or bracelets that typify the Zagros zone, but small numbers of polished stone bowls are present.

Levels C and B have rectangular structures of mud brick and pisé comprising several rooms with hearths and white plastered rooms. Many occupation floors are found. Level A is poorly preserved but yielded a domed oven or kiln with layers of burnt limestone – it was probably a lime kiln for the preparation of plaster. Some pottery from this level is decorated with finger-nail impressions.

Some twenty-six individuals have so far been found buried at Ganjdareh, mainly in level D. They include infant burials below the floor in the cubicles. The dead are buried either flexed or extended and secondary burial may have been practised. One grave, constructed in brick with a mud roof, contained the extended skeletons of an adult, an adolescent and a child, stretched out on a powdery mass of burned limestone (?). One was accompanied by a finely polished stone pendant. The skeletons await study.

The third phase of development in the Zagros zone is represented by Jarmo in Iraqi Kurdistan, Alikosh in Khuzistan, and Tepe Guran in Luristan. The first two sites remained aceramic, whereas the pottery invention of Ganjdareh soon spread to reach Tepe Guran, and later Tepe Sarab. This phase is contemporaneous with late PPNB of Palestine and Syria and with Çatal Hüyük in Anatolia, and compared to the earlier phases it is of relative short duration, some five hundred to six hundred years. As elsewhere this is a period of marked cultural advance, but with marked individuality.

Qal'at Jarmo, 3–4 acres in extent, lies on the edge of a wadi in the plain of Chemchemal, at an altitude of c. 800 m in the oak and pistachio belt of woodlands.[67] Its excavator estimates that the village consisted of not more than 20–30 houses, lasted some four centuries (11 building levels) and housed a population of about 150. The top five (1–5) levels have pottery, the lower eleven are aceramic and radiocarbon tests suggest they date from between 6500 and 6000 B C.[287] These aceramic layers are characterized by stone vessels, baskets lined with asphalt, and possibly by wooden and leather containers – this nearly a thousand years after pottery had first appeared at Ganjdareh!

31d Houses were built of pisé (mud brick was apparently unknown) and had mud floors laid on reeds. A typical house consisted of seven small rooms, packed together in a space of approximately 5 × 6 m with an additional 3–4 m of walled courtyard or working area. Four of these rooms may have been used for storage, leaving about 15 sq. m as living and sleeping area. A sunk clay-lined hearth was found within one room, or rather cubicle – for some were only 1·5–2 m in length. Pot-boilers and fire-cracked stones occur near the hearth; ovens were built into courtyards between buildings. Matting covered floors, and roofs were probably flat and made of reeds with a clay covering. These houses have doors or doorways, unlike the earlier Ganjdareh D structures, but a notable feature even at Jarmo is the small size of the rooms. The dead were probably buried outside the settlement and this may account for the scarcity of human remains;[87] a few skulls showed good teeth, but that is all we know about them. The economy indicates that Jarmo was a permanent village, occupied all the year round.[67] Domestic emmer wheat and two-row hulled barley, surprisingly still morphologically close to the wild forms, were grown and einkorn was also present. Protein was obtained from field pea, lentils and blue vetchling, fat from pistachio and acorn. Snails were eaten in great quantity. The stratigraphic position of the plant material is nowhere indicated in the report. Domestic goat, and to a lesser extent sheep, were herded,[86] dog was present, but aurochs, boar, fox, deer and gazelle were hunted.[89-90]

The ground-stone industry was highly developed; there are the by now familiar mortars and pounders, saddle querns and handstones, door pivots and stone balls, and axes with polished cutting edge. But there are also marble and alabaster rings and bracelets, many with incised and grooved ornament, perforated stone maceheads, beads, palettes for grinding red ochre, perforated discs

35 Characteristic objects of the Jarmo culture: below left, earliest pottery from the upper levels (after Braidwood)

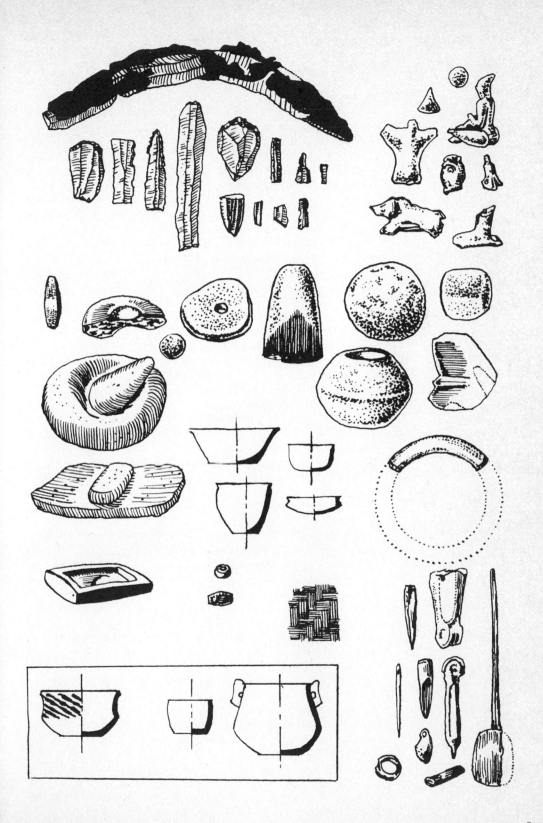

that may have been spindle whorls, and an elegant set of cups, bowls and dishes carved from carefully selected veined limestone and marble.

The chipped-stone industry consisted mainly of blades for composite tools, such as curved wooden sickles in which the blades were set in asphalt. Microliths, such as diagonal-ended bladelets (used as arrows?), side-blow flakes and scrapers, and geometrics such as triangles and crescents were frequently made in obsidian, green from Nemrut Dağ or grey from Suphan, obtained by trade from the region of Lake Van far to the north.[84]

Bone tools included awls and needles, spatulae and rings, beads and pendants. Although pottery was unknown, other baked-clay objects were very common; there are numerous naturalistic female figurines, some almost elegant, others schematically rendered, T-shaped or stalk-like. Many animal figurines were made, taking the form of horned animals, and dogs with curling tails; also spheres, tetrahedrons, discs and cones used in counting. Knuckle-bones were used for games.

ALIKOSH (ALIKOSH PHASE)

The permanent village that occupied the site during this period is estimated to have covered some two acres with a population of about a hundred. It had grown out of the previous semi-permanent encampment of the Bus Mordeh phase. The number of building levels is not known with any certainty, but the multi-roomed *31b* houses have grown larger; rooms exceed 3 sq. m in size and have walls up to 1 m thick. Untempered clay slab bricks ($40 \times 25 \times 10$ cm) covered with mud plaster were used, and floors are of the same material laid over twilled mats of reed and club-rush, as at Jarmo. Courtyards contain domed brick ovens, as at Jarmo and Tepe Guran, and brick-lined waste pits. Niches and doorways are found and alleys separate houses. Wall plaster, painted with red ochre, occurs in the upper level of the site, but there are no red plaster floors or terrazzo mosaics as at Tepe Guran.

Some of the dead were buried in a sitting position, tightly flexed and wrapped in a mat, below the floor of the house. Others were coated with red ochre, as earlier at Asiab. A few articles of personal use were found with them, such as the first copper and turquoise beads, exotica that must have been rare at the time. Secondary burial also occurs. The women of Alikosh practised skull deformation and wore strings of beads, black and white stone discs, tubular beads or sea-shells from the Persian Gulf. Men wore a sort of loincloth, the imperishable part of which was formed by a bell-shaped cover made of lightly baked clay, polished stone or asphalt. Other ornaments included mussel shells, boar-tusk pendants, flat pebbles and strings of disc beads with tubular spacers. A copper bead was made of native copper, cold hammered, cut with a chisel and rolled into shape. Whereas the origin of the turquoise beads points to Maden, near Nishapur in northeast Iran, the native copper may have come from deposits in the same area, or conceivably from the Anarak deposit in the desert area of central Iran.[197] Obsidian (now 2 per cent) was still imported from the Lake Van area – but now not only the green, but also the grey variety – as at Jarmo, Tepe Guran and Tepe Sarab, which may have been the intermediaries from which this material was obtained, a normal distance for transhumant goat herds during the summer. Although contact with other communities is thus clearly indicated, the Alikosh people did not pick up the idea of pottery-making until the next phase in their development. They did, however, now make not only animal figurines as before, but also small human figures, clay cylinders with pinched ends, applied blobs, and punctuations (tattooing ?) rather schematic in appearance.

Instead of pottery, they turned wicker baskets, sometimes lined with asphalt and carved stone bowls from gypsum, limestone and marble. There are limestone trays and flat-based bowls with simple rounded or beaded rims. In this respect also Alikosh ran parallel with Jarmo, Tepe Guran and Tepe Sarab. Some grind-stones were used for the preparation of red ochre, and the wide-spread use of asphalt and red ochre is attested by hundreds of cigar-shaped stones with a smear of red or black colour at one end. A mortar and pestle now occurs in addition to saddle querns; also grooved sandstone rubbers for polishing bone tools – awls, needles and bodkins for basketry – while stone perforated discs were probably used as spindle whorls as before. Then there are limestone balls and flint pestles, abundant pebble choppers for butchery and slicing slabs for cutting up the meat, new forms invented to cope with the increase of hunting that characterizes this period. Chipped flint was still used for composite hunting tools armed with diagonally ended, backed microlithic bladelets (as in the previous phase), for end-scrapers for hide-working, and for sickle blades set into a wooden shaft with asphalt. Drills, burins, reamers, domed core-scrapers and the conical bullet-shaped cores from which such blades were struck, are typical.

The inventory of the Alikosh phase thus presents us with a much greater variety of tools and marks a cultural and technological advance over the more primitive Bus Mordeh phase. This is evidently true throughout the Zagros area but at Alikosh one can also see how it was reflected in the economy.

The main meat supply of the village came from morphologically domestic young goats; these still heavily outnumbered domestic sheep though the latter are more common than before. The establishment of mixed farming led to an increase in the hunting of gazelle, onager and wild cattle, and new butchering tools were invented. Foxes were apparently eaten, but their skins would also have been useful; otherwise small mammals are not important. Birds (duck, geese, crane, heron), fish (carp, catfish), crab, turtle and mussels continued to be exploited.

Whereas in the Bus Mordeh phase wild plants outnumbered cultivated plants in the ratio of 28:1, in the Alikosh phase this had decreased to 1·5:1. The main crops were emmer wheat and two-row hulled barley together with some new naked barley and einkorn, though these were not yet important. Cereals increased from a mere 3·4 per cent in the Bus Mordeh to 40 per cent in the Alikosh phase, at the expense of the small wild legumes, which are down from 95 to 18·5 per cent. Perhaps the land where these were formerly collected was taken over by wheat and barley fields.

Lentils appear, suggesting contact with the mountains where they were beginning to be cultivated as at Jarmo. Wild oats, canary grass, capers, goosefoot as well as weeds were still collected, and reeds and club-rush served as fuel. Surveys in Deh Luran and northern Susiana show only one site, Alikosh, of this period in the area, so its people had no close neighbours.

TEPE GURAN

Tepe Guran, situated at an altitude of 950 m above sea-level, lies in the northern part of the Hulailan valley in Luristan. It is an oval mound, 110 × 80 m with 6–7 m of early deposits containing eighteen building levels, D–V.[76] A radiocarbon date from level U gave 6460 ± 200. The site was occupied for about a millennium from *c.* 6500 to 5500 BC.

The first settlers established themselves in a semi-permanent winter camp of wooden huts, each with two or three small rooms and with straight or slightly curving walls.[77] Matting covered the floors and fire-places were out in the open. They herded domestic goat (80–100 per cent of all the animal bones) and occasionally hunted gazelle, fox and hare, and caught migratory winter fowl – goose, crane and heron which visit the River Saimarreh in wintertime. In summer, these goat herds probably moved into higher pastures. Mortars, querns and sickle blades, tools related to agriculture, were almost totally absent.

About 6200 BC, represented by levels P–N, the situation changed; mud-walled houses appear side by side with the wooden

36 Tepe Guran, Luristan: courtyard paved with white stones laid in red coloured clay, level J

huts, which disappear after level N. The upper part of the mound
contains mud-brick houses built close together to form a village,
and indicates permanent occupation. The houses are divided into
small rooms, and the walls have recesses for low mud benches and
tables, as well as openings to ovens placed out-of-doors between
buildings, as at Jarmo and Alikosh. Walls and floors are covered
with white or red plaster, but floors and courtyards also sometimes   *36, 37*
have a terrazzo mosaic of white felspar pieces set into red ochreous
clay, a technique also known from Beidha VI, Mureybet and, at
its most splendid, Çayönü. Agricultural tools now appear,
together with actual carbonized grain of domestic two-row hulled
barley. Pistachio was collected as well as the common snail (*Helix
salomonica*). The faunal remains change; the number of gazelles
relative to domestic goats, now joined by some domestic sheep,
increases (were gazelles also being herded?). Moreover, as at
Alikosh, there is a significant increase in the hunting of aurochs,
red deer, wild pig, wolf and fox, attesting a greater interest in the
various food resources of the vicinity. At Tepe Guran in *c.* 6200 B C,
we find signs of the transformation of a semi-permanent winter
camp into a permanent village. The occupants of the former relied
on restricted seasonal resources, those of the latter were intent on
fully exploiting the entire area, both the valley floor (cereals,
snails, herding) and the neighbouring hills (herding, hunting,
pistachio collecting).

What distinguishes Tepe Guran from Jarmo and Alikosh is the
appearance on the site, after a short aceramic phase, of pottery in

37 Tepe Guran: plastered walls
and floors of house in level H

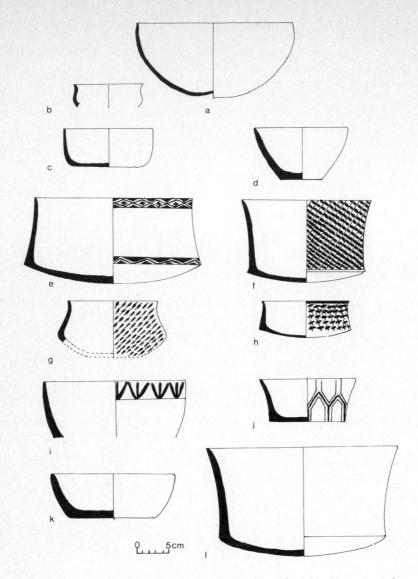

38 Plain and painted pottery from Tepe Guran: (a–d) red burnished ware; (k, l) undecorated buff ware; (e) Sarab style; (f) close-pattern style; (g) Jarmo type; (h) Sarab style; (i, j) archaic painted ware (after Mortensen)

the three lowest levels (V–T). After the discovery of Ganjdareh this is no longer surprising in this region, but one would not have expected mobile goat-herders to have used and developed it. An undecorated greyish-brown ware in the form of coarse thick-walled bowls with vertical or curving sides and wet-smoothed or burnished surface starts off the sequence (levels S, R, Q). In level R a finer, plain buff ware with a straw temper appears, which lends itself to painting. This 'archaic ware' is decorated in red or orange on a buff slip with widely spaced, extremely simple patterns (levels R–O). Bowls and beakers with flat bases and curved or vertical sides are the main shapes.

These developments took place in the goat-herders winter camp, and during the harsh Zagros winter they evidently provided plenty of work. One wonders whether in summer they peddled the pots during their migrations.

With the development of a permanent village economy the pottery flourished. Undecorated buff ware was accompanied by a   *38* new 'standard painted ware' (levels O–M). It has a straw temper and an orange-buff or reddish slip, which is sometimes burnished. Red patterns of obliquely arranged lines made of blobs are typical on bowls with curved sides and a flat base. This pottery was later diffused to Jarmo 5–4 and is often referred to as 'painted Jarmo ware'.[67] Higher up in the sequence (levels L–H) there is a development into the so-called 'Sarab ware',[66] and carinated bowls with flat or rounded bases now prevail.[68] These are decorated in horizontal bands with lozenges, triangles or chevrons on the rim as at Tepe Sarab, or they have more regular obliquely placed patterns as in the earlier 'Jarmo ware'. A little later in 'Upper Guran' levels J–D, the Sarab type develops into a style characterized by close patterns, the greater part of the exterior of the vessel being covered with paint on which the patterns stand out in reverse. Carinated bowls, larger than before, are the main shape, and they are reminiscent of the *later* Khazineh and Hajji Muhammed style of decoration. A red burnished ware – post-Sarab – occurs from level H, the end of which is dated by C_{14} to 5850 $\pm$ 150 BC, to level D. Open bowls and cups of the latest levels, E–D, foreshadow certain shapes at Tepe Siyalk I with dimple bases, *c.* 5600–5500 BC. At this point the site of Tepe Guran was deserted.

Bowls of white and pink marble, semi-globular bowls and truncated conical bowls with flaring rim, were made as in Jarmo. Among the finds were palettes (an evident necessity) and celts and numerous sling-stones of ground stone, as well as a phallus that has a Jarmo parallel. Then there are the familiar bone awls and pins, and stone, shell and mother-of-pearl beads and pendants. The flint industry with some 5–10 per cent of green and grey (type 4c and 1g Vannic) obsidian, the rest local flint, closely resembles that of Jarmo and Alikosh.[84] Microliths such as obliquely ended, backed blades, trapezes and their conical cores occur with wooden-hafted sickle blades with sheen (but not in the winter-camp levels!), numerous notched blades, end-scrapers and borers.

Burials are rare at Tepe Guran; at the bottom of the site a pit was found with a heap of human bones and four skulls, probably a secondary interment. A few single contracted burials occur throughout the levels of the settlement. Funeral gifts are rare and consist of a few beads, perforated teeth pendants and a few microliths.

TEPE SARAB

Tepe Sarab, 7 km east of Kermanshah and 1300 m above sea-level, parallels part of the Guran sequence.[66] Although the site was occupied all the year round on the evidence of the animal bones, and was not just a summer camp for goat-herders as has been suggested, there were no permanent mud-brick structures, but remains of wooden huts like those of early Guran.[68] There was evidence of the domestication of goat and sheep, as well as of emmer and two-row barley, this being accompanied by wild barley which grows in the area. Pistachios and snails (*Helix salomonica*) were consumed in enormous numbers and have left

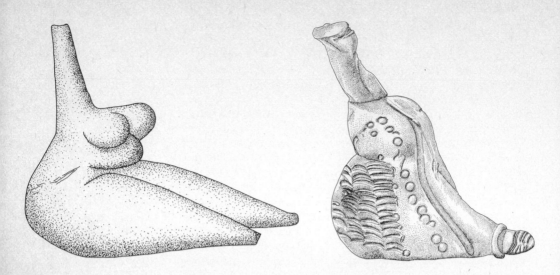

39 Two female figurines from Tepe Sarab near Kermanshah (after Braidwood)

39

35

thick deposits. Some fine Sarab pottery, red burnished and painted and sometimes oval in shape, was found, together with finely carved stone bowls, but the most striking objects are two intact female figurines, with tall necks, no facial features, bulging breasts and thighs. One has impressed decoration of the kind already found at Ganjdareh, which provides the prototypes for such figures. There are also some spirited renderings of wild boar with stab marks suggesting their use in some magical hunting rites in which the quarry is killed through sympathetic magic. The finds included a fine tortoise, a fleecy sheep, and – in the Zagros – the inevitable calculi probably used in the counting of herds. Three C14 dates, 6006±98, 5695±89, and 5655±96 roughly date the settlement.

At the moment it would appear that the vigorous development of pottery just outlined was a feature only of the central Zagros region from which it spread, rather late in the sequence *c.* 6000 BC, both north, west and south, to Jarmo, Tamerkhan and Alikosh. This period is roughly contemporary with the end of the PPNB in the Levant which witnessed a similar diffusion of pottery and a change to new conditions. By the end of the period Jarmo, Guran, Sarab and Alikosh lay deserted.

In the five top layers of Jarmo, pottery appears; in levels 5 and 4 it is decorated with obliquely strung rows of dashes and blobs.[67] This also appeared at Tamerkhan near Mandali,[180-81] on the alluvial Mesopotamian plain but near to the Zagros foothills. This pottery is in turn followed by half-baked local (?) unpainted red ware, among which a jar shape with two vertical lugs is characteristic.[67] This ware also occurs at Ali Agha near Erdebil in the Assyrian plain. It looks as if at last people of the Guran-Jarmo tradition were beginning to exploit the winter grazing potential of the Mesopotamian plain. There are few other innovations in this ceramic phase of Jarmo; stone foundations now occur in the houses and ovens are provided with a flue to extract the smoke. Apart from the domestication of pig, the economy is unchanged.[89-90]

At Alikosh, pottery is introduced in the last, Muhammed Jafar, phase of the mound which certainly comprises more than two building levels and still covers about 2 acres; there are two other mounds of this period in the plain.[75] The houses with their red-ochre walls, are of the same type as during the Alikosh phase, and the cultural inventory is not markedly changed, though there is a great increase in grindstones and obsidian (2 per cent) continues to be imported.

The dead were buried, not under the floor of the house but outside it in a semi-flexed position on their left side, facing west, and red ochre was found on some of the skeletons. One male was buried with a basket containing perishable food (?), others with articles of personal adornment – three to four turquoise beads and a string of beads with bell-shaped pendant at the hips. There is as yet no report on the skeletons themselves. Articles of jewellery were not uncommon – cowries from the Persian Gulf, turquoise from northeastern Iran, stone bracelets of marble and alabaster, lip plugs (labrets) of asphalt, clay or polished stone, and limestone or alabaster phalli, as at Jarmo, Guran and, later, Tell es-Sawwan. Numerous broken clay figurines link this phase with Jarmo and Tepe Sarab, especially the stalk and T-shaped types. Yet the most important feature of the period is the pottery, which appears early in the Muhammed Jafar phase. It is soft, friable and straw tempered and occurs in three varieties: plain buff ware, painted ware and burnished monochrome red ware. Deep round or large oval bowls are typical of the mottled buff ware. The painted ware, which tends to be covered with poorly adhering red ochre, is exemplified by a deep bowl decorated with geometric patterns such as zigzags, chevrons, pendant triangles and lozenges. Some of these bowls are provided with trough-like spouts at the rim. The red burnished monochrome ware took the form of hemispherical or carinated small bowls, some with beaded rims, as well as a few red globular jars with dimple base at the end of the sequence, just as at Tepe Guran. Stone bowls were still in use. The Muhammed Jafar phase is tentatively dated to *c.* 6000–5600 (?) B C. It is interesting to see

40

40 Muhammed Jafar pottery from Alikosh (after Hole, Flannery and Neely)

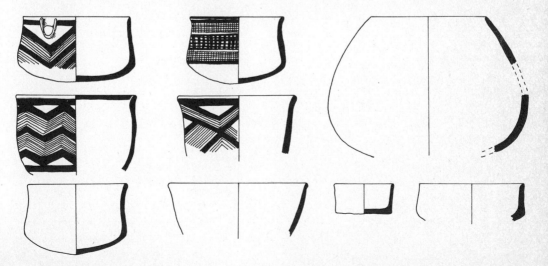

how long it took this pottery to spread from northern Luristan to Jarmo and Alikosh.

The economy of this phase shows signs of stress. Old habits such as the collection of aquatic resources continue, but now small mammals (fox, wild cat and hedgehog) appear in the diet. Herding greatly increases and sheep gain gradually on goat, both fully domestic, and hunting of gazelle, onager, aurochs and wild pig continues. There is a corresponding and dramatic decrease in agriculture. Prosopis (*shauk*), a leguminous plant which flourishes on fallow land and has an edible fruit, is found by the basketful, and gradually becomes more and more important. Small legumes, hardly touched in the Alikosh phase, are again collected in the early stage but are absent later. Emmer and especially two-row hulled barley, occasionally also lentil, are still the main crops, but weeds such as plantain, mallow, vetch, oat and canary grass increase. During the Muhammed Jafar phase the carbonized deposits show a staggering increase of wild over cultivated plants. In the Alikosh phase the ratio of wild to cultivated was 1·5:1; in early Muhammed Jafar it was 28:1, in late Muhammed Jafar 47:1. The excavators claim that farming, while obviously (?) successful, required careful weeding and a reasonable fallow system, which had altered the landscape to a noticeable degree. How successful was the farming? It looks as if agriculture was in decline in favour of pastoralism and by the end of the period Alikosh was deserted. The Khuzistan plain may have suffered from the same desiccation that seriously affected the drier parts of the Levant from *c.* 6000 BC and which made farming, if not impossible, at least an unprofitable pursuit in arid lands.

Chapter Three

Anatolia and Cyprus

ANATOLIA

Anatolia, like Iran, is a great mountain mass bordered by two Alpine chains, the Pontic Mountains in the north, the Taurus in the south. Between these ranges, which approach each other in Transcaucasia, lies the Anatolian plateau with rolling monotonous steppes and fertile basins gradually descending towards the Aegean and the Sea of Marmara, the descent from the plateau being effected by a parallel series of rift valleys carrying major rivers. The natural lines of communication run in an east–west direction, but passes lead through the mountains to the Mediterranean and the Black Sea. On the south coast the rocky piedmont zone of the Antalya area[121] and the alluvial Cilician plain offer a choice of habitat, but the north coast is abrupt, mountainous and heavily forested.

With a few minor exceptions the pre–Bronze Age occupation of Anatolia is confined to the southern half of the country, the Taurus zone, with distinct cultures on the southern shore, or in the wood and grassland belt along the inner flank of the mountains.[135] No Neolithic is known north of the Halys (Kizil Irmak) or in the Ankara-Eskişehir basin, but around the eastern shores of the Sea of Marmara and in the Akhisar–Izmir area there are sporadic finds of Neolithic cultures.[114] Two groups of obsidian-producing volcanoes dominate the southern parts of the Anatolian plateau: the central Anatolian group at the northeastern end of the Konya plain, the source of black obsidian of types 2b from Çiftlik and *11* 1e–f from Acigöl; and the east Anatolian group around Lake Van, the source of green obsidian (type 4c) from Nemrut Dağ, grey obsidian (type 1g) from Suphan Dağ and black (type 3a) from Ararat.[83-5] This clearly desirable material found its way across the Taurus Mountains as early as the Upper Palaeolithic, but more or less regular trade dates from the time of the establishment of the first agricultural settlements in the Early Holocene both in Palestine and the Zagros zone. It continued throughout the Neolithic and was only ousted by the use of metal tools in the Chalcolithic, when it became a raw material, no longer for tools, but for luxury vessels. As a 'guide fossil' for early trade it is invaluable, but it should be remembered that obsidian was probably only one, and not necessarily a main, article of the trade, most of which was probably made up of perishable stuffs, such as food, skins, cloth, etc. Most important, however, would have been the exchange of knowledge and information on new techniques of food production, the raising of crops, and the taming and cross-breeding of animals, as well as new religious concepts which arose in the Neolithic.

Very little is known of the Upper Palaeolithic of Anatolia,[110] especially on the plateau, but there are rich sites in the Antalya area and in the Amanus Mountains.[121] Little has yet been published but the Antalya region seems to have passed through a sequence similar to that of the Levant with a sort of Levanto-Aurignacian – the Kemerian – developing locally into an Epipalaeolithic with two phases, the Belbaşı culture, which resembles the Kebaran, especially in its later geometric phase, and the Beldibi culture, which has Natufian affinities in its first phase (Beldibi C1–2).[105–7] After a gap in occupation, there was a second phase (Beldibi B1–2), possibly of eighth-millennium date, with pottery, obsidian and wall paintings in the top layer, c. 7000 BC (?).

The similarities between the Antalya sequence and that of the Levant suggest at least intermittent contacts along the Mediterranean littoral, if not a cultural continuum. In the absence of reliable C14 dates, the sequence can only be dated by typological comparisons and some climatic observations. The Belbaşı assemblage, in three levels (I–III), is clearly of Epipalaeolithic type, characterized by a microlithic industry of points, triangles and in particular obliquely truncated blades. The Geometric Kebaran A parallels would suggest a date c. 13000 BC. It is followed by the Beldibi culture, after an apparent gap resulting, it is thought, from some climatic event. Beldibi C, with two levels, resembles the El Wad sequence of the Natufian with its microlithic backed blades and lunates. A number of art objects, including a carved fish, were found, and a rock engraving, using natural contours and apparently showing a bull with its head turned back as well as a running stag, may perhaps belong to this phase of the rock-shelter's occupation. After a gap which may mark the transition from the Pleistocene to the Holocene with a rise in temperature, the last occupation of Beldibi, B1–2, possesses imported Çiftlik obsidian and in its top level primitive pottery, a red coarse ware as well as some hole-mouth shapes in black and brown burnished ware. A number of schematic wall paintings show human figures and an ibex. These are painted in red and manganese black, and they partly cover the engraving. At this point the shelter was deserted.

41 Epipalaeolithic art mobilier from the Antalya caves: engraved stone plaques, pebbles and bone object. (c, d) from Kara'In; (a, b, e) from Öküzlü'In (after Anati)

a

b

c

d

e

As far as is known the dwellers in these rock-shelters were primarily hunters of deer, ibex and cattle, and the presence of harpoons in this coastal environment may indicate some fishing though there are no reports of fish bones or shellfish. Some sickle blades and grindstones in Beldibi C may point to the collection of wild grain on the slopes of the Taurus Mountains. Admittedly this is not the proper environment for the beginnings of agriculture – the area is too low lying and covered with pine forest, the soil is rocky and covered with shrub. When agriculture did develop in Anatolia this area was deserted. At the more northerly sites of Kara'In, Öküzlü'In and Çark'In similar microliths have been found but they have not been published. From the first two sites come engraved pebbles decorated with a variety of subjects, geometric, animal and human.[98] One shows a bull and a schematic female figure of a type characteristic of Upper Palaeolithic art. Another shows a bearded man's head, and a second bearded man figures on a bone tool which has a Natufian parallel at Wadi Fallah. A cave at Öküzlü'In contains a great red bull naturalistically engraved, as well as a human (?) figure,[97] while at Beldibi there is the engraving of stag and bull already mentioned.[105] Deep and shallow cup-marks occur on the rock outside the entrance to Kara'In cave.[98]

41

42

All these features of a local Palaeolithic art have much in common with that of the Mediterranean province, and Italy in particular. The absence of art at Belbaşı (and in the Kebaran of the Levant), the affinities with the Natufian which has similar traces of an Upper Palaeolithic art tradition, or with Palanlı and Kobystan, would suggest a fairly late date in the Epipalaeolithic, not before the eleventh millennium B C and, generally speaking, during the Natufian period – the early Beldibi culture. The wall paintings at Beldibi and neighbouring sites in the Lycian peninsula, not yet published, as well as the black stylized goats and a bird (?) in Kürtün'In cave near Suberde in the Taurus Mountains, are clearly later and may belong to the Neolithic period.[132] The presence of Epipalaeolithic art in the Antalya region is of considerable importance, for with similar occurrences elsewhere in the Taurus (Palanlı) as well as Kobystan near Baku on the Caspian, it demonstrates that the Near East was not wholly devoid of Upper

42 Epipalaeolithic rock engravings from the Antalya region, including a bull and deer from Beldibi rock-shelter and a red painted bull from Öküzlü'In (after Kökten and Bostanci)

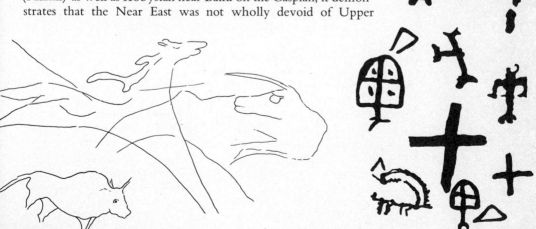

Palaeolithic art, as has often been too rashly assumed. Moreover, the art of the Antalya region provides a suitable ancestor for the Neolithic art of Çatal Hüyük where the old rock art, painted or engraved on rocks, is transferred to man-made buildings, a process which, logical as it seems, has not yet been observed elsewhere. The sporadic presence of Acigöl or Çiftlik obsidian in these three caves suggests some contact with hypothetical Epipalaeolithic groups on the central Anatolian plateau,[84] for the extremely rare occurrence of this material on the south coast does not suggest that its inhabitants made the arduous journey to the deposits themselves. Instead they continued to exploit the inferior local beach chert. With the possible exception of open-air sites on Avla Dağ in the obsidian area[133] and of Macun Çay near Ankara, no Epipalaeolithic sites have yet been located on the Anatolian plateau and the contexts and dates of these sites remain uncertain.[110] A few rolled flints, including some microliths, occur in the sand dunes that once surrounded the great Konya Lake, a stretch of water which occupied most of the plain during the Upper Palaeolithic until it dried up around 16000 B C.

The trade in Çiftlik obsidian began in the Proto-Neolithic layers of Jericho and continued throughout the PPNA and PPNB periods. Evidently there were then people living in the area of the central Anatolian volcanoes; however, what are perhaps the earliest sites in the area, Çiftlik itself and the much larger mound of Aşıklı Hüyük, have not been excavated and there is no surface material to document the Anatolian end of the late ninth-millennium trade route.

Aşıklı Hüyük is a medium-size mound, situated on a river, which has destroyed part of the site. It lies on the Melendiz Çay, east of Aksaray and some 50 km from the Çiftlik obsidian deposits on Göllü Dağ.[134] Mud-brick walls of houses with red lime-plaster floors can be seen, as well as burials below the floors. From these came polished greenstone axes, bone awls, beads and a belt-hook. Not a sherd of pottery was found, but an abundance of tools and flakes made of Çiftlik obsidian. Microliths were not discovered and there was only one piece of flint collected on the surface. Five unstratified radiocarbon dates ran from 7008 ± 130 to 6661 ± 108, enough to show that the site is earlier than the excavated part of Çatal Hüyük, a conclusion typologically confirmed by the different technology of the chipped-stone industry. All tools are in the medium to large range and they consist of stout (spear?) points on blades and flakes, but there are no definite projectile points. Scrapers abound, indicating that skin-working was important. There are borers and many notched blades, the latter usually associated with woodworking. Among the many large blades there are some sickle blades, which are hard to recognize in Anatolia, as obsidian does not acquire a silica lustre like flint. Fire-stones for striking fire have been recognized. There were a few grindstones lying around as well as hackberry pips. Animal bones, none necessarily of domestic animals, indicate the following species: sheep or goat, cattle, onager, red deer and hare. On the basis of these data, which may well be deceptive, Aşıklı Hüyük is contemporary with the early PPNB of Palestine, overlaps with

Çayönü, and is earlier than Çatal Hüyük. For a conjectural account of its economy and its role in the obsidian trade the reader is referred to Jane Jacobs, *The Economy of Cities*, 1969, pp. 19–31.

The earliest evidence for an agricultural settlement in Anatolia comes from Aceramic Hacılar in southwest Turkey, 25 km west of Burdur.[125] Below the later mound, an earlier site was discovered with seven superimposed building levels of which the third from the base (level V) yielded evidence for cereal crops. In addition there is C14 date of 6750±180 (i.e. early PPNB in Levant terms).

Simple dry farming was practised with concentration on two-row hulled barley and some emmer wheat and lentils. Wild einkorn and naked (six-row?) barley also occur, but were not important. There were numerous weeds, and the standard of agriculture is described as primitive, Animal bones are too restricted in numbers to yield any proof of domestication, except for domestic dog. They consist of sheep or goat, cattle and red deer.

Neither pottery nor figurines were found, and though there were a few fragments of polished marble bowls, most of the containers must have been made of basketry, leather or wood. Polished greenstone axes were used, and local red and grey chert was utilized for blades together with some imported obsidian. Polished marbles and knuckle-bones suggest use in games. Clean house-keeping was responsible for a dearth of small finds and no burials were discovered.

No complete house plan was found, but a thick wall of straw-tempered bricks on a stone foundation separated the kitchen area in a courtyard from the living quarters. In the courtyard were hearths and ovens, square bins and post holes showing that the court was at least partly covered. It seems that the dwellings consisted of large rooms surrounded by a few smaller ones, but it is not clear whether they were free-standing or built up against each other, although the latter seems more plausible. The small rooms had mud plaster on walls and floors, the larger ones red burnished lime-plaster floors laid on a bedding of pebbles. The

43

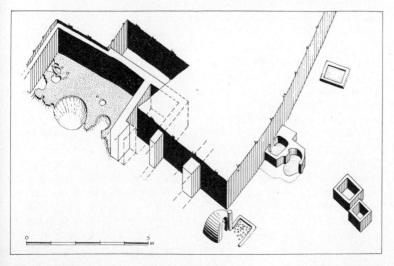

43 Aceramic Hacılar V (after Mellaart)

plaster continued up the walls, probably to form a dado, and two pieces of cream plaster with red bands painted on them suggest the use of wall paintings. A small room contained a circular depression in a red floor with a white band left in reserve at some distance from the wall, forming an oblong around the depression. At a later date the room was redecorated with a plain red floor. Hearths and ovens are not associated with the red floors. Doorways are not in evidence and entry may have been through the roof. Human skulls were set on the edge of hearths or propped up on pebbles in a court but no burials were found with them. Eurafrican and Proto-Mediterranean types are present at Hacılar. The size of the settlement is unknown but it was probably small. Its date probably falls within the first half of the seventh millennium.

A second aceramic site, Suberde,[101] covers half an acre on a rocky knoll beside Lake Suğla in the Taurus Mountains.[104] Pollen tests indicate that the area was heavily wooded. A series of radiocarbon dates shows the site to have been occupied in the second half of the seventh millennium, a little later than aceramic Hacılar. The lower deposits show floors with ashes, but no permanent structures, whereas the upper ones have plaster floors and mud-brick walls, probably contemporaneous with the earliest levels (XII–IX) excavated at Çatal Hüyük. To the unclean habits of its inhabitants the archaeologist owes much information about the hunting activities of these people, whose only domestic animal was the dog.[130] The main quarry was red deer, wild sheep, cattle and boar. Aurochs was butchered where it was killed and the meat cut off, the skeleton being then dragged back by the legs in the animal's hide. Sheep, and occasionally goat, were carried back to the settlement intact. Aquatic resources such as birds, including pelicans, freshwater mussels, fish and the like, were relatively unimportant and no remains of plant foods have yet been recognized. Suberde, only 80 km west of the agricultural centre of Çatal Hüyük, may have been a seasonal hunting camp, though the presence of querns, axes (hoes?) and sickle blades tends to belie such an assumption. Hunting nevertheless stands out as the main activity of the inhabitants and the chipped-stone industry, microlithic and mainly in obsidian (the specific type is not yet known), consists predominantly of various types of arrowheads and scrapers. Some arrowheads have tangs whereas others are leaf-shaped; geometric microliths do not occur. Unifacial retouch is typical. Some crude pottery is reported in the lower level but its use was neither common nor continuous and it soon disappeared. A few baked-clay figurines of women and wild boars were made. Burials have not been found.

Can Hasan III is an aceramic mound with a diameter of approximately 100 m, 6·75 m high with about seven building levels, some of which are below present water-level.[116] An area measuring some 20 × 30 m, representing only about 6 per cent of the site, was fully excavated in the top building level and disclosed a complex of rooms, courts and passages, built of mud brick or pisé slabs without stone foundations or wooden supports. Walls and floors are covered with mud plaster, sometimes painted with red ochre, and some floors are made of a very hard clay reinforced with

44

pebbles. The buildings are of rectangular plan and most of them lack doorways which suggests entry from above, as at aceramic Hacılar and later Çatal Hüyük. Ovens are built into the wall. These buildings of the top level of Can Hasan III are very reminiscent of those of the lower levels (X–XII) at Çatal Hüyük, but no shrines are reported from Can Hasan III. The small finds consist of finely retouched obsidian such as Mersin produced (what does that imply?), end- and flake-scrapers, awls, *lames écaillés*, heavy backed blades, and small backed bladelets, some with obliquely truncated ends – microliths of a type not found elsewhere. There is much waste material and flint also occurs, though less abundantly, with many sickle blades, some of which are denticulated. There are numerous bone implements: awls, scoops, spatulae, pins, pierced spatulae and tubular beads. Burials are not reported.

The animal bones are said to indicate that no species dominated numerically, but cattle was the important meat animal, followed by sheep/goat.[128] Equid, probably onager, and pig are fairly common; red and roe deer are also present besides hare and two species of canids. It has not yet been established whether any of these animals were domesticated, but it would not be surprising to find them so at this period. Among crops the following were identified: bread-wheat and club-wheat, emmer, einkorn, both wild and domestic, two-row hulled and naked (?) barley; lentils, common vetch and bitter vetch, as well as walnut, hackberry, wild grape, prunus and crataegus. Weeds and seeds of medicago, trifolium, scirpus, sedge, etc. were also found. Evidently Can Hasan III had an agricultural economy, but it is far too early to deduce from this limited excavation that bread-wheat took first place over emmer and barley, as at Aceramic Knossos.

The chronological position of Can Hasan III, apparently based not on C14 but on typological comparisons with Suberde or on the absence of pottery, and therefore considered to pre-date Çatal Hüyük and put at *c.* 6500 BC by the excavator, has still to be confirmed. D. H. French may be right, but the possibility that Can Hasan III, a small site, could still have been aceramic at a time that

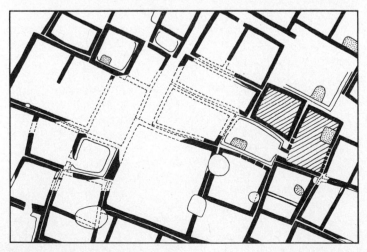

44 Top level of Can Hasan III. Hatched area = red plaster floors (after French)

0   5m

the larger Çatal Hüyük used pottery (albeit in minute quantities) cannot be overlooked. Only further excavations and C14 tests can settle this problem.

More important than such details is the recognition that the aceramic sites of Anatolia – Aşıklı, Aceramic Hacılar, Suberde and Can Hasan III – *may* already have been fully agricultural communities in the seventh millennium – even if the animal remains are still morphologically those of wild ones, as pointed out by S. Payne.[128] Only in this way is it possible that fully Neolithic cultures reached Crete and Greece (Knossos, Franchthi, etc.) by the end of the seventh millennium B C.

Çatal Hüyük

After this tantalizingly vague information about aceramic sites in Anatolia, the reader may well turn with relief to the site of Çatal Hüyük, 11 km north of Çumra in the alluvial Konya plain.[123–4] It is a large mound, approximately 600 × 350 m, covering 32 acres with archaeological remains of the Neolithic period. How much of this vast site, the largest-known Neolithic site in the Near East, was occupied at any one time remains unknown; nor have the lower deposits of the site been reached in the four seasons of work there that the excavators were granted. Fourteen building levels have been excavated in an area that only represents about one-thirtieth of the mound, and more than thirty radiocarbon readings have been obtained for these, which show that they cover a period from *c.* 6250 to 5400 B C. Thick deposits, some possibly aceramic, lie below level XII, the earliest reached, in which pottery is already present.

The Çatal Hüyük sequence then, is comparable in duration and contemporaneous with the late PPNB, plus Amuq A and B in the Levant, or Aceramic Jarmo-Ceramic Jarmo plus Umm Dabaghiyah and Early Halaf periods, cultures that at no other sites except Tepe Guran show an unbroken succession. Yet even Çatal Hüyük is not perfect and one lacks the transition from the aceramic to the ceramic Neolithic period, which here as in Iran may date farther back than expected. This may of course be represented in the unexcavated lower layers.

The economy of Çatal Hüyük was based on simple irrigation agriculture and cattle-breeding, trade and industry. A preliminary study of the crops shows that domestic emmer, einkorn, bread-wheat and six-row naked barley were grown, the latter two cereals being hybrids that had developed as important food crops as the result of irrigation.[119] These cereals provided the starch, and protein came from legumes: field peas, bitter vetch and vetchling. Vegetable fats were obtained from the seeds of crucifers, acorns, pistachios and almonds. Other fruits included crab-apple, juniper berries, hackberry and capers. As early as level XII dog and cattle are domestic,[129] but by level VI the large aurochs-like creatures of the earlier levels had become smaller. Sheep occurred widely, but was morphologically still wild, whereas goat, not an inhabitant of the alluvial plain, was rare. Domestic cattle provided the people of Çatal Hüyük with more than 90 per cent of their meat, as well as transport. The domestication of cattle is reflected in the bull games, painted in great detail on the walls of two shrines in levels V and III, and in the elaborate bulls' heads that are such a feature in the religion of the site from about the time of level X onwards. In addition onager, half-ass, boar, red, roe and fallow deer, bear, wolf and a feline – lion or leopard – were hunted, some for their skins, others no doubt to provide a change from beef. There are bones of mice and shrew, pests rather than food; fresh-water fish, birds (not yet identified except *Gyps vulvus*, the Griffon vulture) and eggshell. To complete the picture one should un-doubtedly add such foods as leave no archaeological traces: dairy products (milk, butter, cheese, yoghurt), green and root vegetables, onions, garlic, herbs, fruit juices, hackberry wine and beer; also grape, pear, walnut, fig and pomegranate which grew wild in Anatolia. Olives, however, do not appear before the fourth millennium.

Compared to other cultures, Çatal Hüyük's specialities are wheat rather than barley, cattle rather than sheep and goat (northern Mesopotamia) or goat (Zagros and the Levant).

All this, in addition to the clear chronological antecedence of its irrigation agriculture over that of Mesopotamia, suggests that we are dealing with a local Anatolian tradition, independent of those of its neighbours and not notably influenced by them. Yet the fact remains that it was only the use of the river on which Çatal Hüyük is situated for irrigation that made agriculture a success in this wide open plain; the wild ancestors of the crops were not at home there. It is reasonable to assume, therefore, that the first settlers came from hilly regions, perhaps from the east or southeast, the area of the obsidian sources and the adjacent parts of the Taurus and Anti-Taurus Mountains.

The population of Çatal Hüyük is in fact mixed.[112] Eurafricans, descended from an Upper Palaeolithic type like Combe-Capelle man, formed about 59 per cent of the population. Proto-Mediterraneans of finer build (17 per cent) are a second doli-chocephalic stock, but the third group consists of brachycephalic Alpines (24 per cent).[111] Such a heterogeneous population accounts in large measure for the inventiveness and the rapid advance in every field of cultural activity seen at Çatal Hüyük.[99] The average adult age was 34·3 years for men, 29·8 years for women. Compared to an Upper Palaeolithic population, such as that of Taforalt (Morocco), man lived one, women one and a half to two years longer, which means that they gave birth more often and spent more time instructing the young. In this respect the presence of some people over sixty years of age is important; they would be the mentors of the society. Child statistics show a parity of 4·2 per woman, and as the death rate per woman was 1·8, there was an excess of 2·4 children. In terms of population growth that repre-sents a multiplication of at least 528 times over 800 years. If the settlement started off with say 50 people at level XII, it would have risen to 25,000 by level I. In real terms we do not know the extent of level XII, but it seems likely that it was considerably larger, nor did the city contain 25,000 people at any time. Conservative estimates suggest that in its heyday Çatal Hüyük may have had a thousand houses, with a population of something like 5000–6000.

It could have been larger, yet even so it is obvious that it produced many emigrants. It may be surmised that with such resources of man-power Çatal Hüyük controlled not only the Konya plain, vital for its food supplies, but also the trade in obsidian and other commodities in all the neighbouring areas. Many towns and villages would owe their origin to Çatal Hüyük's population explosion, and its culture, cults and language may have been widespread in southern Anatolia. Yet the remarkable thing is that these people prospered as they did, for the pathology of the skeletons shows that they suffered from anaemia, causing porotic hyperostosis, a thickening of the blood-carrying parts of the skull. Some attribute this to a dietary deficiency – people do not always eat what is good for them even when they have plenty of food as at Çatal Hüyük – but J.L. Angel suggests that it was caused by *falciparum* malaria, which may have been endemic in the inland drainage basin of the Konya plain. Nevertheless these health hazards were overcome. Dental decay was also rare. Average stature was 170 cm for males, 156 cm for females, a small decrease since the Upper Palaeolithic.

Houses at Çatal Hüyük show a standardized rectangular plan, usually covering about 25 sq. m of floor space (6×4 m, 5×5 m); smaller or larger houses are uncommon.[123-4] They consist of a large living-room and a smaller storeroom, entered through a low doorway (without door) or a port-hole raised above the floor. Access to the house was through a hole in the roof and a wooden ladder fixed against the south wall, which also acted as a smoke hole for the hearth and oven on the floor underneath. Roofs were flat and a veranda of light inflammable material covered part of the roof. Each house had its own walls and roof levels would have been staggered to admit light. Houses were closely built up against each other though there were some courtyards, usually ruined houses of a previous level not rebuilt, to serve for rubbish disposal and sanitation. There were no streets, lanes or alleys, and all communication was at roof level. The furniture was part and parcel of the house: a bench, a series of platforms used for work,

45

45 Diagrammatic view of a typical room at Çatal Hüyük showing timber framework, panelling and platforms, bench, hearth, oven and larder (after Mellaart)

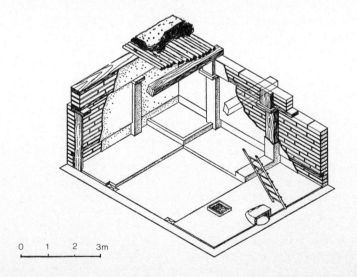

0   1   2   3m

sleep and burying the dead under, and at the kitchen end, ladder, hearth, flat-domed oven and fuel cupboard. Many storerooms contained grain bins of various types.

Shrines distinguished by their decoration, associated finds and burials, do not structurally differ from the houses, nor are they larger in size. They are intermingled with the houses in considerable numbers. All the excavated buildings are houses or shrines and their storerooms; the manufacturing and trading quarter has not yet been located. Animals, with the exception of dogs unfamiliar with steps or ladders, would have been kept outside these quarters. To the outside the city of Çatal Hüyük presented a blank wall, not specially designed as a fortification, but acting as such against enemies as well as floods. Although the later levels show signs of not infrequent fires, there was an uninterrupted cultural development over at least eight hundred years and possibly more. Building materials were mud brick in various sizes; timber, used for posts, roofing, verandas and panelling of the walls; and plaster, both mud and fine white gypsum from the Pleistocene lake bed. Lime-plaster floors, stained a variety of reds were occasionally used. Red painted panels were common in houses and shrines, often to pick out structural details, but floors were of stamped mud covered with fine club-rush matting, and this was also used on many platforms. Wall and floor plaster was renewed annually, which is chronologically useful. The structure of the city did not allow for individual rebuilding; this was done *en bloc*, and old house walls were used as foundations for the new. All this made for limited mobility, which accounts for a fair number of broken bones at Çatal Hüyük; moreover, the too-close proximity of one's neighbours no doubt led to many a broken head – the frequency of head wounds testifies this.

The people of Çatal Hüyük buried their dead below the sleeping platforms in their houses and shrines, which strongly suggests that the dead were still regarded as part of the family. The type of burial, however, is unusual in that the dead were exposed to vultures and insects and after excarnation were wrapped in cloth,

46 Plan and tentative reconstruction of the southeast quarter of the mound of Çatal Hüyük VIB (after Mellaart)

46

47

47 Group of burials below the main platform in house VI.B.34 at Çatal Hüyük

mats or baskets (for children) and then interred. The great majority were buried without any gifts, but when these do occur they consist of personal ornaments, necklaces, armlets, wristlets, anklets of stone or shell (including dentalium as in the Natufian), lead or copper beads, pendants of all sorts of material including mother-of-pearl, for women and children, and weapons for men. There are a number of red-ochre burials, and some, apparently of both sexes, for which blue azurite or green malachite paint was used. High-status burials also occur, usually in shrines, accompanied by precious objects, such as stone vessels, ceremonial daggers, cosmetic sets and obsidian mirrors, fine bone belt-fasteners (for leopard skins?), polished maceheads and quivers of arrows; also wooden vessels and boxes, baskets, metal beads, rings, etc., as well as funerary offerings of food, which included boars' jaws. Such rich gifts are rare; pottery or figurines were never buried with the dead. When the communal grave beneath the sleeping platform was opened to admit a new burial the earlier corpses were frequently disturbed, and the skulls were often re-arranged. One red-ochre burial in level VII had large sliced cowries set into the eye-sockets, as at contemporary Jericho and Tell Ramad. The cowries were probably from the Red Sea.

The equipment consists of ground stone tools made from a great variety of rocks, and a chipped-stone industry with more than 90 per cent use of Acigöl obsidian as well as imported Syrian tabular flint, cream, honey-coloured or brown. In the first group there are mortars and pestles, saddle querns and hand-stones of limestone or volcanic rock; also dolerite hammer-stones, a wide variety of polishing stones in many varied, sometimes exotic, types of rock, and small axes or adzes and whetstones (for polishing bone) preferably made from greenstone and diabase. Sandstone or schist palettes are frequently found together with lumps of red ochre.

The chipped-stone industry[100] is easily the most elegant in the Near East (with Byblos and Syria taking second place).[126] About fifty types of tools and weapons can be distinguished of which the weapons, up to 20 cm in length, are outstanding. Bifacial flat re-touch is typical and there is a variety of arrowheads with or without tangs and barbs, large and small, as well as double-pointed spear-heads, pressure-flaked flint daggers, polished on one side, long thin blades, many side-scrapers, firestones, etc., as well as polished obsidian mirrors. To judge by this industry one would think that hunting and skin preparation was extraordinarily important, but from the bone material we know that hunting was not. Yet the hides of domestic cattle still needed preparing and the killing of a domestic cow or an aurochs cannot have been very different. Many of the weapons are clearly prestige objects, like the numer-ous perforated maceheads of breccia, conglomerate and various coloured rocks. Such weapons would have been useful not only in the hunt, but in human conflict also. Baked clay balls are common in the lower levels, but higher up these disappear and baked sling-stones take their place. In the last levels the stone industry declines, as it seems to have done everywhere after the

48 Ceremonial flint dagger with bone handle carved in the form of a snake. From a male burial in shrine VI.A.29. The flint was imported from north Syria

49 Cache of obsidian spearheads from house V.7 at Çatal Hüyük. The obsidian was brought from Acigöl in central Anatolia

50 Wooden vessels from Çatal Hüyük VI (after Mellaart)

middle of the sixth millennium. There were no microliths at Çatal Hüyük; sickles, mainly of wood, but some of antler, were curved.

The bone industry covers the usual tools; awls, needles, polishers for skin, beads, pendants, tubes, spatulae, toggles, as well as belt-hooks, dagger hafts; also carved animal heads, cosmetic stick and fork, hairpins, and a fish-hook. For containers these people used coiled baskets, with or without covers, leather bags, wooden vessels and boxes with lids of varied shapes, a few luxury vessels in stone, and pottery. There is no evidence for gypsum- or asphalt-lined baskets but pine resin was probably used, together with gypsum plaster, as an adhesive. A sherd of painted 'white ware' shows contact with Syria (level VIB), but this ware was not made locally.

As mentioned earlier, the lowest building level (XII) to be excavated has pottery, and it is quite possible that pottery-making goes back farther still. This earliest recovered ware is cream-coloured and burnished, frequently mottled grey, with some straw temper, coiled and medium fired. Flat-based, oval bowls or circular hole-mouth jars prevail occasionally provided with a knob handle to facilitate manipulation. This ware is undecorated but not coarse and was evidently used in cooking. It predominates from level XII (or before) till level VII. In VIII, however, the first dark burnished ware with a grit temper, better firing, higher burnish and thinner walls, appears but in the same shapes. It is still of local manufacture. By level VII it has ousted the earlier ware. A red wash, already found in level XII, continued to be used, and from level VII a small percentage of the pottery is red-washed or red-slipped. In the later levels – from IV onwards – mottled slips become common, and by level III fine buff-shaped vessels are made in sophisticated shapes. Painting in red is attempted once or twice, but other forms of decoration are virtually unknown. Occasional animal heads on oval cups, a few incised lines along the rims of bowls, ledge handles or basket handles on hole-mouth jars, are the only features that grace this monochrome ware. There is no shell

51 Textile fragment from a burial in shrine VI.A.5, with shawl or fish net weave

impression, nail, finger or barbotine ornament as on contemporary ware along the Cilician, Syrian and Lebanese coasts. The Çatal Hüyük potters never forgot the primary function of the wares they made, namely to cook and serve food in. Many shapes betray origins in other materials, chiefly basketry and wood. In level II, tubular lugs are introduced to tie on a cover, probably of cloth; the idea of making pottery lids never occurred to them, but they might have used wooden ones. The production of excellent textiles[108] with several weaves in wool and/or linen is another feature of Çatal Hüyük,[118, 131] yet these people did not grow flax, nor have we any evidence that they kept domestic sheep or goat.[129] (They probably did, but the animals do not yet show the morphological changes which came later.) The quantity of textiles found among the burials hardly suggests that cloth was an import. There is likewise evidence for string, woven tapes and fibrous rope. Moreover, metal was not unknown, though used, as far as we know, only for trinkets. Lead pendants occur as early as level IX, copper beads in level VIII. Slag from level VIA shows that copper was extracted from ore by this period, whereas some of it was hammered native copper.[127] The use of azurite and malachite paints in levels VII and VI goes hand in hand with this early use of metal for pendants, beads, tubes for string skirts, finger-rings, etc.

Apart from food, mud brick and plaster, salt, and some wood and reeds, the people of Çatal Hüyük had to import everything else they used from at least one day's walk away – the distance to the nearest hills. This included timber for their houses (oak and juniper), raw materials for their stone tools, weapons, beads, statuettes, paints and metals, shells and flint, fruit and berries from the hills, etc. They had, however, domestic cattle[129] and thus a form of transport, which would have facilitated the carrying of obsidian over a distance of 200 km.

Trade and industry, with specialized craftsmen (metal, weaving, obsidian, woodcarving, beadmaking, etc.) is clearly a feature of Çatal Hüyük. It is this creative local economy that ensured the wealth of the city, not just access to material or the success of its

52 Pottery from Çatal Hüyük: straight-sided cream burnished bowl from level II; dark burnished ware cooking pot with two ledge handles from level IV; pot with double vertical perforated lug handles from level III

53 Group of clay stamp seals with incised designs from Çatal Hüyük VIB–II

54 A large baked-clay figure giving birth to a child, supported by two felines, from Çatal Hüyük II

55 A bird of prey in white marble, from Çatal Hüyük VIA

56 A kneeling female figure in white marble, from Çatal Hüyük VIA

agriculture. It imported and exported, it developed new industries, it was able to control the trade through its 'emporia' and colonies, drawn from its expanding population. In fact its culture covers the entire Konya plain as well as a number of outlying areas: the Beyşehir-Seydişehir region, the sites in the Karaman area,[104] and the region of the central Anatolian volcanoes.[139] There is good evidence that Çatal Hüyük owed its importance to more than material prosperity; it was probably also the spiritual centre of the Konya plain.

At Çatal Hüyük it is possible, from the way in which they are employed, to distinguish two groups of figurines. To the first group belong crude, female figurines, with pointed legs, a stalk-like body and a beaked head; these highly schematic renderings of the human figure appear as early as level IX, as do more realistic animal figures – horned bovids, caprids and wild boar – the latter frequently covered with stab marks, probably the result of their use in sympathetic magic during hunting rites. Such boar effigies

are mainly found in pits, but the female figurines – so similar to
those of other cultures – never appear inside shrines; they are
tucked away in crevices in the brickwork of such buildings,
ostensibly with the aim of ensuring fertility. These ex-voto
figurines often clumsily made, are common, but their function
clearly differs from that of the carved stone or modelled clay figures,
which I prefer to call statuettes, that are found as the cult inventory
of shrines, nearly always accompanied by an array of broken-off
stalagmites or stalactites, obtained from caves, the nearest of
which in the Taurus Mountains are situated in the Hadim-
Taşkent area. This association is the closest men or women at
Çatal Hüyük came to sexual symbolism; many of the natural
concretions suggest breasts or phalli, even to the non-Freudian
mind. The carved statuettes range from the aniconic to the
naturalistic, defying any attempt at a chronological typology, and
demonstrating the futility of this sort of approach. Some are
concretions with heads carved into them, others are 'pregnant'

57 A grey schist plaque with
two figures in an embrace on the
left and a mother and child on
the right, from Çatal Hüyük VIA

pebbles with a few incisions to emphasize the meaning; yet others are well carved, though often with a remarkable economy of effort, into clear types. Finally, there are those which represent minor sculpture in the round. The forms of representation chosen are often explicit; a towering concretion with a head suggests a chthonic deity, a well rounded one is clearly pregnant. Some are dressed in cloaks or wear leopard-skin bonnets, kerchiefs or bracelets. Associations are often indicated by grouping: an old woman, a bird of prey and a confident male adult (crone and young god); a young female with leopard in blue limestone and an older female with leopard, and a boy riding a leopard in brown limestone (mother and child, and maiden aspect of the mother; a prototype of Demeter, Kore and Ploutos?). Twin females may represent the same theme, virgin and mother; the concept of twins has no religious connotation. Male figures ride animals; several are seated on what are probably meant to be bulls. Cult themes are always difficult to interpret, however, and historical analogies with similar cultures in the same area provide the only reliable key.

The numerous shrines at Çatal Hüyük take us a step further, for 58 here there are scenes depicted in plaster reliefs that defy materialistic interpretation. Women do not give birth to bulls' or rams' heads, and certainly not on top of a doorway from which peer the ferocious heads of three superimposed bulls, made the more lively by the use of actual horn cores. Nor is it very usual to find 6-foot-tall Siamese female twins, one of which gives birth to a huge bull's head, on top of which there appears another, smaller one. The benches found in several shrines, in which one, three, five or seven pairs of horn cores of aurochs are embedded, are matched in simpler form by the bucrania, brick structures with a pair of horns, set on the edge of platforms, found in others. If one denies the religious nature of these structures, one is faced with the equally implausible suggestion that the people of Çatal Hüyük were masochists trying to make things as awkward for sleeping and sitting as possible. Why should they? There are plenty of houses which show what their normal dwellings were like and common sense demands a different explanation. In the plaster reliefs the female deity alone appears in anthropomorphic form, whereas the male is only represented by his symbols, the bull, the ram, and less commonly the stag or wild boar, the latter two usually shown in incised relief. There are other forms of symbolism: female breasts containing lower jaws of boar, skulls of foxes and weasels, or of Griffon vultures – all animals associated with scavengers, hence death.

Then there are wall paintings, executed in monochrome but more often polychrome mineral and vegetal paints on dead white plaster with a brush. The subjects vary from plain panels and decorative textile-like patterns, which either inspired the design of later rugs, or copied already existing ones, to a landscape with a 59 settlement and erupting volcano, scenes of vultures with human corpses or the celebration of animal games, in which among 60 scenes of festivity (dancing, etc.) bulls, stags, boar, bear, lion, etc. are teased and baited. Hunting scenes, in which red deer are actually

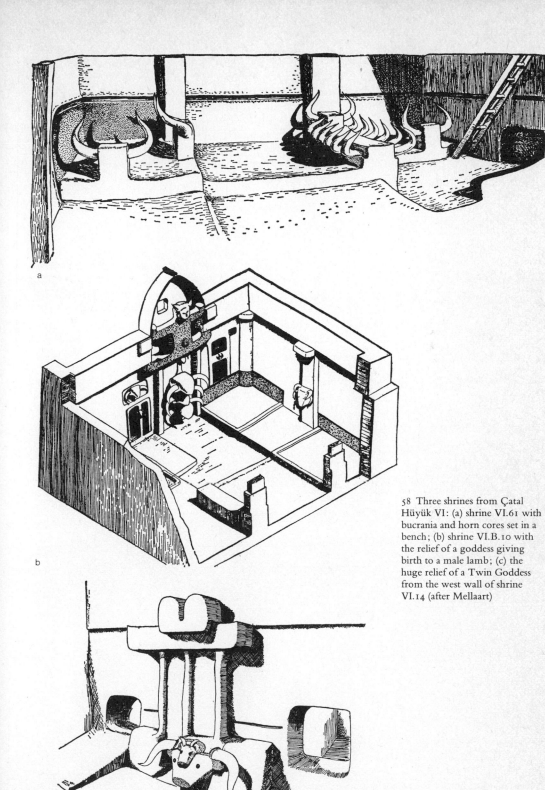

58 Three shrines from Çatal
Hüyük VI: (a) shrine VI.61 with
bucrania and horn cores set in a
bench; (b) shrine VI.B.10 with
the relief of a goddess giving
birth to a male lamb; (c) the
huge relief of a Twin Goddess
from the west wall of shrine
VI.14 (after Mellaart)

shot at or brought down by men, are few. These paintings were not meant to be seen permanently like the reliefs of deities, *61* leopards' and bulls' heads, though they too were sometimes renewed, on a fresh layer of plaster. This suggests that paintings were made in connection with certain events, the precise nature of which we shall probably never ascertain. Çatal Hüyük is thus one of those rare cases in archaeology where man tried to communicate some of his thoughts. For us to read these is another matter.

Enough has been said to put Çatal Hüyük in perspective. It was during this period that the use of pottery, i.e. the dark burnished ware, spread throughout southern Anatolia, westward certainly as far as the edge of the plateau at Tavas, southeastwards to Cilicia, Syria and the Lebanon. In the west it reached the Antalya caves, which were, if not already deserted, soon to be abandoned.[110] The few Neolithic sherds may have been introduced by herdsmen in search of winter pasture, for nothing suggests a local development. This diffusion of Çatal-type pottery culture may have given rise to local developments, e.g. at Erbaba on Lake Beyşehir, [102–4] Kızılkaya and Hacılar in the southwest, at Can Hasan 4–7 in the Karaman area and at Mersin on the south coast, where there is a C14 date of 6000 ± 250 for layer 33, near the base of the mound. At Erbaba, with a C14 date of $5780 \pm$? there is evidence for domestic sheep, goat and cattle (*c.* Çatal Hüyük IVA),[109] but it remains to be seen whether these sites rose above village level.

The period that follows Çatal Hüyük is often called the Early Chalcolithic, a term first used at Mersin for the period of the first

59 Transcript of a wall painting from Çatal Hüyük, shrine VII.14, showing a town in the foreground and an erupting volcano in the background, probably Hasan Dağ (10,672 ft) at the eastern end of the Konya plain, visible from Çatal Hüyük

60 Transcript of a stag- and boar-baiting scene from the north wall of shrine F.V.1 at Çatal Hüyük, decorated with scenes of festivities

painted pottery cultures. In economic terms it is as Neolithic as the preceding one. Technologically, painted pottery, usually red on cream with lighter-coloured monochrome and plain wares, replaces the dark burnished ware; the chipped-stone industries lose their weapons and are reduced to blades; spindle whorls replace scrapers as hunting declines with the domestication of sheep, goat, pig, now added to that of dog and cattle. Copper occurs, but still mainly for trinkets, such as beads and pins. Maces and sling-stones are the only weapons. The dead are buried outside the settlement, and archaic features such as red floors, roof entry, secondary burial, ochre graves, become far fewer. Figurines are preferably made of clay rather than stone. The date of its beginning is roughly the middle of the sixth millennium in C14 terms. The end of the Çatal sequence, Can Hasan 4–7, Mersin XXVI and XXV and Hacılar IX–VI ending with carbonized material dated to 5399 ± 79 B C, is likewise called 'Late Neolithic', a term that marks innovations at Mersin, new settlements in the Hacılar culture, possibly a ceramic phase at Can Hasan, but is not clearly definable at Çatal Hüyük, except that at the end (?) of it, the old site was deserted for a new location, Çatal Hüyük West, across the river. As that site is virtually untouched, no continuous account of cultural developments can be given, nor do the few published details of the Can Hasan sequence come to the rescue. The only full account of a later sixth-millennium site available in detail is Hacılar. It will, therefore, be described first and we shall return later to the Konya and Cilician plains.

61 Clay and plaster relief of a pair of leopards from the north wall of shrine VII.44

The Hacılar Culture

The later mound of Hacılar, which covers the earlier aceramic site, is small, with a diameter of approximately 100 m, containing some thirteen building levels, clearly divided into three main periods: levels IX–VI, V–IIa and Ia–d.[125] Levels VI, IIb, IIa and Ib had been burnt and thus yielded plentiful remains. Hacılar VI dates from about the end of the Çatal Hüyük sequence, and was burnt *c.* 5400 B C. Part of the village plan was excavated enough to give one some idea of its arrangement. Rectangular houses, some measuring as much as 10 × 4 m with walls 1 m thick, were constructed of large plano-convex mud bricks, 50 cm square. Most of these houses were oblong and had a doorway 1·5 m wide in the

62

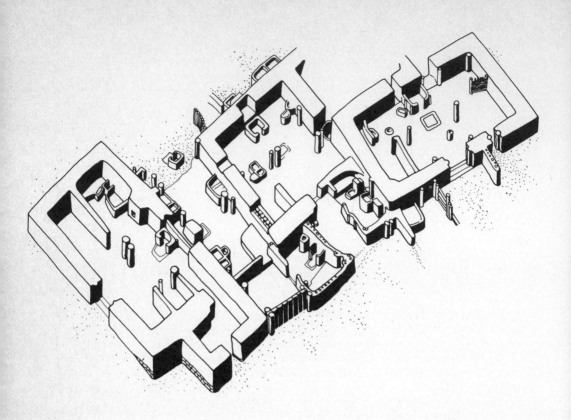

62 Isometric drawing of a group of houses from Hacılar VI (after Goff)

middle of the long side facing a central court, with wooden thresholds and jambs for a double door of wood, about 1·7 m high. Entry by the roof had been abandoned. Against the south wall and facing the entrance stood a flat-topped oven with a hearth 1 m square, with moulded kerb in front of it. Querns and mortars were either fixed in the mud-plaster floor near the hearth or set on a small platform to facilitate the back-breaking job of grinding. Rectangular clay boxes, used as braziers for glowing embers, were found on the floor; these were always placed diagonally to the walls of the room, part of which was screened off with sticks coated with plaster to form a narrow storeroom for sickles, spoons and other tools. Cupboards had been let into the thick walls for further storage, but as all were found empty they may have been used as clothes cupboards. There were no platforms for sitting or sleeping on, as at Çatal Hüyük or Can Hasan, no red plaster floors and no panelling or wall paintings. In only one room was a plastered bull's head found with large almond-shaped eyes, like those of the statuettes, but it had not been provided with actual horn cores. The Hacılar houses had plain walls, perhaps adorned with cloth hangings and rugs on the floor; had matting been used, this certainly would have left a trace in burned buildings. Although the substructure was incredibly solid and had windows in the wall, set at eye-level, the ceiling rested on two stout wooden posts arranged on the long axis, and a number of smaller posts in the corners and along the walls. These supported not just the roof, but an upper storey constructed of wood and plaster, probably consisting of a long open veranda with a view onto the courtyard and small rooms at the back. Access was gained by a flight of mud-brick steps with a parapet on one side leading straight up from the courtyard. On either side of the door there were small lean-to structures of brushwood and plaster used as kitchens, as is evidenced by their domestic equipment: an oven, grindstones, tables, and square grain bins 1 m high made of plaster. The separation of kitchen from main room is reminiscent of similar practices in the aceramic period and might have been devised as a precaution against fire – if so, in vain. The Hacılar houses with all their wood were highly inflammable, and the habit of having a second hearth on the upper storey together with stores of fuel and grain often proved fatal. These houses show two layers of pottery in the ruins, those from the upper rooms, covered by the roof and those of the lower, covered by the ceiling. Some of the work, such as the modelling of figurines in one house, was done upstairs, in addition to much grain storage, drying, etc. There was also a stone-lined well. These houses – no definite shrines could be identified – were built up against each other and faced onto courtyards which communicated with each other through straight or crooked lanes; there is no evidence for fortifications. The site may have contained fifty houses, with an estimated population of perhaps 250, but this admittedly is surmise. Only three burials were found, rather unceremoniously interred in the ruins of the burnt village, perhaps victims of the fire. Two were put in a pit, the other was bundled in a shallow grave. Stone beads and a three-legged marble pot were found with the top burial in the first grave, whereas the second was accompanied by a drinking cup in the form of a human head; this had been wrapped in cloth, which had left its imprint as the result of the fire.

The chipped-stone industry is poor through all levels of the site; blades and sickle blades predominate, but there was a cache of microliths in level VI. Hunting weapons have disappeared and for armament the Hacılar people relied on maces and sling-stones, either pebbles or missiles of baked clay. Spindle whorls occur, but few scrapers, suggesting woven cloth from sheep and goat rather than leather jerkins or leopard skins. Belt-hooks and toggles still occur, and there is some fine craftsmanship in the bone spatulae, the handles of which are frequently decorated with animal or even human heads. Sickles are curved and fashioned from deer antler; blades were made of local chert, never obsidian. The latter did occur, but its provenance is not known; possibly it came from Acigöl. Copper was used, as corroded fragments show, but apparently only for pins and trinkets. If copper tools were known, the inhabitants took great care not to leave them around for the archaeologist to find! The ground-stone industry abounds in querns and mortars, polishing stones of richly varied materials, pounders, chisels, fully polished axes of greenstone of a much higher quality than those of Çatal Hüyük, possibly owing to the presence of fine greenstone supplies only one hour's walk from the site. White marble bowls, up to 40 cm in diameter, are common in Hacılar VI; these imitate pottery shapes, having tubular lugs, flat or ring bases, or three or four stumpy feet. Mending holes

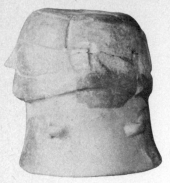

63 A drinking cup in the form of a woman's head, from Hacılar VI

show that they were regarded as precious. Stone figurines, on the other hand, do not seem to have been made. Small pendants of bulls, bull's heads, and beads were made of stone, and mother-of-pearl was used for amulets in the form of a figurine, model fish-hooks or geometrically shaped pendants. Seals were not found.

These people were expert potters and from the very beginning (level IX) they made a fine light-grey or cream-coloured ware, infrequently decorated with simple red linear or curvilinear patterns. The local clay is excellent and the burnishing exceedingly fine; the result is first-rate pottery of much higher quality than the earlier Çatal Hüyük ware. By levels VII and VI the greys had been replaced by red- and brown-slipped or unslipped monochrome wares with attractive shapes, disc bases and vertical tubular lugs for tying on a cover. Painted ware in level VI was still very rare, but included both red on cream, and less commonly, white on red. Far more typical than painting was applied ornament that took the form of animal heads, usually bucrania, but also some bears, an ibex and a scorpion. Some vessels took the form of a woman's head or were shaped like animals: boar, doe, pig, bird, etc. A single sherd shows that occasionally figurines were stuck onto pots, but here only the head and arms survive (cf. Umm Dabaghiyah).

63, 64

The potters also excelled in making statuettes as opposed to the crude figurines, often with a wooden peg head, requiring far less skill. Where it was possible to observe these different groups *in situ*, i.e. not fallen from upper floors or embedded in masses of burnt brick, the crude figurines appear to have been grouped together in a niche, not accompanied by statuettes, a situation that is reminiscent of Çatal Hüyük. There are no animal figurines. The statuettes of Hacılar VI are well known; all represent females, naturalistically modelled in red or buff burnished ware, the latter frequently decorated with paint. Details such as the pupils of eyes or the spots on a leopard-skin dress may be added in black paint as in the later Çatal Hüyük clay figures, which are only a few centuries earlier in date.

64 A ritual vessel in the shape of a recumbent deer, from Hacılar VI

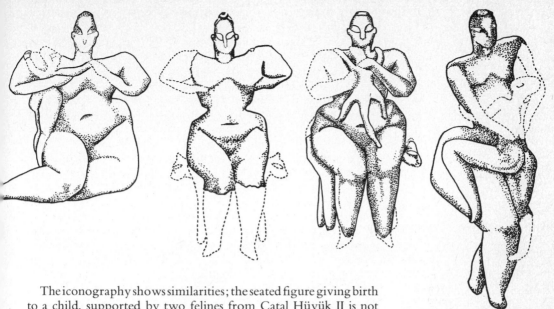

The iconography shows similarities; the seated figure giving birth to a child, supported by two felines from Çatal Hüyük II is not repeated, but two figures at Hacılar are seated on what may be a single leopard or a pair. One of them holds a leopard cub, as does a further standing figure. Age differences, emphasized by hairstyle and dress, are marked at Hacılar, where slim girls in topless 'bikinis', their hair done up in pigtails, alternate with more portly matrons shown in the nude or wearing short skirts, their hair done up in buns at the back of the head or in tiara-like structures. Women with animals or with small children, standing, seated, reclining, or giving birth – all were well observed and neatly modelled These figures seem to have been kept in the houses, and not in communal shrines. One misses the male figures, not rare at Çatal Hüyük. Here, on the other hand, a stone slab with incised facial features seems to have been kept in nearly every house. Whilst two others made of clay and resembling little dolls are clearly female, the sex of the stone slabs is not indicated. They remain unexplained and apparently disappear after level VI.

65 Baked-clay statuettes of the Mother Goddess, some painted, found in the burnt houses of Hacılar VI (after Mellaart)

Such, then, is the 'Late Neolithic' of Hacılar, contemporary with the end of the Çatal Hüyük sequence. There are similarities, yet enough differences to suggest that the culture of Hacılar is not directly in the Çatal Hüyük tradition. It may, or may not, represent an offshoot; the evidence is insufficient.

The next period at Hacılar spans levels V–II, c. 5400–5050/5000 B C, clearly a development of the culture from its earlier beginnings, and without recognizable extraneous influences. The hall-mark of this phase is painted pottery, considerably less monochrome ware, rigid stylization of statuettes now less varied than before, and the substitution of painted for relief ornament with bizarre results. With it goes a decline in stone bowls and in the working of bone, besides a change in house plans, manifest only at the end of the period in the two phases of level II.

Level II shows Hacılar to have been a small walled settlement, approximately 70 × 35 m, containing a number of houses, a

66

granary, a guardhouse, three potters' workshops, and two possible shrines as well as a number of courtyards and a quarter of less substantial habitations and kitchens, following an old and well established tradition of separating the living area from the cooking, and potmaking (?). Several ovens contained painted pots – not the sort of vessels normally used for cooking. However, at Hacılar it is not impossible that these bowls were kept in the oven to keep the soup or food warm; but this is a matter of little consequence. The interpretation of shrines is based on a number of features: a niche in the main room with remains of standing stones, their tops unfortunately broken (were they originally incised like the stone slabs of level VI?); traces of geometric patterns painted in the niches; libation holes in front of the stone in one shrine which is unique in that it contained a number of intramural burials of women with children; and the nature of the contents such as figurines, clay seals and a group of pottery with evidently religious motifs, found in and around the second shrine. The plans are striking; the shrine near the well retains the level VI plan, the other one, opposite the granary, follows the new house plan, roughly that of a megaron, with main room, anteroom and porch. The development is evidently a local one, which took place during levels V–III; both the old arrangement of combined oven and hearth and the screen marking off a place for storage are, however, retained. The potters' workshops, resembling houses but lacking domestic equipment, had red and yellow ochre on the querns and bins containing clay as well as simple modelling tools, palettes and paint cups lying on the floor, besides stacks of obviously unused pottery – cups in one room, jars or bowls in another. Courtyards were attached to these rooms for work such as drying and the like, but no kilns were found. Such a job may well have been done outside the settlement, away from the prevailing wind. Two large ovens in the courtyard outside the granary were probably used for drying grain. This settlement was partly burnt and the eastern half was not rebuilt. The number of houses, or rather hearths was now reduced from twenty to ten at most and the population may have

66 Reconstruction (a) and plan (b) of the Hacılar IIa settlement (after Mellaart)

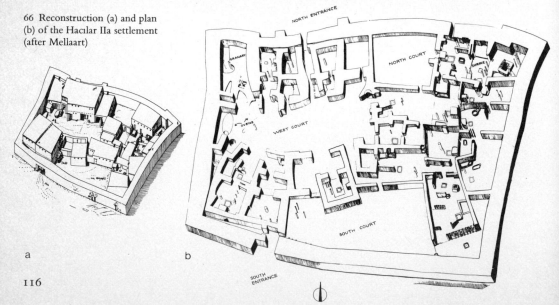

a

b

dwindled from around 100–150 to 50–70. A second destruction
c. 5050 BC was probably caused by the newcomers of Hacılar I.

Characteristic for levels V–II is painted and monochrome ware
using the same shapes, and roughly in equal numbers. Among the
bowls and jars one should note the many oval cups in the shape of
a human head cut off below the nose, and the first occurrence in
level II of anthropomorphic jars and vessels with spouts, often, it
would appear, in the form of an animal head. Handles bear
vestigial resemblances to animal heads, but relief decoration has
disappeared. Red-on-cream ware is in two styles, one with old
relief motifs such as animal heads, and female figures, sometimes
hardly recognizable through stylization, the other using textile
patterns to great advantage. Frequent play was made with negative
and positive painting, full of symbolism and sophistication, worthy
of the Çatal tradition.

The statuettes, on the other hand, are less varied than before and
they clearly fall into standard types; their size increases and many

67 Oval cups and jars decorated
in geometric and fantastic styles
in red-on-cream, from Hacılar
IIa (after Mellaart)

67

68 A selection of painted ovoid jars from Hacılar I (after Mellaart)

are painted, showing details of dress. Animals and children are no longer found associated with them, but there is some evidence that fairly large animal figurines were being made.

A few burials show contracted skeletons of Eurafrican and Proto-Mediterranean type but no other details are known. Some excessive wear of teeth occurs in level II. Funerary gifts were confined to a few beads and pots, plain or painted.

The destruction of level II brought about a complete change in the culture that had developed locally since level IX. Now new-comers arrived with somewhat different traditions, in many respects closer to those of Hacılar VI. They may not have come from afar, but they changed the culture in all its major material aspects: architecture, pottery and figurines. The ruins on top of the mound were levelled to form a central courtyard for a heavily fortified structure consisting of blocks of rooms radiating round the court and separated from each other by minor courtyards with fences and ovens. The structure – that is to say the fifth of it that was excavated and, being residential, contained no shrines or workshops – had at least two storeys of which the basement rooms alone survived. With the exception of a guardroom near one entrance, and a number of passages that almost certainly carried flights of steps to the wooden upper storey, all the basement rooms were entered from above, in the old Çatal Hüyük style as evidenced in contemporary Can Hasan. The basements were fairly empty except for the contents of the collapsed upper storey, suggest-ing that they were used during the winter only. Many had hearths, and thick layers of decayed matter, reeds or felt (?), covered the floors. There was an abundance of pottery – some 75 per cent of which is now painted in red on cream, but in a predominantly linear style, resembling basketry. The old wares have gone, and both a red and a cream burnished monochrome ware and coarse incised potstands are introduced. White-on-red pottery, often bearing a creamy crusted paint, is a recurring feature, but much rarer. Shapes are varied and weird and in general much larger than before; instead of being always round, many bowls and jars are now oval or subrectangular in shape, and there are beakers, wide or narrow, square mugs, ovoid jars like churns

69 An anthropomorphic vessel from Hacılar I

for making butter. Other vessels are decorated with animal heads, or horned handles that look like stylized animals, but the most remarkable vessels are jars in the form of a seated figurine, which *69* occasionally has two heads. The faces, characterized by prominent noses and eyebrows, have painted eyes or eyes made of chips of obsidian, neatly inlaid, the occasional use of which can be traced back through animal handles at Hacılar to a figurine in Çatal Hüyük II. Small schematic figurines, almost violin-shaped, now appear for the first time, but heads show that larger statuettes were still made. A number of animal heads, legs and tails show that fairly large, solid or hollow painted animal figurines were produced. The population of Hacılar I must have been more numerous than ever before – my estimate is about three hundred to five hundred or more – but the very few burials show that, like their predeccessors, the Hacılar people buried their dead outside the settlement. The position of the Hacılar I cemetery is known – it lies a few hundred yards northwest of the settlement – but it has been ruthlessly looted since our excavations came to a premature end.

The economy of Hacılar remains to be discussed. Unfortunately the number of animal bones recovered was insufficient for statistical studies, and until new methods for detecting domestic bone structure are applied to the material, only dog can definitely be said to be domestic.[125] Contemporary evidence from sites like Erbaba and Can Hasan would suggest that sheep, goat, cattle and possibly pig were kept at Hacılar. Botanical evidence, on the other hand, is plentiful and has been published *in extenso*. The Hacılar people practised simple irrigation agriculture and grew the same crops as the inhabitants of Çatal Hüyük.[120] The only innovation was chick-pea, and it is worth noting that some carbonized weevils were found in a grain deposit. The destruction of Hacılar I was followed by some desultory reoccupation (Ic, Id); then the site was deserted for good. This may have been *c.* 4800 in C14 terms. The date has not been ascertained at Hacılar, but apparently has at Can Hasan 2B.

Can Hasan and Çatal Hüyük West

The successors of Neolithic Çatal Hüyük in the Konya plain are represented at Çatal Hüyük West, from which some pottery is known but nothing much else, and at Can Hasan near Karaman. The mounds have diameters of around 380 and 400 m, but how much of each site was occupied at any given time can only be established by thorough excavation. The situation at Can Hasan, on which only a series of brief preliminary reports are available, is as follows.[115] Of the four 'Late Neolithic' levels 7–4, the last two have produced architecture with red-ochre floors. The pottery is the Neolithic black and brown burnished ware and there are some blue beads (apatite) as at Çatal Hüyük. In phase 3 there are three building levels with solid architecture, twelve secondary burials of children and infants, and a red-ochre skull. The first painted pottery appears in red on a clay (brown?) surface or on a white slip together with plain burnished wares. Another three

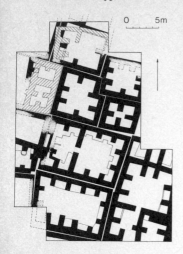

0   5m

70 Can Hasan 2B: plan of the settlement with two houses of levels 2A and 3. Note the absence of doorways, with roof entry in the Çatal Hüyük and Can Hasan III tradition (after French)

71

71 Painted pottery from Çatal Hüyük West, contemporary with Can Hasan 3–2B. Top four rows belong to the later phase, below is the 'Çatal West ware' (after Mellaart)

building levels make up phase 2B, of which the last (2B3) was destroyed by fire *c.* 4900 B C. This was excavated over a large area, and gives us our first glimpse of what Can Hasan looked like, at a period comparable to Hacılar I. Rectangular or square houses built of mud brick with a little wood reinforcement and mud plaster and occasionally red lime (?) plaster are set close together, each house with its own walls, without any intervening courts or passages. Internal buttresses are well developed, sometimes too well, so that the room is divided into four cubicles that could only have been used for storage. Buildings vary in size, but usually consist of one room only. One of the best preserved houses, still standing to a height of 3 m and with its doorway intact, had an anteroom with buttresses and platforms as well as a large main room. The rooms have hearths, but ovens have not been reported. Entry was through the roof, part of which was covered by a lightly-structured upper storey, leaving some space for communication. The upper part of the large house mentioned has a mud-brick upper storey with window casements decorated with plaster painted with geometric patterns.

In this building was found the body of a male forty-five years old, who had been trapped by the fire; near him lay a perforated macehead of solid copper and a copper bracelet. Copper is mentioned as occurring in all the Chalcolithic building levels, a situation similar to that at Hacılar. The pottery of phase 2B consists of red-on-cream painted and plain burnished ware in the first building level. In the second level a vivid red-on-cream ware of Çatal West type is typical, and the first fine burnished and incised pottery coloured grey, black or yellow appears. In the last building level (2B3) red-on-cream ware, the same incised ware and a new dark-on-light ware appears, painted in brown or black on a white-slipped red ware. This last pottery marks the transition to Can Hasan 2A. Pottery with chevrons and hatched bands of foreign appearance occurs in Can Hasan 2B2 and B3, allowing correlations with Mersin XXI and XX across the Taurus. A 'Halaf' sherd is also reported from layer 2B3. The earlier 'Çatal West ware' seems to have been exported to Mersin, where sherds of it occur from level XXIV–XXII.

The material from Çatal Hüyük West consists of an earlier painted 'Çatal West ware' and a later dark-on-light ware, accompanied by plain burnished wares, mainly hole-mouth jars, jars with basket handles and bowls, used in the kitchen.[122] The incised grey ware of Can Hasan is absent (except for two rather coarse sherds with pointillé design), but there are incised coarse-ware potstands of distinctive type and appearance, apparently absent at Can Hasan. Peculiar to a number of sherds of the dark-on-light ware at Çatal West is the use of more than one layer of paint on some pots, which usually hides a crack or other blemish. This is a practice that reminds one of wall paintings, where one painted layer of plaster covers another. Shapes at these two sites are similar but not identical, oval carinated bowls on small ring bases being typical at Çatal West, but not apparently at Can Hasan. Typical vessels of the 'Çatal West ware' are jars with flaring necks, some with an internal ledge (as later at Ras el-Amiyah), perforated

72 Can Hasan 2A painted
pottery, both monochrome and
bichrome. Latest pottery on top,
earliest at the bottom (after
French)

with holes. Some of the large jars have two loop handles, others
have a basket handle. Carinated bowls, flat dishes (lids?), simple
bowls and cups are typical. The decoration in red paint is sometimes burnished and the firing is often uneven. Patterns are
basketry-like: vertical zigzags on rims, chevrons, plain or inter-
woven, and triangles, solid or filled with dots. On the interior of
the carinated bowls crudely drawn human figures sometimes
appear as well as maladroit star patterns. The general effect of this
pottery, though often fine, is somewhat rustic.

The later phase, in which red-on-cream and dark-on-light
decoration appears side by side, is far more sophisticated. The
drawing is much neater and groups of parallel lines are bordered
by broader bands of paint. Metope decoration is introduced with
different patterns in each panel. The effect is sometimes oddly like
Halaf, but the resemblance is superficial, owing to bright colours
and burnishing, panelling, etc.; technique, shape or individual
patterns are unlike those of Halaf ware. A few human figures are
still found, but there are no animals. Applied animal heads appear
in the incised grey ware of Can Hasan, together with incised bands
filled with dots and dashes, and complicated meander patterns
painted on plaster in the house already mentioned and known
before from the clay seals of Çatal Hüyük. Some very fine
statuettes were produced at Can Hasan during phase 2B. One
calcite or gypsum figure is in the Çatal Hüyük tradition, but the
clay figures are not. A large intact example shows an enthroned
figure with a very long neck, its head swathed in a turban. Several
incomplete and smaller figures, all of them painted, seem to
represent the same type. Not less remarkable are large heads with
high foreheads, delicately modelled features and great almond
eyes. They show no sign of having been attached to a body. Again
they bear traces of paint. There is no report yet on the plant
remains from Can Hasan, but the inhabitants evidently practised
agriculture; sheep, goat, cattle, pig and dog are all domestic. Bone,
antler, chipped- and polished-stone industries, beads and ornaments occur, but no details are yet available. It would appear from
the pottery that Can Hasan was engaged in trade across the Taurus
with Cilicia, probably through the Calycadnus valley, which
offers the easiest route to the south coast. The rarity of burials
rather suggests that there must be a cemetery at Can Hasan and it
is to be hoped that this will be found and excavated. Human
skeletal material would be extremely welcome, to show how the
population of the Konya plain fared after Çatal Hüyük.

It is not known what caused the destruction of Can Hasan 2B,
but the site was not deserted, and houses of the same type continued to be built in 2A, a phase divided into five sub-phases.
Much of this material comes from open areas and scoops, filled
with rubbish – a feature already present in the later phase of Çatal
West. This 'Middle Chalcolithic' period is roughly contemporary
with Mersin XIX–XVII and Late Halaf, and it is post-Hacılar. In
C14 terms it may be dated between *c.* 4900 and 4500? BC.

This is a period in Anatolia about which little is known and we
cannot say for certain what corresponds to it in the west of the
country. Surface material from the Uşak region may suggest that

there is a post–Hacılar phase here (or is it contemporary with Hacılar I?) with red-on-cream as well as black-on-red ware.

The first phase of Can Hasan 2A is ceramically characterized by the final appearance of the 2B red-on-cream ware, the disappearance of the grey incised ware and the dominance of dark-on-light painted ware, always accompanied by plain wares. In the third sub-phase of 2A, however, polychrome ware appears, and progressively increases in quantity. Large elaborately decorated jars are typical of phases 2A3–5. Monochrome black and red burnished bowls occur in the last two sub-phases. The polychrome pottery is most attractive, fired grey and orange rather than red and black. The material is unfortunately fragmentary but the illustration shows the range of shape and ornament, which is highly attractive and first drew my attention to this site in 1951. At that time polychrome ware was only known from Mersin XVI–XV, where the use of such sophisticated colour was attributed to Halaf influence. With polychrome painting established in the Konya plain at Çatal Hüyük, at least a millennium and a half before Can Hasan 2A3, the claim for Halaf influence no longer stands unchallenged. Unless it can be shown that Halaf influence occurred beyond Mersin, the case for a local development should be given priority. Once again not a single shape or pattern is definitely of Halaf origin. There are no reports of Halaf imports in Can Hasan 2A, and very little is known of this culture; a bracelet possibly of ivory is reported and there was a cache of 'jewellery', consisting of pendants of semi-precious stone, cardium shells with faces cut into them, a number of bull's-head (?) pendants and a fine ram's head in carved stone. Copper is said to occur, as well as fine work in bone. The last building level, 2A5 has links with Mersin XVII. Then the site was apparently deserted, or occupation shifted, for I retrieved two sherds of Mersin XVI ware from the surface of the mound before excavations began. One was a rim sherd of a jar with typical brown-on-cream ware decoration, the other a good piece of multiple-brush ware. As a few similar sherds were found on other sites in the Karaman area, there was presumably occupation during the period of Mersin XVI. At Can Hasan there is possibly an erosional gap, and when reoccupation takes place in level I, *c.* 4300 B C, it is a different culture, the 'Late Chalcolithic', that supplants the older tradition in the Konya plain.

There can be little doubt that Can Hasan is a key site in the archaeology of southern Anatolia and it deserves to be excavated rather than trenched; moreover, the habit of extramural burial means that there must be cemeteries from the 'Late Neolithic' to the 'Late Chalcolithic', a period of several millennia, which could yield much information vital to Anatolian archaeology.

Mersin

John Garstang's excavations just before the Second World War at Yümük Tepe, northwest of Mersin in the plain of Cilicia[117] should have opened archaeologists' eyes to the importance of Anatolia, but its position south of the Taurus and its proximity to north Syria, added to our lack of knowledge about early conditions on the Anatolian plateau, resulted in a tendency to 'explain'

Mersin in Syro-Mesopotamian terms, and designations like Syro-Cilician were coined. In the light of the evidence then available, this is understandable, but now that things have drastically changed through the discovery of an 'Anatolian tradition', a reappraisal must be made. Fortunately this can be carried out without detriment to the work done in contingent fields. The site of Mersin, on the bank of a river, measures some 200–250 m. The sequence which concerns us runs as follows: Early Neolithic (XXXIII–XXVII), Late Neolithic (XXVI–XXV), Early Chalcolithic (XXIV–XX), Middle Chalcolithic (XIX–XVII and XVI) and finally Late Chalcolithic (XVb–XIIa). The terminology, frequently used in Anatolia, was made for Mersin. There is one C14 date – for XXXIII – of 6000 ± 250, about equal in time to Çatal Hüyük VIII. Our knowledge of Neolithic Mersin is based on a 2 m-wide trench which yielded about 9 m of deposits of stone-walled rectangular structures, floors, pottery and obsidian and flint tools. The pottery is of the dark burnished type, often chocolate-brown, one-tenth of which is decorated with impressed, shell-impressed or rouletted ornament. The shapes seem a little more squat than at Çatal Hüyük, but are otherwise the same. The origin of this ware is clearly Anatolian, but the process of decoration is local Cilician, matched in Syria. A gritty, plain buff coarse ware is likewise local, the stone industry has weapons of Çatal type in obsidian from Çiftlik and Acigöl, but unlike on the plateau, local flint was used for sickle blades. There are no details of the economy, which could have been very interesting; the Cilician plain readily lends itself to simple irrigation agriculture. The whole of the Neolithic in Cilicia, both ceramic and earlier, needs proper investigation.

The first painted sherds on the gritty buff ware begins to appear in level XXVII, and in the next two building levels there is an influx of much finer, black and red burnished wares, about which we know all too little. The foundations of a fairly large house in level XXV are the first to have a recognizable plan. From XXIV to XX, the characteristic feature is painted pottery in red on cream; its few shapes show a rather limited repertoire of patterns. Generally speaking, this 'Early Chalcolithic' is a poor reflection of the plateau wares, contact with which was established early. In my opinion it has nothing to do with Hassuna or Halaf. Concurrently with the painted ware a black or brown burnished ware with white-filled incised patterns appears, probably an adaptation of the old dark burnished ware which disappeared with or during the 'Late Neolithic'. Patterns and colour change somewhat during the 'Early Chalcolithic'; horizontal bands of hatching are typical of the later phases and so is darker fired paint, brown or black instead of bright red. Burnishing disappears. The architectural remains of this early painted pottery phase are disappointing: silos in XXIV and some rectangular structures in XXII–XX. From levels XXII–XXI come emmer and six-row erect barley. Copper pins are also known. Contemporary though it was with Can Hasan 3 and 2B, Çatal West and Hacılar, Mersin seems to have been little more than a small township or village. With the Halaf orientation of northern Syria at this period, Mersin's obsidian trade may have suffered a reverse since it was east Anatolian obsidian that was now used in the Levant. It looks as if Mersin was averse to contact with Syria at this period (Amuq C and early D) for there is no trace of Halaf influence. But Mersin XX was destroyed by an enemy, as is evidenced by the finding of bodies (of Eurafrican type), thereby breaking this isolation, and polychrome Late Halaf pottery appears throughout levels XIX–XVII in the 'Middle Chalcolithic'. Besides the imported pottery, there seem to be local copies of somewhat inferior quality, but the local dark-on-light ware shows links with Can Hasan 2A. Architectural details are lacking and the ceramic picture is somewhat confused; one would have liked to have seen some percentages of imported Halaf, local imitations, and other local wares, painted and plain. Has, for example, the dark incised ware disappeared, or did it linger on, to reappear in Mersin XVI? Evidently Mersin XIX–XVII was not a Halaf site in the classical sense, any more than Tell Judeideh or Ras Shamra, but at no time was north Mesopotamian influence stronger. One would have liked to know more; was the destruction of Mersin XX related to a takeover by newcomers? Were there signs in the economy of eastern traits, such as Vannic obsidian or even tholos structures? One or two bow-rims of Amuq D type were found, but was there any red ware of this period? Such questions are not academic in view of what followed. J. Garstang believed that the little fortress of Mersin XVI was the culmination of the Halaf settlement, whereas the pottery shows quite clearly that a different cultural origin must be sought for this, which I think is to be found in the area of the Konya plain, although one cannot yet prove it. The date of Mersin XVI with its three phases would be *c.* 4500–4300/4200 B C, namely post-Halaf and pre-Late Ubaid. There are some links with Ras Shamra IIIC which ends at 4184 ± 81.

73   The fortress of Mersin XVI was only partly excavated to preserve an overlying 'Hittite' structure which has since eroded away. As the result of a destructive fire, followed by changes in culture and therefore probably connected with enemy action, the top building level of Mersin XVI yielded a rich supply of information, whereas virtually nothing is known of the earlier two phases.

73 Isometric drawing of a section of the fortress of Mersin XVI (after Lloyd)

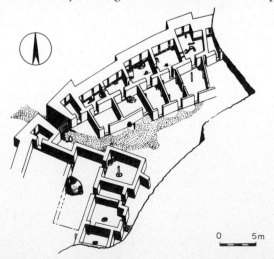

0   5m

The little fortress was set on top of the steeply sloping mound, with a path or ramp leading up to the water gate above the river. This was flanked by two projecting towers, and in the open court inside the walls was a structure divided into several rooms and connected with a courtyard containing an oven. Set against the thick circuit wall was a series of barrack-like rooms, originally communicating but later turned into individual dwellings. Each had its own enclosed yard on the inner side, opening onto the central court. All the rooms were provided with a slit window – very much like the arrow slits in later fortifications though the bow-and-arrow appears to have been unknown to these people, who were armed with slings which would be very effective when operated from the flat roof that covered this series of houses. The rooms had the usual domestic equipment, grindstones raised on mud-brick platforms, hearths, etc. Pottery was found in profusion, and for the first time there were heavy copper tools: axes and a chisel. Yet the most distinctive feature of the culture was its pottery, which can be divided into painted cream burnished ware, 74 polychrome ware, black burnished ware with white-filled incised patterns and monochrome burnished ware, cream, red or black. The earlier wares, including Halaf imports, seem to have disappeared completely in this last phase, and the cream burnished ware appears already in Mersin XVII. This is most striking pottery comprising large jars with funnel necks and two strap handles as well as simple bowls with handles rising above the rim. The first appearance of handles on pottery should be noted; they are not a Halaf feature but occur in the Late Chalcolithic cultures of the Anatolian plateau, where they have simple ancestors, for example in Hacılar I, Çatal West and Can Hasan. Red, brown or black paint covers a pale red surface or more often a thick cream slip, which is burnished. Patterns are simple and include loops hanging from a horizontal line, a feature appearing on the inside of bowls in the Halaf pottery; wavy lines, frequently in bunches painted with a multiple brush; vertical groups of parallel lines – a peculiar style hitherto unknown. Sherds of this material occurred at Can Hasan and a few other sites in the Karaman area. The polychrome ware is also familiar with its predominantly orange motifs outlined in grey on a buff slip, but the jars with flaring rims have shapes known from Halaf, where the rosette pattern is characteristic of the late phase. The handles, on the other hand, are new and striped in red or black paint. The black burnished ware is fine and includes bowls with horned and 'tab' handles rising above the rim; the latter resemble stylized bulls' heads as found on Can Hasan 2B incised grey ware, whereas the horned handles are in general a Late Chalcolithic feature. The white-filled incised technique had occurred before in Mersin XXIV–XX and may well be local, but the shapes of the monochrome burnished ware have analogies in the Late Chalcolithic of the Konya plain. Chronologically, Mersin marks the transition from Middle to Late Chalcolithic. A few jars with simple decoration do not look out of place, but have been hailed as the first 'Ubaid' ware. The definition of 'Ubaid' should, however, be applied on the basis of clearly stratified and dated material; at Ras Shamra, where this

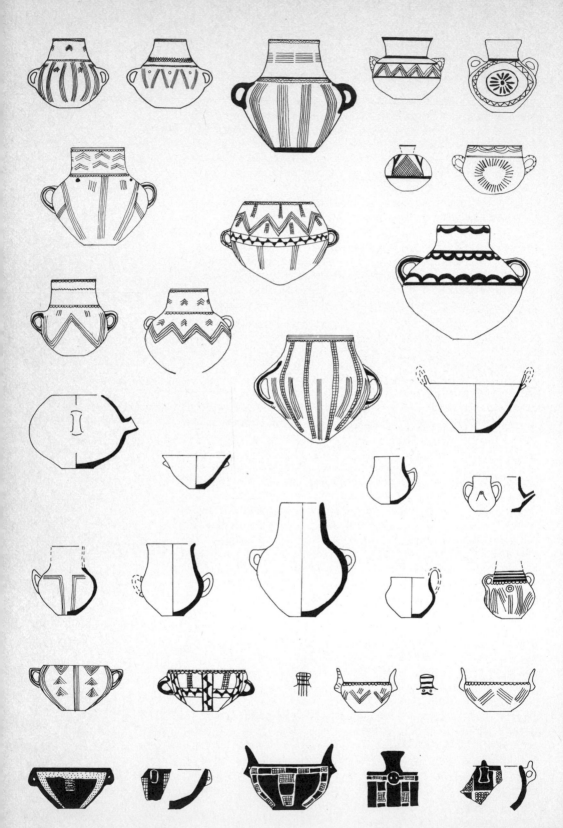

has been done, 'Ubaid-like' pottery (IIIB) equates with Tell es-Sheikh ware and that of the bottom layers of Gedikli Hüyük near Sakçagözü. It overlies the strange and crudely painted pottery of Ras Shamra IIIC, which has some analogies, in the first use of handles, wavy line decoration, etc., with Mersin XVI, but also shows many other motifs that cannot be derived from there. Found with this pottery was red burnished ware of the earlier Ras Shamra IVB–A and Amuq D (Tell Kurdu) tradition. So the Syrian material from the coast seems to show a mixture of several strains which, as several authors have pointed out, should not be classified as northern Iraq Ubaid; 'Syrian Ubaid' might be a better term if the eastern links are to be stressed, but it looks as if the old tradition of Halaf was stronger than were the new innovations from the east. There is nothing similar in the Mersin XVI tradition, and it should not escape attention that neither at near-by Tarsus, nor at any other site during the Cilician survey, was there any further trace of the Mersin XVI culture. For the moment it is confined to Mersin itself, and the few northern links, to which may be added the new use of metal for tools – not found until later in Syria – rather points to Anatolian plateau influences. Cilicia is conspicuously lacking in metal resources and the rich ore deposits of the Taurus Mountains are controlled from the plateau, and not from the coast.

The destruction of Mersin XVI opened the way for new influences, this time clearly from the east. For a while the polychrome ware (and perhaps some of the other kinds?) survived but then monochrome painted ware of a not very inspired 'Ubaid type' gains the ascendancy in level XV, though the fine Tell es-Sheikh pottery is lacking. The 'Late Chalcolithic' had arrived, and Mersin XVI, perhaps somewhat arbitrarily, may be regarded as the end of an earlier tradition.

CYPRUS
The island of Cyprus, geologically an extension of the outermost Taurus range most of which now lies below the Mediterranean, is clearly linked to the Amanus Mountains and Jebel Akra in northern Syria. Situated half-way between Cilicia and Syria it is clearly visible from the Turkish coast, and from the tip of the Karpass peninsula in Cyprus the Syrian coast can often be seen.

The Khirokitia Culture

The earliest culture yet known on the island is that of Aceramic Khirokitia,[137] earlier Palaeolithic or Epipalaeolithic remains not having yet been located. There is likewise no clear evidence that the wild ancestors of wheat and barley, sheep or cattle ever existed on the island, but wild goat and fallow deer were clearly native. The Khirokitia culture, which is well distributed throughout the island, appears to have been fully agricultural and though no actual remains of grain or plant material were found, there were abundant querns, mortars, grindstones and sickle blades indicative of agricultural pursuits.[136–7] Among the animal bones, those of goat, sheep and pig are said to show domestication, but this is not certain; fallow deer was hunted.

74 Pottery from Mersin XVI (after Garstang)

Three radiocarbon dates give an average of 5650±150 BC, which suggests that the culture, with two distinct building levels, falls in the first half of the sixth millennium BC and is approximately contemporary with part of the Çatal Hüyük and Mersin Neolithic on the one hand, and with Amuq A and early B, Umm Dabaghiyah, and final PPNB in Palestine on the other. With the exception of the last-named, all the contemporary cultures made full use of pottery; but if we ignore some sherds of crudely made ware found in the bottom layer of Khirokitia, pottery appears not to have been used and the culture remained staunchly aceramic. This deficiency was offset by some of the most elegant and striking stone ware produced anywhere in the Near East, and the discovery of a fragment of such a stone vessel in Amuq A shows that these products were occasionally exported. The culture was clearly seafaring and one of the sites, Petra tou Limniti, lies on an island off the northwest coast. Central Anatolian (Çiftlik) obsidian was imported from Cilicia in small quantities.

The population of Khirokitia consisted entirely of brachy-cephalic Alpines,[137] a racial peculiarity which – until the same Alpine stock was recently found to be present in considerable numbers (40 per cent) among the population of contemporary Çatal Hüyük – seemed to emphasize the idiosyncrasies of this culture even more.

The culture reveals archaic traits in at least two aspects: architecture and the chipped-stone industry. The latter worked predominantly in local flint, with a small admixture of Anatolian obsidian, but it is utterly unlike those of its Anatolian and north Syrian neighbours. There are no fine arrow and javelin heads, and no daggers; the industry consists almost entirely of blades and flakes including burins, scrapers, tanged flakes and axes, as well as some of the by now indispensable sickle blades. The ancestry of this stone industry, to which microliths are foreign, remains obscure. Perforated maceheads of polished stone served as weapons, and among the bone tools are handles for stone tools as well as awls, pins and needles. Weaving is attested by the presence

75 Reconstruction of part of the Aceramic Neolithic settlement of Khirokitia in Cyprus, showing the domed houses, corridors, workshops and the main road through the settlement (reconstruction painting by Gaynor Chapman)

of spindle whorls made of limestone; garments sewn with needles and fixed with pins were probably of wool and leather. There were ground and polished axes for woodwork and a number of stone vessels may have been copied from wooden prototypes.

The houses of this culture were round, their diameters varying from 3–4 m to 7–8 m. Local limestone was used for the lower part of the wall, pisé, mud brick or light materials for the upper part and the dome. There were houses with double walls, the outer casing probably serving as a retaining wall. Some of the largest houses contained two stone pillars with niches – which may have been used as cupboards – supporting a semicircular loft, accessible by ladder, on which people probably slept. Hearths, pits and sleeping platforms were set into the stone-paved floor, but many domestic activities were carried out in walled courtyards outside the buildings. In one complex there were circular stone tables, covered corridors and subsidiary round houses used for grinding corn, storage, or serving as kitchens and workshops. A few stone steps led down into the rooms over high thresholds designed to keep out rain and mud. Short ramps led to a 200 m-long stone-paved roadway that diagonally traversed the hill-top settlement. Some fifty houses were excavated, but the total number is estimated to have approached a thousand. The site had a diameter of about 250 m and evidently Khirokitia was more than a village, even if evidence for social strata is lacking. Floors were frequently relaid and repairs and rebuildings suggest lengthy occupation.

75

The architecture of the Khirokitia culture looks like a highly refined descendant of the earlier and simpler round-house tradition of the Natufian Levant at sites like Ain Mallaha, Wadi Fallah or Mureybet, but Cyprus is peculiar in that it should have retained this archaic form of building long after the period in which all its neighbours had changed to rectangular structures in wood or mud brick. Yet at an even later date we find similar round-house traditions reappearing in the Middle Halaf culture of northern Mesopotamia and in the adjacent regions of Transcaucasia. It would seem that this traditional form of architecture, which can probably be traced back to the Upper Palaeolithic, survived only in the more peripheral parts of the Near East after the end of the Natufian tradition *c.* 7300 BC.

The people of Khirokitia buried their dead beneath the floors of their houses, usually in single graves and in a tightly contracted position. These are primary burials and there is no evidence for skull cults as on the mainland. Stones were sometimes put on the body to prevent the dead from rising and a number of objects appear to have been ceremonially broken before deposition as grave goods. Stone vessels were buried with the body as well as articles of jewellery: stone-bead necklaces, pendants and bracelets of carnelian, steatite, picrite and dentalium shells. Copper, a commodity which later gave its name to the island, was not yet exploited. In the upper layers a few burials of mother and child occur. The rich gifts that accompanied the women's burials suggest equality of status with men.

The population was entirely brachycephalic, and artificial cranial deformation is also attested. The stature of males was

76 Necklace of carnelian beads and dentalium shells from a woman's grave at Khirokitia

161·4 cm, that of females 151 cm; the average adult age at death was 35·2 for males, 33·6 for females. That is to say, they were less tall than the people of Çatal Hüyük, but they lived longer. This information was obtained from some 123 skeletons, 34 of which were infants, 11 children 1 to 14 years of age, and some 78 adults, only 4 of whom reached an age of between 45 and 54. The Khirokitia skeletons are one of the few groups of Neolithic men and women that have been studied.[137]

Very little indeed is known of the religion of these people. They made stylized anthropomorphic figures of stone without an indication of sex and there is one unbaked-clay head of a woman, but the usual category of 'mother-goddess' figurines appears to be lacking. There are carved stone cones and pebbles with engraved intersecting lines but we do not know to what use they were put; they bear a slight resemblance to similar decorated pieces in the Yarmukian culture of northern Palestine.

77 Spouted bowl and basin of andesite, a volcanic stone, from Khirokitia

The most striking feature of the culture lies in its stone vessels, for which andesite and other volcanic boulders present in the near-by river bed provided a handy source of material. Many of these are large, and there is a great variety of forms: elegant spouted basins and deep bowls, dishes, ladles, mortars and possible lamps. Some are decorated in relief with rows of knobs, raised chevrons, crosses and other geometric motifs suggestive of basketry or woodwork. Others have intricate handles with thumb grips, or heads of humans, sheep and bulls in high relief. The decorative style, as opposed to the shapes, is sometimes faintly reminiscent of similar workmanship in the Natufian tradition of Ain Mallaha, Mureybet and Çayönü, all of which produced stone vessels; whereas the animal heads on stone vessels and pottery have faint Anatolian parallels. Taken as a whole, however, the Khirokitia culture stands on its own.

The origin of the Khirokitia culture probably remains to be sought in the island and it has been suggested that the large site of Kataliondas may be earlier in date.[139] The end of the culture is as obscure as its beginning; though the sites were apparently deserted, there are no signs of violence or destruction.

The Philia Culture

It is only in the last few years that excavations at Philia (Drakos site A) have revealed a different and evidently later culture with pottery that in origin at least was clearly derived from the mainland.[140–41]

In the pits that are associated with house floors of the first building level, Philia I, a dark burnished monochrome ware is found, including some red pattern-burnished sherds of the type associated with Mersin XXV, Amuq B and Ras Shamra VA, but lacking the characteristic mainland form of impressed or rouletted decoration. Just as on the mainland, the next phase, Philia II, sees the arrival of a red-on-white painted ware decorated with chevrons, etc. which has its closest parallels in Mersin XXIV and Ras Shamra IVC, but the Middle Halaf pottery found there does not apparently reach Cyprus. This may suggest that the influence came from Cilicia, rather than from northern Syria. Dark burnished ware remains in use until the next phase. Stone bowls, simpler than those of the Khirokitia culture occur, and may be an indication of local island strains. This is also noteworthy in the pottery shapes decorated in red on white, such as tall-necked bottles and spouted bowls, shapes that are characteristic of the island, and less common though by no means absent in Cilicia.

Philia I and II appear to have used rather flimsy structures built of sticks smeared with clay, or of pisé, and it is only in the upper levels, III and IV, that square houses with rounded corners and similarly constructed walls on stone foundations are found. These may be free-standing or built in terraced rows. They have plastered floors, kerbed hearths and grindstones on platforms. In level III the settlement appears to have been enclosed by a wall and ditch, and by a simple wall in level IV.

The pottery development of these later levels proceeds along local lines and remains within the red–on–white tradition on the

78 Pottery of the Philia culture: painted and red burnished vessels (after Watkins)

same shapes, and the dark burnished ware drops out. Characteristic of Philia III is the use of wavy lines arranged in parallel rows. After a small hiatus in occupation a new way of painting known as 'ripple painting' executed with a multiple brush replaces earlier forms in Philia IV. This handsome pottery with its varied designs is clearly a local development and owes nothing to its mainland neighbours.

Apart from the adoption of pottery, first the dark burnished and then the earliest red-on-white ware, Philia seems to have shunned overseas contact. The obsidian trade of the previous Khirokitia culture was discontinued and only local materials were used. No details are yet available of the local economy and in the absence of a cemetery nothing is known about the bearers of this culture.

Another settlement of this period, Ayios Epiktitos Vrysi, on the north coast is in the course of excavation.[138] Like Troulli farther east, it is one of many unexcavated sites on headlands along this coast, from which Anatolia is clearly visible. Houses and work-shops of somewhat irregular shape, built of rubble with wooden posts and supports and coated with mud plaster (and roof entrances?) are preserved up to heights of 3 m. They were in-habited for a considerable span of time and four to five super-imposed floors are not uncommon. Benches and platforms, bins formed by upright stone slabs and circular rush mats as well as a fixed hearth and subsidiary fire-places form the regular built-in furniture of the house. Other rooms were used as workshops for the manufacture of bone beads, stone axes and chisels. Then there are querns, grinders, antler picks, flint blades with sickle gloss, chert tools, a little obsidian, bone awls, needles, shell and cowrie beads, etc. Among the animal bones there are large numbers of sheep and goat, as well as deer, cattle, pig, fox, fish and birds. Seeds and grains include, provisionally, emmer and bread-wheat, barley, peas and lentils, and grape and olive. Evidently this was an agricultural community, which supplemented its food supply by fowling, fishing and shellfish (limpet) collecting.

Pottery is abundant and close to that of Troulli and Philia-Drakos, but it would appear from the published drawings that it links up mainly with the later phases at Philia (IV with ripple painting) or with Troulli-type reserved circle decoration. Shapes are similar, and some combed and painted and combed pottery also occurs. A number of C14 dates from the penultimate phase of occupation fall in the early fourth millennium (e.g. Birm. 182 3875 ± 145) or around 4000 B C. With calibration such dates would correspond roughly to *c*. 5000 B C or a little later, in comparative terms early in the Late Ubaid, or in Anatolian terms about Mersin XV? It should perhaps be pointed out that, whatever its origins may be – and at Philia they would seem to include Anatolian ceramic elements – the main development is evidently a Cypriote one and native to the island, eschewing contact with the Asiatic mainland.

Chapter Four

Cultures of the Mesopotamian Lowlands

The Umm Dabaghiyah Culture

In the triangle of arable land south of Jebel Sinjar in the Jezireh, there are more than sixty sites of the Hassuna–Samarra culture, once thought to be the earliest occupants of the Assyrian steppe. At the extreme southern margin of the triangle, some 26 km west of Hatra, lies a series of pre-Hassuna sites of which Umm Dabaghiyah,[160-62] a mound measuring approximately 100 × 85 m with a height of 4 m, is the southernmost.

The site has four main building periods of a single culture, the earliest yet discovered in the north Iraq plain. Each period has a number of phases and with every rebuilding the site decreased in size. Umm Dabaghiyah IV (phases 12–9) was the best built and yielded the richest variety of pottery, both plain and painted. Building period III (phases 8–6) presents rich architectural detail, but period II, which was fully excavated, shows a decline in building and culture in general in its four phases (5–2). Of the top level (I) only a few ruined walls have survived the erosion to which sites, in this region of high winds, sudden thunderstorms and generally unpredictable climate, have been exposed for thousands of years. Tell Sotto and Telul et–Talathat are sites of the same culture farther north.

The earliest occupation at Umm Dabaghiyah consists of small circular or oval gypsum-lined bins and basins cut into virgin soil and not associated with any buildings. They may represent temporary shelters while the settlement was being built, comparable to the pits and hollows which occur on virgin soil on many other sites such as Ganjdareh E, Tell Ramad and Beidha.

Early in period IV, permanent tauf (i.e. clay slabs or clay pads) structures appear in the southwestern quarter of the mound, consisting of storage ranges grouped around a rectangular court entered from the west. To the north there was a row of domestic dwellings, all but one of which were demolished in the middle phase of period IV when large storage ranges were founded in the centre of the site around a central open space. Two new houses were built to the west of the one surviving house and a series of three or more walled enclosures, without buttresses and with wide doorways, were constructed, possibly for keeping the domesticated flocks of goat and sheep. The purposes of the storage blocks, which consisted of rows of unplastered cubicles set along corridors and entered through trapdoors in the roof, appears to have been for cold storage of onager hides (and meat) after the carcases were dismembered with polished greenstone or basalt axes in the open central space and the hides dried on structures consisting of a series of low parallel walls.

In a late phase of period IV the central houses fell into disrepair and may have been deserted for a while before they were reoccupied and replastered in period III. Other small houses were built near the southern storage block (III) and a further group of houses were built at the southwestern perimeter tucked in between the earliest storage block of period IV. At the end of period III the site was deserted by its inhabitants who blocked their doorways, perhaps intending to return at a later date. This did not happen, however, and a grey ashy layer, the result of periodic squatting or camp-fires, extends over the settlement. On top of this ash layer build-ings of period II were eventually erected. Period II represents a less tidy rebuilding on a smaller scale of the plan of the previous period. Traces of red paint on the plaster floors are still present, and the main courtyard was paved with blocks of clay. In a late phase a rectangular enclosure, presumably for domestic animals, was built in it. Period I is only represented by ruined walls.

The domestic architecture of Umm Dabaghiyah is exceptionally neat; the three central houses of periods IV–III are oriented N–S and each have individual walls although they are built up against each other. They consist of a living-room, probably a kitchen, and one or two other rooms, 1·5–2 m in size and almost square, built in tauf without stone foundations. They have internal buttresses forming doorways, arched or occasionally square, 50–75 cm wide and high. The walls and internal features are always plastered. The south rooms have an oven built on to them on the outside with an opening into the room, forming a hearth with plaster curb, sur-mounted by a plaster chimney hood. Semi-circular gypsum-plastered depressions, sometimes provided with grinding stones, served in the preparation of food and there are fuel cupboards in the wall, plaster boxes sunk into the floor, niches and occasionally (in the house on the southwest) round plastered windows. Steps of plastered clay set in a corner, surmounted by plastered toe-holes in the wall, led to a trapdoor in the roof. Some houses may have been entered from the roof but in others there is evidence for a normal door. One room was divided in two by an arch spanning the whole width of the room, the earliest known arch in existence! Traces of red paint are found on the plastered floors of the buildings of periods IV, III and II, but much more significant is the discovery during the 1974 excavations of wall paintings *in situ* on house walls of the IV/III period, illustrating the main occupation of the Umm Dabaghiyah onager hunters. A frieze of five running onagers, painted in red ochre, covers the east wall of the kitchen in the middle house of the central block. The animals are almost surrounded by a series of hooked figures, interpreted as wooden stakes fastening a net into which they have been stampeded by hunters brandishing weapons (or torches), two of which appear on another fragment. In the middle room beside the doorway leading into the north room there are patterns of clusters of parallel wavy lines, either decorative or a schematic rendering of vultures – a familiar sight to the onager hunters. Above the lintel of the door is a spider-like pattern above a cluster of large red dots, the 'spider and eggs painting', perhaps a rendering of a creature prominent among the Umm Dabaghiyah fauna – a spider of the *Solifugidae* family.

The paintings were executed in red, black and yellow paint and occasionally there were two layers separated by layers of white plaster as at contemporary Çatal Hüyük. Some of the patterns are not unlike those found on the painted pottery and the onagers are paralleled in the relief-decorated pots, some of which show pregnant onagers.

A fine example of architectural sophistication is shown by the storerooms of Umm Dabaghiyah, the best preserved complexes of which date from period III. A courtyard is surrounded on three sides by blocks of storerooms, some arranged along corridors, of regular dimensions (about 1·5–1·75 m). These small rooms have mud floors, and were usually entered from above; few have doors leading into other rooms or into corridors. None were provided with hearths or ovens and they clearly did not serve a domestic purpose, except when alterations took place, e.g. in the northern projection, and some family installed itself. This complex of storerooms, to which access could only be gained from the domestic area to the west, has yielded little evidence of its original purpose, for most of the rooms were found empty. Storage vessels are rare, but one room contained an arsenal of over 2400 baked-clay sling missiles, as well as heavy clay balls of unknown purpose. The roofs of the single-storeyed storeroom complexes were probably of branches and reeds covered with plaster, and they must have been flat with trapdoors leading into the rooms. The small size of these structures is probably the result of the dearth of trees in this region; although some timber must have been available for roofing the occasionally somewhat larger rooms of the domestic quarter that lay immediately to the west of the courtyard, the coolest position as the prevailing winds blow from the west. The absence of burials within the settlement presupposes the existence of a cemetery not yet located.

Situated at the limit of a dry-farming area in a region where the gypsum subsurface made irrigation agriculture impossible, the economy of the people of Umm Dabaghiyah not unnaturally shows some peculiarities. The evidence for agriculture is very scanty and though there is some evidence for emmer, einkorn and barley, pea, lentil and bread-wheat must have been imports as they would not grow in the treeless steppe.[155] Querns and sickle blades, indications of agriculture, are very rare; hoes of Hassuna Ia type do not occur. There is a dearth of good fuel and tree charcoal is virtually absent, hence our lack of radiocarbon dates. It would seem that shrub produced most of the fuel, together with reeds that somehow managed to grow along the few watercourses in this gypsum- and salt-covered steppe. Morphologically domestic sheep, goat, cattle, pig and dog are found, the first two species predominating; cattle is the only newcomer among the local domesticates, though not yet of economic importance.[148] For meat the people relied on the local wild fauna, restricted in species in this barren environment to onager, gazelle and wild boar with an occasional aurochs and badger, inhabitants of the forest steppe to the north in the foot-hills of the Jebel Sinjar. The main quarry was onager, subjected to intensified hunting on a scale unparalleled at any other Near Eastern site (68·4 per cent

79

of all animal bones found, with gazelle 11·4 per cent), yet showing no sign of domestication. The special role of the onager in the Umm Dabaghiyah economy is obvious and requires further elucidation.

The chipped-stone industry made use of local flint and imported grey or green obsidian from Lake Van.[160] Blades and blade cores, end- and flake-scrapers and sickle blades occur together with side-blow flakes in obsidian, the only feature reminiscent of Zagros traditions. Genuine arrowheads with Syrian parallels occur here, pointing to western contacts or origins. Among the polished stone tools made of imported materials are beads, maceheads, basalt axeheads and greenstone axes. A number of veined alabaster vessels from level I are reminiscent of similar vessels at Tell es-Sawwan I.[161] There are bone awls, points and spatulae, clay sling-stones and balls (roof weights?) and gypsum pot-lids and spindle whorls.

A few baked-clay female figurines were found, all in the lower

79 Plan of the settlement at Umm Dabaghiyah: (top) level II; (below) level III (after Kirkbride)

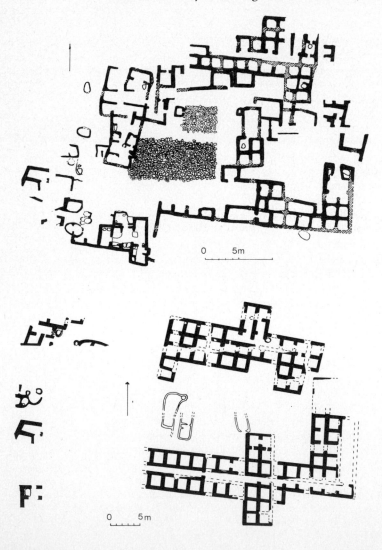

0   5m

0   5m

levels; one has a concave base, another wears what looks like trousers and a third sports garments with red dots on an ochre slip.

The great innovation at Umm Dabaghiyah is the widespread use of pottery; some of it like the fine burnished ware of Amuq A type possibly imported, the bulk, primitive, lightly baked ware probably made on the spot.[160–61] Hand-made and coil-built, it is heavily tempered with straw and mostly undecorated. Cream or white slips are found only on medium and fine ware. Burnishing, painting and applied relief decoration were all found, but incision only occurs in the latest levels. Shapes are generally simple, flat bases prevail, but many vessels have a rounded carination. In the upper levels (II–I) large carinated vessels, more than 50 cm high and with oval mouths, were used for storage and 'husking trays', oval vessels with rough ridges or round pit-marks inside hitherto considered a hall-mark of the later Hassuna culture, appear together with round and oval lids to keep out dust and insects. Incised pottery with simple patterns or crosses is late,

80

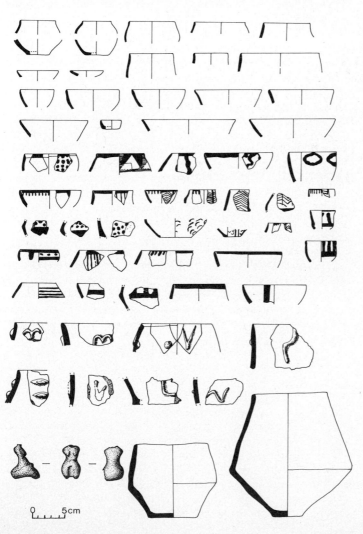

80 Pottery from Umm Dabaghiyah: fine burnished ware; red-on-cream painted ware; plain coarse ware or with applied decoration; incised coarse ware (after Kirkbride)

whereas the high-quality burnished ware, grit tempered and hard fired and usually of a pinkish-brown colour, but occasionally grey or black, is confined to the early levels. This appears to be a lighter-coloured version of the dark burnished ware of Anatolia and north Syria (Amuq A), altogether a different fabric from the local Umm Dabaghiyah ware and the other soft chaff-tempered fabrics of the Zagros zone, Iran and Transcaucasia. It is suggested that this fabric is an import from the northwest.

In the local painted ware red ochre is used as a pigment which fires brown to reddish brown, mustard colour or orange and is mostly applied to a cream slip, which can be absent. Red-painted triangles alternating with cream ones on a reserved slip occur and other patterns include dots (very popular), circles, squiggles, ticks and a variety of linear patterns including chevrons. In phase 7 (level III) herring-bones framed by thick vertical lines appear and these continue into the upper levels, where painting declines into a restricted repertoire of stripes, chevrons and herring-bones. Some pieces decorated with a fugitive paint, familiar from the Zagros, occurs also in the lower levels.

Very typical of all periods is pottery – mainly fine ware – with applied decoration, some of it simple like knobs, ledges, horizontally pierced lugs, but some far more ambitious with animal heads (ram, oryx, bull), snakes, crescents, human faces (eyes and ears). Some pots have representations of entire onagers affixed and others full-face female figures with hands below the breasts. Umm Dabaghiyah forms an important new link in the religious artistic development of the region with its change of medium from cave wall to pottery; the old animal heads have moved from the walls (Mureybet, Ganjdareh, Çatal Hüyük) to the pottery and so have the female figures (as from Çatal to Hacılar VI). Soon the relief figures on the pots, whether whole animals or their heads only, will be translated into painting (as in Early Halaf) or into theriomorphic vessels (as at Hacılar VI, Samarra or Halaf). The roots of the Near Eastern Neolithic-Chalcolithic art traditions evidently date back far into the past.

The Umm Dabaghiyah culture – there are at least seven other sites in the Hatra-Jebel Sinjar area – is the earliest culture so far traced in the Assyrian steppe west of the Tigris.[160] Its discovery throws new light on the beginnings of civilization in Mesopotamia and considerably modifies the views that have been expressed on this subject.

Umm Dabaghiyah material is known from two other sites – the bottom levels at Telul et-Talathat, carbon-dated to 5570 ± 120, and Tell Sotto[169] which is still in the course of excavation. In the absence of charcoal, and therefore of C14 dates, the date of Umm Dabaghiyah can only be established by comparison with other sites. The Telul et-Talathat date, however, appears low unless it dates the very end of Umm Dabaghiyah.

The relationship between the Umm Dabaghiyah culture and Hassuna Ia presents problems and needs further elucidation. Evidence from Tell Sotto and Yarim Tepe I may help in this respect, as here certain features of the earlier culture are definitely present – for example, storage buildings with roof entry, parallel low walls for drying, carinated vessels, knobs and crescents on pots, husking trays, etc. These similarities are, however, outweighed by the differences between the two cultures and it would seem unlikely that Hassuna developed out of Umm Dabaghiyah. Moreover, in the light of the latest evidence, Diana Kirkbride now feels that Hassuna Ia is later than Umm Dabaghiyah and does not overlap it in time. The first half of the sixth millennium, possibly including also the end of the seventh, appears to be the most likely date for Umm Dabaghiyah.

Many of the features of the Umm Dabaghiyah culture – red and white plaster, tanged arrowheads, grit-tempered burnished pottery, relief decoration, painting in red-on-cream technique, baked-clay sling missiles – point to the late PPNB and early PNA of the Levant. The few Zagros features are late and relatively unimportant; at best they prove contact with the Zagros cultures, but little else.

Behind the development of the Umm Dabaghiyah culture there must lie some as yet unknown aceramic culture, contemporary with later PPNB and therefore later than Çayönü, about which all we know as yet is that it was probably engaged in the obsidian trade between Lake Van and Bouqras. Alikosh, Mureybet, Tell Abu Hureyra and, somewhat later, El Kowm and Bouqras have shown that in favourable circumstances it was perfectly possible for aceramic cultures to settle on the winter grasslands of northern Mesopotamia and Khuzistan, long before the invention of irrigation. Many more aceramic villages will no doubt be discovered especially in the north, which had and has a greater rainfall.

North Mesopotamian Cultures after c. 5500 B C

After the end of the Umm Dabaghiyah culture, the classic trio of Hassuna, Samarra and Halaf, frequently regarded as a chronological sequence with some overlaps, are found to cover most of northern Mesopotamia. Each of these cultures is represented by an impressive number of sites, but few have been scientifically investigated. The type site of the Hassuna culture is Tell Hassuna, southwest of Mosul, now joined by Yarim Tepe I near Tell Afar in the Sinjar district, at present in the course of excavation. The type site of the Halaf culture is Tell Arpachiyah near Nineveh, now joined by Yarim Tepe II. The main Samarran sites are Tell es-Sawwan, near Samarra, Chogha Mami near Mandali and Tell Shemshara, submerged through the Dokan dam in the northern Zagros. Other sites in which soundings have been made are Chagar Bazar, Brak, Banahilk, Gerikihaciyan, Yunus near Carchemish, Tell Aswad on the Balikh and Tilki Tepe on Lake Van, to mention only the most important. Then there is the bulky material from a large number of archaeological surveys extending from the Mediterranean coast to the Persian Gulf, and often overlapping into the surrounding hills and mountains of Turkey and Iran, a territory which, with little regard for local susceptibilities and less archaeological justification, is referred to by some as Greater Mesopotamia. With the notable exception of a recent

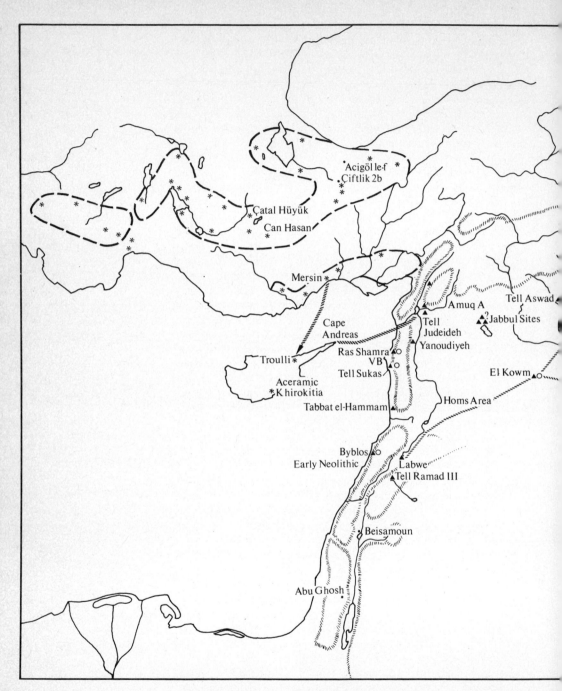

survey in the Mandali area,[180-81] all these surveys have one thing
in common: they either are inadequately published or not at all.
A list of sites, at best a good map or a series of maps, are released
but few or no illustrations of the material on which conclusions are
based and from which other archaeologists might possibly benefit.
This is and remains a most serious drawback in the study of early
Mesopotamian cultures. Until chronological and geographical

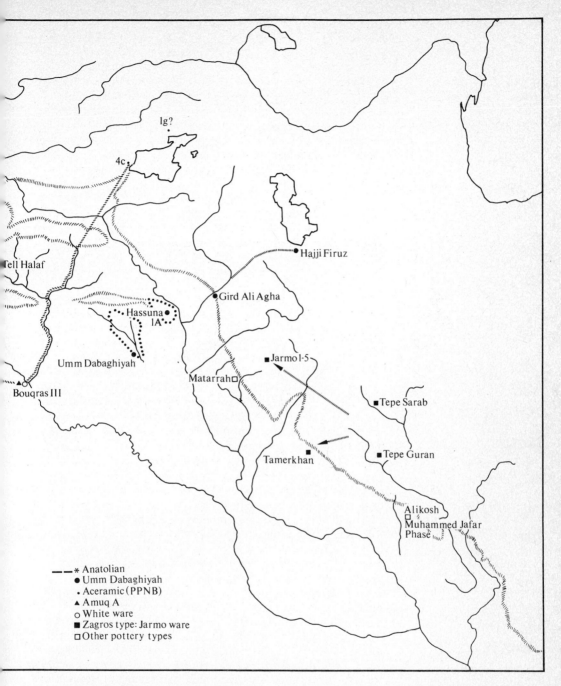

lg?

4c

Tell Halaf

Hajji Firuz

Gird Ali Agha

Hassuna
IA

Umm Dabaghiyah

Jarmo I-5

Matarrah

Bouqras III

Tepe Sarab

Tamerkhan

Tepe Guran

Alikosh
Muhammed Jafar
Phase

—— * Anatolian
● Umm Dabaghiyah
. Aceramic (PPNB)
▲ Amuq A
○ White ware
■ Zagros type: Jarmo ware
□ Other pottery types

distributions are sorted out with modern methods, much of the
northern Mesopotamian cultural development of this period will
remain blurred and obscure, consequently the account that follows
will undoubtedly need some corrections.

The chronological relationships of these three cultures have
recently been re-examined[171] and it would appear that what
looked like three successive cultures in the Tell Hassuna sequence

81 Pottery distribution in the
Umm Dabaghiyah–Ceramic
Jarmo phase

represents in fact the interaction, i.e. cultural contacts and influences upon each other, of three independent and virtually
contemporary cultures: Early Halaf in the north, Samarra in the
south and Hassuna in between.[184] This reinterpretation, well
supported by evidence and C14 dates, immediately introduces the
question of geographical distribution to explain this mosaic of
interaction. Here the published evidence from surveys is found
wanting. It is for example not clear which sites show Early, as
distinct from Middle or Late Halaf occupation. Likewise one
would like to know at which of the 'Hassuna-Samarra' sites
evidence for pre-Samarran Hassuna was found, and which have
evidence for the later Samarra wares of either the classical or the
Hassuna variant. Such information is clearly essential and the
minimum one needs is clear distribution maps of each of the three
phases of the Halaf culture, two for the Hassuna culture, i.e. before
the coming of Samarra influence and during it, and at least three
for the Samarra culture – the monochrome phase, the classic
Samarra phase and the Late Samarra phase of Chogha Mami (and
Chogha Sefid).

The distribution of these cultures can thus be seen to present
difficulties. That of the Hassuna culture is perhaps the easiest to
define as the Sinjar triangle and the adjacent Mosul area on both
sides of the Tigris, up to the Rowanduz gorge and the passes leading to Lake Urmia. Definite Hassuna pottery has not yet been
located in the Khabur area, as far as I am aware, nor farther west.
Its southern boundary east of the Tigris is ill-defined and it is here
that contact with the Samarra group becomes a possibility. As a
hypothesis one might suggest that the Lower Zab becomes the
border with Samarra. Reports of 'Hassuna' pottery rather than
'Hassuna period' pottery which includes Samarra, e.g. in the
Chemchemal valley, need checking for such elements as 'archaic
painted ware' which have no parallels in the Samarra culture. Only
by greater precision can such settlement patterns of various culture
groups be satisfactorily defined. This is not an academic argument,
it is essential to the elucidation of cultural origins. If Hassuna and
Samarra had shared the same origins, cultural boundaries might not
be very important, but if it should be proved that they had not,
then lines of demarcation might well acquire relevance.

The third culture, Halaf, is definitely the northernmost in a
general distribution that takes no account of the chronological
subdivisions of the culture, and it covers a vast area from Banahilk
in the hills east of the Tigris to the western bend of the Euphrates at
Yunus/Carchemish. It tends to stick close to the well-watered
foot-hills of the border ranges with Turkey suggesting the old
agricultural pattern of dry farming – like Hassuna, but unlike
Samarra which practised irrigation agriculture, at least in the
plains, but not necessarily in the uplands. This distribution of
Halaf along the Turkish foot-hills gave rise to the suggestion that
Halaf people descended from the mountains, including the Tur
Abdin, into the plain.[166] This hypothesis may be essentially correct,
but there is still no proof and surveys in the Upper Tigris basin
between Diyarbakir and Siirt as well as westwards to the Euphrates
have yielded relatively few remains of Halaf wares (and no

82

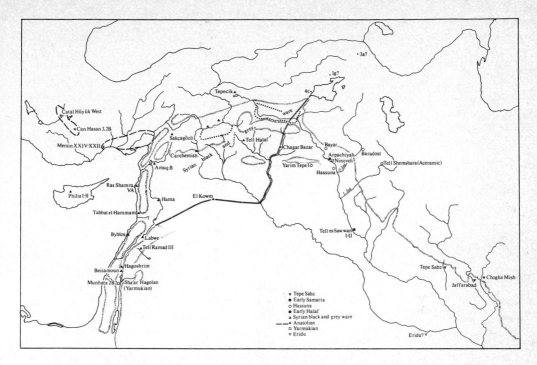

82 Pottery distribution in the Early Halaf–Hassuna–Early Samarra phase

Hassuna). Instead there is much grey burnished ware, rather coarser than that found in Amuq A–B, the eastern counterpart of Amuq B dark burnished ware, contemporary with Early Halaf at Arpachiyah. By Amuq C times, there is an abrupt change in culture and Middle Halaf wares spread westward as far as the Mediterranean (Amuq C, Ras Shamra IVC).[244, 251] Middle Halaf occurs superimposed on grey and black burnished ware at Yunus,[256] Sakçagözü[245] and Chagar Bazar in the Khabur, and at Tell Turlu 3;[247] in the Jabbul it is found on buff and brown burnished ware.[246] The change to Halaf may not have come in these parts till Middle Halaf, but a modern excavation would be required here to establish whether this represents a general pattern. The status of Halaf pottery in the Adiyaman region, west of the Euphrates, needs investigation; was it native there or again superimposed in Middle Halaf times, as the presence of dark burnished ware in the area, e.g. at Gendere, suggests?

Earlier painted pottery in red-on-cream technique may precede the Halaf or Halaf-inspired local wares in the Malatya region. At what date did Halaf appear here on the Anatolian plateau? At a number of sites in the Elazig region east of the Euphrates, e.g. at Korucu and Tepecik, local dark grey or black burnished wares of Amuq A–B affinity suggest that Halaf was intrusive. At Geriki-haciyan, a site under excavation near Ergani, south of the Taurus Mountains, painted Halaf pottery forms only a small percentage of the total ceramic bulk, whereas at Arpachiyah it was said that unpainted ware hardly existed.[51]

The general impression one gains of the Halaf distribution in Syria is that it succeeded earlier native monochrome grey or black burnished ware traditions. In Iraq, on the other hand, these are absent, except in very small quantities at Umm Dabaghiyah, the eastern counterpart of the dark burnished wares.

The Hassuna Culture

Tell Hassuna is a fair-sized mound, measuring some 200 × 150 m, 35 km[163] southwest of Mosul, and Yarim Tepe I, 7 km southwest of Tell Afar in the Jebel Sinjar area, is a small mound some 100 m in diameter.[167-70] The first has seven (Hassuna Ib–VI), the second ten building levels with Hassuna pottery superimposed on deposits resembling coarse ware of the Late Umm Dabaghiyah period (Hassuna Ia with three phases and similar material from the bottom of the stratigraphic trench at Yarim Tepe I). The architectural remains from these two settlements start with an early and little-known phase in which simple round and rectangular structures exist side by side (Yarim Tepe I, levels X–VII, Hassuna Ib, Ic with some round buildings). The buildings are of pisé or clay blocks, not yet mud bricks formed in a mould, and they are covered with gypsum plaster. Some of the round buildings at Yarim Tepe I, level VII reach diameters of about 6 m, but usually they are smaller, as in level VIII where a group of them, 2·5 m in diameter surround a rectangular two-room house measuring 10 × 2·5 m. One of these round structures had three contracted burials below its floor. Other features of this early phase are numbers of low parallel short walls, probably the foundations for a granary or a structure for drying grain, such as occurs regularly in contemporary settlements of the Jeitun culture east of the Caspian.[229] In level VII was found a two-storeyed pottery kiln with an underground firing chamber, a thick plate with numerous holes and a domed upper chamber. Round and long semi-cylindrical bread ovens are regular features of the early levels, X–VII at Yarim Tepe I.

Developed from these early stages are larger and more sophisticated buildings with more rooms, e.g. in level VI at Yarim Tepe, but the fullest picture of part of a settlement of this period is provided by level V at this site. Passages and courtyards, gypsum-plastered like the buildings, separate large multi-roomed houses with interior courtyards, work-rooms and living-rooms as well as a number of storerooms. Buttresses strengthen walls, doorways are provided with pivot stones and thresholds, and the roofs were probably flat to provide extra working space for the cleaning and drying of grain, and other household pursuits. There is no evidence for second storeys. At the northern end of the excavated area lies a communal (?) storage building reminiscent of Umm Dabaghiyah with rows of rectangular rooms without doors and evidently entered from the roof. Many alterations indicate intensive occupation and frequently resulted in a change of plan with passages blocked, rooms subdivided and courtyards encroached on as the population increased. Cult rooms have not yet been identified and most of the dead were probably buried outside the settlement, as graves other than those of infants are rare, both here and at Hassuna. There three adults of Eurafrican type were excavated,[94] buried with a few pots, probably containing food and a few beads. In level IV at Yarim Tepe I groups of kilns were found together with a roughly circular structure provided with a number of

83

internal buttresses, possibly a working area (for storage or drying of pottery?) which has no parallels elsewhere.

Yarim Tepe I has yielded evidence for the economy of the Hassuna culture; as at Umm Dabaghiyah these people kept domestic sheep, goat, cattle and pig, but there are as yet no details as to which were the mainstay of the economy. Dry farming of emmer, einkorn, bread-wheat and two-row hulled barley is well attested. Spindle whorls suggest spinning and weaving, but it is not known whether flax was already grown. Meat was obtained by hunting wild cattle, boar, gazelle, hare and other species.

The stone industry is poor and consists of blades of local flint, but with some imported Nemrut Dağ obsidian. Sickle blades, set in curved wooden hafts, are common and so are flint axes with polished bits and side-blow flakes, the exact use of which is unknown. Arrowheads are very rare and the few pieces found at Hassuna are probably imports, but clay sling-stones are common. There are fine beads of marble and chalcedony, turquoise and carnelian, small toilet sticks of stone, and small stone seals with criss-cross decoration (Yarim Tepe I, levels VIII, IX; Hassuna II), possibly imports. At Yarim Tepe I, copper ore and beads occur in levels IX–VII, as they do in the Samarra culture of Tell es-Sawwan I in the south. Stone vessels have not yet been reported. Incised marks on cattle bones are interpreted as evidence for counting.

Compared to the primitive soft-baked pottery of Umm Dabaghiyah the Hassuna pottery shows marked technical advances. Kiln-baked hard and even over-fired wares with grit or straw

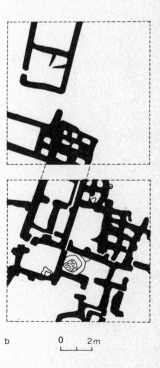

83 Hassuna culture: house plans from Yarim Tepe I, (a) level V; (b) level VI (after Merpert and Munchaev)

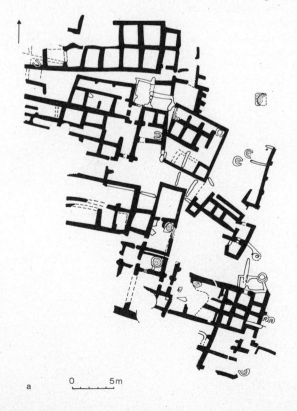

a   0   5m

b   0   2m

temper show cream, buff or even light-green fabrics. Shapes are simple and unambitious and round bases are common. Most

84 characteristic is the incised ware with its globular jars, provided with short offset necks, covered in simple designs like herringbones and hatched triangles or in early examples at Yarim Tepe VII–VIII with rows of pecked incisions. No less distinctive is pottery painted with red or black motifs on a cream slip in linear designs like chevrons, herring-bones, etc., patterns reminiscent of basketry. Early examples have glossy red paint and are frequently burnished, features that disappear in the later specimens. The pottery classification distinguishes 'Hassuna archaic' (Hassuna Ib–II, Yarim Tepe I, levels X–VI) from the later 'Hassuna Standard' wares (Hassuna III–VI, Yarim VI–I). A combination of painted and incised ware occurs from Hassuna II and Yarim VI onwards.

In Hassuna III–VI and at Yarim from the transition from VI to V and lasting until level I, Samarran ware occurs. It remained less common than the local wares, but was better made and not locally imitated and it is possible that some Samarra potters were allowed to set up workshops in the Hassuna settlements. This northern Samarra ware is less rich in shapes and motifs than in its homeland farther south. Finally there is much coarse ware, especially in the earlier phase, Ia, and this includes such agricultural implements as husking trays inherited from the Umm Dabaghiyah culture.

The Hassuna culture as known at present conveys a picture of almost rustic simplicity; houses and furnishings are neat, pottery shapes and décor rather unimaginative compared to Early Halaf, Samarra or Eridu. The influence of basketry on many of the designs is suspected, but more original decoration such as animal or human figures, as had already occurred on Umm Dabaghiyah pottery, never occur. Yet a fine series of small baked-clay female

85 figurines recently discovered at Yarim Tepe (levels II–VI, but mostly from V) show a fine aptitude for modelling. Some wear elongated head-dresses (?) or hair-styles and most of them show details of clothing resembling flounced skirts. There are some similarities here to figures from Tell Ramad III in Syria, but these

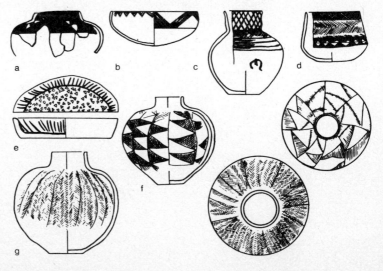

84 Pottery from Tell Hassuna: (a, b) painted ware; (c, d) painted and incised ware; (e) husking tray; (f, g) standard incised ware (after Lloyd)

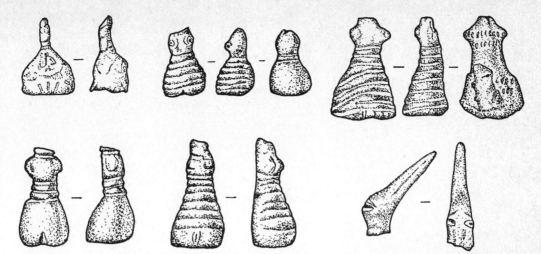

85 Hassuna culture: baked–clay figurines from Yarim Tepe I; top left from level II, the rest from level V (after Merpert and Munchaev)

Hassuna figurines are quite unlike those of the Halaf or Samarra cultures; a similar head-dress appears, however, on a painted Halaf sherd. One other cult object must be mentioned; a cigar-shaped terracotta object pierced with regular holes like a whistle. One end is c-shaped and painted red; the other end is in the form of a ram's head. It was found in level V at Yarim Tepe.

The origin of the Hassuna culture is by no means clear. It evidently did not develop out of the Umm Dabaghiyah culture and is different in every aspect from contemporary Early Halaf. Its presence west of the Sinjar area has not been satisfactorily demonstrated and the few western manifestations (Amuq B-type seals and some grey-ware sherds in Hassuna IV and VI) may signify trade links. The stone industry does not suggest an origin in a Jarmo-like milieu. It is tempting to postulate that Hassuna and Samarra are related, especially if the earliest pottery from Matarrah, that from the pits and scoops on virgin soil, is regarded as a form of early Hassuna incised ware, finer than that found in the north.[150] The earliest pottery from Tell es-Sawwan, however, is a coarse and plain ware, closely linked in shape to the numerous alabaster vessels. Some globular incised Hassuna jars are found here, but the spirit, quality and design of the later painted Samarra ware are utterly unlike that of archaic or standard Hassuna, and there is no equivalent for these at Tell es-Sawwan, where Samarra pottery has no painted predecessors.

Architectural traditions, the use of mud brick, the eminence of alabaster vessels and figurines, the remarkable Samarra pottery and clay figurines – all these differ markedly from those of the Hassuna culture. If one insists on the similarities and regards Hassuna and Samarra as close relations, there can be little doubt that Hassuna was the poor relation. There is, however, not enough evidence yet to elucidate the origin of the Hassuna culture.

The Samarra Culture

Only since the excavations at Tell es-Sawwan has it become evident that Samarra ware is not just a luxury class of pottery, but part of a distinct culture.[149] Tell es-Sawwan, situated on a bluff

86 Plan of the Tell es-Sawwan settlement showing circuit wall of level IIIA and multi-roomed houses of level III (after Abu al-Soof)

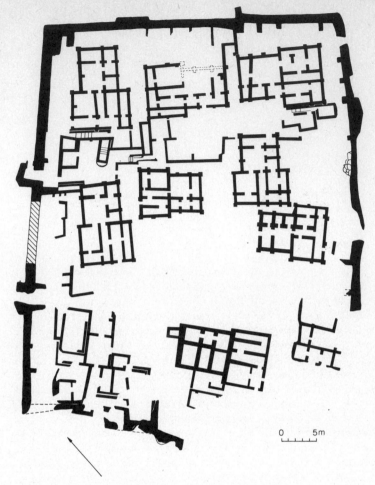

0   5m

on the east bank of the Tigris is a fairly large oval site (220 × 110 m) and Chogha Mami, near Mandali at the foot of the Zagros, measures as much as 350 × 100 m.

At Tell es-Sawwan,[146-7] painted pottery characterizes the upper levels (III–V), whereas the earlier two have only produced crude ware, some of it incised.[188-90] The plain ware shows close similarities to large quantities of stone vessels found in a cemetery below the structures of level I and belonging to it. At Chogha Mami, on the other hand, where layers earlier than those with classic Samarra pottery have not yet been excavated, the site was not deserted at the end of that period; it has a Late Samarran level as well as a further sequence of great stratigraphic importance having links with various other cultures. Thus, three phases can be distinguished: Early Samarra (without painted pottery), the classic Middle Samarra, and at Chogha Mami, a Late Samarra in which naturalistic design disappears.

The earliest settlement at Tell es-Sawwan (I) was rectangular, and defended by a ditch, but already before the end of the period buildings were encroaching on the now useless defences. Three buildings have been excavated; beneath no. 1 were discovered about 130 graves, mainly those of infants, but including a number

87

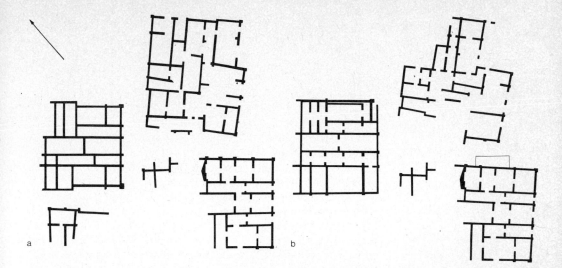

a

b

87 Tell es-Sawwan: plans of buildings of (a) level I and (b) level II (after Abu al-Soof and al-Wailly)

of adults. The building contained no household goods, but an alabaster statuette was found in a niche in one of the rooms. The excavators have suggested that it was used as a shrine connected with the underlying cemetery. Architecturally it does not differ much from the other two buildings; they are all large, containing many rooms with thin walls and built of proper mud brick cast in a mould, an innovation in Mesopotamia. Walls and floors were covered with mud plaster. All three plans are simple, consisting of rows of rectangular rooms of various sizes, but lacking such features as hearths, ovens, benches, etc. Buttresses on the exterior of the walls not only broke the monotony, but served to support the beams of a presumably flat roof of reeds and clay. Building 1 was destroyed by fire at the end of level I but it was shored up with buttresses and re-used in level II; building 2 was reconstructed. Building 3 in level II again had infant burials in shallow graves beneath it. These large structures, then, are characteristic of the Early Samarra phase at Tell es-Sawwan I–II. A C14 date of 5506±73 BC from a level I floor places the beginning of the settlement at *c.* 5600 BC.

In the level I cemetery the dead were buried in a contracted position wrapped in matting and in a number of cases red ochre was used on the skeletons. The dead were buried with personal ornaments: dentalium shell, bivalve mussel, and asphalt, alabaster and greenstone beads strung together in striking colour patterns – black and white or red carnelian combined with turquoise or copper – for necklaces and bracelets. Pottery was not buried with the dead but there were numerous stone female figurines, mostly in the standing position and generally made of alabaster; also phalli and hollow headless squatting female figures, buried with infants and adolescents alike, together with a vast variety of alabaster (gypsum) vessels, bowls, jars, ladles, palettes, etc. The rarity of pottery in the earliest level of the settlement suggests that these stone vessels were not only buried with the dead but were in common use among the living. Most of the coarse ware was no doubt used for cooking and storage, some lined with gypsum, though baskets lined with

88

89

90

88 Sketches of graves 201a (left) and 201b (right) in the cemetery of Tell es-Sawwan I (after al-A'dami)

asphalt and gypsum were probably still in vogue. The use of veined alabaster may have retarded the need for painted pottery, and many of the pottery vessels imitate stone vessels. Actually Tell es-Sawwan gives one the impression of a society in the transition stage from aceramic to ceramic Neolithic. The variety of stone vessels is much greater than in the Jarmo period. The chipped-stone industry is undistinguished, a feature shared with the Hassuna and the Halaf cultures; there are neither microliths nor arrowheads. Sickle blades, side-blow flakes, straight knife blades are the most common tools and the ground-stone industry is the old traditional one with querns and mortars, grindstones, pestles, etc. Obsidian was imported from a new source (4a) believed to lie at Doğu-bayazit at the foot of Mt Ararat.[85] Baked-clay figurines of standing and squatting women are fairly crude but there is a fine seated figure of a male.[179]

11

The people of Tell es-Sawwan kept domestic sheep and goat and had domestic dogs,[146] and though hunting is relatively un-important, gazelle, red deer, fallow deer, aurochs and onager were occasionally caught.[154] The presence of deer suggests woodlands not too far away from the Tigris. Deposits of carbonized plant material from the ditch show that the Samarra people, unlike their northern neighbours, practised simple irrigation agriculture.[156] They grew emmer wheat, six-row naked and hulled barley, some einkorn and bread-wheat, as well as flax. The six-row barleys and bread-wheat are hybrids which are thought to have developed by mutation under the influence of early irrigation practices. The large-seeded flax developed similarly. Caper, prosopis and certain thistles were collected. It was due to the development of early irrigation farming that Samarra man was able to settle in the middle Tigris area, where the rainfall is insufficient for the growth of crops by dry-farming methods. Where the new techniques were acquired is not known, but one suspects that it was in the margin of the Kurdish hills east of the Tigris that man started to practise with artificial watering of crops on unproductive land.

In the Middle Samarra phase (Tell es-Sawwan IIIA) a buttressed fortification wall was built lining the old course of the ditch. Eight buildings of T-shaped plan have so far been excavated and from the finds made in the rooms it is clear that they were houses with storerooms for agricultural products. These structures are smaller than those of the previous period, but they have the same thin walls and were probably single-storeyed and contained numerous small rooms. Later in the period (level IIIB) gypsum plaster came to be widely used and one of these T-shaped buildings is constructed over the wall and ditch, which presumably had lost its defensive

89 Alabaster figurines from the Tell es-Sawwan cemetery with inlaid eyes and caps of asphalt

90 Stone vessels (mainly alabaster) from the cemetery of Tell es-Sawwan I (after al-A'dami)

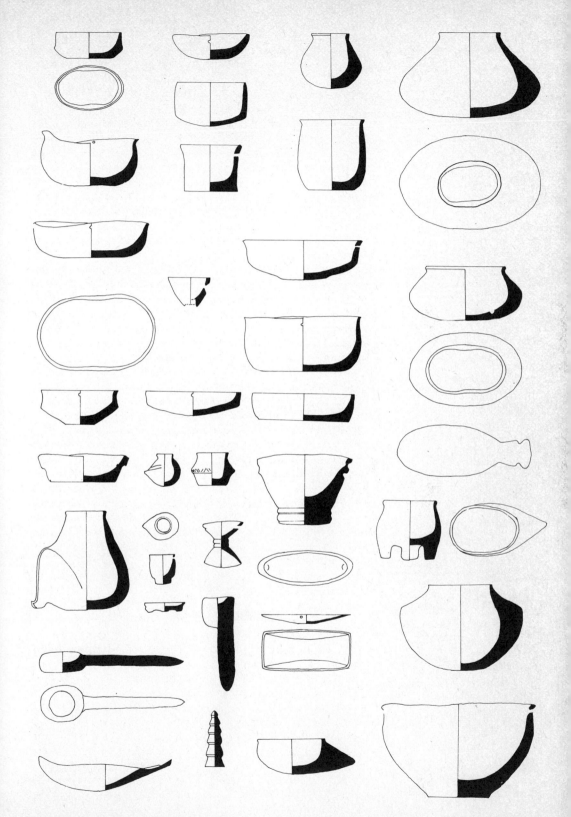

function and had fallen into disuse. Besides houses, there are courtyards with ovens and storage pits, later used for rubbish disposal. Burials are apparently absent, but a Samarra cemetery of this phase was found at Samarra itself. Stone vessels have disappeared and pottery is now common, both the old coarse wares with grit and straw temper used for cooking purposes, and the new classic painted and incised wares. A few sherds of painted pottery found already in level II seemed to suggest that the development was local, rather than the result of outside influences. At the same time classic Samarra influences are now felt in the Hassuna and to a lesser extent in the Early Halaf of Arpachiyah. In both these instances they are clearly intrusive from the Samarra area. At Baghouz on the middle Euphrates a Middle Samarran site is founded,[149, 171] and Samarra pottery accompanies the Middle Halaf expansion to the Khabur[165] and the Carchemish area.[256] The classic Samarra phase at Tell es-Sawwan comprises levels IIIA, IIIB, IV and V. The last two levels are less well preserved, but there are a number of burials with worn-down teeth, the result of excessive cereal diet. Halaf pottery occurs sporadically in levels IV and V, as an import from the north.

91

The painted Samarra pottery is highly distinctive; it is decorated in matt paint, sometimes fugitive, of a chocolate-brown or light or dark grey colour (rarely in both, except at Baghouz) on a smoothed buff slip or washed surface.[158] Large and small bowls, deep or shallow, pedestalled bowls and jars are the most common shapes. Patterns are arranged in horizontal bands and each is filled with different motifs, some flowing to the left, others to the right. Many of these patterns are strongly reminiscent of basketry and woven textiles, which may have provided the inspiration for the strongly geometric motifs, but others such as the wavy lines may represent water, for the Tigris dominated the view. Occasionally reeds, rushes and trees are shown and on the interior of large bowls there are numerous representations of human beings, especially dancing girls with flowing hair, groups of figures holding hands (on rim interiors), water-fowl catching river fish, deer among

91 Pottery from Tell es-Sawwan: (a, b, d) plain ware from level II; (c) from level I; (e–g) classical Samarra ware from level III (after al-A'dami)

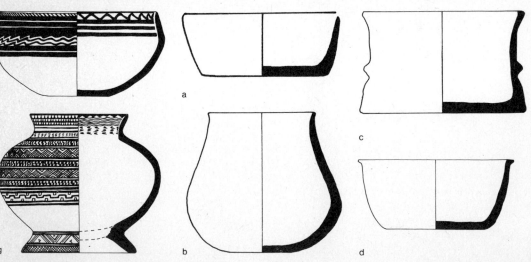

trees, goats, crabs, spiders and scorpions. Often the arrangement is in a dynamic whirling style and in certain traditional scenes like that of deer and goat around a water-hole, a progressive schematization from naturalistic to almost abstract pattern can be observed. Potters' marks also occur. Among the jars there are some decorated with female faces, with wavy hair, cowrie-like eyes and what appear to be painted or tattoo marks. Such effigy vases, common at Tell es-Sawwan in level III, occur also at Chogha Mami, Serik[180-82] and even at Hassuna V.[163] They may be the descendants of the squatting female stone vases of level I. The stone phalli too are imitated in pottery decorated with horizontal red bands. The naturalism seen in Samarra pottery is rare in Mesopotamia and some scholars, misled by this, have suggested an Iranian origin;[195] but in Iran nothing similar has yet been found at this period and the idea of Iranian influence had better be abandoned. A local origin seems far more likely. Samarra pottery was buried with the dead in the Samarra cemetery, but no anthropological study has yet been made of the bearers of this culture. With the excavation of Samarra sites in progress, this aspect of the culture demands investigation.

The economy of the Middle Samarra phase offers little that is new. At Tell es-Sawwan III there is an emphasis on fishing and an increase in gazelle hunting but apparently less sheep and goat herding. At Chogha Mami in the same period there is now evidence for domestic cattle side by side with domestic sheep and goat;[182] there is also evidence for the same wheat and barley crops and flax, grown by irrigation, as at Tell es-Sawwan.[157] A series of small ditches on the very edge of the site, at several superimposed levels, show the extreme simplicity of this early form of irrigation farming.[184] Flax could have been used for the extraction of oils and the fibres may already have been woven into linen. At Tell Shemshara 13, an imprint of a plain-weave textile was found (as before at Jarmo and at Çatal Hüyük).[172] Clay spindle whorls occur at most sites of this period. The excavations at Chogha Mami complement the evidence from Tell es-Sawwan in a most satisfactory way.[182] House plans show rectangular structures with external buttresses, thin walls and two to three rows of rooms. They vary in size from 9×7 m with twelve rooms and two doorways, to 7×6 m with nine rooms and three doorways or 8×4.5 m with eight rooms and two doorways. This suggests that more than one family lived in these houses. Particularly important is a rich find of highly sophisticated, painted clay figurines of females with elaborate coiffure, wearing nose and ear plugs of stone (some examples were found), painted or tattoo marks and coloured garments. These elaborate figures have no counterparts in the Hassuna or Halaf cultures.

At present the main feature of Late Samarra, isolated only at Chogha Mami, is the disappearance of naturalistic ornament and its replacement by purely geometrical patterns of a somewhat less fussy type than those that had prevailed before; chevrons now play a large part in the new decorative scheme. By this period Tell es-Sawwan was probably already deserted. How and why this occurred we do not know, but Baghouz may have suffered the same fate. Much remains to be learned about the Samarra culture.

92 Chogha Mami: head of a figurine of the classical Samarra phase

92

At Arpachiyah, a small mound situated east of the Tigris north of Nineveh, the Halaf sequence was divided into three phases: Early Halaf (Arpachiyah pre-TT10) with at least five building levels and probably more; Middle Halaf (Arpachiyah TT10–7) and Late Halaf (Arpachiyah TT6 and 5).[166] The earliest building levels are said to have been characterized by insubstantial huts, of which no plans have been published, nor any further description given. Only the pottery and the seals were published. Subsequent excavations at other Halaf sites have thrown no further light on Early Halaf habitation, but perhaps the Russian excavations at Yarim Tepe II will clarify the structures of this period. It would certainly be interesting to know whether these insubstantial huts were round like those of the Middle Halaf or of a different plan, and whether they had been made of reeds or sticks and plaster, pisé or brick.

93, 94 Early Halaf pottery is inferior to the later products, both in baking and clay temper and the number of shapes and design motifs is very restricted. A slip is in common use and much of the pottery is burnished. The paint is a lustrous red–brown or brown. Many of the vessels are small, including the characteristic cream bowl, the jars with flaring neck and oval orifice; sharp profiles are common. Metallic prototypes have been suggested, but there is no definite evidence for metalworking in the Halaf culture; if Early Halaf pottery imitated vessels in other materials, it is only stone,

94 *Opposite* Early Halaf pottery from Arpachiyah (after Mallowan)

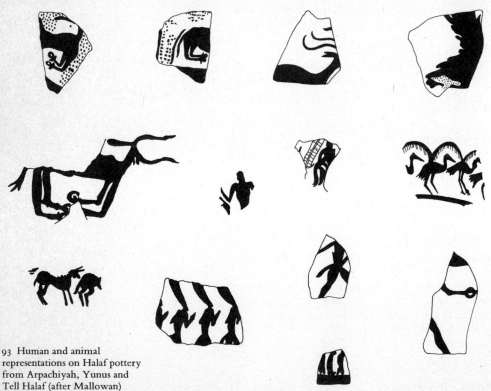

93 Human and animal representations on Halaf pottery from Arpachiyah, Yunus and Tell Halaf (after Mallowan)

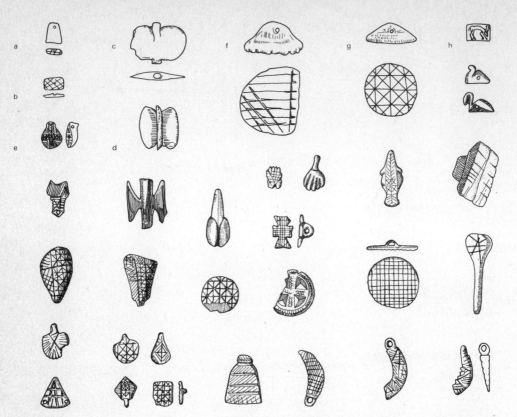

95 Early Halaf seals and amulets: (a) from Mersin XXVII; (b) from Hassuna II; (c, d) from Tell Dhahab, Amuq; (e, h) from Tepe Gawra; (f, g) two large seals from Tell Judeideh XIV (Amuq A–B); the rest from Arpachiyah (after Mallowan)

wood, basketry or leather that can be legitimately considered. Naturalistic renderings of animals occur among the designs; deer, leopard, onager, birds, fish, snakes, and an occasional human figure (all earlier than similar designs on Samarra ware). These are said to be typical only of Early Halaf at Arpachiyah, though elsewhere this animal style probably survived into Middle Halaf,[170] e.g. at Tell Halaf, at Yarim Tepe, levels III–IV and at Yunus near Carchemish,[256] or perhaps in the west in general. Other typical motifs are stylized animal heads, including those of bulls and moufflon; such motifs are rendered in relief on Umm Dabaghiyah pottery, but are here transmitted in painting. Among geometric motifs, there are 'leopard spots' (a circle surrounded by spots) and egg-and-dot patterns, while decorative panels filled with herring-bones, wavy lines, etc. are exceedingly common on bowls. The latter bear a striking resemblance to pattern-burnished panels on north Syrian Amuq B ware. Squares filled with pointillé dots are also typical and are matched in the white-filled incised ware of Mersin XXIV–XX,[117] and at Sakçagözü at the end of the Early and the beginning of the Middle Halaf period.[245]

These western design parallels, although executed in totally different techniques are not irrelevant, for there is good evidence for western contacts with Early Halaf at Arpachiyah in the form of the numerous small sealstones and pendants, often carved with fine geometric ornament, in steatite or serpentine. These are confined to this phase at Arpachiyah, and are as common there as they are in Amuq B in northern Syria,[244] which controlled the

95

greenstone supplies from which they were made. Similar seals were also found in Hassuna II,[163] and Yarim Tepe I, as mentioned above. Obsidian may already have been present, but there is no precise information as to when it first occurred. Likewise nothing is known about the physical characteristics of the people or their economy.

Middle Halaf

As the excavations at Yarim Tepe II[167-70] have not yet reached Early Halaf levels, it is only at Arpachiyah that the transition to Middle Halaf can be observed and though this later phase is much better known, there is no evidence for a break in the sequence.[174-7] At this site there are four building levels (10–7) with round structures, the earliest of which lack the rectangular annex, ante-chamber or open courtyard, which produced the typical 'keyhole' plan, also found at Tell Turlu, Yunus near Carchemish, Geriki-haciyan and in one case at Yarim Tepe II. At the latter site there are at least six building levels of round houses (levels II–VII) with diameters varying from 2·5 to 5 to 6 m. They have thin pisé walls, on average 25 cm thick, covered with gypsum plaster, in one case painted red. One of these buildings has a rectangular niche in the wall and all have doors with threshold and door pivot. Hearths are common, but bread ovens like pottery kilns are located outside in the open air. There are also short sections of parallel curved walls, which suggest foundations for drying-sheds or granaries near a *tholos* in level VI, of a type known from Yarim Tepe I and the Jeitun culture. Storage-rooms also occur in a number of *tholoi* – bell-shaped pits at Tell Turlu, internal sub-divisions at Yarim Tepe II. At this site there is also evidence for rectangular buildings, with square rooms 3·5 m wide or rows of rectangular rooms, while in the centre of the settlement in level IV there is a still enigmatic structure of rectangular plan, at least 8·4 m long with buttresses and several small rooms; as it has associated burials but no domestic rubbish, it is therefore tenta-tively interpreted as a shrine. Other unusual structures include a *tholos* with a very low pisé dome, ante-room and side chambers at Arpachiyah level 8, and a set of kilns with flues, ashes and wasters in a trench at Yunus. There appears to be little evidence of planning in these Middle Halaf settlements and the round houses, though free-standing, huddle together in a way not much different from the much earlier settlements at Ain Mallaha, Mureybet or Wadi Fallah. Only at Arpachiyah do stone-paved paths lead to the structures on top of the mound; what the houses of the slope looked like is not recorded.

96

It is often assumed that the large *tholoi* of Arpachiyah with their stone foundations carried a pisé dome,[166] but the thin walls of the Yarim Tepe structures could not have supported such a weight and a roof thatched with reed seems more likely.

A number of burials accompanied by pots and painted clay figurines were found outside some of the Arpachiyah *tholoi*, but their number does not account for the population of the settlement and cemeteries must have existed. At Yarim Tepe, besides a few intramural burials, two such cemeteries have been found, one on

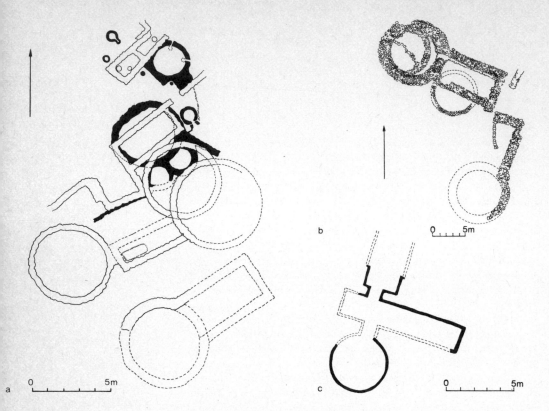

a

b

c

96 Structures of the Halaf period: (a) kilns and the superimposed series of tholoi at Yunus near Carchemish; (b, c) Middle Halaf tholoi at Arpachiyah near Nineveh (after Woolley and Mallowan)

the slope of the mound, the other on the deserted earlier site. Here the dead were buried, sometimes in shaft-graves with a lateral chamber, accompanied by pottery vessels, stone vases, pig's-head beads, mace- and axeheads of polished stone. It will be interesting to see to what physical type these Halaf people belonged.

The great expansion of the Middle Halaf culture westward and northward has already been noted and it would appear that this was owing to a population increase resulting from successful agriculture. As the amount of available agricultural land surrounding a site is frequently limited, excess population hives off and founds new settlements in previously unoccupied areas and thus the culture is able to expand. On the evidence of economic details alone this process cannot be demonstrated for the Halaf culture, for far too little is known. At Arpachiyah 'wheat and barley' are said to have been found in all levels,[166] but no details are given until emmer wheat and 'barley' are specifically ascribed to Late Halaf (level 6). Flax also occurred at Tell Brak. At Gerikihaciyan (Middle and Late Halaf), north of Diyarbakir, there is evidence for domestic sheep and goat, pig and wild cattle;[51] at Banahilk (Late Halaf) for domestic sheep and goat and domestic cattle.[67] At Yarim Tepe II (both Middle and Late Halaf) there are domestic sheep, pig and cattle, as there had been before in Yarim Tepe I. The preoccupation of Halaf potters with bulls' heads right from the beginning suggests that the domestication of cattle was in progress or had just been achieved – details may have varied from site to site. The less numerous rams' heads do not reflect the numerical inferiority of domestic sheep – bones show that their numbers had increased – but wild sheep do not engender the same emotion as wild cattle. Middle Halaf influence in northern Syria is associated with the appearance of domestic sheep at Ras Shamra IVC,[251] to which dog was added in IVB and pig in IVA, yet these events need not be correlated as domestic sheep was already present in Amuq B.[244] Detailed faunal reports from Ras Shamra are not yet available.

From the little information at hand it would seem that the basis of Halaf agriculture was dry farming of emmer, barley and perhaps einkorn, and stockbreeding mainly of sheep, goat and pig, with cattle in a subsidiary role here and there, supplemented by some hunting of aurochs, boar, onager, gazelle and seasonal birds. The evidence for hunting is mainly derived from the pottery. There is no evidence (yet) for domestic dog, and no apparent interest in fish or snails. This admittedly fragmentary economic picture does not support the theory that the Halaf people were great cattle-herders and derived their wealth from these beasts, like the earlier population of Çatal Hüyük. Nor is there any evidence that they practised irrigation agriculture like their southern Samarra neighbours.

Yet there is ample evidence for a flourishing material culture; the vast territory now occupied by the Halaf people must have facilitated communications and it may be surmised that it was their luxury pottery that was chiefly sought after, together with foodstuffs, sheepskins, wool, linen and woven garments that were exchanged in the barter and trade for raw materials. The many fine textile-like motifs now found on Middle Halaf pottery to the exclusion of almost anything else except animal heads, certainly

97

97 Pottery distribution in the Middle Halaf, Middle Samarra and Late Hassuna phases

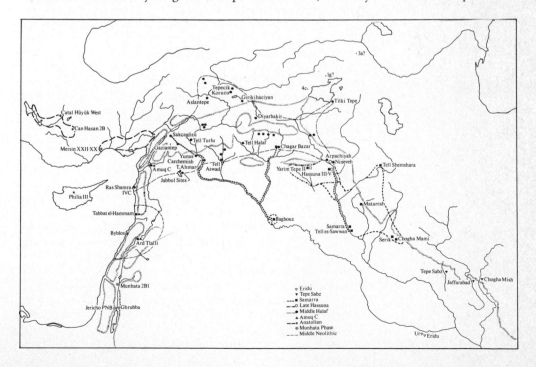

98 Middle Halaf pottery from
Arpachiyah (after Mallowan)

resemble weaving, stitching or embroidery (on linen?) and it
would not be surprising if the later Mesopotamian textile trade
had its origin in this period. Many of the small motifs, such as the
hour-glass or double axe, the leopard spots, the quatrefoil, etc.,
already had figured in the Çatal Hüyük wall paintings of Anatolia,
but the use of these old motifs on gaily coloured textiles might
have occurred in the Halaf area. It is an interesting fact that the
prevalence of these small-scale patterns, often floral or geometric,
striped or checkered like a carpet of spring flowers in the foot-hills
of the Taurus and Zagros, should still be found as the most
common textile design today from the Amanus in the west to
Iraqi Kurdistan, exactly the region of maximum extension of the
Halaf culture some seven thousand years ago. Precise and neat,
minute but repetitive, the Halaf designs formed an overwhelm-
ingly rich brocade, which contrasts with the bold and imaginative
larger patterns preferred by the peoples of the plateau, be it in
Anatolia (Hacılar) or Iran (Dalma), the simple but unimaginative
peasant basketry style of Hassuna or the dynamic and naturalistic
styles of Samarra.

98   Middle Halaf pottery shows greater technical competence and
the simple Early Halaf shapes and patterns are abandoned or
enriched. Light-on-dark effects come into play in the second half
of the period as white paint is introduced on a brown ground,
usually in the form of stippled designs, a straight translation of
white-filled pointillé on dark burnished ware, common in northern
Syria and Cilicia. The small-scale floral and geometric patterns
alternate with stylized animal heads and fine naturalistic scenes
are found at Yarim Tepe, levels III and IV, Tell Halaf and Yunus,
where all the pottery consists of wasters from the kilns.

The similarities of Halaf animals on pottery may help to date the
final phase of rock art in the Taurus Mountains in which the
99   animals are not engraved but pecked into the rock, from Palanli
near Adiyaman west of the Euphrates to the regions of Hakkiari
(Şat) and Çatak, south of Lake Van. [98] In these areas Middle Halaf
settlements now appear (Adiyaman sites, Tilki Tepe on Lake Van)
to control the trade in raw materials – stone, copper (?) and
obsidian, green (4c) from Nemrut Dağ, grey (1g) from Suphan
and black (3a) from Ararat. Gerikihaciyan is suspiciously close to
the native copper and malachite ores of Ergani-Maden and Halaf
interest in the Malatya-Keban area may conceivably be linked to
the raw materials of that area which included copper and gold.
Whether timber already interested these people – as it did their
Ubaid successors – is doubtful, but with growing familiarity with
the forested area and its inhabitants who would have used timber
in rectangular structures, the idea of building larger rectangular
houses and roofing them with flat roofs may have penetrated. At
Arpachiyah in Late Halaf the round houses were apparently replaced by rectilinear structures.[166] The Halaf people must have been
ultra-conservative to have kept to the round-house tradition for so
long. Middle Halaf also shows contacts with the south; its pottery
occurred in small measure in Tell es-Sawwan IV and V, well after
Samarra had made its way north, accompanying the Middle Halaf
expansion as far west as Sakçagözü II, Amuq C, Carchemish/

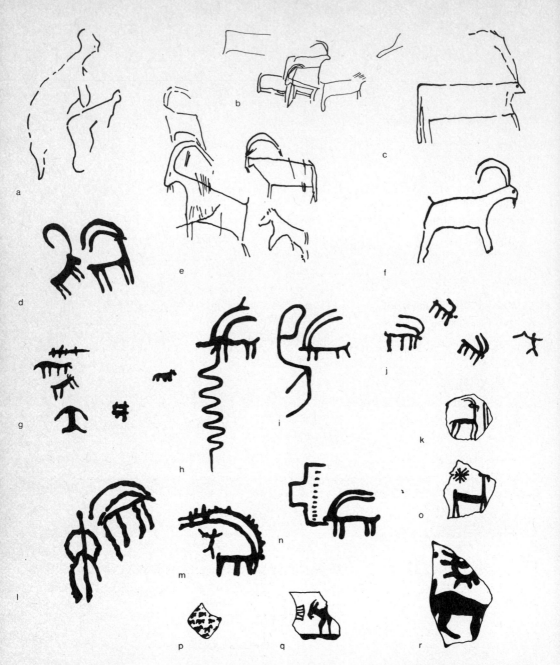

99 Rock engravings from
Palanlı caves near Adiyaman:
(a–c, e, f) style I; (d,l) style III
(after Anati); (g–j, m, n) from
Şat Mountains in Hakkiari;
(k, o, p–r) Halaf sherds from
Chagar Bazar (after Mallowan)

Yunus and Chagar Bazar 14–13.[165] The Halaf expansion was
probably matched by a Samarra expansion farther south; Baghouz,
for example, was implanted in the strategic Mari area where the
Khabur trade routes reach the middle Euphrates. Proper mud-
brick architecture with rectangular houses containing rooms were
built at Baghouz.[171] There may have been a symbiosis between the
two cultures in the Khabur area, but they never assimilated
culturally and we have no Halaf pots with Samarra patterns, nor
the reverse.

The Late Halaf period is best known for its splendid polychrome pottery from Arpachiyah 6 (and 5)[166] and Tepe Gawra. The distribution of Late Halaf appears to be less extensive and less dense than in the previous phase although there is a notable extension eastward and southward connected with the disappearance of the Hassuna and Samarra cultures. Halaf now appears in these regions up to Shemshara in the east and its influence does not stop there but reaches Chogha Mami[182] and even the Hajji Muhammad culture of the far south.[185] In more central and western areas Late Halaf is certainly attested in the Khabur at Tell Halaf, Chagar Bazar, Brak, etc. and beyond at Gerikihaciyan (with a C14 date for final Halaf (?) of 4515 ± 100 B C) and Sakçagözü, but at many other sites typical Late Halaf features have not been recognized. Where local Middle Halaf wares continued uninterruptedly the chronological division might well remain obscured and local features are clearly observable in the Khabur if one compares Arpachiyah wares with contemporary pottery from Chagar Bazar. Late Halaf polychrome ware was imported, however, for the first time into Cilicia, where it is found in addition to local wares in Mersin XX–XVII.[117] This shows that a cultural continuum still existed although there are now clear signs in northern Syria,[244] from Tell Turlu to Ras Shamra,[255] of a new culture – Amuq D, a reaction against the Middle Halaf-influenced Amuq C – with many local peculiarities such as jars with bow-rims, a new red monochrome pottery, etc. The distribution map of this phase is, like most maps of this kind, but a poor reflection of such cultural complexities.

100

100 Pottery distribution in the Late Halaf, Hajji Muhammed phase

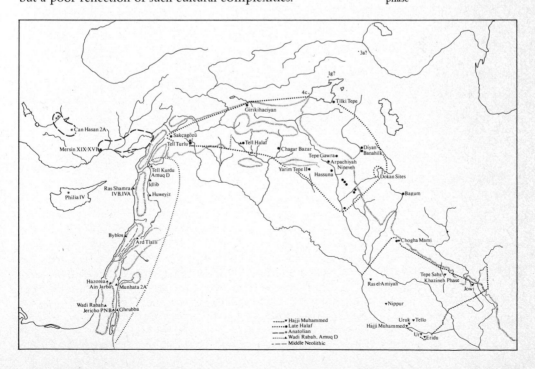

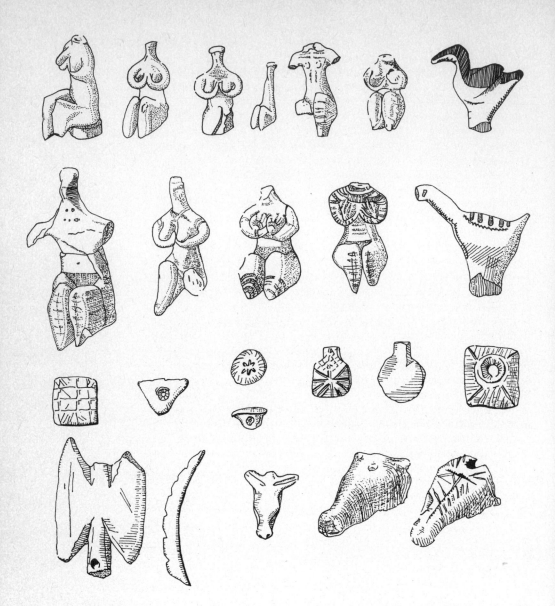

101 Halaf baked-clay figurines, stone seals and amulets, from Chagar Bazar in the Khabur area (after Mallowan)

Economic details are as scanty as before and there are no notable changes. With the domestication of cattle in many areas the prevalence of bulls' heads on the pottery sharply declines. Animal decoration is not a feature of this period in the central area, but here and there it is adopted in areas which have newly come under Halaf influence, such as Tell Shemshara or Ras el-Amiyah. Bucrania even reach Khuzistan.[75] A novelty of the period is the first attested use of lead and copper in the form of pendants and fragments of pins in Arpachiyah 6.[166] This seems surprising after the much earlier use of copper at Çayönü, Çatal Hüyük, Alikosh, Muhammed Jafar and Tell es-Sawwan. New also is the use of rectangular buildings in pisé (but not mud brick) at Tell Aswad, Yarim Tepe II and Arpachiyah 6. At the last-named site the top of the mound was occupied by an important building, ruined and destroyed by fire, consisting of a large hall surrounded by storerooms and workshops for pottery and stone vessels. It also contained a possible shrine with a female statuette, amulets in the form of phalli and human finger bones, all carved in stone. A small room at Tell Aswad contained part of a bull's skull with horn cores, perhaps once mounted on the wall in a fashion familiar from Mureybet, Ganjdareh and Çatal Hüyük. Another rectangular shrine is reported from Yarim Tepe II, but no details are available.

Recorded from the burnt building of Arpachiyah 6 were variously shaped vessels made of stone including obsidian, jewellery with long perforated obsidian beads, painters' stone palettes (already seen at Tepe Guran, Jarmo and Tell es-Sawwan), stylized stone figurines of females (side by side with the red-striped, seated and faceless Halaf clay figurines), baked-clay sling- *101*
stones and a blade industry in flint and obsidian.

The main distinction of the Late Halaf is its pottery. The splendid polychrome plates, bowls and jars, decorated in red, *102*
brown and white on an apricot slip, seem confined to the region east of the Tigris, whereas the Khabur and the west in general has somewhat more provincial shapes and less spectacular ornament.[144] Yet they share a number of features among which there are vessels with corrugated patterns and added painting, resembling basketry, which reach from the Mediterranean at Mersin to east of the Tigris. Earlier shapes such as the popular 'cream bowl' have virtually disappeared. Whereas the fine textile patterns with small motifs continue to be made in level 6 – the transition from 7 to 6 is not abrupt at Arpachiyah – the new eastern style makes use of very daring designs on thin plates, among which rosettes, Maltese crosses, large quatrefoils surrounded by multiple bands of varying design are characteristic. Loose quatrefoils, rendered almost naturalistically, are more typical in the western group. After *103*
enduring for about a millennium – probably as a potters' centre for near-by Nineveh – Arpachiyah 6 was destroyed by an unknown enemy, who looted and smashed the settlement before setting fire to it. In level 5 there were traces of rebuilding, but the Halaf pottery is mixed with later material and there may be an erosional

102 Polychrome Late Halaf plates from Arpachiyah (after Mallowan)

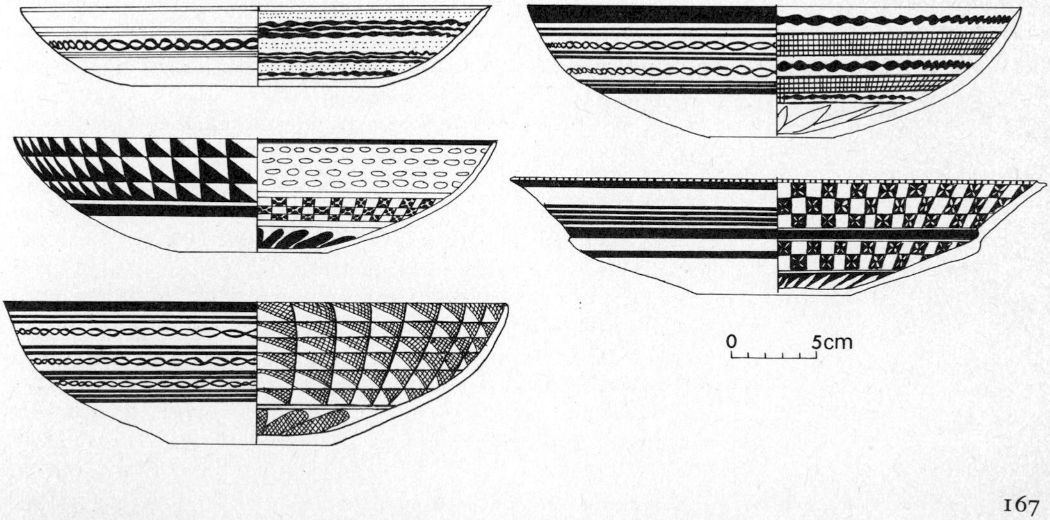

103 Middle and Late Halaf pottery from Chagar Bazar (after Mallowan)

hiatus between level 5 and the reoccupation in the Late Ubaid period in level 4. At Tepe Gawra, however, Early Ubaid occupation follows, which still shows clear traces of Halaf influence.[145] At other sites, for example in Syria, Ubaid influence did not immediately follow the end of Halaf and the same is the case at Mersin. When Ubaid influence is actually found, it is that of Late Ubaid and not the early form best known in the north from Tepe Gawra. Serious consideration should therefore be given to the possibility of a hiatus in the stratigraphy on many sites between the end of Halaf and the Late Ubaid reoccupation. The old explanation given, that the Halaf culture was destroyed by Ubaid newcomers from the south conflicts with evidence from Syria and Cilicia and may not even apply to Arpachiyah itself.[166] The events that led to the breakdown of the Halaf culture and the reoccupation after a possible hiatus are problems demanding further investigation, with due consideration paid to alternatives to southern invasion.

If the causes for the end of the Halaf culture are obscure, the origin of the culture is not much clearer. Halaf appears at Arpachiyah on virgin soil without previous antecedents. Its distinctive pottery shows no similarities to that of its neighbours, the Hassuna and Samarra cultures, which belong to a different tradition. A copying in paint of the pattern-burnished black and grey wares of northern Syria (and Chagar Bazar 14 in the Khabur) in the Amuq B period has been suggested as an origin for Halaf painting;[166] though some of the herring-bone, wavy line and other patterns could derive from such a source, the decoration in animal style does not. Animals and animal heads do not occur in northern Syria or Cilicia at this time, as far as we know, although such representations were still current on the Anatolian plateau at the end of the Çatal Hüyük culture. On the basis of a faulty chronology, the author in a previous work did attempt to link Anatolia with Halaf,[97] but it now appears that the beginning of Halaf does not come after Hacılar I, as was suggested there, but overlaps with the end of Çatal Hüyük. The similarities, however, remain and might perhaps be explained by similar environmental factors; both cultures were domesticating cattle and thus showed a natural interest in bulls and bucrania, shared to some extent by other useful animals such as sheep, goat, deer, onager, etc. Beliefs associated with these may also have been held by cultures such as Amuq A, though they did not express it on their pottery, which was dark burnished and therefore hard to decorate; on the other hand, they might have had shrines with modelled heads or even paintings. Of this culture virtually nothing is known except its pottery. The discovery of the Umm Dabagiyah culture allows one to view the origins of Halaf in a somewhat different light. Here is a culture contemporary with Çatal Hüyük and Amuq A with western links such as rectangular houses, plaster floors, red paint, a light-coloured pottery decorated with animals and animal heads in relief and red-on-cream painted wares with dots, herring-bones, squiggles, etc., that could conceivably have given rise to something like Early Halaf. Some of the pottery shapes could also be regarded as ancestral. The similarities are undeniable, but a technical gap remains during the late phase of the culture, when there is nothing but decline at Umm Dabaghiyah. This might obscure the crucial period of the transition. Yet, tempting as some of these similarities are, there remains the obstacle of the round-house tradition and this would appear to be rooted in very early traditions. The northern location of the Halaf sites also tends to suggest that in origin their occupants were hill people who had ventured into the plain in pursuit of agriculture and stockbreeding like their Hassuna neighbours, but who were loath to sever their connections with their old homeland and native building tradition. The symbiosis with the people of the Hassuna group in the Assyrian steppe seems surprising and one can only guess that it involved mutual benefits. Could it be that the Early Halaf settlers had come originally from the mountains between the Assyrian steppe and the Lake Van area, where for thousands of years, from Epi-palaeolithic times on, they had engaged in the obsidian trade? Once settled on the northern edge of the plain they might still have controlled the trade with their relatives to the north, now becoming the middlemen. Does this explain the early contacts with the Umm Dabaghiyah culture, and its development into Early Halaf and its subsequent wealth, its north Syrian and Anatolian links and the apparent absence of any settlements on the obsidian-producing volcanic plateaux of the north apart from Tilki Tepe?

If the Halaf people were the controllers of the east Anatolian obsidian trade, many features of the culture fall into place. This is only an hypothesis and nothing more, but on analogy, it would explain another similar development to the north of the obsidian area, where in late Middle to Late Halaf times another culture arose in the Ararat plain and the Tiflis region, once again characterized by round-house complexes similar to those of the Halaf culture. The parallel development took place on either side of the obsidian-producing area, which because of its altitude of approximately 2000 m above sea-level, and the recent lava flows, bore little tree cover, was not really suitable for agriculture and was sparsely inhabited. It was not these few inhabitants of the area, but their neighbours, the Halaf people in the south and the bearers of the Neolithic of Soviet Armenia and Georgia in the north, that reaped the benefits of the obsidian trade. The cultural developments in Transcaucasia in the Neolithic period are described in Chapter Six.

South Mesopotamian and Khuzistan Cultures after 5500 B C

THE ERIDU CULTURE
The Eridu culture is known from a number of sites in the monotonous alluvium of the Euphrates valley around Eridu and Ur, separated from the coast of the Persian Gulf and the Khuzistan grasslands at the foot of the Zagros Mountains by a wide area of marshes. In spite of much exploration, we have still no evidence for earlier settlement in southern Mesopotamia than the Eridu culture. Admittedly remains of hunting and fishing communities in this area, flimsy mud huts or reed shelters, may lay buried deep below the alluvium, but no signs of these have yet been discovered, not even flints or chance finds like those gathered along the south shore of the Persian Gulf, for example in the Qatar peninsula, a developed stage of which is dated to *c.* 5000 B C.[159] On the other hand it is equally hard to maintain, on present evidence, that the Eridu culture (levels XIX–XV of the Eridu sounding),[164] founded on virgin soil with its simple but effective mud-brick architecture and its sophisticated painted pottery, was the product of autochthonous development.[178] This culture does not look like the fumbling beginnings of a settled community freshly emerged from the hunting and gathering stage of development. There is no parallel for such a cultural leap forward anywhere in the Near East; and if, as it would appear, the Eridu culture arrived in the region fully fledged, ancestral phases must be sought elsewhere. One may reasonably postulate earlier phases with pottery of a less spectacular kind, and the chances are that we must look farther north for the origins of this culture.

Unfortunately, the economy of the culture was not investigated and though fishing was undoubtedly important, it is unlikely to have been the sole mode of subsistence at this period. Mixed farming with irrigation agriculture (dry farming is impossible in this setting) and stockbreeding of cattle and sheep (as in Ubaid times?) might account for the new settlements.

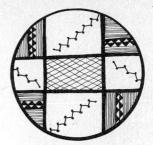

The archaeological remains are scarce: four parallel mud-brick walls and a circular oven or kiln in level XVIII, a square room just over 3 m wide with two or possibly three internal buttresses and a platform, interpreted as a shrine, and accompanied by another oven or kiln, in level XVII. In level XVI there was a similar, but larger building with a broad alcove at the back containing an altar with a platform in front of it. Once again there is an oven or kiln outside. Above this in level XV there was a much larger structure (*c.* 7 × 5·5 m) with many internal buttresses, another platform inside and a kiln or oven outside. These superposed structures from XVII to XV may have been village shrines that preceded the temples of the Ubaid period, below which they were located. What private houses looked like we do not know, but they could hardly have been of simpler plan. The use of mud brick, sometimes with finger imprints on top, is interesting, and so is the use of rectangular plans.

The published pottery found in these buildings could hardly be described as rustic, although the greater number of coarse green pottery sherds and a simple decorative style in the lowest level (XX) may indicate rapid local development.[178] The typical Eridu ware has a very fine buff- or cream-slipped fabric, which is decorated in thick, almost glossy paint, most often chocolate-coloured, but varying from dark brown to black or red. With it occur painted and unpainted coarser wares, as well as a coarse, green-coloured ware. In the earlier levels, bowls are often ornamented with chevrons and zigzags outside and with large plain triangles ending in tassels inside. Designs are geometric, never naturalistic, and there is a tendency towards reserve decoration. The use of multiple horizontal bands with varied motifs and central cruciform compositions are reminiscent of classic Samarra pottery, but the shapes, which are very varied, are not. These include a variety of bowls, some with ring bases, and large dishes, sauce-boats (cf. Tepe Sabz and Jaffarabad) and beakers, as well as collared globular jars with short necks, a type that also occurs at Samarra. The inspiration for much of this pottery may have come from gaily coloured basketry. Husking trays occur and the pottery may have been fired in kilns. The red ochre or haematite used as paint must have been imported. The suggestion that this pottery had an ancestor similar in some respects to that of the Samarra ware is intriguing, but needs to be substantiated by new discoveries in the intervening territory. At present Eridu ware is only known from the type site, Ur, and three sites or more near Usaila, 8 km northwest of Eridu, but it may well be present at the bottom of a much larger number of sites. 'Eridu ware' has recently been reported at a number of sites in Saudi Arabia[151] opposite the island of Bahrein, but this is more likely Hajji Muhammed ware. At Chogha Mish in Khuzistan a new sequence is reported with three successive Archaic phases,

104 Reconstructions of Eridu ware (after Lloyd and Safar)

followed by Early Susiana wares.[152] The painted burnished ware of Archaic 1 is still without close parallels; the chevron painted ware of Archaic 2 can be connected with the wares of the Deh Luran plain and Luristan and in Archaic 3 there are parallels with the pottery of Chogha Mami as well as remains of a massive structure built of mud bricks with finger-marks on the top. These have parallels at Eridu and elaborately painted shallow bowls that occur in the Early Susiana levels are a further link with Eridu. Terracotta heads and animal heads on bowls of this period also point to relations with Chogha Mami and Tell es-Sawwan.

There are no C14 dates to fix the absolute chronology of this culture, but it is not likely to be earlier than the Samarra painted pottery and could be a little later. A date in the last quarter of the sixth millennium may not be far out.

The Tepe Sabz Culture of the Khuzistan Plain

At the end of the Muhammed Jafar phase the old site of Alikosh was deserted, perhaps around the middle of the sixth millennium. A gap of unknown length intervenes in the archaeological record of the Deh Luran plain. Radiocarbon dates of 5510 ± 160 and 5250 ± 100 from Tepe Sabz, a small site about 140 × 120 m, 16 km to the northwest of Alikosh, suggest that this site marks the beginning of reoccupation of the area soon after the middle of the sixth millennium.[75] Since then, a new and earlier site, Chogha Sefid, has been sounded and though nothing has yet appeared in print, it would appear that the material from this site is closely related to the Late Samarra phase of Chogha Mami.[182] This suggests a post-Samarra date for Tepe Sabz, somewhere around 5000 B C. The culture represented at Tepe Sabz is found at at least six sites in the Deh Luran plain and at thirty-four others in the Susa region, e.g. at Jaffarabad 4–5 and Chogha Mish.[152] It may also occur in Luristan at Bog-i-No near Khurramabad.[74] Surface pottery from Chia Zargaran and Chia Siyah in southern Luristan may belong to this same cultural phase that preceded the Tepe Giyan culture of Luristan.[198] It is therefore a distinct possibility that the Sabz culture was not confined to the Khuzistan lowlands, but also occurred in the Zagros Mountains, just as did Halaf in the north. Tepe Sabz provides a useful stratigraphic sequence; Sabz material lies at the bottom and is followed by Khazineh, which has Hajji Muhammed affinities, and this is overlaid by two phases of material related to Mesopotamian Ubaid, locally named Mehmeh and Bayat.[75] Unfortunately no architecture of the Sabz phase was encountered in the test trench, but the information about the economy of the period is crucial. Tepe Sabz sees the introduction (unless this had already started at Chogha Sefid) of irrigation agriculture, domestic cattle and dog into Khuzistan. This is accompanied by many new tools; for example, a flint hoe, ground smooth and fixed with asphalt onto a wooden handle, an implement used to open irrigation ditches. Only a few implements were found that could be linked to the Muhammed Jafar tradition. If newcomers did arrive, as seems likely, it is clear that this time they did not descend from the Zagros Mountains, for all the cultural and economic bonds are with the riverine Samarra culture and the newly founded Eridu culture, itself perhaps a Samarran offshoot. Here lie the origins of the later Ubaid tradition of the southern lowlands.

Many sites of the Sabz culture are situated where advantage could be taken of sources of irrigation water, but not all the villages in Susiana did so and rainfall was still important in some dry-farming areas. The Sabz people grew free-threshing (hexaploid) bread-wheat, as well as emmer and two- and six-row barley, flax, lentils, vetch and vetchling – as at Tell es-Sawwan. They also gathered or grew almonds. They kept domestic goats with helically twisted horns, fewer sheep with small curly horns and some domestic cattle (only 5 per cent) of a much smaller variety than the wild aurochs. Dogs, still the size of wolf and with curled tails, assisted in herding; the remains show that they were not eaten. Hunting had greatly declined but gazelle and some onager and wild boar were still taken. Fish, mussels, turtle, birds, fox and hedgehog occasionally augmented the diet.

105 Tepe Sabz painted pottery (after Hole, Flannery and Neely)

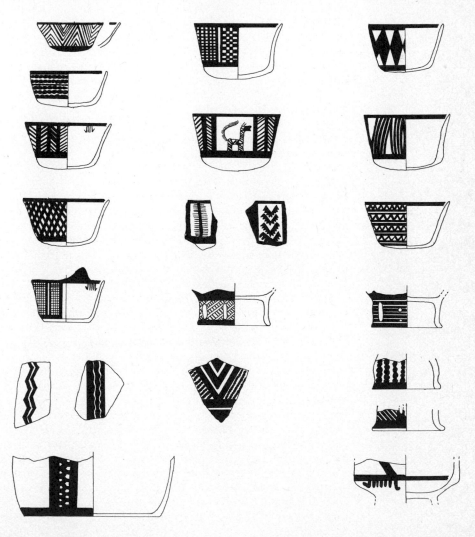

106 Khazineh ware from Tepe Sabz (after Hole, Flannery and Neely)

Whereas agricultural tools, querns, grinding and slicing slabs continue, as expected, there is a notable decline in weapons associated with hunting – just as in the north Mesopotamian cultures after the end of Umm Dabaghiyah. Inferior flint is now used and obsidian disappears. Knife and sickle blades predominate, microliths for hunting weapons such as crescents still occur, in contrast to the north. There is a decrease in skin-working tools, balanced by an increase in spindle whorls, which suggests the wearing of woollen and linen garments rather than sheepskins. A few stone bowls are still found, but pottery is now mainly used for containers, not the crumbling soft-baked, straw-tempered wares of the Muhammed Jafar phase, but hard, sand-tempered, thin new fabrics of a buff colour, fired in a kiln. Some coarse, chaff-tempered oval bowls and hole-mouth jars survive, as well as red-slipped burnished bowls, but these classes are now in the minority. The buff ware includes new shapes, a bowl on a pedestal with fenestrations, as at Samarra, sauce-boats with tab handles, convex-walled bowls, etc. These have geometric designs in black paint in the form of herring-bones, chevrons, cross-hatching, etc. Some small bowls are almost smothered in paint, producing a reserve effect, more typical of the following Khazineh phase. Compared to Eridu ware, the Sabz products look provincial. Figurines are still of the old type: T-shaped or stalk-like figures. Asterisk-shaped spindle whorls are typical and scrapers are made of potsherds. The people used lip plugs of clay, asphalt or stone as in the Muhammed Jafar phase and at Chogha Mami. Stone bracelets have new shapes; they are flattened bands with incised parallel lines. No burials have been found.

105

THE HAJJI MUHAMMED AND KHAZINEH CULTURES

In the period that follows the neighbouring but unrelated Eridu and Sabz cultures close contacts are established across the area of the marshes. The Khazineh culture covered the whole of northern Khuzistan with a dozen sites in the Deh Luran plain and not less than 102 in Susiana, some of them large (Tepe Musyan(?), Chogha Mish), suggesting on the basis of 100 persons per village a population of at least 10,000 in Khuzistan.

The Hajji Muhammed culture covered a much larger area than its predecessor, and stretched over the whole of southern Mesopotamia, from Sumer to Akkad, or rather from Eridu[164] to Ras el-Amiyah near Kish,[185] but the presence of thick alluvial deposits does not allow one to estimate the number of settlements, nor the size of the population. This manifest increase in population can only be ascribed to the benefits resulting from the introduction of irrigation agriculture, probably affecting southern Mesopotamia as much as Khuzistan, though we still have no factual evidence for it there. In Khuzistan, however, dry farming, small-scale irrigation of bread-wheat, two- and six-row hulled and naked barley, lentil, flax, vetchling and vetch, and the herding of sheep and goat in equal numbers as well as some cattle, were the main agricultural occupations. Probably transhumance was practised into the upland summer pastures of Luristan, the Bakhtiari country and Fars. Hunting of gazelle and onager had greatly declined. Micro-

liths disappeared, the flint industry consisting mainly of blades and sickle blades – obsidian is absent – and the ground-stone industry became less varied, but hoes continued. Coiled basketry was introduced; star-shaped spindle whorls, labrets, pottery scrapers were all very much as before. There were no graves as in the Sabz phase and people were probably buried outside the settlement as in the north. Mud brick was used for walls on cobble foundations but no house plan was recovered in any of the three building levels.

106   It is the pottery that is the most distinctive feature of the Khazineh culture. There was still the home-made, straw-tempered, red burnished pottery with hole-mouth jars, and dimple-base, open and carinated bowls. The highly fired black-on-buff painted pottery would seem to have been made by specialists. It consists of large carinated bowls, some with complex geometric patterns, including rosettes of Late Halaf inspiration, others with basketry designs, sauce-boats with handles, and convex bowls like those of Tepe Sabz. Large areas of the pots were now covered with black, greenish-black or reddish-black paint leaving patterns standing out on the plain buff surface in reserve. A plain buff ware occurred in the same shapes. This Khazineh pottery is closely related to that of Hajji Muhammed and Ras el-Amiyah,[185] which overlaps with the next Khuzistan phase, Mehmeh. At Ras el-Amiyah, a small mound below the alluvium, a trench disclosed five building levels with remains of rectangular huts or houses arranged around court-

318   yards which contained ovens. These are the only architectural remains of this period, for no buildings were found in the Hajji Muhammed levels (XIV–XII) at Eridu. Hajji Muhammed pottery was imported into Chogha Mami in the later phase of the transitional period, after the Late Samarra pottery that is linked to Choga Sefid.[182] This is the period of the Late Halaf expansion to the south and east, and Halaf elements (bucrania, rosettes) filtered through into the Hajji Muhammed culture and the Khazineh phase of Khuzistan. After an interval with local Chogha Mami wares, Late Halaf also reached Chogha Mami. There it was succeeded by Iranian wares of the Mehmeh phase, as at Khazineh, and these also reached the Early Ubaid of Ras el-Amiyah. There can be no doubt whatsoever that at Eridu the Hajji Muhammed pottery developed out of the Eridu ware. In Khuzistan the change from Sabz to Khazineh ware was gradual, but the Hajji Muhammed elements became typical and more pronounced in the later part of the period and they continued during Early Mehmeh.

The Early Ubaid Period in Southern Mesopotamia and the Mehmeh Phase in Khuzistan, c. 4500–4200/4100 B C

The black-on-buff ware development in the two areas continued without a break. Hajji Muhammed designs persisted for a while in both areas, together with such specialized shapes as jars with an internal ledge, and then disappeared. Once nearly the entire vessel had been covered with paint, new methods had to be devised, and a much more sparing use of paint characterizes the Ubaid style. Only the upper part of the vessel is decorated, or in the case of bowls only the interior or exterior, but not both. The

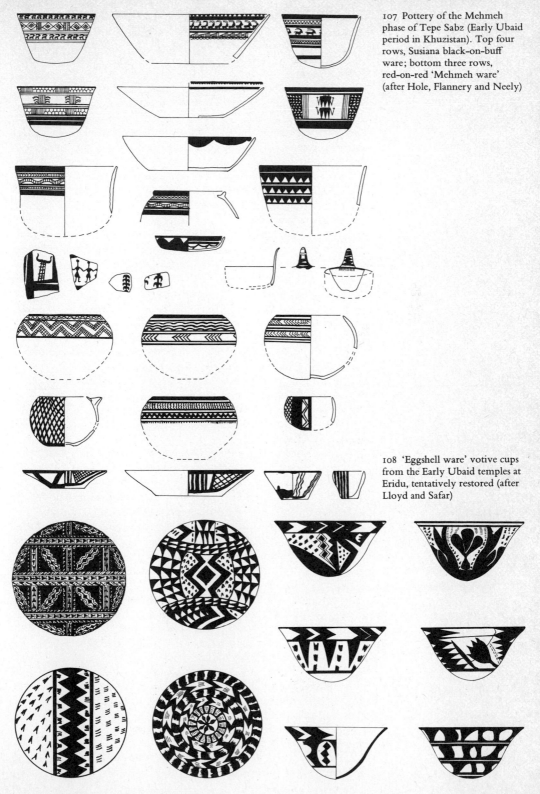

107 Pottery of the Mehmeh phase of Tepe Sabz (Early Ubaid period in Khuzistan). Top four rows, Susiana black-on-buff ware; bottom three rows, red-on-red 'Mehmeh ware' (after Hole, Flannery and Neely)

108 'Eggshell ware' votive cups from the Early Ubaid temples at Eridu, tentatively restored (after Lloyd and Safar)

107

108

designs are simplified, and close style patterns are abandoned. In the Ubaid culture the patterns remain linear, but renewal of contact with the Iranian highlands in Khuzistan leads to the adoption of animal motifs into the Mehmeh pottery.[74] Bell-shaped bowls of extremely fine quality, probably fashioned on a wheel, show rows of wild goats or groups of dancing men. Similar shapes, but with geometric motifs only, appear at Ras el-Amiyah. These fine vessels are matched at Eridu by 'eggshell votive bowls' from the Early Ubaid temples in levels IX–VIII, as richly decorated geometrically as the spouted 'tortoise vases' found filled with fish offerings, which are still decorated in the traditional close style. Some of the patterns on the votive bowls show resemblances to Iranian designs. In the same Eridu temples painted pottery horns, like those of bulls, occur as well as clay nails, of unknown use, which crossed the marshes to reach Tepe Sabz.

Another innovation is the appearance of Mehmeh 'red-on-red ware', which occurs imported in small quantities at both Chogha Mami and Ras el-Amiyah, both easily accessible from Iran. This ware is straw tempered and is decorated in dark red to purplish paint on a soft pale-red slip. Hole-mouth jars with dimple bases are shapes typical of the Iranian plateau. Some of these jars had spouts and there are also wide, shallow bowls and small cups. At the same time as this pottery made its appearance in Khuzistan the red burnished Khazineh plain ware went out of use, thus ending a tradition that had begun in the Muhammed Jafar phase.

Other signs of Iranian influence in the Mehmeh phase can be detected in the appearance of copper (not seen since Alikosh!) in the form of pins with diamond-shaped heads, like those of Siyalk III. Obsidian also reappears after an absence during the Sabz and Khazineh phases.

31f

Architectural remains are confined to houses at Tepe Ashrafabad and Tepe Sabz,[75] and a fine set of temples at Eridu in levels XI, IX and VIII.[164] The Ashrafabad house is rectangular, approximately 5×10 m, and built of mud brick on stone foundations. It had a door with a pivot stone in the middle of the long side and was provided with platforms, storage areas and partitions. The clay floor was covered with twilled-reed or club-rush mats. The earliest temple found at Eridu, that of level XI, stood on a platform approached by a ramp, which was later extended. It was a complicated structure with thin mud-brick walls strengthened by external buttresses. One room contained an offering table. The temple of level IX, of the same type but better preserved, was complete with altar and offering table in a similar position. The best example came from level VIII; it measured over 20 m in length by about 12 m in width. These large buildings show that Eridu at this period was probably no longer a village.

A cemetery of the Late Mehmeh period that continued into use during the following Bayat phase was recently excavated at Hakalan in Luristan.[186] The cemetery, possibly that of nomads who had their summer quarters here on the Kabir Kuh and who wintered in the Deh Luran plain, consists of cist graves, covered with slabs of stone. These served for multiple burials; the earlier occupants were pushed aside without much ceremony, and only their skulls were rearranged. Burial gifts consist of pottery, both the black-on-buff ware and the black-on-red Mehmeh ware, stone perforated battle axes and maceheads as well as button seals.

In the Mehmeh phase the same crops were grown and the same animals herded as in the previous Khazineh phase, but at Ras el-Amiyah the herding of small domestic cattle was of greater importance than that of sheep (and goats?).[185] In both these cultures hunting had become unimportant, though gazelles are more common at Mehmeh than at Ras el-Amiyah and scenes of the hunt as well as animal tracks occasionally appear on Mehmeh pottery. There were no innovations in the Mehmeh tool-kit. The population of northern Khuzistan with nine villages in Deh Luran and about one hundred in Susiana, including towns at Tepe Musyan and Chogha Mish, is thought to be around 12,000, that of southern Mesopotamia remains unknown. The spread of Early Ubaid culture to the north, where it is well attested at Tepe Gawra, does suggest a sizeable population. Typical features of Early Ubaid, apart from the pottery, are the introduction of baked-clay sickles and 'nails' of unknown use. Cast copper objects, lizard-headed figurines, and in the north stone stamp seals with figurative decoration (Tepe Gawra) are not yet a feature of this culture, but they belong to the Late Ubaid phase, dated by several C14 samples to c. 4200 B C.

It is in this period that the Ubaid pottery of the south goes into a sharp decline and grey and red Uruk wares make their first appearance. This transition to a new, vigorous 'Chalcolithic' age starts in Late Ubaid, a period characterized by the establishment of widespread trade contacts with northern Syria for timber, with southern Iran, for copper, and actual seafaring in the Persian Gulf, where Ubaid pottery dated to c. 4207 ± 238 (calibrated to 5057 ±288 B C) was recently found on thirty-two sites in Saudi Arabia in the area opposite Bahrein.[151, 187] Most of these lie in the salt flats of the coast, but some are more than 65 km inland. Some of these are sizeable mounds (200 × 50 m and 7 m high) with remains of reed-impressed plaster, sometimes painted black, and thick layers of oyster shells suggesting not only food but a quest for pearls, the much prized 'fish-eyes' of the Sumerians. Evidence for trade is further supported by the presence of Ubaid pottery on all sites, and Vannic? obsidian on five sites, where it was used side by side with local flint, worked into arrowheads, or triangular tanged and barbed forms, used in hunting and fishing. Local straw-tempered coarse pottery with knobs and plain rims occurs and the use of straw and querns suggests at least a modicum of agriculture. Among small objects were shell beads and pendants, and human knuckle-bones, but no burials are reported. One site yielded painted pottery reminiscent of Hajji Muhammed ware, which if confirmed would suggest contact with southern Mesopotamia.

Ubaid contacts with their southern neighbours, recently disclosed, as well as increased contacts with their northern and eastern neighbours no doubt contributed to the firm and lasting establishment of urban civilization in Mesopotamia, the description of which, being a post-Neolithic development, falls outside the scope of this book.

Chapter Five

The Highland Cultures of Iran

The Central Zagros

In the central Zagros Mountains the sequence of Tepe Guran came to an end *c.* 5600–5500 B C. It is after the end of the earlier group of cultures – some aceramic, others, such as Guran and Sarab, ceramic – that there seems to have been an expansion of the ceramic Neolithic to other parts of Iran: to Azerbaijan (Hajji Firuz culture), to Fars (Tal-i-Jarri B and Tal-i-Mushki), and to northern Iran (Tepe Siyalk culture), the origins of which in each case are still obscure. In the central Zagros area itself, the transition from Guran to Tepe Giyan may be represented at four sites, Bog-i-No in the Khurramabad area[74] and Chia Zargaran, Chia Siyah and Chia Sabz in western Luristan.[198] Excavations have only been carried out at Bog-i-No, but most of the material has not yet been published. Bog-i-No has yielded evidence for domestic emmer and bread-wheat, two- and six-row barley, and for the collection of pistachio and jujube.[74] The cereals were probably grown by dry farming. Goat and sheep herding may be inferred, but is not yet documented. The pottery is painted and resembles that of Tepe Sabz.

The other sites yielded straw-tempered wares in the old Zagros tradition, heavy, unpainted and coarse, as well as two finer fabrics: a pinkish ware painted in fugitive red paint (cf. Muhammed Jafar) and a dark brown on buff, hard-fired and grit-tempered ware, a mixture of old and new as found at Tepe Sabz.[198] At Tepe Siyah there is a hard-fired straw-tempered ware with a yellow slip painted in purple geometric patterns. Meanders suggest Samarra influence, while hatched bands have Sabz affinities. Goats and headless human figures holding hands appear, again familiar from Samarra ware. At these same sites pottery of Giyan V type appears, which seems to indicate that these wares are earlier than Giyan VA. Excavations are clearly needed to elucidate the transition period between Guran and Giyan.

Giyan

A second phase is represented by Giyan VA,[201] which has a distribution covering the greater part of Luristan, but at Kozeragan in Saimerreh, just north of Susiana, Khazineh ware appears. Close contact with Khuzistan is now well established and the fine grit-tempered fabrics of Giyan VA are similar to the black-on-buff ware of Susiana, and although there are similarities in the close style of the Khazineh period, the Luristan shapes and patterns are on the whole different.[75] The evidence does not indicate strong Ubaid influence as some authors have suggested, but the presence of 'superimposed antlers' and 'dancing men' at Giyan VA clearly

109

109 Giyan VA pottery: approximate reconstructions of pots and patterns (after Contenau and Ghirshman)

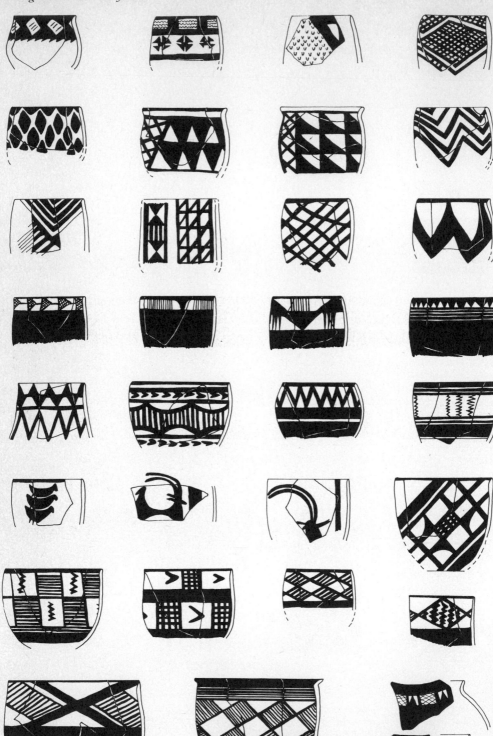

influenced the following Mehmeh style of Khuzistan. If this second phase falls somewhere in the first half of the fifth millennium, the third phase, represented by Giyan VB, is approximately contemporary with Early Ubaid and Mehmeh.[195]

DALMA

At Giyan, the sequence is interrupted and two new types of pottery, painted and impressed ware, of the Dalma culture are introduced.[192, 198] Thick, straw tempered and poorly fired, the painted ware has a maroon-slipped interior and decoration in glossy black paint on a red wash or a cream burnished surface. Bold geometric designs, sometimes with several patterns in metope arrangement, occur on the same vessel. A red-slipped coarse ware may bear impressed patterns, punctuated designs, finger imprints, nail impressions, barbotine, etc.[198] The shapes consist of hole-mouth bowls (as in Giyan VA), deep bowls and shallow bowls, some with knobs and lugs.

111

This Dalma ware, painted, plain and impressed, has a striking distribution in Iran: it extends from Giyan and Seh Gabi, where a deposit 8 m thick was excavated in 1971,[217] and Siyahbid near Kermanshah to the Solduz valley near Hasanlu, where Dalma is situated, and as far as Yaniktepe, which, however, has yielded only a few sherds. To the northeast it does not cross the hills which border the Zenjan valley. Dalma influence, it would appear, reached well beyond Yaniktepe and, if correctly identified, was noted in the Mil steppe at Ilanli, Shahtepe, Kiamiltepe and elsewhere, either in impressed or painted variants.[212] A C14 date for late Dalma of 4036±87 is confirmed by clear Dalma influences on some Late Ubaid pottery from Tepe Gawra XIII,[192] and by the discovery of imported Ubaid-like ware at Dalma itself.[218] Here there were only two building levels. A series of small rectangular rooms were built around a courtyard containing hearths, bins and storage jars. The material was pisé, not mud brick. Intramural burials below the floors comprised adults as well as infants. Among the small objects obsidian tools were rare, most of the blades being of chert. Granite was apparently used. Loom weights and spindle whorls of clay indicate weaving, an activity which may be deduced from the many patterns on pottery that resemble textile designs. Bone awls occur as well as whetstones for sharpening them. This culture evidently did not grow out of the Hajji Firuz culture and it may be as intrusive in Azerbaijan as at Giyan VB. Excavations at Seh Gabi may eventually establish its origins.

120

In later Giyan VB the Dalma elements disappear[201] and the vitrified brown- or black-on-buff ware of the VA tradition developed.[195] Hole-mouth bowls, bowls with slightly flaring sides, and jars with everted rims are typical shapes. The close style disappears and the geometric motifs are varied, but simple: hatched diamonds, Ubaid-like rows of triangles, chevrons and loops. The first representation of a goat appears, an Iranian innovation seen also in the Mehmeh pottery. Red-on-red Mehmeh ware, another Iranian product, does not apparently occur at Giyan, where the later VB ware is more closely related to the Siyalk II wares of the Tehran-Qazvin plain, its northeastern neighbour.

110 Giyan VB: approximate reconstructions of pots and patterns (after Contenau and Ghirshman)

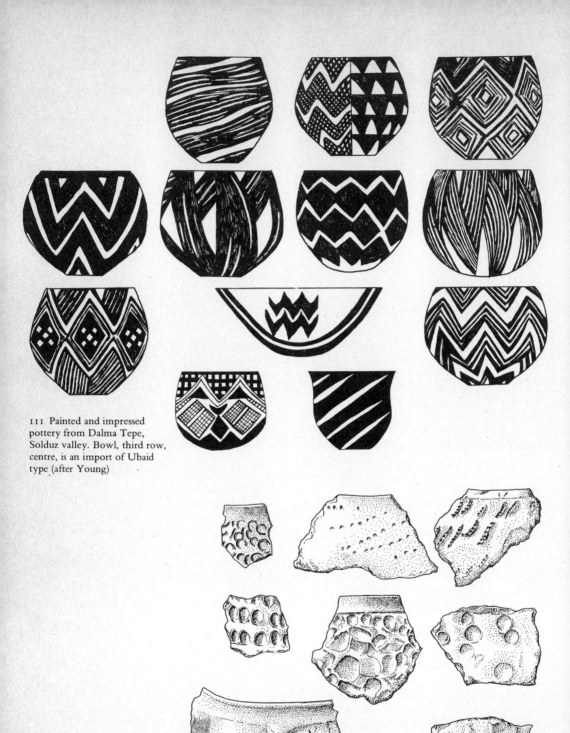

111 Painted and impressed pottery from Dalma Tepe, Solduz valley. Bowl, third row, centre, is an import of Ubaid type (after Young)

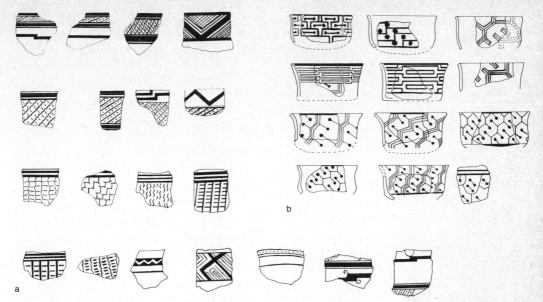

a

b

112 Tal-i-Jarri B (a) and Tal-i-Mushki pottery (b) from the plain of Persepolis in southern Iran (after van den Berghe)

In the fourth phase, the Late Ubaid period is reached with Giyan VC; the pottery degenerates and as geometric ornament becomes simpler and repetitive, more goat motifs are introduced. This phase of development can now be studied at Seh Gabi, where architectural remains of a village with rectangular houses, etc. is in the process of excavation. At Giyan itself only the pottery was recorded.

Fars

Soft ware is reported from a number of sites in the Kazerun valley west of Shiraz on the road to Khuzistan, but no details are yet available. Northeast of Shiraz in the Merv Dasht plain of Persepolis, two successive painted-pottery cultures were discovered, of which Tal-i-Jarri B is the earlier, and Tal-i-Mushki the later.[200] In the absence of radiocarbon dates, these cultures have been variously dated, but I believe that the former may be of the same period as Sabz and the latter of the period of Khazineh, Giyan VA and Siyalk II. The stratigraphical evidence shows that both cultures preceded the Tal-i-Bakun culture (B2), the later phase of which (A1–4) is clearly of Ubaid date and technically linked to the black-on-buff ware of Khuzistan. No buildings are reported from these two cultures, suggesting perhaps that they were confined to lightly built structures. Only a limited amount of the pottery has been published. The Tal-i-Jarri B pottery is a *112* thick, coarse ware with straw or sand temper, yellowish grey in colour and painted in black or dark brown. The paint is fugitive and has a tendency to flake off. Bowls and dishes with flaring sides and flat or dimple bases are the main shapes; some of these are faintly reminiscent of Siyalk I. The patterns are geometric and suggest basketry. This pottery is fairly widespread in the Persepolis plain.

The Tal-i-Mushki pottery, which at Tal-i-Jarri B overlaps with the earlier pottery, is better fired, red-brown or deep red with a red polished slip. It is decorated with black paint, a black-on-buff version being less common. The shapes are almost confined to small bowls, not unlike some Khazineh-Hajji Muhammed vessels, a resemblance that is probably fortuitous. The decoration is ingenious and unique as illustration 112 shows.

Until more detailed reports on these early culture become available the early cultural development of Fars cannot be understood.

Kerman

C14 dating indicates that the Bakun, Iblis and Tepe Yahya cultures begin in the Early Ubaid period. At Iblis the earliest pottery (level O) is a coarse-tempered, red burnished ware, quite different from the earliest pottery of Fars, and once again we find storage jars with undercut profiles, perhaps connected with the use of basket moulds.[206] The Tepe Yahya VIC–E pottery falls into the same early class[207] and so does that of Bakun BII, which is still unpublished. Painting does not occur until a little later, in Iblis I, Yahya VIB and Bakun A1–4, which come at the end of a long soft-ware tradition. Dark maroon, black or fugitive red paint are used on a buff ground. In Iblis I, painted pottery accounts for only 5 per cent.

113

Tepe Yahya VIE shows part of a village with mud-brick architecture consisting of four rows of rectangular rooms with abutting party walls on either side of a narrow entrance into the village. The rooms had no doorways and were entered from the roof. A parapet (?) or low wall surrounded the settlement. This village was rebuilt many times and in level VC a different type of architecture with large multi-roomed houses appears; these are thin-walled and single-storeyed but have normal doorways. They are carefully plastered and hearths are set in the corner of one of the rooms. Similar houses are typical of Iblis I and each of the houses there contained a group of storerooms in the centre, surrounded by several living-rooms with red plaster floors, a feature of great antiquity which only on the Iranian plateau had managed to survive into the fifth millennium. This sort of elaborate architecture must have had ancestors, perhaps in Fars, about which nothing is known. Infant burials were found in Tepe Yahya VC below floors, and at Iblis I the earliest crucibles for copper-smelting appear. Copper pins and turquoise necklaces – the nearest source of the latter is Maden near Nishapur in northeast Iran – also occur in Tepe Yahya VC, before 4000 BC, and indicate that trade routes crossed the central Iranian desert. Clay figurines of aurochs were found at Iblis I, and at Tepe Yahya VID a large steatite female figure was found together with three bone tools, sixty-three flints and three grooved whetstones, suggesting offerings in a village shrine. Iblis I provides some economic details. Domestic dog, goat and possibly sheep and cattle were kept by the villagers, whereas aurochs, gazelle, onager and horse were hunted. Bones of turtle, lion and Griffon vultures have also been found. In this area, at present semi-desert and 7000 feet above sea-level, domestic bread-wheat and probably emmer were found as imprints on the level O coarse ware, showing that the economy of the village was mixed farming; this was combined with the extraction of several

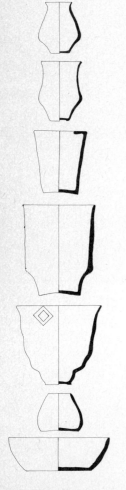

113 Lalehzar coarse ware from Tal-i-Iblis O, Kerman area (after Caldwell)

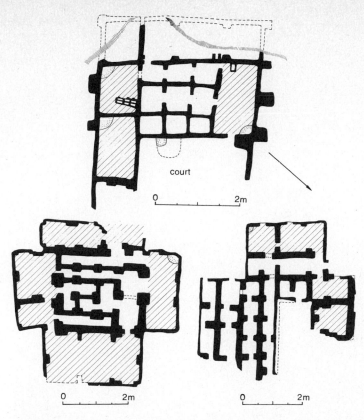

114 House plans from Tal-i-Iblis
I. Hatched areas = red plaster
floors (after Caldwell)

court

0   2m

0   2m   0   2m

raw materials, copper and steatite, which soon were to supply the
markets of the expanding civilizations in Khuzistan and southern
Mesopotamia.

The Siyalk Culture

The Siyalk culture occupies the triangle Qazvin-Tehran-Kashan
on the north Iranian plateau and is bordered by the Elborz Mountains to the north, the eastern foot-hills of the Zagros near Kashan
and the central Iranian desert, the Dasht-i-Kavir to the east. To
the west lies the Hamadan steppe with the Giyan and Dalma cultures, but the narrow corridor between Qazvin and Tabriz was
apparently unattractive to early settlers.

Siyalk is a large mound some 6 km south of Kashan.[202] It
measures 320×110 m is $11 \cdot 8$ m high and contained eight building
levels, five of the Siyalk I, three of the later Siyalk II period. Siyalk
III occupation shifted to another mound south of the earlier one
at a date comparable with the Early Ubaid period.

Siyalk I has five strata, of which the earliest, level I,1, consisted
of layers of ashes and remains of light structures made of reeds,
branches and mud, no plans of which were recovered. The next
four levels, I,2–I,5, had mud floors and pisé walls, but once again
as at Giyan nothing is said about plans. Throughout Siyalk I the
dead were buried below the floors and the skeletons lay in a
contracted position on their side, with the hands placed on the
abdomen, or with one or both hands before the face. The orienta-

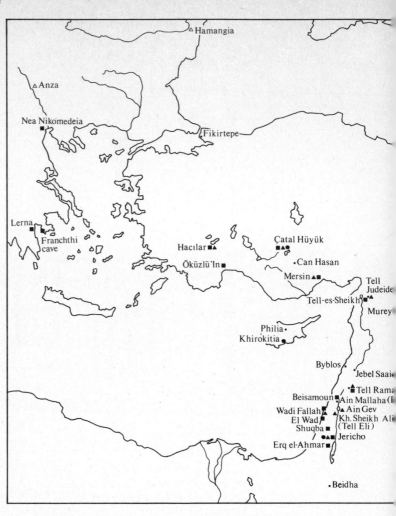

tion was often from east to west and all skeletons were covered with red ochre. Infants were buried in the earth or in small jars. Funeral gifts are absent, except for one instance where a burial was provided with a stone axe placed between the hands and two jaws of sheep deposited opposite the head.

The population of Siyalk I shows two racial strains: Eurafrican and Proto-Mediterranean. Tooth decay occurred as the result of an excess of cereal in the diet. In level I,2 two-row hulled barley was found as well as evidence for domestic goats. Hoes and sickles occur already in the lowest deposit, suggesting that agriculture was practised right from the beginning, at a date that may tentatively be put at *c.* 5500 B C. Gazelle, wild sheep and cattle were hunted with sling and mace, but there were no microliths, arrowheads or spearheads. Axes and hoes were made of grey rock, whereas knife blades, sickle blades, scrapers, piercers for skin-working, polishers and querns were made of flint. Only one piece of obsidian was found; its source is unknown, but must lie far to the northwest. The handles of reaping knives, one of which was carved in the form of a human figure (level I,1), were made of bone or of a blue-

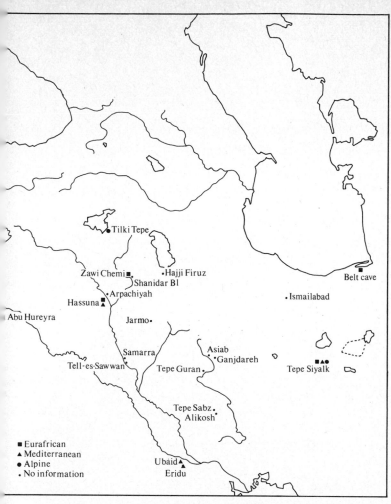

Tilki Tepe

Zawi Chemi
Hajji Firuz
Shanidar B1
Belt cave
Arpachiyah
Hassuna
Ismailabad
Abu Hureyra
Jarmo
Samarra
Asiab
Ganjdareh
Tell-es-Sawwan
Tepe Guran
Tepe Siyalk
Tepe Sabz
Alikosh

■ Eurafrican
▲ Mediterranean
● Alpine
. No information

Ubaid
Eridu

115 Map showing distribution of early racial types in the Near East

grey stone decorated with incised patterns. Ovoid maceheads of white marble, occasionally carved with double chevrons (level I,2), were obviously ceremonial weapons and are frequently coated with red ochre. Stone vessels are rare. Personal ornament consisted of bracelets of grey sandstone or black volcanic rock, rings of local gypsum (alabaster) and beads of white limestone and marble. Small cosmetic mortars and pestles are made in pottery or grey or blue stone.

From Siyalk I,3 come the first copper artifacts, a hammered awl with a round section and another with a flattened bulbous top. Pins and needles with biconical heads occur in level I,4 and another such pin and a spiral were found in level I,5. The copper is thought to come from the Talmessi mine at Anarak, 225 km southeast of Kashan in the central desert, where native copper occurs in abundance.[197]

142a

These early Siyalk people made straw-tempered pottery: a coarse plain ware, very thick and crumbly, a monochrome red ware, often with dimple bases, a very rare monochrome black variant and two painted wares. Of these the earliest, beginning in

116

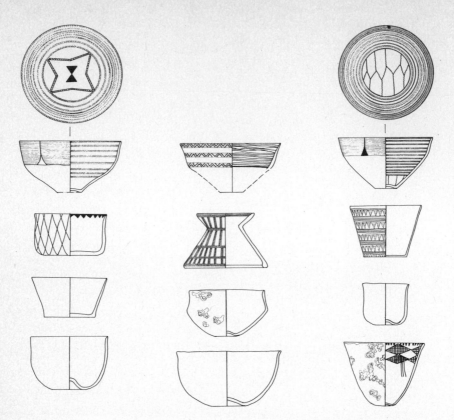

116 Siyalk I pottery (after Ghirshman)

level I,1, is black-on-buff ware, and this remains the more common, but from level I,2 onwards black-on-red ware also appears.

Many of the large deep bowls of the black-on-buff ware look remarkably like copies of coiled baskets (cf. Tal-i-Jarri B). All patterns are simple and geometric and there are good parallels with the Anau IA culture of southwest Turkmenistan, which is thought to be somewhat later in date and may have been founded by Siyalk I elements. The red monochrome bowls with dimple bases are reminiscent of the last layers at Tepe Guran, but, as we have seen, these are characteristic also of Muhammed Jafar and the later offshoots of the soft-ware Zagros tradition.

The origins of the Siyalk culture are still unknown, but the new excavations at Zaghe and Tepe Sagzabad, 64 km south of Qazvin, have now revealed an earlier pottery and even an aceramic layer, as well as red-ochre burials, which may be ancestral to this important culture.[205] A single pre-Siyalk C14 date of 5179 (TUNC 12) BC would seem to be too low.[203] Further details are found on page 194. The presence of earlier cultures in the area is further suggested by copper and turquoise beads in the aceramic Alikosh phase, c. 6500–6000 BC,[75] of turquoise in the following Muhammed Jafar phase, and of copper and turquoise beads in Tell es-Sawwan I. The turquoise points to northeast Iran, the copper could come from the same area or from Anarak. Whatever its origin, the routes by which these materials reached the lowlands must have passed through the area later occupied by the Siyalk culture.

Siyalk II, tentatively dated to the first half of the fifth millennium, is a development of Siyalk I and is represented by three building levels (II,1–3).[202] The houses consisted of rectangular structures of pisé walls on mud-brick foundations. Finger imprints on top of the mud brick helped to make the mortar adhere more firmly, a method used from PPNB Jericho to Eridu 15 and Tepe Yahya. The walls were plastered and painted red, but no complete house plans have been published. Red-ochre burials continue to be placed below house floors, unaccompanied by funeral gifts. A new brachycephalic Alpine strain now occurs side by side with the previous Eurafrican and Proto-Mediterranean types, and there is a marked increase in dental decay. Agricultural data are scarce, but domestic dog and possibly pig occur – and presumably the goats of Siyalk I continued to be herded – while gazelle and wild sheep were hunted as before with mace and sling. There is evidence for weaving and basketry and there is more copper than before, in the form of hammered needles, awls, pins, etc., which show no great technological progress. Incised stone bracelets of the type known from Tepe Sabz are now made, and beads of carnelian and turquoise show contact with the Nishapur-Meshed area whereas *Pteroceras* shells came all the way from the Persian Gulf.

The Siyalk II pottery is technologically more advanced than that of the previous period; the firing improved gradually and though black cores continued, the pottery may have been fired in kilns. Black-on-red painted ware predominates and as it is rather

117

117 Siyalk II pottery: complete vessels (after Ghirshman)

porous the paint is slightly blurred, which creates a not unpleasant charcoal effect. Plain red ware, used for smaller vessels, is now rare. The decoration of Siyalk II ware has become much more sophisticated, and includes numerous animal motifs, both naturalistic and stylized. There are flying birds (storks?), salt-loving wading birds (flamingoes?), wild boar, goats and onagers, gazelle, dogs and fish. Even human figures occur, but there is a marked absence of cattle. Egg-and-dot patterns, wavy lines and Dalma-like finger-nail patterns also occur, as well as common textile patterns such as hatched checkerboards, lozenges, etc.

118

Some of the finest pottery of this period comes not from Siyalk itself, but from Ismailabad, Karatepe and Cheshme Ali in the Qazvin-Tehran area.[204] Many of these vessels show more variety in shape and design and greater naturalism than the Siyalk pottery. The explanation might be that this material is a little later than the abandonment of Siyalk II, and falls in a gap between Siyalk II and III, or it could equally well represent a more lively northern variant. Some of the Siyalk II pottery shows links with the Dalma ware, with Giyan VB, and with the red-on-red Mehmeh ware, but the animal style, so characteristic of Siyalk II, is absent or rare in these cultures. Many of the more interesting shapes, such as basket-handled jars, pedestalled bowls and goblets, conical beakers and huge painted storage vessels have no counterparts in these cultures. Siyalk II pottery spread eastward towards the Caspian and has been recognized in Hotu cave.[231-2] It likewise influenced the culture sequence in southwest Turkmenistan, where Anau IA shows Siyalk II elements in the pottery.[225]

119

118 Siyalk II pottery: reconstructions from sherds (after Ghirshman)

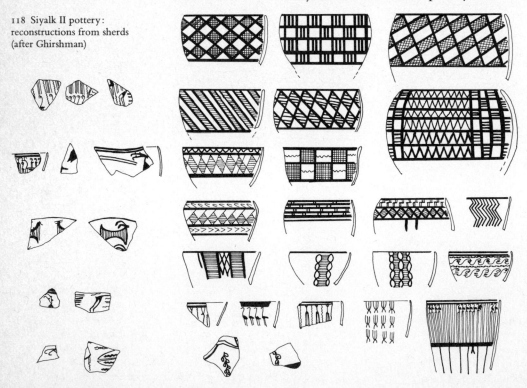

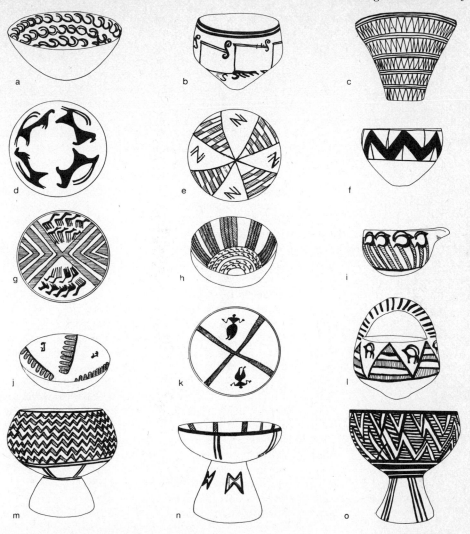

119 Ismailabad ware (Siyalk II period) from the Tehran area: (a–c) from Cheshme Ali; (d–f, h, j) from Karatepe; (g, i, k–n) from Ismailabad; (o) from Save (after Maleki)

The Siyalk III culture, which may have begun *c.* 4500 B C, shows new cultural elements and is found on a new site, the southern mound of Siyalk.[202] Mud-brick architecture with complex plans and multi-roomed structures, and new hard kiln-fired black-on-buff pottery with flower vases, goblets and pedestalled jars appears, while intramural red-ochre burials cease. The period is a long one and its first phases, III,1–3, roughly equal that of Early Ubaid, Mehmeh in Khuzistan, Dalma in northwest Iran. Somewhat later in the period, in levels III,4–5, there are further innovations: the casting of copper into moulds, the first wheel-made pottery, and the use of stamp seals with geometric motifs. These features were to percolate into southern and northern Mesopotamia in the Late Ubaid period, the beginning of our 'Chalcolithic', and not, as has so often been assumed, the other way round.[192] A C14 date of 4133 ± 84 B C shows that Siyalk III,4–5 is contemporary with Late Ubaid (Warka 4120 ± 160 B C), with the Bayat phase of Khuzistan (Susa A), the equivalent of Late Ubaid (4110 ± 200 and 4220 ± 200), and the end of Ras Shamra IIIC (IIIB = Late Ubaid period) with a comparable date of 4184±173 BC. This disproves the suggestion that Siyalk III, 4–5 was contemporary with the Uruk period of Mesopotamia. These same technological advances that ushered in a new development of the Chalcolithic period also made themselves felt farther east, at Hisar IB near Damghan, part of the Siyalk III culture area, and beyond in southwest Turkmenistan where they appear in the Late Namazga II and Geoksyur periods.[225]

The presence of a Bactrian camel on Siyalk III pottery may show the method of transportation used by the inhabitants. With these developments we have reached the end of the Neolithic period in the region.

Excavations now in progress on the Iranian plateau have revealed seventh-millennium remains at Tepe Zaghe south of Kazvin and at Tepe Sang-i-Chakmak near Shahrud. At Zaghe the top layer has Cheshme Ali (Siyalk I–II) ware and levels 2–4 have new archaic painted ware and the use of fugitive paint. Levels 5–17 are aceramic. Small rectangular houses and a number of workshops were found indicating industrial activity. They are built of pisé or mud brick and have plastered platforms and red panels. Extended intramural burials occur, laid on a bed of red ochre. A C14 date of 6269±150 has been obtained.

There are two mounds at Sang-i-Chakmak. The earlier, western tepe has five building levels, with a C14 date of 5850 BC for level 2. Characteristic are well-built rectangular houses with floors of beaten earth or lime plaster, frequently stained red. Raised platforms for sleeping or work, and raised hearths, ovens and benches are other features. Not all houses have a hearth or oven. The architecture is reminiscent of Umm Dabaghiyah and Çatal Hüyük with its built-in furniture, but entry is at floor level. Pottery is virtually unknown. Clay female figurines were found. The flint industry has blades, awls and cores. Some imported obsidian was found but there are no microliths.

The eastern tepe has six building levels. In the uppermost level four adult female and three infant burials were discovered, associated with Siyalk II pottery. Levels 2–3 are poorly preserved but yielded unpainted and coarse wares and husking trays, unknown in the earlier levels, as well as animal figurines. Levels 4–6 clearly belong to the early (and middle?) phases of the Jeitun culture, having the same painted pottery, stone industry with microliths, small objects and bone sickles. New is the fine naturalistic carving of fox, wild cat and lizard figures on the end of sickle hafts. Brick houses have open courtyards with kilns and oblong rooms divided by cross walls into several chambers, differing from the standard square plan of the Jeitun culture. Walls are painted black or red. The excavations at this site show that the Jeitun culture is probably the eastern equivalent of Siyalk I, and is now also represented on the Iranian plateau.

Chapter Six

Early Cultures in Transcaucasia and Azerbaijan

The greater part of eastern Turkey, Transcaucasia and Iranian Azerbaijan consists of high mountain plateaux, covered with recent lava flows, rugged mountains and a number of large and small lakes, only one of which, Lake Sevan, contains fresh water. Lake Van, central to a group of volcanoes with obsidian, contains washing soda; Lake Urmia (Rezayieh) has evil-smelling salt and black mud. A number of rivers are tributaries of the Euphrates, others join the large rivers Kur and Araxes that run down to the Caspian sea through the lowland area of Shirvan, now called the Mil and Moghan steppes. Areas favourable for early settlement are restricted to river valleys, and as usual the settlers tend to avoid the mountains, once heavily forested and inhabited by wild animals hostile to man. The greatest enemy of man in these high regions is the climate, hot and dry in the short summer but bitterly cold during the very long winters, when deep snow covers the land from the Caucasus to the Taurus.

120

TRANSCAUCASIA

In the more favoured spots, such as the southern slopes of the Caucasus in Colchis, the Baku region or the middle Araxes valley – the Ararat plain – there is abundant evidence for Palaeolithic occupation, some of it going back to its early stages. Around Mt Alagöz (Aragats) a volcano that guards the middle Araxes with its nearby twin, Mt Ararat, obsidian was the usual raw material for tools since the Lower Palaeolithic.[220] There evidently is also much Upper Palaeolithic and Epipalaeolithic material in this area, as elsewhere in Transcaucasia, but its stratigraphy and possible links with the Zarzian or Baradostian are not yet clear. Some of the local microlithic industries seem to include familar types, and it should be remembered that Vannic obsidian trickled through the mountains south to Shanidar and Zarzi at these periods. Equally important perhaps is the existence of a tradition of rock engraving which stretches from the Kars region in Turkey, through Soviet Armenia to the rocks of Kobystan on the Baku peninsula.[220-22]

Kobystan

Here there are thousands of engravings on the rocks, dating from many periods; these A. A. Formozov has divided into four groups, the last two of which are Bronze Age and Medieval.[221] The earliest occur on the upper terrace of the limestone rocks of Beyuk Dash, some 60 km west of Baku and about 5–10 km from the Caspian shore. Some of the rocks form natural shelters of which the largest (rocks 29–31), close to a spring, has a back wall measuring 7×3 m.

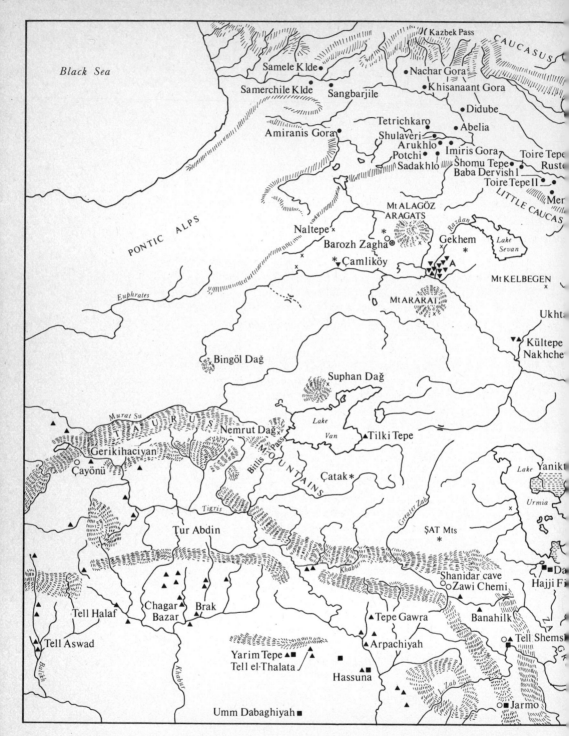

Black Sea

Kazbek Pass

CAUCASUS

Samele K Ide
Nachar Gora
Samerchile K Ide
Sangbarjile
Khisanaant Gora
Didube
Tetrichkaro
Abelia
Amiranis Gora
Shulaveri
Arukhlo
Imiris Gora
Toire Tepe
Potchi
Shomu Tepe
Ruste
Sadakhlo
Baba Dervish 1
Toire Tepe II
Mer

LITTLE CAUCAS

PONTIC ALPS

Mt ALAGÖZ
ARAGATS

Naltepe

Razdan

Lake
Sevan

Barozh Zagha
Gekhem

Çamliköy

Mt KELBEGEN

Euphrates

Mt ARARAT

Ukht

Kültepe
Nakhche

Bingöl Dağ

Suphan Dağ

Murat Su

T A U R U S

Lake
Van

Tilki Tepe

Yanik

Nemrut Dağ

Urmia

Gerikihaciyan

Bitlis Pass

M O U N T A I N S

Çayönü

Çatak

Tigris

Greater Zab

ŞAT Mts

Tur Abdin

Khabur

Shanidar cave
Da
Zawi Chemi
Hajji F

Chagar
Bazar
Brak

Tell Halaf

Tepe Gawra
Banahilk

Tell Aswad

Balikh

Arpachiyah
Tell Shems

Khabur

Yarim Tepe
Tell el-Thalata

Hassuna

L Zab

Jarmo

Umm Dabaghiyah

Hollowed out of its surface are some of the earliest representations of human figures – tall males 0·8–1·5 m in height, wearing loin-cloths and armed with bows and quivers, possibly engaged in a ritual hunters' dance. To the right of the scene, balancing the composition, are smaller female figures drawn in profile, as opposed to

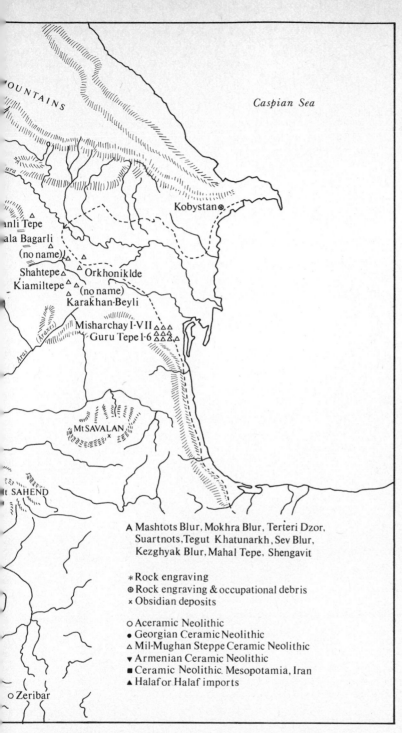

Caspian Sea

MOUNTAINS

Kobystan ⊕

...anli Tepe
...ala Bagarli
(no name)
Shahtepe △ △ Orkhoniklde
Kiamiltepe △ △ (no name)
Karakhan-Beyli

Misharchay I-VII △△△
Guru Tepe 1-6 △△△△

(Kura)
(Araxes)
Aras

Mt SAVALAN ×

Mt SAHEND

▲ Mashtots Blur, Mokhra Blur, Terteri Dzor,
   Suartnots, Tegut Khatunarkh, Sev Blur,
   Kezghyak Blur, Mahal Tepe, Shengavit

∗ Rock engraving
⊕ Rock engraving & occupational debris
× Obsidian deposits

○ Aceramic Neolithic
● Georgian Ceramic Neolithic
△ Mil-Mughan Steppe Ceramic Neolithic
▼ Armenian Ceramic Neolithic
■ Ceramic Neolithic, Mesopotamia, Iran
▲ Halaf or Halaf imports

○ Zeribar

120 Map of Transcaucasia,
northwest Iran and eastern
Turkey

the men who are shown full-face. Human figures of this type
occur on numerous other rocks on the same terrace, for example
on rock 39, where a row of them accompanied by smaller figures
are shown holding hands in a round dance, or again on the outer
wall of rock 29 and on rock 27.

121 Rock engravings from the upper terrace at Beyuk Dash, Kobystan: (a–c) engravings in the first style with hollowed-out human figures and deeply engraved superimposed animals; (d, f) second style with smaller animals and more schematic lively figures. The pictures of boats are later Bronze Age additions. (a) back wall of sanctuary 5, rock 29; (b) outer wall of sanctuary 5, rock 29; (c) rock 39; (d) sanctuary 5, rock 31; (e) rock 45; (f) rock 72 (after Formozov)

122 Rock engravings from Beyuk Dash, style 2: (a) sanctuary 3, rock 45, with a wild ass hunt; (b) rock 42, with aurochs and superimposed goats; (c) rock 9 of the lower terrace, with men holding hands and driving cattle into a net; (d) sanctuary 3, rock 46, with two figures of the first style above a later dancing and battle scene (after Formozov)

These human figures are in all instances the earliest, but they are frequently covered by deeply engraved figures of bulls, drawn in characteristic Mediterranean Late Palaeolithic style (cf. Levanzo), some of which are again very large, varying from 80 to 100 cm to a full 2 m, on the back wall of rock 29. Figures of bulls are common *121* but their treatment varies from naturalistic to 'cubist' and more schematized representations, for which again there are good Italian parallels. Associated with this second style are smaller human figures, schematically rendered in profile, but often very lively. In a small shelter into which one could enter on all fours, one rock (45) shows bulls being attacked by men with bows and arrows, *122* the other (46) lively scenes of small figures, dancing and fighting, below two hollowed-out figures in the earlier style. Engraved on another side of rock 45 are a row of horses or wild asses (*kulan*), wild boar followed by a dog, a hunting scene with a net, human figures and asses, reminiscent of the wall paintings in a shrine of Çatal Hüyük V, *c*. 5650 B C.

In this smaller sanctuary deposits of archaeological material – the remains of visits but not settlement occupation, for which there was no space – covered the lower part of the engravings. There were a number of stone and shell amulets, some very coarse pottery and lumps of red ochre, suggesting that these engravings may once have been painted. The flints, comprising thin, well facetted blades, Gravettian-type blades with a blunted edge, pointed tools, implements with dented edges, end-scrapers, trapezes and a few gravers and segments, are dated in the Caucasus to the Late Mesolithic and the Neolithic. Formozov concludes that the deposits and the engravings of the second style are Early

a

b

c

123 Rock engravings from Naltepe on Mt Aragats in Soviet Armenia: (a) bowman and goat, ostrich, deer and dogs; (b) archer and deer; (c) large scene with cattle, deer and wild goats, dog and several human figures. Aceramic to ceramic Neolithic period (after Sardarian)

Neolithic, possibly even Late Mesolithic, and he attributes the first style to the Early Mesolithic at the latest.

These conclusions seem wholly acceptable, if we substitute the terms used in this book: Late Epipalaeolithic (Zarzian and Natufian farther south) for Early Mesolithic; aceramic Neolithic for Late Mesolithic, leaving ceramic Neolithic, from the mid-sixth millennium onwards, unchanged.

Art traditions are notoriously difficult to confine within chronological limits and though cave and rock engravings and paintings are traditionally linked with hunting economies, Çatal Hüyük, Umm Dabaghiyah and North Africa show that they can and do last into the Neolithic, linked to hunting, domestication and pastoralism. As Transcaucasia seems to have entered the Neolithic age at a fairly late stage, in the sixth millennium, one must reckon with the survival of this type of art in that region until perhaps as late as 5000 B C, if not later. It may be possible to define the various stages of this essentially Late Palaeolithic art through a series of comparisons. At Palanlı cave near Adiyaman the very last pictures of animals are roughly pecked into the walls of the cave and they resemble similar representations of animals on Early to Middle Halaf pottery (found on several sites near by).[98] If this link is valid, those last figures could be as late as *c.* 5000 B C in this area. As the same style is found in the petroglyphs of Çatak, south of Lake Van and in the Şat Mountains of Hakkiari, on the obsidian trade route still used during the Halaf period, they could be of roughly the same age. This would suggest that the representations of goats in 'cubist'
99 style typical of the earlier Palanlı engravings are earlier than 5000 B C, though it would be hard to say by how much. The same 'cubist' treatment also appears among some of the Kobystan engravings of the second style, suggesting a rough synchronism, but other more naturalistic scenes are comparable to Çatal Hüyük V, dated to *c.* 5650 B C. Both lines of argument lead to sixth-millennium dates, and the Early Halaf representations of animals are on the whole very naturalistic, again suggesting that 5500 B C is a minimum date for the second Kobystan style.

The pre-Halaf animal figures from Umm Dabaghiyah in the first half of the sixth millennium, applied to pottery, show rather rigid stylization with occasional faulty attempts at perspective, and human figures also occur on pots, but they are too fragmentary to compare with the rock engravings. The small-scale figures of
123 the second Kobystan style and those of the Armenian rock carvings[220] could certainly come down to the sixth millennium, but it will be hard to establish when this second style begins. The presence of the dog in some pictures might suggest the Neolithic, but we have no certain evidence that it was not domesticated before this. Domestic dog is now reported in the Zarzian.[92a] In the absence of analysed bone material, such arguments tend to be of a somewhat inconclusive nature. More important in establishing the date of the first style at Kobystan is the Upper Palaeolithic character of the rendering of the bulls at Kobystan (cf. Levanzo), the female figures (cf. Mezine, Peterfels, Antalya) and the tails shown on some of the men's loin-cloths (cf. Kostienki I, Gagarino, Lespugue figurines, but also at Çatal Hüyük, Sakçagözü and

dynastic Egyptian kings!). The presence of human figures, which here are the dominant element, would suggest a fairly late Palaeolithic date in Europe, but European canons are not necessarily binding for the Near East.

Late Palaeolithic art in Italy, for example at Levanzo and Addaura where it probably approaches the beginnings of the Holocene, is variously dated between 8500 and 8000 BC. In Near Eastern terms that is the end date of the Natufian, which falls between 10000 and 8500–8000 BC. The engravings and *art mobilier* from the Antalya region have not been properly dated, but one would agree with E. Anati that they are likely to fall in roughly this period and not earlier.[98] Although comparisons over vast areas are hard to establish, one would be inclined to put the Antalya material and the Natufian *art mobilier* a little earlier than the large human figures of the first style of Kobystan, for the former are still closer to the Magdalenian tradition. We may not be far wrong if we put the Antalya group in the Natufian period at the end of the Pleistocene, and the first style of Kobystan, perhaps closely followed by the large bulls of the beginning of the second style (as on rock 29), early in the Holocene, i.e. at *c.* 8000 BC – a period at which even on the remote shores of the Caspian Sea man starts to dominate nature in his art.

Not enough is known about the cultures that produced this Early Holocene art in Transcaucasia for us to say whether any attempts were being made at herding or domestication; but it is clear from Kobystan, where at one site 50 per cent of the bones belonged to wild ass, that hunting was probably the main source of food there.[222] The area with its precipitous rocks was a natural hunting ground until the last century.

Aceramic and Ceramic Neolithic

An aceramic culture is also reported from Soviet Armenia;[220] it is in evidence at a number of cave sites, at an obsidian workshop and on several open-air sites of which Barozh and Zaghe on the slopes of Mt Aragats are the most important. Stratified sequences suggest a local development from a hunting and gathering culture to an agricultural one. Wild wheat and barley, native to the area, were collected and wild animals – deer, aurochs, goats and sheep (?) – were hunted. The presence of stone-walled structures suggests a certain permanence, perhaps of seasonal encampments. Microliths, as well as larger obsidian tools, arrowheads, borers and scrapers were found, but the ground-stone industry does not appear until the upper levels, when the animal bones suggest domestication. These developments took place in a hilly environment with barren lava flows, much fine black obsidian of Kars-Erevan (1e–f) type,[83–5] and pine forests in the valleys.

With the development of agriculture settlements move into the fertile alluvial Ararat plain, which contains some of the best land in all Transcaucasia. Small villages of round and sometimes rectangular houses are founded, pottery is invented or introduced and we find the by now familiar items such as bone sickles with denticulated sickle blades, small querns and mortars and storage

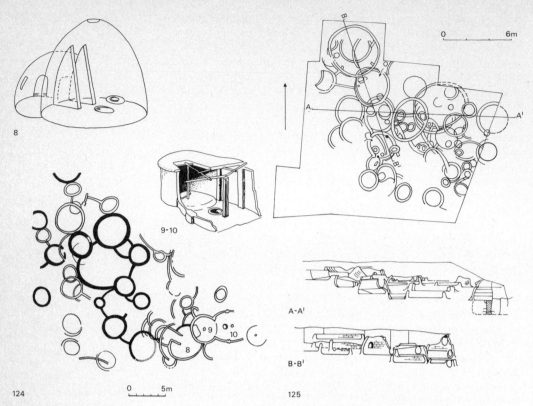

9-10

124

125

0   5m

0   6m

A   A¹

A-A¹

B-B¹

124 Shulaveri culture: plan of
the settlement at Imiris Gora and
reconstruction of double tholos
house 8 and flat-roofed house
9–10 (after Dzhaparidze and
Dzhavachnishvili)

125 Neolithic houses and section
at Shulaveri (after Dzhaparidze
and Dzhavachnishvili)

pits. There are antler hoes and polished axes of local basalt and
greenstone. Microliths now disappear and the new obsidian
industry is dominated by large blades and flakes, and arrowheads.
Wheat and barley grains (no specification) have been recovered;
sheep, goat, cattle and dog are said to be domestic. A great number
of rock engravings, some fairly naturalistic, others more schematized, show hunting or herding scenes of deer, goats and cattle by
humans accompanied by dogs; and, therefore, presumably mainly
of Neolithic date.

The beginning of the ceramic Neolithic in the Araxes valley
probably dates to the sixth millennium, perhaps as early as 6000
B C, more likely around the middle of the millennium as at Shomu
Tepe in the Kur valley to the north. The better known Shulaveri
Neolithic, south of Tiflis, has fifth-millennium dates (4660± 210
and 3955± 300 B C) and may represent a somewhat later stage.[209]
At the eastern end of Transcaucasia, in the Mil steppe west of the
Caspian, a number of sites show links with the Dalma culture of the
Urmia region to the south, which is dated by C14 to the second
half of the fifth millennium.

The entire Transcaucasian Neolithic complex, of which some
fifty sites are known, may have lasted for a few millennia.[212–13]
Possibly this accounts for the lack of homogeneity in the pottery
which tends to exhibit not only regional but also chronological
differences over a period from the sixth to the fourth millennium.

Transcaucasian houses are round or oval, and built of mud brick
on stone foundations. The size of the mud brick varies from place

to place; pisé is not used. A diameter of about 3 m is most common (Shomu Tepe, Tegut, Shulaveri, Imiris Gora) but some are as large as 4·5 m. In the Erevan area diameters of 8–9 m have been reported, and there are rectangular structures of up to 10 × 13 m. Each round house contains a hearth, a feature absolutely essential in this cold climate, and several houses have annexes or outhouses, either curvilinear or rectangular in plan, not unlike the Middle Halaf 'keyhole' plan. When one domed structure is built against the other, internal buttresses take the thrust. Many of these houses are partly subterranean and entered by a few steps, as in the Natufian tradition of the Levant. Developing late in the sequence we find double-roomed houses with buttressed walls and wooden posts to support heavy flat roofs (Imiris Gora house 9–10). These foreshadow the Transcaucasian house plans of the Early Bronze Age.   *124*

The number of building levels varies; in the Ararat plain Mashtots I, Keghyak I, Terteri Dzor and Shengavit I have only few,[220] but in the Tiflis area Shulaveri and Imiris Gora are proper mounds, 4–6 m high, with five and six superimposed building levels respectively. Shulaveri, measuring some 100 × 80 m, is   *125* thought to have had a population of 400–500 people, assuming a family of five to eight persons per house.[209] Imiris Gora, 89 m in diameter, may have housed 200–250 people. Arukhlo, 100 × 150 m, was larger than either.

Local materials were exploited for the manufacture of tools and weapons. At Shomu Tepe in the Kur valley fine black obsidian came from Mt Kelbegen, east of Lake Sevan;[208] in Soviet Armenia local black obsidian from Alagöz or the Razdan river valley was used and obsidian blades and cores abound.[220] Fine polished axes made of basalt or serpentine were found, together with perforated hammer-stones. Hoes and picks, probably used in tilling the soil, were made of bone and antler, so were spatulae, knives, bodkins, awls, chisels, polishers, spearheads and sickles. The last-named had the teeth set diagonally as in a saw, and not edge to edge as farther south. Sometimes animal jaw-bones were used as sickles (Shomu Tepe).[211] Matting was widely used, as is evident from mat impressions on the bases of pots. Mixed farming was practised at all these sites, but rock engravings show that hunting was not entirely neglected, even if arrowheads are virtually absent; bone points or wooden spears might have been used. Clay figurines of horned animals occur. From Soviet Armenia domestic sheep, goat, cattle and dog are reported,[220] and from the Kur valley sites there is ample evidence for floral remains. Two-row barley and *Hordeum pollidum* came from Shomu Tepe, perhaps the earliest site of the complex. Emmer and wild barley, *Triticum turgidum*, *Triticum durum*, bread-wheat, *Hordeum pollidum*, vetch, *Vica villosa*, *Lolium*, all these came from Toire Tepe near by. Bread-wheat, *Triticum durum*, and *Hordeum pollidum* were found at Rustepe, *Triticum durum*, *Hordeum pollidum*, bread-wheat and vetch at Ilanli Tepe in the Mil steppe, perhaps a fairly late site. Finally *Triticum sphaerococcum* occurs only at Kültepe near Nakhchevan in the Araxes valley.

It is in the pottery that the individuality of the various settlements is most marked. At Mashtots I and Keghyak I in the Ararat plain soft-baked and grit-tempered wares appear in the form of round-based bowls, jars and cups with incised sprig motifs.[220] At Shomu Tepe, on the other hand, black and drab-red vessels with wide, flat bases are common, sometimes decorated with impressed ornament of circles and dots made with end of a reed or a stick, resembling the later Dalma impressed ware from Iran.

126 The Shulaveri group near Tiflis has coarse vessels with a grit or pottery temper, mat-impressed bases, often spreading at the foot.[209] Crinkled rims and applied decoration of knobs, bars and crescents, very primitive at Arukhlo, more sophisticated or developed at Shulaveri where it is accompanied by some incised ornament, is characteristic of this group. The widespread use of applied ornament is reminiscent of that of Umm Dabaghiyah, but evidently much later in date and probably quite unconnected. Kültepe (Nakhchevan) also has crude pottery with many oval shapes and flat bases, and among this imported Halaf stands out in a conspicuous manner. At Tegut near Echmiadzin, again in the Araxes valley but higher up, the coarse ware is accompanied by a highly fired thin pottery, light red or orange-buff in colour painted in burnished red. Technique, quality and in some instances the shape suggest Halaf influence, which is felt as far as the Kur valley.

Later on, Dalma influence from the Urmia region penetrated into the steppe west of the Caspian where the Kur and the Araxes meet. At Ilanli Tepe there are large red-slipped pots which frequently bear a jabbed decoration of triangles like impressed Dalma ware. At several other mounds, Shahtepe, Kiamiltepe and others, simple geometric patterns such as stripes and chevrons in a purplish-brown to black paint decorate a buff ware, the shapes of which have not yet been published. There may be some resemblances to painted Dalma ware.

127 Human figurines in baked clay, not unlike some from Yarim Tepe I, are known from Shulaveri; from Arukhlo come pebble heads, some primitive and not unlike those from Ain Mallaha, others quite accomplished with an almost humoristic touch. The other regions do not appear to have yielded human figurines yet.

126 Pottery from Shulaveri (after Kushnareva and Chubenishvili)

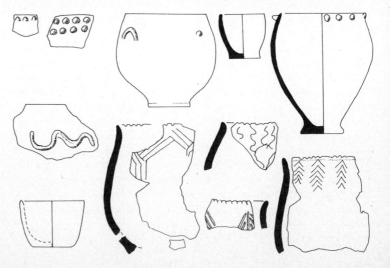

The absence of graves, except at Kültepe (Nakhchevan) and Tilki Tepe (Van) where red-ochre burials are reported, suggests that the dead were buried outside the settlement.[208] Unfortunately nothing is known of the physical characteristics of these early Transcaucasians.

None of the resemblances to more southern cultures are strong enough to suggest more than intermittent contacts with the south, except perhaps at Tegut situated across the river from Mt Ararat, the 3a obsidian source, which was first being exploited in Halaf times. Along with the green (4c) type from near-by Nemrut Dağ, it occurred at Tilki Tepe, south of the town of Van, founded perhaps as a trading emporium by the Halaf people. From there it crossed the eastern Taurus to Arpachiyah and Chagar Bazar, and reached Tell es-Sawwan down the Tigris.[85] This was probably the way Halaf influences penetrated to Tegut and Kültepe in the Araxes valley, and beyond. Although much of the Transcaucasian tradition of round houses and monochrome pottery may only belong to the late sixth, fifth and fourth millennia B C, earlier stages of settlement will undoubtedly be found, and the remarkable rock engravings of the pre-agricultural period will no doubt, when fully published, throw much more light on the early phases. This is evidently an area of considerable importance; it contained the ancestors of wheat and barley, sheep, goat, cattle, pig and dog, as well as valuable raw materials, and there is no reason to suggest that its development was not a local one. Mesopotamian or Iranian influence can hardly be said to have contributed much to its development. On the other hand, the round-house tradition of the Halaf culture may well have originated in this area, if, as I believe, the Halaf people came from the regions between Lake Van and the Assyrian plain, as descendants of the earliest obsidian traders in this area whose activities can be traced back to the Upper Palaeolithic. Incidentally it may be noted here that round houses continued in use in Transcaucasia till the end of the Early Bronze Age, when there is increasing evidence to regard the people of this area as Hurrians.

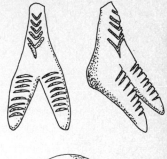

127 Figurine from Shulaveri and carved stone head from Arukhlo (after Kushnareva and Chubenishvili)

The Hajji Firuz Culture of Azerbaijan

The Urmia basin occupies the northwest corner of Iran and this province of Azerbaijan is closely linked to Transcaucasia on the one hand and the rest of the Iranian plateau on the other. Communications with either offer no hardships and the old silk route ran from the east through Sultaniye, Tabriz, Nakhchevan, Echmiadzin to Ani and Erzerum, north of the modern road through Maku and Doğubayazit. Mountain passes link the Urmia basin with the uplands around Lake Van in Turkey and with the Assyrian lowlands.

The two earliest sites known in the area are the mounds of Hajji Firuz near Hasanlu in the fertile Solduz valley south of the lake,[214–16] and Yaniktepe in the more arid Aci Çay valley west of Tabriz.[219] Four radiocarbon dates, 5184±82, 5297±71 from Yaniktepe, 5319±86 from Hajji Firuz VI and 4945±83 from Hajji Firuz II, place the beginning of this culture around the middle of the sixth millennium, a date not inconsistent with evidence from northern Mesopotamia and Transcaucasia. At least five building levels occur at Hajji Firuz as compared with some nine phases of occupation at Yaniktepe. Earlier sites are not yet known and it is, therefore, uncertain whether the first permanent settlements were introduced by newcomers or represent a local development from simpler semi-permanent camps of hunters and gatherers.

The economy of the Hajji Firuz culture seems to have been based on irrigation agriculture of domestic emmer, bread-wheat and barley; sheep and goat, and probably pigs, were domestic.[214-15] There is, however, no evidence for dogs and aurochs, and red deer were hunted. Birds were also taken. There are querns and grind-stones, but very few sickle blades. Husking trays were found in the early levels and grain was stored in pots and bins of ogee type as at Umm Dabaghiyah and Hassuna Ia. The teeth of a number of skeletons showed marked wear, which would suggest excessive cereal diet.

The settlement at Hajji Firuz seems to have been an open village with detached single-roomed houses, separated by lanes and court-yards. The yards contained outhouses built of packed mud, append-ages to the main house. The houses were approximately square in plan, measuring some 6.5×4 m, built of mud brick and mortar. They had stamped mud floors of a clean yellow clay that was sometimes stained with red ochre. Internal brick buttresses and wooden posts supported a roof of beams, reeds and clay, which the excavator thinks may have been pitched. Hearths were surrounded by a low kerb and set against the wall on a raised platform. A partition wall separated the hearth from a storage area. In some houses storage jars were sunk into the floor. A doorway with a single step led into the room, which was divided into living, working and storage space. Reed matting is deduced from impressions on the bases of pots and there is evidence of coiled basketry. Baskets were used as moulds in pottery-making; they were coated with clay and removed once the clay had hardened, the basket imprints being then obliterated with a coating of finer clay, after which the surface was burnished and sometimes painted. In this way many of the biconical or double ogee-shaped vessels were constructed by placing one basket on top of the other. These types recur all over Iran (Tal-i-Iblis, Tepe Yahya) and south-west Turkmenistan (Anau IA) among the earliest pottery pro-ducts; the result of a primitive method of manufacture, they are not a significant chronological criterion. The pottery is a poorly fired buff ware and all vessels, except the coarse storage jars, were burnished; some carry a thin red slip, others are decorated with red or brown paint applied in simple bold motifs of chevrons and triangles.

Yaniktepe offers a similar picture of a village of rectangular, well-built houses of mud brick, but here lime-plaster floors occur.[219] Pottery is scarce, straw-faced and soft-baked, lightish buff or greenish in colour. The ware is plain and the shapes are limited to heavy bowls, hole-mouth jars, flat-bottomed dishes and some carinated bowls. Painted pottery occurs in the upper layers: the chevron-painted ware of Hajji Firuz and a red burnished ware

128

with a decoration in chalky white paint also known from Tepe Sarab, far to the south in Kurdistan.

The three basic types of pottery, coarse unburnished, burnished monochrome, and painted, are of course familiar to most cultures and the chevron ware has been compared with Hassuna archaic painted ware, the white-on-red to Tepe Sarab. The general stone tradition is also of the Zagros pattern, especially at Yaniktepe where alabaster bowls, bracelets, beads and figurine heads are manufactured from the amber-coloured gypsum found at Maragheh. Ground stone celts occur and there is a simple blade industry in local chert and imported obsidian (type 3c) from a local source perhaps near the town of Rezayieh. Baked-clay female figurines occur at Hajji Firuz; they are modelled in a novel and abstract style and wear short skirts ornamented with finger-nail or punctated designs (cf. Ganjdareh and Tepe Sarab). Animal figurines are found as well. There is a bone industry with awls, needles, beads, etc. and numerous biconical spindle whorls also occur.

At Hajji Firuz intramural burial was common.[214-16] In level II, a collective grave contained the bones of thirteen individuals, buried in a bin over a period of time, the bones being covered with red ochre. Grave goods included spindle whorls, small pots, chipped and ground stone tools and a small rectangular stone decorated with linear geometric patterns, as well as animal bones and plant remains (food?). Beneath the floor in a house of level III were found at least three human skeletons, and in the burnt level II the remains of twenty-eight massacred bodies distributed over three graves, again covered with red ochre. An analysis of the skeletons is not yet available. Red-ochre burials are also known from Tilki Tepe (level?) and Kültepe, Tepe Asiab, Zaghe and especially Tepe Siyalk I–III. In the lowlands they occurred at Alikosh and Tell es-Sawwan. Red-ochre burials thus look very much a part of the Zagros tradition, but they had of course appeared in the Natufian (Tell Abu Hureyra) and at Çatal Hüyük. The distribution of the Hajji Firuz culture is evidently centred around Lake Urmia, but may have extended north to the Araxes. It is not apparently found south of the Solduz valley. What followed the Hajji Firuz culture is not known and there may be a hiatus in the record until the arrival of the Dalma culture with its highly distinctive painted and impressed wares.[218]

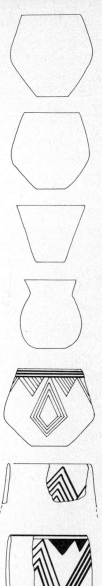

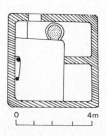

128 Hajji Firuz, Azerbaijan: house plan, figurine and plain and painted pottery (after Dyson and Smith)

Cultures of the Transcaspian Lowlands

At the southeast corner of the Caspian Sea the Near East meets Central Asia in the Turkoman plain of Gurgan. The Elburz Mountains and their eastern continuation, the Kopet Dagh, form the divide between the high Iranian plateau and the lowland steppe of Gurgan and the Karakum desert. Strangely enough, neither the fertile upland valleys from Meshed to Bujnurd nor the region between Sabzavar and Nishapur to the south, rich in copper[194] and turquoise, have yet yielded any Neolithic or earlier sites in spite of exploration. Yet evidence suggests occupation of a sort at least since the middle of the seventh millennium BC when turquoise first appears at aceramic Alikosh. A number of cave sites in the Beshar area at the southeast corner of the Caspian, Belt, Hotu and Ali Tappeh caves,[230–32] and also Jebel and Damdam Cheshme in the Balkan Mountains on the east coast, have furnished a framework for the development from the Epipalaeolithic to the beginning of farming in this region (the Jeitun culture), a period covering more than five thousand years, from c. 11000–5500 BC.

129

In terms of Near Eastern development the Caspian caves add little to what is known elsewhere in the Levant or the Zagros zone, but the meticulous study of the materials from Ali Tappeh cave provide probably the fullest environmental picture obtained for any similar site in the Near East and its climatic sequence can be linked with that of northwestern Europe. Nowhere else in the Near East is this possible except in Egypt, where similar work is under way, and between these two countries and the somewhat less complete sequence in Palestine it should eventually become possible to reconstruct a series acceptable for the whole Near East, which would obviously be appreciated by archaeologists.

The second important feature revealed by the exploration of these caves is the way in which they illustrate man's adaptation to his various food supplies throughout a period of repeated climatic changes. It would be foolhardy to dismiss the idea that this area too could have been the scene of a local cultural tradition from food-gathering to food production, as both the potential animal and plant domesticates are native to the region.

Epipalaeolithic Ali Tappeh

The earliest period in Ali Tappeh cave (I), linked to Oldest Dryas of northwestern Europe (c. 10500 BC) and roughly contemporary with the beginning of the Natufian, had a cold climate with a dominance of gazelle (60 per cent) over goat and sheep (20 per cent).[230] This 'gazelle optimum' could be due to preferential hunting of this animal, but it is not impossible that gazelle herding was beginning. In period II, a warm oscillation related to Bölling saw a notable decline in gazelle bones (less than 40 per cent), which is compensated for by seal, horse and pig, jackal and fox, and finally sheep and goat. Around 10000 B C, period III saw a second 'gazelle optimum', which corresponds to the dry cold spell of the Older Dryas, with a corresponding increase in cattle and pig. Period IVA marks a warming-up phase, related to Alleröd, giving rise to a dramatic increase in the number of seal seeking refuge in the deeper and colder waters of the southern Caspian, with the result that the hunting of seal largely takes preference over that of gazelle, sheep and goat. In IVB, however, gazelle gains on seal and in period V (*c.* 9300 B C) another cold phase, the so-called final Ice Age of the Younger Dryas, there is a third 'gazelle optimum' accompanied by a peak in sheep and goat. At this point (*c.* 9000 B C) just before the end of the Glacial period in Europe, Ali Tappeh cave is deserted and this technologically Zarzian-like culture comes to an end, just as the Zarzian did at Shanidar in northern Iraq. The possibility of early gazelle, sheep and goat herding in this area should not be ignored, especially as there is evidence for domestic sheep at Zawi Chemi a little later, and that in an environment not naturally suitable for sheep.[89] The origin of sheep domestication may well lie in Iran east of the Zagros and from here it could have spread westward to Zawi Chemi and Bus Mordeh as well as eastward to Ghar-i-Asp in northern Afghanistan.[73]

In the various Caspian caves there is a gap in occupation that corresponds in time to the Pleistocene-Holocene transition. At Hotu and Belt caves, reoccupied around 7500 B C on the evidence of C14 dating, the patterns have changed and sickle blades indicate an interest in probably wild but native cereals, barley and some emmer. During the warm Pre-Boreal and Boreal stages animal bones show a steady increase in caprids (sheep and goat) from Hotu 4 with 50 per cent, through Hotu 3 with 72 per cent to Belt cave (layers 7–9) with 84 per cent. In the Atlantic phase, after *c.* 6100 B C, soft-ware pottery appears and soon afterwards all the caves are deserted. Farther north, levels 2–4 at Jebel show a predominance of gazelle, but by *c.* 6000 B C in layers 5–6 there is again a complete change to sheep and goat, followed by desertion of the cave.[225] Fortunately there are now two settlements at Tepe Sang-i-Chakmak that might illustrate the development to the Jeitun culture, see page 194 and *Iran XII* (1974), 222.

The Jeitun Culture

By the middle of the sixth millennium, if not before, there is plentiful evidence for the establishment of early farming villages along the piedmont of the Kopet Dagh, where streams water a narrow strip of fertile soil between the mountains and the black sands of the Karakum desert.[225–8] This early farming culture is known as the Jeitun culture, and its distribution is not confined to southwest Turkmenistan; it also occurs in the Gurgan plain, at Yarim Tepe and Tureng Tepe. The conditions in these areas are typical of lowlands where agriculture is said to be impossible without irrigation. This would suggest that earlier stages of wild-

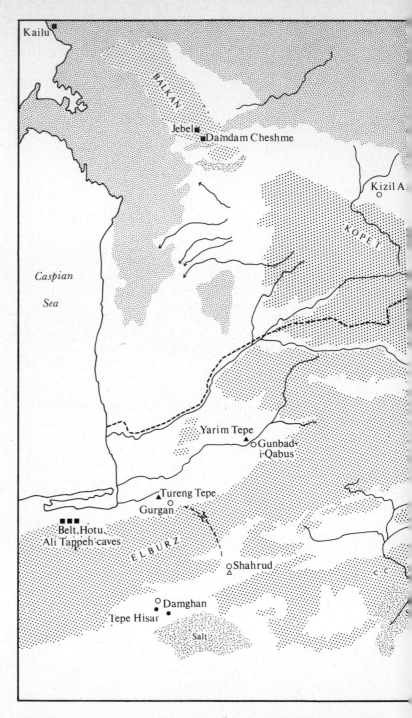

129 Map of eastern Iran and southwest Turkmenia

grain collection followed by dry farming in the uplands preceded the exploitation of the alluvium of the plains, but the only evidence for this is the finds of sickle blades in the Caspian caves *c.* 7500 B C. For these earlier phases the uplands of Khorasan, already engaged in trading contacts with the west, still need to be investigated.

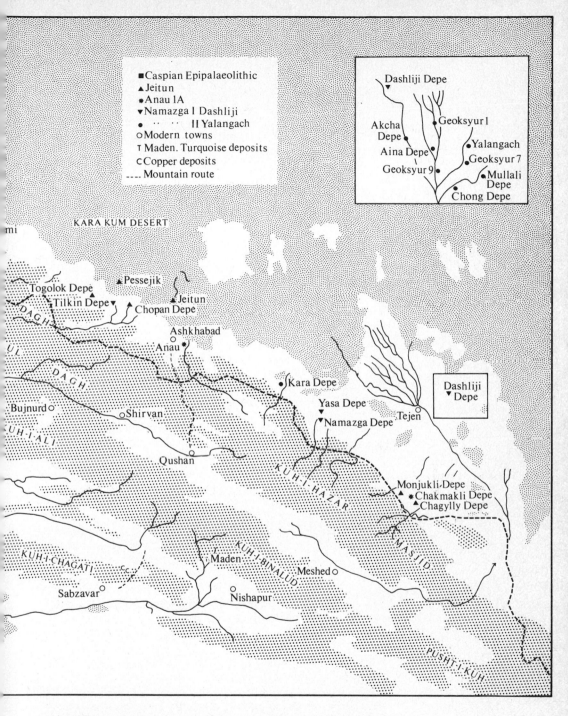

Inset map labels:
Dashliji Depe
Akcha Depe
Aina Depe
Geoksyur 9
Geoksyur 1
Yalangach
Geoksyur 7
Mullali Depe
Chong Depe

Legend:
■ Caspian Epipalaeolithic
▲ Jeitun
✳ Anau 1A
▼ Namazga I Dashliji
• ····· II Yalangach
○ Modern towns
τ Maden. Turquoise deposits
c Copper deposits
---- Mountain route

KARA KUM DESERT
mi

Togolok Depe
Pessejik
Tilkin Depe
Jeitun
Chopan Depe
DAGH
UL
DAGH
Ashkhabad
Anau
Kara Depe
Bujnurd
Shirvan
Yasa Depe
Namazga Depe
Tejen
Dashliji Depe
KUH-I-ALI
Qushan
KUH-I-HAZAR
Monjukli Depe
Chakmakli Depe
Chagylly Depe
KUH-I-CHAGATI
c.c.
Maden
KUH-I-BINALUD
Meshed
MASJID
Sabzavar
Nishapur
PUSHT-I-KUH

The Jeitun culture is known from excavations at not less than
eight sites and can be divided into three phases: Early Jeitun,
including Jeitun itself and the lower levels of Chopan and Togolok;
Middle Jeitun, represented by Pessejik, upper Chopan and
Togolok, Bami and Novaya Nisa, lower Monjukli and Chagylly

Depe; Late Jeitun, best illustrated by the upper levels of Chagylly Depe. There is a radiocarbon date of 5370 ± 100 BC for Middle Jeitun from Togolok and another of 5086 ± 100 (or 5050 ± 110) BC for Late Jeitun from Chagylly. The beginning of the culture, therefore, may go back to *c.* 5600 BC if not farther. The economy of the Jeitun culture is that of fully settled farmers. From Chagylly Depe come the grains of two-row barley, *Triticum vulgare* and *Triticum compactum*, i.e. bread-wheat. Jeitun itself lies on the delta of a large mountain stream, and it is thought that by damming the run-off from small streams the Jeitun farmers practised primitive irrigation agriculture.[224] With an annual rainfall of not more than 285 mm dry farming would have been difficult if not impossible, and environmental studies do not suggest that conditions were any better in the sixth millennium BC. Even in the early phase at Jeitun itself domestic goats and sheep provided most of the meat in the diet, and the domestic dog probably helped in the pasturing; domestic cattle appeared at Chagylly by Late Jeitun. In the early phases hunting was by no means abandoned, gazelle being the favourite game. Onager, wild pig, sheep and fox, cat and wolf were hunted, the last three probably for their fur. In later phases hunting declined, so that nearly all bones from Chagylly are those of domestic animals. The stone industry consists of chipped flint tools with microliths, especially trapezes which could be used as arrow tips, as well as lunates and triangles. The microlithic element is strong in the early phase and along with notched gravers and burins, provides a link with the earlier cave materials. Though microlithic scrapers are very important in skin dressing, sickle blades set in straight reaping knives of bone were by far the most important single element, amounting to 37 per cent of all tools at the beginning of the period at Jeitun and 31 per cent at its end at Chagylly. Some of the earlier blades are trapezoidal; in the middle period they become larger and heavier, with a development from unretouched blades to denticulation. As in the Iranian cultures there are no arrow- or spearheads, but the sling is widely used. A decrease in the number of scrapers in Late Jeitun is believed to be connected with weaving. Awls and needles, polishers, etc., were made of bone. In the heavy class of ground-stone implements, there are sandstone querns and mortars, pestles, smooth flat discs of irregular shape, axe-adzes and chisels useful in woodwork. From the distribution of artifacts in the settlement it can be established that there was as yet no recognizable specialization of labour and according to the excavators each household made its own tools in the courtyards that were used as a working area.[229]

The village of Jeitun, in its second building level, consisted of thirty detached houses without a protecting circuit wall. The *130* houses were of rectangular, almost square plan with an average floor space of 20–30 sq. m, or about 4×5 to 5×6 m; some occupied only 13 sq. m, others as much as 39 sq. m. This early village, though completely excavated, did not contain a central building or shrine. Each house had a courtyard containing outhouses, or shared one with a neighbour. In various parts of the village there were structures consisting of two or three parallel walls, which probably supported platforms for grain storage raised well above the ground to keep the damp out. The building material was primitive straw-tempered mud brick, 60–70 cm long and 25 cm wide with an oval section. The walls were coated with mud plaster, and sometimes painted red or black like the floor which was made of lime-plaster. Inside the house, to the right of the doorway, which was probably closed with a mat, was a large rectangular hearth or oven and between the doorway and the hearth there usually stood a large rectangular bin for storage. The wall opposite the hearth carried a projection, just above the floor where there was a niche. In many houses this projection was painted red or black like the floors. The hearths stood against either the north or the east wall. These single-roomed houses are characteristic of the Jeitun culture as a whole; a single family of five to six people appears to have occupied each dwelling, so that Jeitun would have had a total population of about 150–180 individuals.

Similar houses were found in the Middle Jeitun period at Pessejik,[226] Chopan and Togolok Depe;[228] occasionally, as at

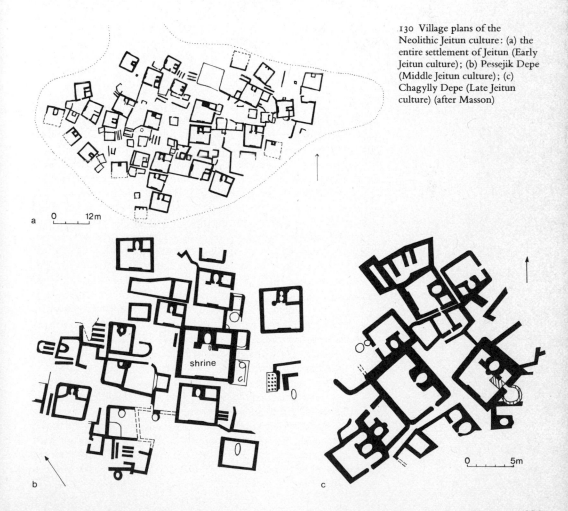

130 Village plans of the Neolithic Jeitun culture: (a) the entire settlement of Jeitun (Early Jeitun culture); (b) Pessejik Depe (Middle Jeitun culture); (c) Chagylly Depe (Late Jeitun culture) (after Masson)

shrine

a   0   12m

b

c   0   5m

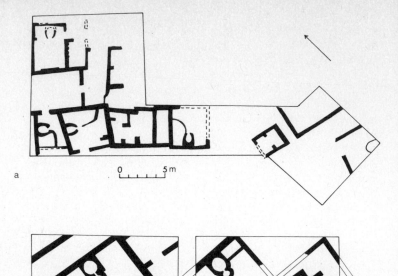

a

b

131 Buildings of the Jeitun culture: (a) Chopan Depe; (b) Togolok Depe, left, first building level; right, second building level (after Masson)

131 Chopan, party walls are found with communal courtyards. House floors are less consistently made of lime-plaster, mud covered with woven reed mats being also used. In the middle of the settlement at Pessejik a building was found twice the size of the normal house (64 sq. m) but of the same plan. It had a white, lime-plastered floor, *132* and walls decorated with polychrome wall paintings of stylized animals and geometric motifs.[227] The small number of domestic artifacts and the painted wall decoration suggest that this was a village shrine. The Late Jeitun phase of Chagylly Depe is represented by a small settlement of about twelve to fourteen houses, and here also a larger structure was found in the centre, which may have been used as a shrine though it has no wall paintings. Flat bricks now come into use and stone door-sockets indicate the use of hinged doors, but the floors continue to be painted red or black.

The Jeitun people made coiled chaff-tempered pottery with a carefully polished surface. In the early period about 12 per cent was decorated in red on a yellowish background. Shapes are simple, taking the form of oval bowls and cups, while a square bowl with curving sides suggests a basket copied in pottery. There are flat, raised, ring or dimple bases. The motifs are unsophisticated *134* but pleasing; vertical rows of wavy lines or brackets predominate in probable imitation of basketry. In the middle period the forms become more varied and the decoration grows richer; triangles and dotted patterns are more common than before. In the third period the patterns become minute, but these also cover the interior of vessels and show tree-like motifs, vertical zigzags and undulating horizontal lines.

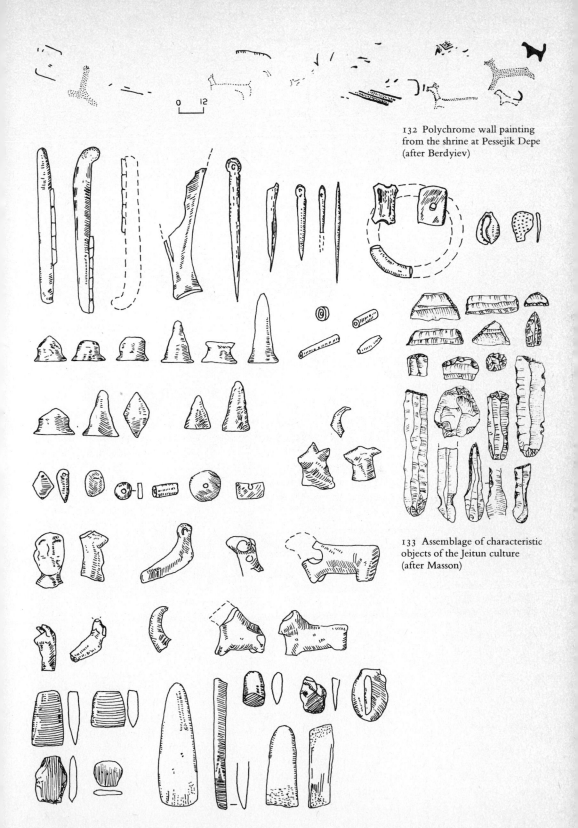

132 Polychrome wall painting
from the shrine at Pessejik Depe
(after Berdyiev)

133 Assemblage of characteristic
objects of the Jeitun culture
(after Masson)

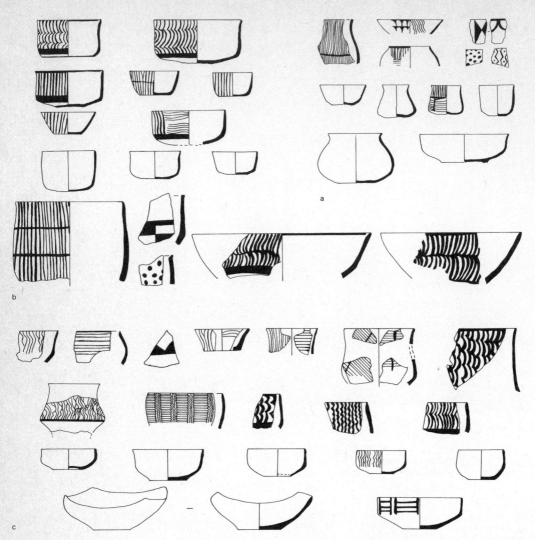

134 Pottery from the lower and middle stages of the Jeitun culture: (a) Chagylly Depe, middle; (b) Pessejik Depe, middle; (c) Jeitun, lower (after Masson and Berdyiev)

133

Human and animal figurines, as well as human heads, were made of baked clay. Some of the animal figurines represent goats, others bovids; in many of them holes have been pierced during some ritual of hunting magic. There are also small clay pieces in the shape of cones, truncated cones, etc. which served as counters in the Zagros and at Çayönü, Çatal Hüyük and Hacılar. A variety of bone beads and pendants, sea-shells, animal pendants and beads of stone including turquoise were found, which attest trading connections across the Kopet Dagh. Small mortars and pestles also occur, as in Siyalk I, but obsidian is absent.

No graves having been found during these numerous excavations, we may assume that people buried their dead outside the settlement. Consequently nothing is known of their physical appearance, but they may well have been descendants of people related to those who used the Caspian caves for this purpose. One Eurafrican skeleton covered with red ochre was found in Belt cave.[231-2]

Until recently these phases were known as the Anau IA culture, but it now appears that the arrival of Iranian elements resulted in a more complicated situation than was once thought;[225] for two different types of pottery, that of Anau IA and that of Chakmakli Depe occur.[226] Of the first group little is known except its fine, sand-tempered, kiln-fired pottery; this has black-on-red geometric decoration – large patterns filled with hatching – on bowls with concave bases which resemble those at Karatepe and Cheshme Ali in the Tehran oasis. These are also found at Havuz Tepe, north of Meshed in Khorasan, to the west of Anau.

Material of the Chakmakli Depe group also comes from Monjukli Depe and Koushut, and this eastern group has sand-tempered, well-fired pottery comprising thin, red- or yellow-slipped and sometimes burnished hemispherical bowls with flat or concave bases. Applied in black paint are hatched triangles or these combined with parallel slanting lines, in a style not unlike standard Hassuna (IV–V) – a similarity that is undoubtedly fortuitous. This rather simple pottery does not compare with the sophisticated designs of Anau IA, and is obviously not derived from the earlier Jeitun ware. With the new pottery came baked-clay spindle whorls, used now in much greater quantities than before, as well as a number of heavy copper tools such as awls and piercers; fragments of a double-bladed knife were also found. As no copper is known in the northern Kopet Dagh the raw materials must have come across the mountains from northeastern Iran. Among the stone tools are sickle blades, drills, scrapers and burins in white translucent flint; new types include chisels used for wood-work and black stone hoes for tilling the soil. Querns, pounders and mortars are also found.

At Monjukli Depe the upper building level consisted of two rows of living- and working-rooms with single-roomed houses of Jeitun tradition, but separated by a central lane into two large agglomerated complexes. At Chakmakli Depe, on the other hand, *135* a large area of the second building level from the top (there are five in all) with more than thirty living and working areas was cleared.[224] They were divided by a narrow central lane into two tightly clustered complexes, each having two types of rooms – small kitchens with a hearth in the corner and larger, elongated living-rooms with numerous buttresses. Some of the rooms led into one another and in each of the complexes one of them had walls and floors painted red. It is suggested that these rooms had ritual significance and were used as shrines. The buildings were constructed of large mud bricks, 50 × 20 × 10 cm, and walls and floors were covered with plaster. The economy of the period is similar to that of Jeitun. At Monjukli Depe domestic sheep, goat and cattle formed 60 per cent of the animal remains, and the numerous spindle whorls suggest that the production of textiles was well under way. Wheat and barley were grown and one suspects that they were the same irrigation crops as grown in the earlier Jeitun culture.

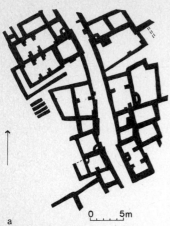

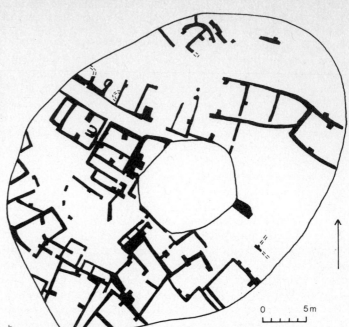

135 (a) Plan of the settlement at Chakmakli Depe; (b) plan of the settlement at Monjukli Depe; (c) Anau IA pots (restored); (d) Chakmakli Depe sherds; (e) Late Jeitun pottery from Chagylly Depe (after Masson, Berdyiev and Sarianidi)

The architectural remains of this phase are particularly interesting in that they may perhaps give us a clue as to the nature of the buildings of the Siyalk II culture, bearing in mind that the preceding Jeitun houses were not unlike those of the Hajji Firuz culture.[214] Whatever differences there may be, the cultures of Transcaspia seem to fit well into the Iranian tradition. The newcomers were soon absorbed into the local community and there is abundant evidence for an increase in population and growing prosperity in the following culture of Namazga I, which may represent the result of the amalgamation of the two earlier cultures.

The Namazga I Culture

This culture is roughly the equivalent of most of Siyalk II, Khazineh, Hajji Muhammed and Late Halaf, in the early fifth millennium B C.[233] A chain of about twenty sites now stretches along the foothills of the Kopet Dagh, and among the small villages there are now large sites such as Namazga or Kara Depe with an area of 35 acres or more and populations totalling some 2500. Late in the period the Geoksyur oasis on the Tejen river was settled, perhaps to accommodate a surplus population from the culture's southeastern settlements. Dashliji Depe is one of the sites *136* in the oasis and provides the best picture of a small settlement of this period. It covered an area of 45 × 38 m and had three building levels with small brick houses which in plan are still very much in the Jeitun tradition. One larger structure may have been the village shrine; it has a platform next to the hearth and a floor painted black and red. Each house has a courtyard with outhouses and there is evidence for a pottery-producing area as well as drying platforms for grain. A local form of pottery is characterized by a *137* light-coloured slip and specific patterns such as triangular chevrons, parallel arches and horizontal chevrons along the rim. Figurines are highly stylized and plaque-like, in contrast to the realistically modelled figurines of Namazga I at Kara Depe.

136 Dashliji II and III, Geoksyur oasis: plan of the village in the middle (a) and lowest (b) building levels (after Chlopin)

Although little is known of the houses of the central settlement group there are two shrines. The one at Anau is decorated with

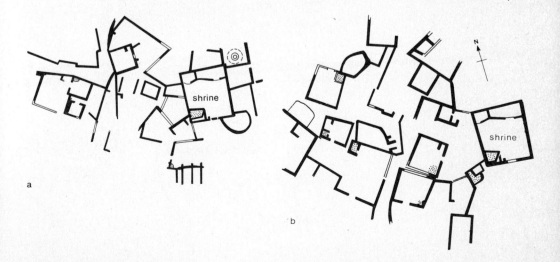

two rectangular panels of wall paintings, one with red triangles in black frames, the other with checkered squares. At Yasa Depe in *138* the centre of the village a larger shrine consisting of two adjacent rooms connected by a passage was found. One of the rooms, in which there were fragments of wall paintings, had a hearth of Jeitun type which may have been used as an altar. The second room had a colonnade of wooden pillars along two of its walls; the third wall contained the doorway and the fourth, opposite the entrance, was decorated with wall paintings several layers thick. The earliest layer had vertical rows of lozenges, alternately red and black and enclosed in black frames. In one of the later paintings there were vertical rows of triangles in red, bordered with white alabaster (gypsum) incrustation. The patterns were undoubtedly inspired by textiles, for which there is abundant evidence. Sheep and goat predominate in the economy and biconical spindle whorls of clay abound, some of which are decorated. On the other hand bone tools used in skin dressing have almost disappeared.

139 Namazga I pottery returned to straw-tempered wares after the grit temper of the previous period, but the use of kilns probably continued. The coarse ware includes large storage jars with undercut bases, often painted in bold designs. Among the fine ware,

137 Painted pottery in the Dashliji style from the type site (Late Namazga I period) (after Chlopin)

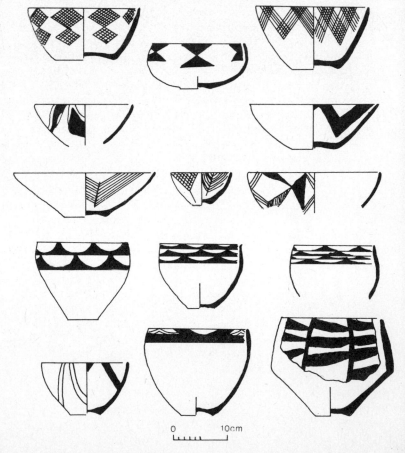

0   10cm

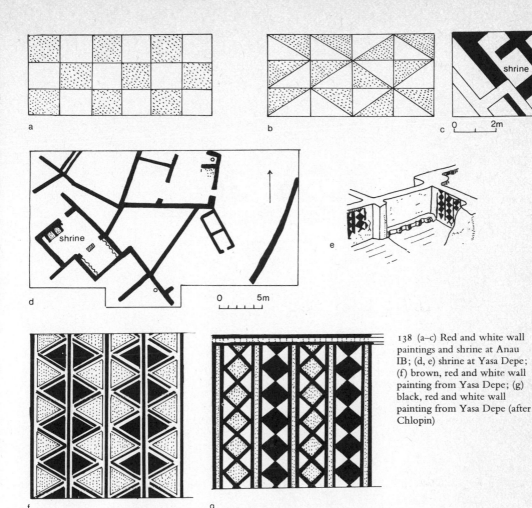

138 (a–c) Red and white wall paintings and shrine at Anau IB; (d, e) shrine at Yasa Depe; (f) brown, red and white wall painting from Yasa Depe; (g) black, red and white wall painting from Yasa Depe (after Chlopin)

some 30 per cent is painted in black on red or – less common – in black on buff. Simple geometric patterns are used, but at Kara Depe the first representations of goats and plants, an onager and a horse appear. Some vessels are painted inside and out. Namazga I ware shows clear links with the earlier pottery of both the Jeitun and the Anau IA periods. Flint tools are gradually replaced by copper: pins, awls, needles, chisels, knife and sickle (?) blades. Only .20 per cent of the animal bones at Dashliji Depe can be attributed to hunting. *Triticum vulgare* (wheat) and two-row barley were grown as before and there is evidence for the use of digging sticks weighted by stone rings. Ornaments include pins with pyramidal copper knobs, beads and pendants of semi-precious stones, including carnelian and turquoise. Trade across the Kopet Dàgh was obviously maintained.

In this period the dead were buried inside the settlement and both children and adults lay in a contracted position with the head facing south. Funerary gifts are almost all confined to articles of personal adornment: beads, copper tubes, etc. There are no details about the racial types represented.

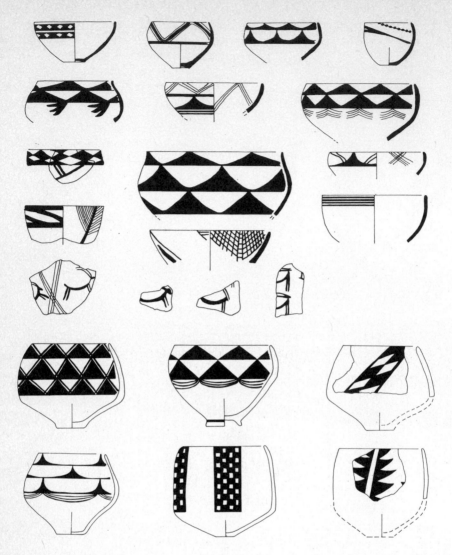

The Namazga II Period

139 Painted pottery of the Namazga I (Anau IB) culture (after Chlopin)

On the evidence of a Late Namazga I C14 date from Tilkin Depe of 4631 ± 110, the Namazga II period (Anau II) probably began c. 4500 BC. It is approximately contemporary with Siyalk III and Ubaid, and like these two cultures it is divided into two phases.[236] As in the previous period two variants are found, Early Namazga II in the piedmont, and the Yalangach culture in the Geoksyur oasis. Typical of Early Namazga II is polychrome painted pottery, but this only occurs as imports in the Yalangach culture where the local wares derive from Dashliji ware. The polychrome ware in

140
141

black and red on buff is decorated with friezes of small geometric figures, and occasionally human figures and goats. The origin of this pottery has been much debated, but it is extremely likely that it is local and imitates the polychrome wall paintings of the previous period. At Kara Depe 4–6 polychrome ware formed 62 per cent of the pottery; next came monochrome ware painted with friezes of goats (10 per cent). Also found are highly burnished, red-slipped hemispherical bowls, a small proportion of polished grey ware and coarse-ware vessels and bowls.

Better evidence for the architecture and the economy of this period is provided by the Yalangach culture.[234] The population of the Geoksyur oasis, which had by now doubled, was concentrated in a capital, possibly walled, designated Geoksyur I,[224-5] and eight other settlements of which Yalangach and Mullali Depe have been extensively excavated. Yalangach is a small mound, measuring 130×95 m. The top level contained two shrines with two-tiered ovens (podia), a round house filled with burned brick and a series of parallel walls of the type that supported drying or storage platforms for grain, enclosed by a defensive wall with round towers. To the northwest remains of a less well-preserved complex of this type were found. In the lower building level were two complexes separated by a thick wall. In the eastern one a large central room was surrounded by smaller rooms, reflecting a tendency, as at Kara Depe 3–5, towards the development of multi-room blocks instead of individual single-roomed houses. This eastern complex at Yalangach was possibly a shrine, whereas the western one was used as dwellings. No circuit wall was found at this level, but being exposed to erosion on the edge of the mound it may simply have disappeared. At Mullali Depe, such a wall with round towers is well preserved and the community lived in some 17–20 houses, with an estimated population of between 90 and 120. At Akcha Depe and Geoksyur remains

143

140 Namazga II polychrome pottery (after Masson)

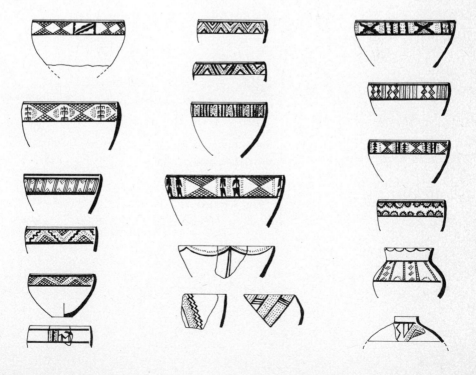

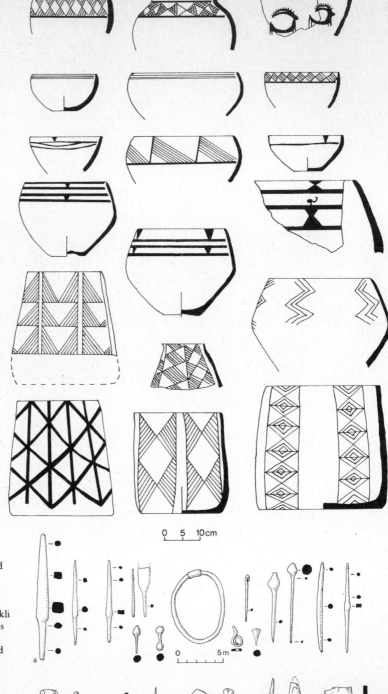

141 Namazga II monochrome ware from Yalangach (after Chlopin)

142 Highland Iran and lowland Turkmenistan, early metal objects: (a) awls, pins, bracelets etc. from Siyalk I and II; (b) pendant and pin from Chakmakli Depe (Anau IA period); (c) pins and chisel from Namazga I (Anau IB period); (d) chisel and dagger fragment from Dashliji (Late Namazga I period); (e) chisel, spearhead and axe from Yalangach (Namazga II period) (after Ghirshman, Masson and Sarianidi)

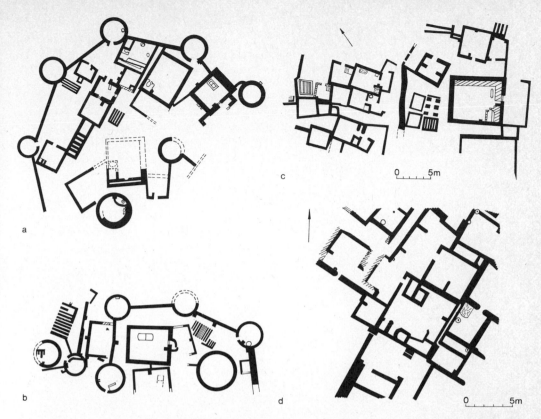

of ditches have been excavated at the foot of the defensive wall. The need for defensive walls throughout the oasis is interesting; the Yalangach people obviously considered the possibilities of attack by bands of hunters and gatherers or pastoral nomads, possibly attracted by the new-found but simple wealth of the agriculturalists of the oasis. There are other signs of prosperity. At Yalangach bread-wheat, two- and six-row barley were grown, with barley outnumbering wheat in the ratio of 30:1. Domestic cattle formed 41–54 per cent of the animal bones, followed by sheep and goat (25–49 per cent), with pigs only 2–20 per cent. Hunting of gazelle, horse, deer, boar and fox had become quite unimportant. Denticulated flint sickle blades and arrowheads are now found, the usual querns, etc. occur.

Metal tools had become more varied and they include a heavy axe, spearheads and a possible razor. They were made from copper extracted from ore and annealed to increase the hardness of the metal, processes learnt elsewhere. Luxury objects included ornaments of carnelian, agate, azurite and turquoise, all products of northeastern Iran. Yalangach yielded a fine painted clay statuette of a seated female deity; it has a length of 28 cm, whereas most of the others are only 10–12 cm long. Painted on these figures are concentric circles and goats. Animal figurines have also been found. Burials of this period are rare, except at the capital site, and it is possible that the villagers took their dead to be buried at Geoksyur I.

143 Architecture in the Namazga II period: (a) the fortified settlement of Yalangach (upper level); (b) the fortified settlement of Mullali Depe in the Geoksyur oasis; (c) complex at Yalangach (lower level); (d) part of the town site of Kara Depe 3 (after Chlopin)

142

The development into Late Namazga II and Namazga III and the Geoksyur group in the oasis[235] is of absorbing interest but falls outside the time span covered by this book. Compared to Mesopotamia or the Levant, southwest Turkmenia had long ago reached a Chalcolithic culture, even though it had no copper deposits of its own. Behind this remarkable cultural development from the Epipalaeolithic to the Chalcolithic there must, one feels, lie a wealth of material in Gurgan and Khorasan awaiting excavation.

Chapter Eight

Early Pottery Cultures in the Levant

The Early Neolithic

Having traced the cultural development in the Levant up to the end of the aceramic period in the first half of the sixth millennium B C, we will now discuss subsequent developments in Syria, Lebanon and Palestine up to *c.* 4200 B C. It would be optimistic to claim that the various cultures of the 'Pottery Neolithic' in this area are well known. Most of our evidence consists of pottery and flints; architecture, economic data and information about the physical characteristics of the population are scanty in the extreme. Large-scale excavations were only undertaken at Byblos and Munhata.

In our account of the end of the PPNB culture we have already drawn attention to the shift of culture towards the north, to Lebanon and Syria and to the coastal areas in particular, where the onset of drought and desiccation had presumably little effect. New cultures sprang up along the hitherto sparsely populated coastal area of Lebanon where the Early Neolithic Byblos culture shows ribbon development of settlements from Batroun to Sidon. *148* Farther north settlement is somewhat less concentrated but is found at Tabbat el-Hammam, Tell Sukas and Ras Shamra VB as well as at several places in the plain of Antioch, a culture known as Amuq A.[254] Other sites along the Orontes include Yanoudiyeh, Hama and a site near Homs; there are probably many more, for no archaeological survey has ever been made in this area. Numerous sites occur in the Beqa'a,[240] among which soundings were made at Labwe and Ard Tlaïli.[242] In the Damascus area Tell Ramad III marks the last occupation of the site.

The area falls into two main culture provinces, northern Syria, and Lebanon with southern Syria; these were joined somewhat later by Palestine as a third province. Although Ras Shamra provides the best stratigraphic sequence for northern Syria,[251] the use of the old Amuq sequence, incomplete as it is, is frequently followed, despite the fact that Amuq A and B were found below water-level.[244] The type site for Lebanon is Byblos, and in Palestine the longest sequence comes from the recent excavations at Munhata.[5]

Although generalizations are notoriously dangerous it would appear that most of the Pottery Neolithic cultures of the Levant were supported by the growing of crops and the herding of domestic animals. Other pursuits, such as hunting and gathering of wild foods may have varied in importance from area to area. Most of the sites so far explored seem to have been villages, but the presence of towns, especially in the north, seems reasonably certain. The main innovation was pottery and though a small

144 Early Neolithic cardium-combed dark burnished bowl and jar from Byblos

quantity of 'white ware' is still found at the beginning of the period, for example at Byblos, Tell Sukas and Ras Shamra VB, it is soon superseded; the new pottery, a dark burnished, coiled ware, hard fired, with a grit temper and a dark brown, chocolate, grey-brown or blackish burnished surface, is accompanied in places by a red burnished ware that may have a slip, and frequently by a coarse, hard, gritty buff ware, which in Amuq A may carry a red wash.

The distribution of this pottery stretches from the Lebanon and the Damascus area, north to the Keban region around Malatya and Elazig and eastwards as far as the Khabur ('Syrian grey-black wares'). It is equally characteristic of Cilicia, and the south Anatolian plateau from the area of the central Anatolian volcanoes to the western edge of the plateau near Tavas. With the exception of Beldibi B and Çatal Hüyük, earlier pottery has not yet been encountered anywhere and the sequence of pottery cultures starts with the dark burnished ware. Its origin probably lies on the Anatolian plateau, but the hard buff wares, absent there, are almost certainly of Cilician/Syrian origin. However, even if the Levant borrowed the technique and some of the shapes from Anatolia, the decoration they applied was their own. None of the plateau ware was decorated, but from Cilicia southwards impressed ornament of various kinds is commonly found. At Mersin in Cilicia it amounts to about 10 per cent; farther south it seems more frequent. In Amuq A, the impressions are both on the dark burnished ware and on the red-washed buff ware. Roulette ornament, done with the edge of a shell and impressions made with bird bones, etc., are typical of Cilicia and northern Syria, but in the

144

Early Neolithic of Byblos pottery was combed all over – below a smooth rim – with a cardium (cockle) shell.[241] Round-based vessels are not uncommon there, but farther north and in Anatolia bases are flat. The Cilician and Levantine forms of decoration often produce a basket texture; was this perhaps inspired by local attempts at pottery manufacture in a basket mould, which was removed when the pot had dried in the sun? If such vessels were made before the superior Anatolian product was introduced, the combination of local ornament and new fabric could have occurred, yet it must be admitted that no actual pieces of such simple pottery have ever been found. In earliest Byblos the use of white plaster on the inside (and sometimes also on the outside) of dark to red

145 Heads of baked-clay figurines from Tell Ramad III (after de Contenson)

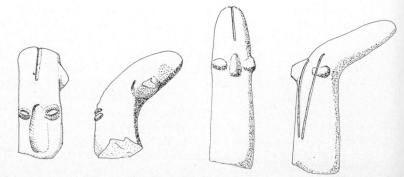

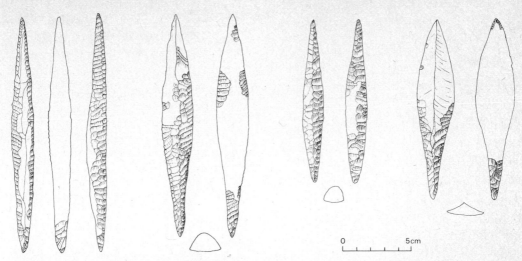

burnished pots is reminiscent of the technique of lining baskets with gypsum and asphalt known from the PPNB. Apart from knobs and ledge handles this pottery is smooth and neither relief ornament nor painting as yet occurs. At Byblos there is also some incised pottery; it has herring-bone patterns between borders on the fine ware, and triangles filled with hatching or dots on the coarse. Shapes are simple and include hole-mouth jars; carinated or hemispherical bowls are the most common.

Clay figurines of animals or humans are rare but, with the exception of the Ramad figures with pointed heads,[18] reminiscent of comparable Hassuna ones, are unremarkable. At Byblos pebble figurines with crudely incised faces were current,[241] as in the later Yarmukian culture. Such types go back to the Natufian tradition, as represented by Ain Mallaha and Wadi Fallah. Byblos also produced clay stamp seals with geometric motifs (as found at Çatal Hüyük); others were made of greenstone, like those of Amuq A and B (and Arpachiyah Early Halaf), a material that does not occur south of Jebel Akra and indicates trade connections. Further contacts are with Anatolia in the form of Çiftlik and Acigöl obsidian, but it is not known whether this reached Byblos by land or sea.[85]

145

Other imported raw material at Byblos consists of a fine tabular flint of chocolate or off-white colour used in the manufacture of weapons: daggers, javelins and arrowheads,[237] It is of Syrian provenance but its precise origin is not yet known. The Byblos stone industry is new, and not related to that of the PPNB though paralleled in Syria and Anatolia (Çatal Hüyük). Taking the products in order of numerical importance, we start with sickle blades with coarse teeth and truncated blades for reed-cutting or reaping grain made of greyish flint from the local beach, with burins for bone-working coming next. Then we come to the weapons: daggers, lanceheads and various types of arrowhead, some tanged and many pressure-flaked in the exotic Syrian materials already mentioned. (Does the chocolate flint imitate obsidian?) Next on the list are axes and chisels made from purple flint found in a near-by wadi; these were used in woodwork,

147 Flint lancehead from Early Neolithic Byblos

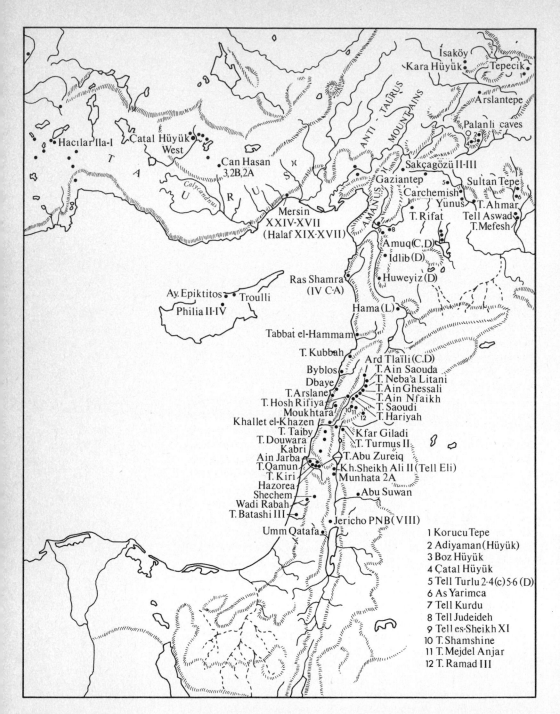

Map of the Levant and neighbouring regions during the Halaf, Amuq C–D and Wadi Rabah cultures

İsaköy
Kara Hüyük   Tepecik
Arslantepe
Palanlı caves
Hacılar IIa–I
Çatal Hüyük West
Can Hasan 3,2B,2A
Sakçagözü II–III
Gaziantep   Sultan Tepe
Carchemish   T.Ahmar
Mersin XXIV–XVII (Halaf XIX–XVII)   Yunus   T.Mefesh
                                    T. Rifat Tell Aswad
Amuq(C,D)
İdlib(D)
Ay. Epiktitos   Troulli   Huweyiz(D)
Philia II–IV
Ras Shamra (IV C·A)
Hama (L)
Tabbat el-Hammam
T. Kubbah
Ard Tlaïli(C.D)
Byblos   T.Ain Saouda
Dbaye   T. Neba'a Litani
T.Arslane   T.Ain Ghessali
T. Hosh Rifiya T.Ain Nfaikh
Moukhtara   T. Saoudi
Khallet el-Khazen T. Hariyah
T. Taiby   Kfar Giladi
T.Douwara   T. Turmus II
Kabri   T.Abu Zureiq
Ain Jarba
T.Qamun   Kh.Sheikh Ali II (Tell Eli)
T. Kiri   Munhata 2A
Hazorea
Shechem   Abu Suwan
Wadi Rabah
T. Batashi III
Umm Qatafa   Jericho PNB (VIII)

1 Korucu Tepe
2 Adiyaman (Hüyük)
3 Boz Hüyük
4 Çatal Hüyük
5 Tell Turlu 2·4(c) 5·6 (D)
6 As Yarimca
7 Tell Kurdu
8 Tell Judeideh
9 Tell es-Sheikh XI
10 T. Shamshine
11 T. Mejdel Anjar
12 T. Ramad III

148 Map of the Levant and neighbouring regions during the Halaf, Amuq C–D and Wadi Rabah cultures

and only the cutting edges are polished. Of lesser importance by now are blades, scrapers, borers, etc. made of black pebble flint. Straight wooden reaping knives, 40–50 cm long, holding ten to twelve blades set end to end were found, an indication of the importance of agriculture (emmer wheat and barley unspecified). The importance also of hunting, mainly deer, but apparently some cattle and goat is revealed by the proportion of weapons found. Grapes were collected, but no fish are reported. This colourful equipment is matched at other Syrian sites, for example those of the Homs area,[254] but in the Amuq A and B culture obsidian is much more common than farther south.[244] At Byblos only eighteen fragments of Çiftlik and Acigöl obsidian were found in Early Neolithic levels, while none at all came from the Lake Van area.[237] Unique at Byblos is an axe made of basalt, the nearest source for which lies in the Homs gap north of Tripoli.

Byblos Early Neolithic

Byblos is the only Levantine site which has yielded architecture in the Early Neolithic.[241] The settlement lay on a consolidated sand dune, and spread over an area of 100 × 30 m with a freshwater spring and a harbour. Its flimsy detached buildings constructed of finger-thick reeds, flat-roofed or more probably vaulted, all took the form of a single room with a plaster floor, frequently stained red, a traditional PPNB feature. These floors had been renewed up to five times, but as there was ample space between houses, rebuilding on the same spot was not practised; consequently the total number of building levels of the period cannot be ascertained. The period may have lasted some five centuries from *c.* 5800–5300 B C. Level 43, representing the middle of the Early Neolithic period, was recently dated by C14 to 5410±70 B C.

Byblos appears to have been a conservative settlement where the new pottery developments evident in the north, from Ras Shamra VA to Amuq B, were not immediately reflected. C14 information from Ras Shamra gives 5736±112 BC as the date of Amuq A-Ras Shamra VB, and 5234±84 for the end of Amuq B-Ras Shamra VA. The change from Amuq A–B may have come *c.* 5600 B C when the Halaf, Hassuna and Samarra cultures began farther east. To the previously mentioned Amuq B links provided by 'Syrian grey ware', the greenstone (steatite) seals in Hassuna II and Early Halaf Arpachiyah, may be added 'husking tray' fragments from the Hassuna culture found at Tell Halaf and Ras Shamra VA. Such contacts were not new, similar relations having existed between Amuq A and Umm Dabaghiyah. This 'Syrian grey ware' (often black or even red) is now frequently decorated with pattern-burnish, a process by which the burnished portion *149* stands out in dark on the light unburnished ground. Farther north, at Sakçagözü I[245] and Carchemish,[256] incised ornament was used on black and brown ware, and a 'colony' or trading post with this ware was found at Chagar Bazar in the Khabur on virgin soil (level 14).[165] From here the Syrian imports may have reached the new sites in the Assyrian plain. Less common than pattern-burnished ware was coarse incised ware, at present confined to the Amuq, as well as an early ware 'brittle painted' in red on a white slip with simple motifs, which was also found at Ras Shamra VA[250] and Tell Aswad;[248] this local but little-known predecessor of Middle Halaf ware that was to spread over northern Syria in the next period. Side by side with these innovations, the old dark burnished ware with its impressed decoration remained in full use. The few fragmentary house remains reveal rectangular rooms

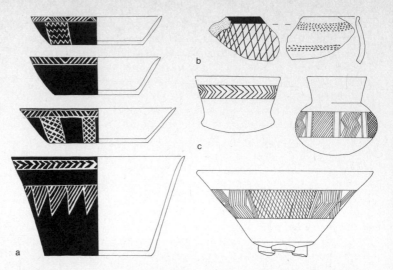

149 (a) Sakçagözü I grey burnished incised ware; (b) Sakçagözü II pointillé and pattern-burnished ware; (c) grey and red pattern-burnished ware of Amuq C type (after Garstang and Braidwood)

with walls of pisé, but plaster floors are no longer found. Grain silos are also reported. Only the briefest information about the economy in the north is available: in Amuq A domestic goat and pig, at Ras Shamra VB emmer and barley and domestic cattle, sheep and pig, in Amuq B domestic sheep, and at Ras Shamra VA domestic cattle.[251]

The 'Middle Neolithic' and the Halaf Impact

During this period there is a growing gap between northern Syria on the one hand and the Lebanon with the Middle Neolithic Byblos culture on the other. This is the result of the expansion of Middle Halaf culture to the west, which involved not only a change in pottery, but also in the chipped-stone industry. The fine Amuq A–B tradition comes to a sudden end, to be replaced by long 'Canaanite' blades with parallel edges, and baked-clay sling missiles.[244] This rather suggests a decline in hunting, but there is no faunal evidence to support this view. The arrival of domestic sheep at Ras Shamra IVC need not mean much, since they were present in the Amuq in the previous phase. There are no architectural remains at Tell Judeideh (Amuq C) and only fragmentary rectangular structures at contemporary Ras Shamra IVC, but at Yunus near Carchemish and at Tell Turlu farther north Halaf *tholoi*, with (or without) antechambers, appear. This looks like an intrusion of newcomers establishing a bridgehead across the Euphrates between Carchemish and Birecik, traditional river crossings to this day. The pottery recovered from Yunus – evidently locally made as it consists of wasters – is pure Middle Halaf, and it may be that Yunus was the pottery producer for Carchemish just as Arpachiyah was the manufacturing centre for Nineveh. Farther west there is no evidence of Halaf *tholoi* and since pattern-burnished ware continues, but on newly adopted Halaf shapes, and local painted ware imitates Halaf imports in design and decoration at Tell Judeideh,[244] influence rather than shifts in population is indicated. At Ras Shamra the Halaf impact is

96

150

strong in the beginning (IVC) and the pattern-burnished ware disappears, but in the next stratum (IVB) imports have ceased and local Halaf wares prevail together with other local features such as the beginning of a red-wash ware.[250] House plans are not affected. At Sakçagözü II, between Maraş and Gaziantep, Middle Halaf pottery occurs with some Samarra (also found at Yunus), but the local pattern-burnished wares persist and a new local black burnished ware is introduced, having pointillé designs with a white fill, imitating Halaf (?) or inspiring the white stipple on brown of later Middle Halaf pottery (?).[245] There are other interesting features here: a boat-shaped vessel, like the wooden ones of Çatal Hüyük, appropriately decorated with excised designs imitated in Halaf painting, and fragments of stone vessels in easily carved chlorite schist incised with Halaf rosettes and other designs. Architectural remains are absent, but the new stone industry prevails.

151

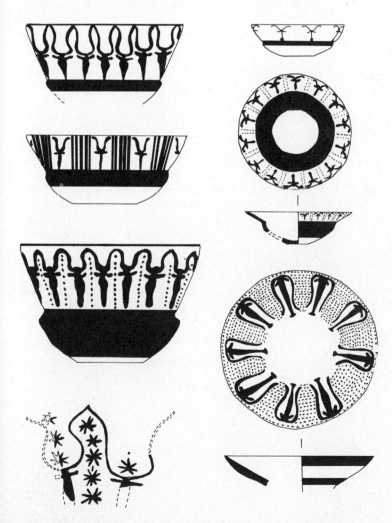

150 Middle Halaf pottery from Yunus near Carchemish (kiln wasters) decorated with animal heads (after Dirvana)

Everywhere in northern Syria the evidence published so far from the various soundings is wholly inadequate for documenting the course of events during the Halaf period. At Ras Shamra IVB and IVA local painted ware, decorated in blackish-brown paint on a white slip follows the Halaf imports of the previous phase.[250] Domestic sheep and dog are recorded for IVB, pigs for IVA. A red-wash ware, sometimes polished, now appears. It is characterized by bow-rim jars, stout lug handles, mat-impressed bases and pedestalled bowls. This distinctive pottery, plain or painted, is also found at Tell Kurdu, which represents Amuq D, after the desertion of Tell Judeideh (where Amuq A–C were present).[244] It also occurs at Tell Turlu 5 and 6, above the *tholoi* with key-hole plan of levels 3–4,[247] as well as on a number of unexcavated sites (near Idlib and Huweyiz) in the Orontes valley. This pottery (Ras Shamra IVB–A and Amuq D) seems to represent the native Syrian reaction to the Halaf impact. Rather austere in style, it shuns the typical Halaf motifs such as bucrania, moufflon heads, double axes, egg-and-dot patterns, etc., and is decorated instead with horizontal bands containing geometric or floral designs. The quantity of red ware increases in Ras Shamra IVA and is alone represented at Tell Kurdu. This Syrian bichrome-painted ware and the red-wash ware are seemingly the approximate equivalents of Late Halaf (*c.* 5000–4500 B C) which probably lingered on in the more northerly areas at Turlu, Sakçagözü III, etc. For these are situated on the trade route from the Euphrates to Cilicia which passed north of the Amuq. In this way Late Halaf imports, many in polychrome ware, reached Mersin XIX–XVII from *c.* 4900 B C.[117] Bow-rim jars also occurred at the unstratified site of Tell Halaf itself, and one came from level XIX at Mersin; among the Late Halaf ware, corrugated and painted 'basket ware' was found. On the Anatolian plateau, beyond Mersin, which guards the western end of the Cilician plain, local versions of Halaf imports are rare, the finds being limited to two sherds at Can Hasan, a few sherds from the Konya plain survey and one unstratified (level I?) sherd from Hacılar. There is also one complete bow-rim jar, reputedly from Hacılar.

To the south, stratified Halaf pottery was found at Ard Tlaïli, a small mound at the source of the Orontes in the Beqa'a valley of

151 (a) Fragments of oval boat-shaped vessel in Halaf ware, from Sakçagözü III. Shape and decoration suggest a wooden origin; (b) fragment of a chlorite bowl with excised zigzag pattern and incised Halaf rosettes, from Sakçagözü III, (c) incised sherds with hunter wearing animal skin, from Sakçagözü II, comparable to painted Halaf sherd from Carchemish (after Garstang and Woolley)

Lebanon.[242] The lower levels contain rectangular architecture, pottery of Byblos Middle Neolithic type, dark burnished with a great variety of incised, impressed and other decoration, local painted pottery and red wares, as well as a number of genuine Halaf imports. In the upper levels bow-rim jars appear in red-wash ware. A series of C14 dates suggest *c.* 4900 BC for the end of the earlier phase, which probably equals Amuq C, and there is one date of 4710±130 for the later phase with bow-rims that is equivalent to Amuq D, Late Halaf and Mersin XIX–XVII. The animal remains from the site have not yet been examined, but the lower levels yielded bread-wheat and six-row barley, the hybrid crops associated with irrigation agriculture and not previously noted in the Levant. The material from Ard Tlaïli is significant in that it is to all intents and purposes identical with that of the Wadi Rabah culture of Palestine. Both these cultures show the southern-most impact of the Middle Halaf culture, which evidently followed the easy route through the Great Rift valley and not – as one might have expected – the coast.

152

Byblos Middle Neolithic

Changes were also taking place along the Mediterranean littoral in Lebanon. A fine stratigraphical transition from Early to Middle Neolithic was found in a funerary structure with plaster floors that effectively sealed several deposits of intact human skeletons in red clay, and others of skulls in a corner, and contained flints and pottery. The lower floors were associated with impressed wares, the upper with new, red burnished and red-wash wares, long flint axes and fine-toothed sickle blades. In the middle layers the pottery overlapped. This evidence shows that the cultural change was a local one.[241]

The new pottery is abundant: flat-based jars with straight or bow-rim necks and lugs or small handles, carinated vessels, oval vessels and others of evident Halaf inspiration. Black- and red-slipped surfaces are burnished, others are covered with a red wash, or plain reserve bands are left on the red-washed surface, which is decorated with impressed or incised ornament much like that painted in bichrome farther north. Shell-impressed wares are now on the way out, and stabbed and incised, finger- and nail-impressed

152 Middle Neolithic incised, impressed and painted pottery from Ard Tlaïli (after Kirkbride)

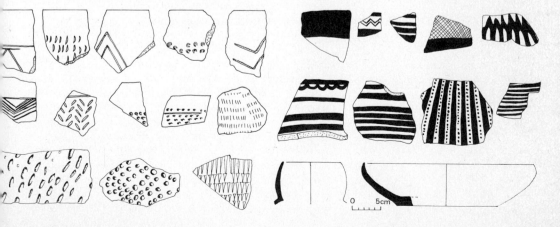

wares appear in a great profusion of techniques as in lower Ard Tlaïli. These are usually arranged in horizontal bands with incised designs in the form of filled triangles and herring-bone patterns between lines. Less commonly, pattern-burnished red and grey ware is found and there are some sherds with red- or black-painted chevrons.

The practice of individual burial continued from the Early Neolithic except in the mortuary structure, where collective burials were found. The physical type of the Byblos people has not yet been studied.

Remains of houses are few, but they are still rectangular. Plaster floors are only found in the funerary structures; in the houses floors are of mud.

The stone industry includes numerous fine-toothed sickle blades, an abundance of burins for bone-working, and a few scrapers. Hunting weapons show a marked decline. Only small arrowheads survive, the finer and larger pieces having all disappeared, though the bones of wild animals are still numerous. An increase in axes and chisels suggests the greater importance of timber and woodwork – not surprising in the forested Lebanon. A new pink or red flint of unknown origin is used, together with all the previous varieties. Obsidian still occurs, but significantly it includes none of the central Anatolian types.[85] Instead it is now of types 3a and 1g, the black obsidian from Ararat and the grey from Suphan on Lake Van. These are the types associated with Halaf trade, and the new orientation is significant. It shows conclusively that the Middle Neolithic saw the Levant move out of the Anatolian sphere of influence into the northern Mesopotamian one.

At Byblos pebble figurines continue to be made as before. As in previous periods the immediate links of the Byblos Neolithic are with the Orontes valley, the Beqa'a and northern Palestine. Secure behind the forested ramparts of Mt Lebanon, Byblos maintained a certain conservatism and painted pottery did not become as important as in the regions farther north, or even the Beqa'a.

The Late Neolithic

The sudden end of Halaf culture about 4500 B C had, it would seem, a disastrous effect on Syria. The reasons for this collapse remain obscure, and as has already been mentioned, the current explanation of conquest of northern Mesopotamia by an expanding Ubaid population from the south seems too simple to account for such widespread changes between the Zagros Mountains and the Mediterranean. One is tempted to blame other factors, hypothetical of course, such as soil exhaustion, animal disease, droughts, nomad incursions and the like, factors that have often affected life in these areas in historical times, for the destruction and more often desertion of once prosperous settlements and the general impoverishment evidenced by the sites that survived, such as Ras Shamra IIIC[255] or Byblos in the Late Neolithic.[237] There is no climatological evidence for a new dry spell, but there seem to be plenty of signs of unrest: population shifts and new influences from the Konya plain on Anatolia's high plateau (end of Çatal West, Can Hasan 2A), Cilicia (newcomers in Mersin XVI),

Cyprus (end of Philia culture) and northern Syria (newcomers in Ras Shamra IIIC), the desertion of the Halaf settlements of northern Mesopotamia, the arrival of Early Ubaid elements at Tepe Gawra, of Iranian elements and influences in central Iraq (Chogha Mami, Ras el-Amiyah) and Khuzistan in the Mehmeh phase, or the spread of Dalma ware into Azerbaijan and the arrival of new settlers in the south Iranian areas of Fars and Kerman. Not all these may of course be related, yet they spell out a series of changes that mark the beginning of a new period, the Ubaid.

Whatever caused the Halaf collapse, the decrease in the number and prosperity of sites may have led to a disruption of trade and industry, undermining the former economy. It may have taken a few centuries, until the beginning of the Late Ubaid period, dated by C14 to *c.* 4200 BC (calibrated into real calendar years, *c.* 5200 BC), before the old trade patterns were restored and prosperity returned, with new markets. It marked a new era in which metals, especially copper, enhanced by new casting techniques, began to play an important role; known as the 'Chalcolithic', it formed the basis for the Bronze Age economy of the Near East. Even Egypt entered this commonwealth as a newcomer from somewhere in Asia, and by introducing irrigation agriculture into what was potentially an exceptionally fertile country, finally overcame the climatic drawbacks which for millennia had retarded her development and forced her into somewhat provincial isolation. By *c.* 4200 BC the Neolithic of the Near East had come to an end.

As examples of the cultural decay that occurred in the Levant at the time of Early Ubaid in Mesopotamia, we may instance Ras Shamra IIIC and Byblos Late Neolithic. Above the burnt 'Late Halaf' level IVA there are seven successive building levels in Ras Shamra IIIC with miserable remains of rectangular houses characterized by mud-brick walls, pisé hearths and patches of stone-paved floors, but there are signs of a revival in level IIIB with Late Ubaid-style pottery. Sickle blades attest agriculture and bifacially retouched arrowheads for hunting replace the slingstones of the Halaf period. Fully polished axes of greenstone (serpentine and steatite) show that woodworking was practised, and a perforated macehead of haematite was found. Stylized figurines of soft limestone are new, and clay and stone spindle whorls suggest spinning and weaving. Obsidian still occurs and is now used for making beads, but its provenance is unknown. Bone tools are common. The pottery is red-wash ware, as in level IVA–B, but here it predominates and includes bowls, jars with bow-rims, lugs or large strap-handles. It is decorated, not with paint as before, but with finger imprints or impressed raised bands. With it occurs a new painted ware comprising bowls and handled jars, decorated in a crude style with wavy lines in multiple-brush technique, parallel bands, hatched lozenges, solid triangles, etc. – geometric and rather uninspired patterns. A certain similarity to the pottery of contemporary Mersin XVI across the Mediterranean in Cilicia is unmistakable,[117] but there the cream-slipped ware with multiple-brush designs applied to a number of different shapes is better made than the Ras Shamra IIIC pottery which is clumsy and crude. So far no parallel for this pottery has been found in Syria – it is missing in the Amuq sequence – but its stratigraphical position and a C14 date of 4185 ± 81 for the end (?) of the period shows that it is contemporary with Early Ubaid of Mesopotamia to which it bears no real resemblance.

At Byblos too the Late Neolithic is a period of decline. Large rectangular houses still occur, but small cellular structures are also found.[241] There are no graves apart from a few infant burials in pots. Basalt maceheads and rams'-head pendants of stone are probably imports from the north. Burins and the bone industry are impoverished. The stone industry shows important changes; long axes, hoes, chisels and antler sleeves, miniature celts of greenstone, and a vast abundance of tools for precise woodwork, such as reamers and piercers, predominate.[237] Sickle blades, too, are found, but offensive weapons are exceedingly rare, indicating that the wild animals still found on the site must have been caught by other hunting methods. The new emphasis on woodworking, the products of which have not survived, is noteworthy and might to some extent account for the decline of the pottery into cooking vessels. It looks as if the Byblites were already turning towards that prize source of their future wealth, timber and woodwork from the forests of Lebanon. There is still no trace of metal at Byblos or elsewhere in Syria or Palestine, and with stone vessels long obsolete wooden plates and dishes may have been used. The pottery is in full decline, burnishing has ceased, and the only concession to decoration is the careless application of red-ochre bands to round pots with large handles, as in Ras Shamra IIIC. There are flat-based flower pots and jars of coarse fabric with rough finger imprints on raised bands, as in the north. Despite this decline Vannic green and grey obsidian still occurs, as well as some Çiftlik obsidian from Anatolia.[85] Does this mean re-established contact with the north? Or did someone dig up a piece from an earlier period? Obsidian analyses could perhaps benefit from stricter stratigraphical controls.

Palestine in the Pottery Neolithic Period

The incidence of a hiatus between the end of the PPNB culture of Palestine and the arrival of several groups of newcomers with pottery from the north or northeast is well established. Suggestions that this gap in the record lasted from *c.* 6000 to 4500 B C[261] are based on vague correlations with climatic events in western Europe and a faulty Mesopotamian chronology, which is emphatically contradicted by C14 dating. Palestine was not uninhabited until 4500 B C, the beginning of the Early Ubaid period!

The site of Aceramic Beisamoun on Lake Huleh[5] has rows of rectangular rooms with stone foundations, pebble-paved floors and courts, and plastered skulls but no plaster floors.[243] It has a late PPNB flint tradition, in which a scarcity of arrowheads is offset by an abundance of sickle blades with coarse teeth, flint axes with polished bits, bifaces, picks, etc., indicative of woodwork, as at Khirbet Tannur and the adjacent forest cultures of southern Lebanon.[239]

This sounds like a transition from PPNB to Early Neolithic Byblos unaccompanied by northern features of pottery and hunting weapons. All animals are said to have been wild.

At the next site in the succession, Hagoshrim, at the foot of Mt Hermon,[5, 243] cattle constitutes more than 60 per cent of all the animals present and may possibly have been domesticated.[53] Here there are querns in the PPNB tradition, many flint axes, greenstone and obsidian seals with incised geometric patterns, and other objects similar to Amuq B. Clay sling-stones (typical only of Amuq C), such as were used much earlier in Anatolia and Cilicia, also occur. Pottery now appears for the first time in Palestine; most of it is very coarse and fragile, but some red and brown burnished ware is found. The links of Hagoshrim are clearly with the north though the material from Beisamoun and Hagoshrim is only known from preliminary notices.

More satisfactory evidence is available from Munhata in the Jordan valley, south of the Sea of Galilee.[259–61] A hiatus separated the last PPNB level (3) from a well stratified Pottery Neolithic sequence with three main periods: level 2B2, the Sha'ar Hagolan phase (= Yarmukian culture), level 2B1, the Munhata phase (cf. Jericho Pottery Neolithic A or Jericho IX) and level 2A with three building phases of the Wadi Rabah culture (cf. Jericho Pottery Neolithic B or Jericho VIII).

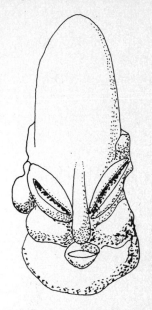

153 Head of a Yarmukian figurine from Sha'ar Hagolan (after Stekelis)

THE YARMUKIAN

Round semi-subterranean huts, 3–4 m in diameter and furnished with a paved area, a hearth and a bench, as well as bell-shaped storage pits, 1 m deep and 1–1·5 m wide at the base, characterize the Yarmukian at Munhata (2B2). Coarsely serrated sickle blades and large axes with polished butts can compare with Byblos Early Neolithic, but javelin points and arrowheads are badly made. There are flat, oblong basalt querns, incised pebbles (at Sha'ar Hagolan) and pebble figurines, again reminiscent of Byblos. Typical of the culture are grotesque clay figurines of women with *153* tall peaked heads, coffee-bean or cowrie-like eyes, exaggerated versions of the heads from Tell Ramad III or the Hassuna figures from Yarim Tepe I. Among figurines representing animals are humped cattle, which would suggest domestication.

The pottery consists of bowls and jars with lugs, and is rather coarse, sometimes painted in red with simple chevrons, but more commonly decorated with herring-bone patterns incised on a *154* border of zigzags left in reserve on the red ground. Among the vessels with lugs are deep bowls but, like those of Labwe III, they are of coarser fabric. This Yarmukian pottery has distinct affinities in decoration with late Early Neolithic and early Middle Neolithic Byblos, which is one of several features suggesting that the influences came from the Lebanon and southern Syria.

THE MUNHATA PHASE

In the following Munhata phase (level 2B1) dwellings occupy shallow scoops with diameters of 10–12 m filled with basins and silos. In the centre stands a circular hut, 3 m in diameter, constructed of bun-shaped bricks (15 × 8 cm) on a stone foundation.

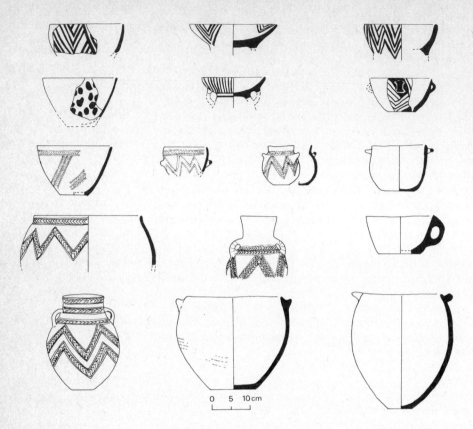

0 5 10cm

154 Yarmukian pottery from Munhata and Sha'ar Hagolan in northern Palestine (after Perrot and Anati)

Similarly built huts are known from Jericho Pottery Neolithic A. The pottery shows more use of red paint clumsily applied on jars and bowls, with some incised ware and mat-impressed bases; it compares unfavourably with the Jericho ware, which is competently made with burnished red-painted triangles and chevrons on bowls and jars.

At Munhata the rest of the equipment resembles that of the previous phase, but axes have disappeared and the grotesque figurines are no longer made. On the basis of what has been published, this would seem to indicate a decline. These single occupation levels, 2B2 and 2B1, hardly suggest more than intermittent settlement, perhaps seasonal when winter and spring offered refuge and pasture to people whose economy is said to have principally relied on herding and hunting. None of the animals of the Yarmukian and Munhata phases are osteologically domestic. In order of numerical importance they are: gazelle (25 per cent), pig (22·3 per cent), cattle (19·9 per cent), wild sheep (19·5 per cent), roe deer (6·7 per cent), and goat (3·3 per cent).[53] The reference in the published material to wild sheep seems strange in a country that ostensibly had none. The reports contain no mention of plant food, yet sickles, querns and the large silos could hardly have been used for anything else at this period.

The excavator of Munhata equates Jericho Pottery Neolithic A and Ghrubba (lower) with his Munhata phase and Ghrubba (upper) with Wadi Rabah. These southern sites present the same unsettled picture of semi-permanent huts, scoops and silos (Ghrubba, lower),[258] but the southern pottery, both at Jericho and Ghrubba seems far superior to that of the Munhata phase and, to judge by the published drawings, is quite different. Either there are far more 'phases' in this period or one is dealing with various tribal units, each with a ceramic tradition of its own. The Munhata phase may be contemporary with the early part of Byblos Middle Neolithic, but it is certainly not related to it. Painted pottery was always rare on the Lebanese littoral, and the origins of the various 'cultures', or rather groups, of the Munhata phase must be sought elsewhere. The lack of domestic animals and the presence of wild (?) sheep – not native to Palestine – seem to point to the marginal steppe-lands or hills of the northeast beyond the Great Rift valley, regions from which at a later date the Ghassulians and the Amorites were to invade Palestine.

THE WADI RABAH CULTURE

By this period, contemporary with Byblos Middle Neolithic, the Ard Tlaïli culture appeared in the Beqa's valley;[242] it had certain affinities with Amuq C and D. During its later phase, when the bow-rim jar was most popular, it seems to have spread to Palestine, where it is represented at Munhata 2A, in the Wadi Rabah culture, perhaps at Ghrubba (upper),[258] at Jericho Pottery Neolithic B, at Ain Jarba[257] and a host of other sites.

At Munhata rectangular houses measuring 4 × 9 m appear, with two or three small rooms and stamped clay floors. Ovens, semi-circular in shape are built up against the long walls on a pebble base. Similar rectangular structures occur at Ain Jarba, but at Jericho round huts continue. Economic details are almost absent, though domestic (?) sheep and goat are reported at Jericho.[52]

There are no figurines, but anthropomorphic and serpent ornamentation is applied to pots. Axes and hoes (for irrigation agriculture?) predominate in the tool-kit, and there are some arrowheads as well as sling-stones.

The pottery, red, brown or black burnished ware is quite different from that of the Yarmukian or Munhata phases. At Ain Jarba, bow-rim jars and small carinated bowls are black; heavy pedestalled bowls, inverted-rim bowls, flat dishes and jars with everted rims in Halaf tradition are typical of the red burnished ware.[257] Ledge-handles with finger imprints occur on large jars. Decoration is varied: incised, pointillé, impressed, combed, as at Ard Tlaïli and Middle Neolithic Byblos. Decoration on bowls appears below an amber-coloured rim. Applied decoration takes the form of human figures on vessels at Ain Jarba and a few painted sherds (and pots) of Halaf type, as in the Lebanon, have been found. From Kabri comes a group of luxury objects of this period found in a partly disturbed cist grave.[6] They include a polished limestone bow-rim jar, several heavy limestone pedestalled vessels, a fine obsidian mirror with a carved strap-handle, a large obsidian core of Vannic obsidian, a bearded male figure carved out of bone, and a broken macehead of red granite, a material that points to Sinai or Egypt. Evidently this must have been the grave of someone of importance.

155

156

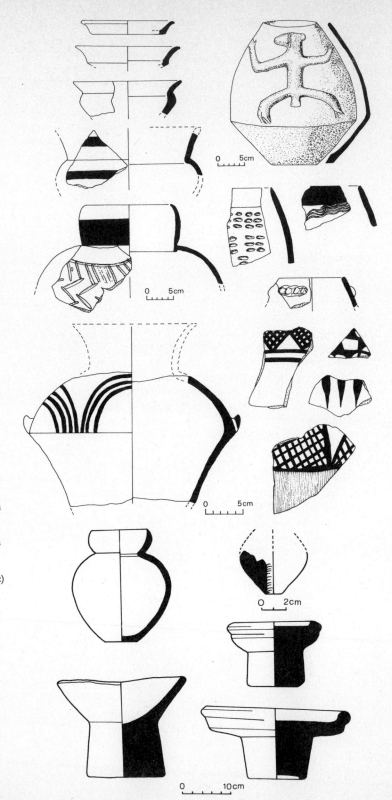

155 Wadi Rabah pottery from
Ain Jarba (after Kaplan)

156 Gypsum and basalt vessels
and granite macehead of the
Wadi Rabah culture, from cist
tombs at Kabri (after Prausnitz)

The Wadi Rabah culture is evidently derived from the Ard Tlaïli group in the Beqa'a, but it is not known when exactly it established itself in Palestine. A C14 date from Ain Jarba of 3740± 140 B C strikes one as impossibly late. Nevertheless with the Wadi Rabah culture some measure of stability and uniformity is re-established in Palestine, from the present Lebanese frontier (Kabri) to the Vale of Sorek and the Dead Sea. A later develop-ment of Wadi Rabah pottery is seen in the Tell es-Shuna ware (also known as Beth Shan XVIII), widespread in the northern Jordan valley as far as Tell es-Sayidiyeh, and characterized by large jars with funnel necks or bow-rims, two lug-handles and simple horizontal bands of red paint, and coarse-ware storage jars with thumb-indented ledge-handles. Also typical are axes and hoes, rectangular structures and bell-shaped silos. This culture (or phase?), recently named Neve Ur,[5] seems to mark the beginning of the Ghassulian period, which ushered in a new era in the prehistory of Palestine with the introduction of metalworking, new stone industries and economies based on herding of sheep, goat and cattle and cultivation not only of cereal crops, but of olives and grapes. The Chalcolithic Ghassulian culture, which I feel is the equivalent of Late Ubaid and Early Uruk in Mesopotamia, must have begun nearer to 4000 than to 3500 B C on the radiocarbon scale.

Chapter Nine

Southeastern Europe: the Aegean and the Southern Balkans

Herodotus, in his account of the Persian wars, was the first to draw attention to the contrast between Europe and Asia, a political concept foreign to earlier periods. Geographically, southeastern Europe is linked to Anatolia and Asia, and the dividing seas, the Aegean and the Sea of Marmara, are geologically-speaking recent accidents. Once man had invented boats, the Bosphorus and the Dardanelles invited crossing, while the chains of Greek islands formed useful links. Recent evidence suggests that seafaring developed in the seventh millennium B C, as is proved by the discovery of Melian obsidian in strata of that date in Franchthi cave on the shores of the Argolid.[267] It reached Crete late in that millennium and the earliest settlements, such as Nuriye and Moralı near Manisa in western Anatolia in the next millennium were importing Melian obsidian.[114]

In theory at least there is no reason why the wild ancestors of sheep and goat, wheat and barley should not have occurred on all three sides of the Aegean prior to the foundering of the connecting chains and basins in the Pliocene. Strangely enough, this does not seem to have been the case, and it appears from the archaeological evidence that these animals were not locally domesticated but introduced, evidently from the Anatolian shores to the east, from the late seventh millennium onwards. There is as yet no evidence whatsoever for local domestication in southeastern Europe nor in the lowlands of western Anatolia, where like in Egypt, certain economic limitations were forced on the population by the environment. However, when settlers with established agricultural practices arrived here, they began to flourish, until eventually they surpassed their masters in the artistic and intellectual climate of the Late Bronze and classical periods, just as western civilization was to surpass classical civilization. In cultural development no group remains dominant for ever; in due course the torch of civilization is passed onto others to take over – *de nihile nihil est*. The Neolithic of southeastern Europe appears to present us with a clear and obvious case of culture diffusion from Anatolia, but this diffusion is limited to the practices of dry farming and animal domestication, and certain techniques like that of toolmaking and pottery-making. Shapes and decoration soon diversify and there is never any question of slavish copying – such a deplorable feature of the modern world.

During the last decade evidence has been accumulating to show that southeastern Europe was inhabited by Epipalaeolithic hunters and gatherers. In many areas the material is still very scanty and one has the impression that such people were not very numerous.

The islands of the Aegean have not yet shown any signs of pre-Neolithic man, but earlier occupation cannot be ruled out, especially in the case of Melos with its rich obsidian deposits. The most instructive site for tracing early developments is Franchthi cave near Porto Cheli on the southern shores of the Argolid.

Franchthi Cave and Aceramic Knossos

In the tenth millennium B C, coeval with the Natufian of Palestine and Syria and Beldibi C in the Antalya region, Franchthi cave was occupied by hunters of probably Eurafrican type.[267] By choice they hunted red deer, but their quarry also included an equid and the aurochs and from time to time they brought back hare, boar and ibex. Radiocarbon dates for this Epipalaeolithic occupation are 9980± 168 and 9143± 260 B C.

The cave was then deserted and not reoccupied until the 'Mesolithic period', *c.* 7500 B C, by which time agricultural settlements in the Near East extended from the southwest Anatolian plateau eastward to the Zagros Mountains, and southward down to the Dead Sea. For these 'Mesolithic' layers, representing a period of some fifteen hundred years, twelve radiocarbon dates ranging between 7527± 134 and 5947± 88 B C have been obtained; the hunting of red deer still predominates in the lowest layers, but gradually the diet diversified and besides venison (still 85 per cent) aurochs, fox and pig, hare, wild cat and wolf appear. Seafaring, indicated by the appearance of Melian obsidian, coincides with fishing (especially tunny) and shellfish-gathering. Land snails were now also collected as well as quantities of pea and vetch, pistachio and almond. The tools were made of local red and grey flint, greyish chert and, in the later half of the period, obsidian; notched flakes predominate, with tools for cutting and sawing, but neither burins nor end-scrapers, and virtually no blades or blade-lets occur. There are a few geometric microliths: triangles, crescents and trapeze forms, probably arrowheads in both flint and obsidian. A number of contracted burials were found without funerary gifts, showing the people to have been of Eurafrican type, dolichocephalic, but less rugged than the Natufians.

Around 5900 B C (5844± 140) an abrupt change takes place in Franchthi cave. The bones of sheep and goat appear in large numbers, ousting the local fauna. As these animals were hitherto unknown, this can only mean that domestic, or at least tame, sheep and goat were introduced. In Crete also the earliest aceramic settlement at Knossos[265] was founded by people who brought with them not only domestic sheep and goat, but some domestic cattle, pig and dog.[268] Sheep were apparently four times as numerous as goats. In terms of the weight of meat, sheep (with goat) provided 49·4 per cent, cattle 31·1 per cent and pig 19·5 per cent of the animal protein of the diet. The first cereal crops now appear, above all bread-wheat, but also emmer, einkorn, six-row naked barley and lentils. Evidently the first farmers arrived by sea with their domestic animals and crops; bread-wheat and six-row barley are clear Anatolian products of this time, dated to 6100± 180 and 5960± 140 B C. The first settlement on the hill at Knossos

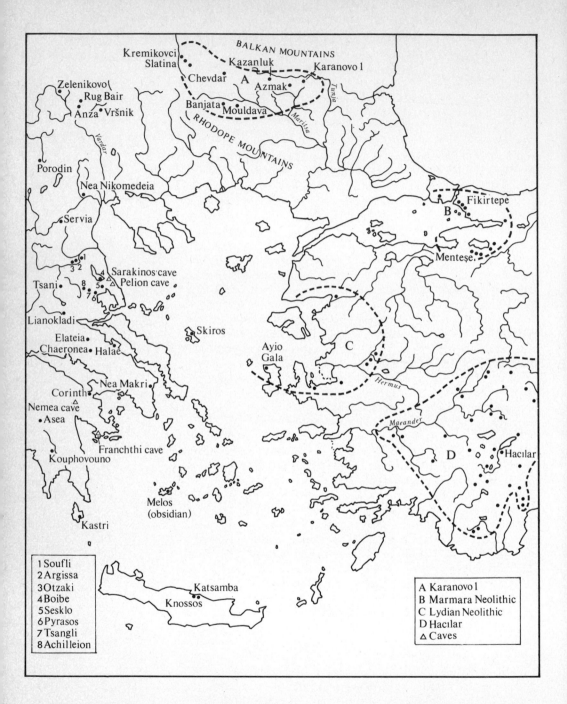

157 Map of the Aegean area

1 Soufli
2 Argissa
3 Otzaki
4 Boibe
5 Sesklo
6 Pyrasos
7 Tsangli
8 Achilleion

A Karanovo 1
B Marmara Neolithic
C Lydian Neolithic
D Hacılar
△ Caves

covered only half an acre, and had a population of fewer than a hundred people, but it grew gradually throughout four building phases to twice that size.[266] Now rectangular houses made of stones (often old querns) and mud brick, and mud plaster, were erected. Pottery was still absent, but two female baked-clay figurines were found. Melian obsidian blades were in use and ground stone querns were manufactured.

There may have been a gradual transition to the next phase (Knossos IX), in which pottery was in full use. This Early Neolithic period, with a C14 date of 5620±150, lasted until 4200 BC, during which time there was repeated rebuilding of rectangular houses.[265] The abruptness of the appearance of dark coloured wares suggests, not a local development but importation from elsewhere, and though no similar material is known at such an early date it is generally thought to come from the unexplored and partly submerged coastlands of western (southwestern?) Anatolia, where at a later date we find many of the typical Knossos features. Pointillé decoration has parallels in Cilicia at Mersin XXV–XXIV,[117] which is again later in date than the Cretan pottery! The home of the Knossos Neolithic ware cannot yet be pin-pointed. Could it be local after all?

In the Peloponnese, the aceramic of Franchthi cave is likewise succeeded by an Early Neolithic ceramic culture with a C14 date of 5754±81.[267] Sheep and goat are now domesticated and domestic barley was grown. There is a blade industry (the aceramic flints resemble those of the Mesolithic with obsidian blades, geometric microlithic, notched and denticulated tools) producing knife and sickle blades in local honey-coloured flint and imported (23 per cent) brown Melian obsidian, as well as scrapers for working hides, and arrowheads without tangs. Here the grit-tempered pottery consists of brown to red burnished ware, with hole-mouth shapes, sometimes decorated with knobs and ribs. This class of pottery, previously described as 'rainbow ware' is quite different in shape and decoration from that of Knossos EN I, and much closer to that of Çatal Hüyük. As during the Mesolithic period, contracted burials of Eurafricans were found.

Painted pottery starts appearing towards the end of the period but is still very rare. Stone vessels also occur. This Early Neolithic culture is known from many other sites in southern and central *157* Greece, such as Nemea, Corinth, Ayiorgitika, Halae, etc.[264] Female clay figurines are also made.

In Attica, the site of Nea Makri has stone vessels and black-incised burnished-ware bowls unrelated to this Early Neolithic and evidently representing a different and local (?) tradition.[277] Comparisons with Mersin do not strike one as convincing. Animal bones from the site indicate the importance of domestic sheep and goat (80 per cent!) as compared with cattle and pig.

Thessaly and Greek Macedonia

Farther north, the fertile Thessalian plain is studded with Neolithic settlements and an aceramic phase has been identified at a number of sites: Argissa, Sesklo, Soufli, Ghediki and Achilleion. In the absence of radiocarbon tests this aceramic phase can be only tentatively dated to *c.* 6200–6000 (?) BC at Argissa.

These farmers kept domestic cattle at Argissa and grew emmer, einkorn, two- and six-row hulled barley and oats, supplemented by peas and lentils, vetch, pistachio, acorns and wild olives.[270–72]

A series of oval storage (?) pits cut into bedrock were found at *158* Argissa, and later there is a rectangular house plan with hearth and

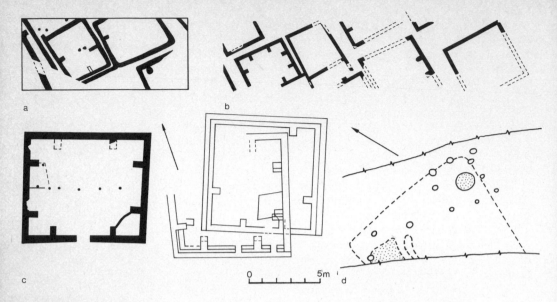

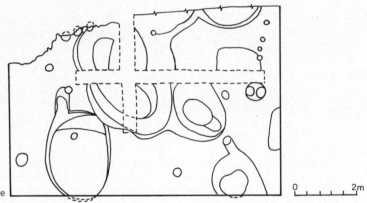

158 House plans from Thessaly:
(a, b) clay and wood mud-brick
houses of the Sesklo period at
Otzaki; (c) mud-brick houses of
the Sesklo period from Tsangli;
(d, e) post and plaster structure
and semi-subterranean huts from
the Aceramic Neolithic at
Argissa (after Titov)

storage pit, but built of light materials. Primitive sun-dried pottery
is reported from Sesklo, though the use of firing is not unknown
as clay-missiles are already a feature of this period. Baked-clay
figurines, still of an old Upper Palaeolithic shape like those of
Peterfels, Mezine, Kobystan or Çatal Hüyük IV, are found at
Sesklo.[276] More up-to-date ornaments include stone plugs for
inserting into the ear, nose or lip, or for use as small cosmetic
pestles. The stone industry, at least at Argissa, seems undistinguished; transverse trapezoidal arrowheads predominate, but
there are also short retouched blades and a few geometric microliths
such as crescents and triangles.

   In the next phase, divided on the basis of pottery into Early
Ceramic and Proto-Sesklo, there is evidence for domestic sheep
and goat. At Sesklo, Soufli and Achilleion, emmer, einkorn,
barley, pea and lentil were grown as at Argissa in the aceramic.[271–2]
The earliest pottery at Argissa is a deep-red or red-brown grit-
tempered burnished ware comprising simple bowls, hole-mouth
vessels and a few jars.[270] Some of the vessels have simple lugs. The
fabric of this pottery resembles that of Early Neolithic southern

Greece, though it lacks the conspicuous mottling, and is like Çatal Hüyük and early Hacılar ware, while different from that of the Early Neolithic I at Knossos.

In the later Proto-Sesklo phase much more sophisticated vessels were produced. There are bowls with beaded or everted rims, on ring bases or short pedestals, in red- or pink-slipped ware. Painted pottery now appears in a red-on-white style with simple but effective patterns of chevrons, zigzags, triangles, lozenges and even a frieze of running figures. Certain parallels in shape, fabric and patterns suggest perhaps some contact with 'Late Neolithic' Hacılar, the monochrome pottery of which is known to have reached the Aegean coast and the island of Chios in the Izmir area, and there are a few more specific elements such as relief decoration in the form of an arm with outstretched hand found both at Sesklo and in Hacılar VI. It may well have been through the trade in Melian obsidian that the new centres in Greece maintained contact with fashions and new technological development across the Aegean.

The richest Proto-Sesklo site explored is Nea Nikomedeia, 60 km west of Thessaloniki in Macedonia.[273-5] The site lies on a knoll on the western side of a lake and about half an acre has been excavated. Four successive building levels, divided into two main Early Neolithic periods, were found without any break in the stratigraphy or any significant change in the culture. A series of C14 dates of 5830 ± 270, 5607 ± 91, 5331 ± 112 suggest that they are approximately contemporary with Hacılar VII–VI and V (?) (5820 ± 180, 5590 ± 180 and 5399 ± 79) and parallel with the end of Çatal Hüyük.

Nea Nikomedeia shows an open-settlement plan with free-standing structures like those of the Karanovo I culture in Bulgaria. Rectangular buildings were erected round a framework of vertical oak posts with reeds and rushes, coated on both sides with mud mixed with straw, forming the walls. Mud brick was apparently unknown. Floors were of mud laid over reeds, and roofs made of the same material were probably pitched with broad eaves. The houses are oriented east–west to avoid the prevailing northerly winds. These structures were large, two of the earliest being square with sides 8 m long, while a third measured $8 \cdot 5 \times 6$ m. The latter had a large central room, a porch on one side, and a narrow room at the other containing a raised platform with a hearth basin and a storage bin. A fourth building, only partly excavated, was 8 m wide and at least 11 m long, and seems to have been subdivided by a series of very large post holes 8 m from the east wall; it has internal buttresses to support the roof beam. There were two ovens inside an enclosure outside the north wall of the building. These four houses appear to have been grouped around a much larger structure, measuring approximately 12×12 m, presumably a shrine. It was divided into three by parallel rows of large posts, forming two aisles on either side of a large central room with internal buttresses. Five baked-clay statuettes and a number of unique objects were found in the building though, following a fire, it had been reconstructed on the same plan. The second building phase shows a slight change in orientation and single- or two-roomed houses continued to be built, but the shrine disappeared.

159

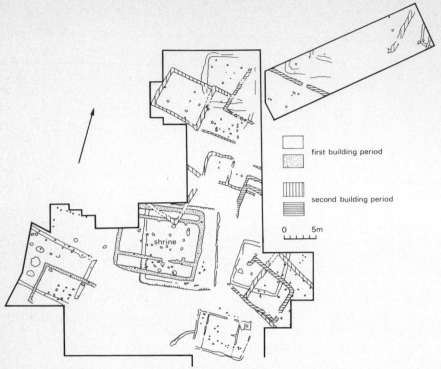

first building period

second building period

0   5m

shrine

159 Structures of four successive building levels at the Early Neolithic site of Nea Nikomedeia in Macedonia (after Rodden)

The best preserved building consisted of two rooms, each 8 m square. Clay-lined basins filled with ashes and much carbonized grain suggests that they may have been used for parching.

Emmer, six-row naked barley and lentils were the main crops, but einkorn, peas and bitter vetch were also known.[278] There is, however, no bread-wheat and no hulled barley. Collected fruits included acorns, dogwood and *Prunus* cf. *spinosa*. Among domestic animals, sheep and goat were the more numerous and domestic pig and cattle played a minor role. Arrowheads, with trapezoidal tips were used to hunt aurochs, boar, deer and hare. Bones of small rodents, carnivores and canids were also found and the local aquatic resources of a lakeside site were fully exploited; fish bones and fish-hooks were found, and shellfish, especially cockle (*Cardium*), occur in large quantities throughout the site.

The settlement was fully ceramic from the beginning. Plain burnished ware, dark grey, beige, or dark reddish brown in colour is most common. There is a slipped ware, also burnished, which is pink, pale orange-red or red-brown, colour variations that may be due to irregular firing or to a deliberate desire to produce such 'rainbow' effects. Nearly all vessels have round, oval, ring or disc bases and four horizontally or vertically perforated string-hole lugs are common on smaller bowls. Miniature vessels, including *askoi* are not uncommon. Relief decoration takes the form of human faces or miniature human female figures (cf. Umm Dabaghiyah, Hacılar VI, effigies in Samarra and Hacılar I cultures). Together with the monochrome wares, painted red-on-cream ware is found as in Thessaly in the Proto-Sesklo phase, and in addition a less common ware painted in white on red-brown monochrome, and an impressed pottery as in the neighbouring territories to the north, with which Nea Nikomedeia evidently kept up contacts.

Large baked-clay statuettes of females of a very distinctive kind were made – some by pegging together several parts. The eyes, which are incised, often take a slit or cowrie-like form; pregnancy, emphasis of the navel and fat buttocks are common. Heads, sometimes with a mouth (which is frequently omitted in statuettes), may occur by themselves, as at Can Hasan, and animal heads of goat and lamb are also found. These figures were all discovered in the shrine together with two greenstone axes, 20 cm long, two large caches of over four hundred flint blades, two *askoi* and several hundred 'roundels' (calculi?) of baked clay. If the figurines are a little rough, there are some extraordinarily fine stamp seals with geometric motifs, as typical of the Early Neolithic of southeastern Europe as they are of Anatolia, and here again the patterns invariably differ from those found on the painted pottery. Even more remarkable are the finely worked pins of local marble, and the 'studs' of blue and green stone and marble, possibly used as nose- or ear-plugs, to be seen for example on Chogha Mami statuettes. Beads, toggles and double perforated beads were very popular, and shell necklaces were common. Also found were polished stone axes, adzes, chisels and three carved frogs, all made from local serpentine. Flint and chert were used for sickle blades, set in bone or wooden handles. Scrapers and trapezoidal arrow-heads of Mesolithic ancestry were used and some Melian obsidian was found. Clay sling-stones were more common than the arrowheads. Bone tools include awls, needles, spatulae, pins, fish-hooks, and belt fasteners as at Çatal Hüyük, Hacılar and Sesklo.

161f, g

There is ample evidence for the use of twined and occasionally twilled matting and impressions are common on the flat-based pots. The dead at Nea Nikomedeia were buried in a contracted position in shallow pits outside the houses or in ruined buildings. Grave gifts are absent, but in one case a pebble was stuck between the jaws of a skeleton. Single burials are not as common as those of adults accompanied by children, or groups of children. A preliminary reference reports that the people were of a Eurafrican racial type and suffered from *porotic hyperostosis* attributed to *falciparum* malaria as at Çatal Hüyük.[99] It is not clear at present how long Nea Nikomedeia was occupied, but it has been suggested that it spanned Proto-Sesklo as well as Pre-Sesklo in north Thessaly.

The Pre-Sesklo culture of north Thessaly[269] – in the south Proto-Sesklo continued – is clearly intrusive from the north or northwest (?)[276] and is characterized by the appearance in considerable quantities of impressed wares (such as were present at Nea Nikomedeia);[264] initially these were of barbotine and nail-impressed type, then fine ware with cardium-shell impressions. These are found on shapes somewhat different from those that were in use before the painted Proto-Sesklo ware disappears. The figurines of the period are crude pear-shaped females with no facial features and incised decoration. According to some scholars this culture represents an incursion from the Hungarian plain, where this type of pottery is said to be the earliest. It interrupted a painted-pottery tradition in Serbia and Macedonia and reached as far as north Thessaly. The specialist in the field must decide whether this material justifies the assumption of such a widespread movement, but the Dalma episode in Iran offers a parallel for similar events, showing how a 'fringe culture' with an inferior ceramic tradition can temporarily overrun the territory of a neighbour with a higher culture until the 'barbaric' elements are assimilated and disappear. In Thessaly this happened with the beginning of the Sesklo period *c.* 5000 B C, when the older tradition prevailed and the impressed ware and the crude figurines disappeared.[262-3] Only a few traces of the former were embodied in an attractive painted and impressed ware, but the latter were replaced by the old anthropomorphic figures.

Square or rectangular houses, arranged in rows but without party walls, occur at Otzaki in a village plan less open than that of Nea Nikomedeia.[269] They are either built of posts, mud and wattle, or in mud brick. Internal buttresses are a feature of the square-house type of this period, but oblong buildings consisting of a square room with portico, the so-called megaron plan, also appear. Others, for example at Tsangli, may have had a row of posts dividing the room into two sections as at Nea Nikomedeia.

Sesklo yielded some pointers concerning the economy in the form of emmer, einkorn, barley and acorns, with sheep and goat the main domestic animals.[271-2] The painted pottery now reaches its climax in the solid or linear styles with bold step and flame patterns on cups and jugs with real strap-handles, and bowls with everted rims. Foreign influences have totally disappeared and the Thessalian Neolithic has shed its Anatolian stamp. White-on-red ware as well as red monochrome wares also occur and there are a number of regional variants in the painted pottery (Otzaki, Tsangli, Lianokladi, etc.).[269] The settlements appear to have greatly increased in number, but details of modern surveys have not yet been published. The use of metal is still unknown, unless the flat axe from Sesklo really belongs to this period, which is rather doubtful.

In central and southern Greece, not affected by the Balkanic irruption into northern Thessaly, the Early Neolithic now develops into the Middle Neolithic, as exemplified by Franchthi around 5300 B C (5244±112); here too the old Anatolian connections are being severed.

In the early phase of the Middle Neolithic at Franchthi the pottery still consists mainly of monochrome-slipped ware, but 'Urfirnis', coated with a glossy thin reddish wash now appears.[267] New shapes are found: carinated bowls, tall cylindrical vessels on flat disc or pedestal bases, jars with proper handles as well as pottery ladles. Decoration of the monochrome ware still consists of ribs, knobs and pellets, but the painted pottery – not more than 20 per cent in this early phase – shows simple linear patterns, which will become more complicated later. In the late Middle Neolithic period pedestalled bowls with flaring profiles appear and fenestrated 'fruitstands', with pattern-burnish introduced as another form of decoration, increase in numbers. 'Urfirnis' ware, a characteristic product of the Peloponnese, was exported to central Greece and Thessaly, during the Sesklo phase (Middle Neolithic). There has been much speculation about the origin of the 'Urfirnis' technique and the use of this slightly lustrous paint has been linked with Halaf through maritime contact with Cilicia or Syria. It is not only the technique that is new, but also the shapes and the idea of painting, and it is hard to believe that borrowings would be so selective. It seems far more likely that this pottery was invented in the Peloponnese at such sites as Corinth, Lerna or Asea without the benefit of oriental influence. There are other features that are clearly local, such as the hut or house with a pitched roof shown on a Franchthi pot, or the striking marble statuettes from Sparta (-Kouphovouno?)[262] and Franchthi.[267] By the Middle Neolithic period Greece and also the southern Balkans were developing local talent and the effects of their Asiatic origins and schooling were no longer felt. Dry farming and stockbreeding in the Peloponnese (Franchthi) were producing approximately the same food as in the north: sheep and goat, emmer, barley and lentils.[267]

At a date which is not yet clearly defined by C14 tests but which may be as early as *c.* 4300 BC, that is, contemporary with the beginning of Late Ubaid, the Middle Neolithic of Greece gave way to new influences that mark the Late Neolithic period.

A matt-painted pottery of central Greek type spread throughout the country together with a very fine black burnished ware evoking metal vessels.[264] On the other hand metal does not yet

160

160 Early and Middle Neolithic pottery from the Peloponnese. Middle Neolithic: (a, c) from Asea; (b) from Corinth; (d–g) from Franchthi cave; Early Neolithic: (h, i) from Franchthi cave; (j) bowl from Corinth; (k–o) from Nemea cave (after Jacobsen and Titov)

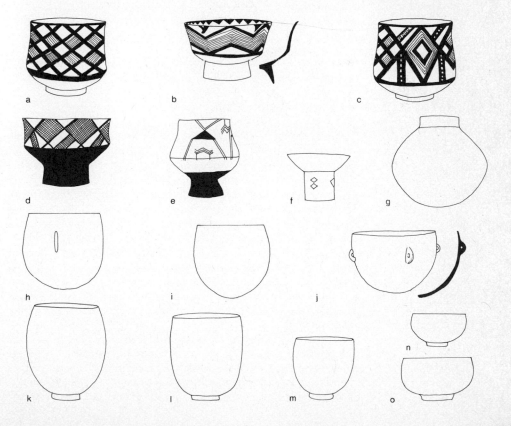

appear, and in this respect Greece certainly lagged behind its eastern neighbours. Anatolian influence has been postulated for the black burnished wares of the Late Chalcolithic, which probably at varying dates supplant or appear side by side with the various painted-pottery cultures during the fifth millennium. This phenomenon – the gradual change-over from painted to dark burnished wares – is not confined to Anatolia or Greece, but takes place in most areas of the Near East; Uruk monochrome ware comes in during Late Ubaid and then supplants the painted wares; in Khuzistan the Susa A ware is followed by Uruk fabrics; red wares take over from Syrian Ubaid and Late Chalcolithic red and grey wares supplant the sparsely painted Ghassulian ware of Palestine. Returning to southeast Europe, this same process was at work in Bulgaria[282] where the Middle Neolithic painted ware of the Karanovo I culture is replaced by grey, black and buff burnished wares of the same shapes in Karanovo II, evidently a change in ceramic fashion and a local process.[286] During Karanovo III more sophisticated shapes evolved and spread across the Rhodope Mountains to the northern Aegean where they occur at Paradimi near Komotini and in the lowest level (I) of Sitagroi. Farther west these same influences led to the formation of the earliest Vinča monochrome wares,[283-4] dated at Anza IV in Yugoslav Macedonia to 4300 BC (C14).[289] In central Greece, at places like Elateia and Drachmani, are found vases on incised legs which have been shown to derive from the Danilo culture on the Dalmatian coast.[264] With such clear evidence for northern connections the presence of dark burnished ware need not be sought farther east.

To trace these developments in further detail and consider the possibilities of ethnic movements into Greece would take us beyond the chronological limits of this book.

The Karanovo I Culture of the Thracian Plain

Between the parallel ranges of the Balkan Mountains and Rhodope lies the Thracian plain, watered by the rivers Maritsa and Tunca and their tributaries.[286] Open to the east, it was one of the natural highways into Europe and an easy pass leads from the Sofia basin to the Morava valley in Serbia, and thus on to the Hungarian plain. The earliest known farming culture of Bulgaria, Karanovo I, stretches from the Sofia basin to the Tunca, but avoids the hilly country between the river and the Black Sea. Neither this culture nor its equivalents have yet been located in Greek and Turkish Thrace. The sites take the form of mounds situated in or around the alluvial plain, such as Karanovo, Tell Azmak, Chevdar and Kazanluk, to mention but four of those recently investigated. At its widest Karanovo measures 250 m and at no point is it less than 150 m across!

Tell Azmak, a small mound some 80 m in diameter, was excavated in its entirety and was found to contain five building levels of the Karanovo I culture and one level of Karanovo II.[282] A fine series of C14 dates places Karanovo I between *c.* 5000 and 4329±120 BC; in other words it is comtemporary with the Middle Neolithic and

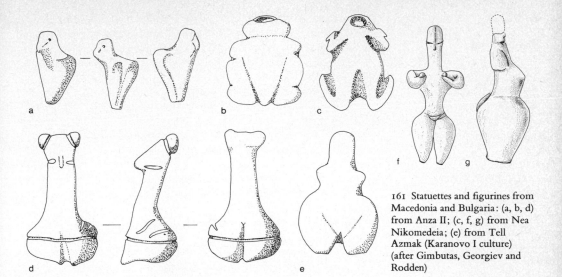

161 Statuettes and figurines from Macedonia and Bulgaria: (a, b, d) from Anza II; (c, f, g) from Nea Nikomedeia; (e) from Tell Azmak (Karanovo I culture) (after Gimbutas, Georgiev and Rodden)

Sesklo cultures of Greece, and with Hacılar I, Can Hasan 2B and 2A in Anatolia.

The Azmak settlement was circular in plan and surrounded by a wall of stamped clay 1 m wide which supported a palisade. In the northeastern part of the settlement, in the earliest level, thirteen burnt houses were found, consisting of a single square or rectangular room varying in size from 5·4 × 4·5 m to 8·2 × 6·2 m. The houses were oriented east–west, set close together but separated by narrow passages 1 m wide, and entered from an alley through a doorway facing the oven; they were built of sturdy oak (and some elm and ash) posts, wattle and clay – exactly as at Nea Nikomedeia. Ovens, occupying about 1 sq. m, were horseshoe-shaped and stood on a platform near to which querns were set in the mud floor. Stone mortars were placed near by and storage jars, 0·5–1 m high, up to eight in a row, were likewise concentrated at the kitchen end of the building. Floors and ovens were frequently relaid. In level 2 were found two burnt buildings measuring 6·7 × 4·9 m and 7·3 × 7·2 m. In the latter, domestic equipment was altogether missing and relief decoration appeared on the southwest wall, suggesting a different function for this building; it may have been a shrine. In the third layer a large house, 15·2 × 7 m, contained three rooms, but the buildings in the last two levels are fragmentary with houses 7·4 × 5·9 m and 7·6 × 6·1 m in size.

Curved sickles made of antler with flint blades set like saw teeth, as in Transcaucasia or Tell Aswad, are common and so are scrapers, fully polished axes and adzes, bone awls, needles, chisels, spatulae, etc. Antler was much used, but the chipped stone tools are of flint as the culture evidently lay outside the range of the Melian obsidian trade.

Loom weights and sling-stones were made of baked clay. Mat impressions occur on the bases of pots and there are the familiar oval clay stamp seals with incised designs. Figurines are mostly made of clay and have prismatic form, but stone was also used in their manufacture; a fine marble figurine was found as well as a

161

schematic and frog-like greenstone figure (cf. Nea Nikomedeia). Relief decoration in the form of faces and human figures occurs on pots, though rather late in the sequence, and a large therio-morphic painted vessel in the form of a deer comes from Mouldava near Plovdiv.

162

The pottery of this culture consists of coarse ware with nail impressions, barbotine, knobs and pellets and fine burnished mono-chrome ware, red or red-brown, grey or black. Rippling of the surface (through burnishing?) is common, and this is to develop into the fine fluted ware of Karanovo II, when the painted pottery disappears. Monochrome wares include jars with vertical necks, others with four vertically perforated tubular lugs and flat or deep bowls on ring bases or pedestals, quatrefoil pedestals or four stumpy feet.[281−2]

The accomplished painted ware is decorated in matt white paint (often chalky and encrusted) on a red-slipped and burnished surface. In the latest levels black or brown paint also occurs on a red ground. The patterns are geometric, but sophisticated; there are hatched pendant triangles, spirals and lattice patterns and floral ornament – a quatrefoil marsh plant is to be seen on a dark polished beaker. Among the painted shapes tulip beakers or carinated and gently curving bowls on ring bases, pedestals, or four feet are the most common. Incised decoration is rare and virtually confined to triangular boxes on three feet used as lamps to light the houses. Meander patterns are most common. A few vessels are made of stone or marble and are said to show Aegean or Anatolian influence.

The animal bones have not yet been studied but both domestic and wild animals occur. The farmers grew emmer, einkorn, bread-

162 White-on-red painted pottery of the Karanovo I culture: (b, c) beakers from Tell Azmak; (a, d) bowl and deer from Mouldava; (e, f) footed bowls from Slatina and Kremikovci (after Georgiev and Detev)

wheat, six-row naked barley as well as vetch, pea and lentil and collected acorns and fruits: grape, cornelian cherry, blackberry.[280]

Intramural burials, mainly of children interred in a contracted position, occur at all levels of the site, but most of the dead must have been buried outside the settlement in a cemetery.

The Karanovo II culture sees the disappearance of the painted ware and a corresponding increase in the fine fluted red, buff, grey and black burnished ware, of the same shapes as before but some now with simple handles.[286] At Karanovo, the house plans show no appreciable change and the development is evidently one of internal growth. Bulgarian archaeologists have not yet established the origins of this Thracian Middle Neolithic, but it is evident that such an accomplished pottery must have had earlier antecedents. These point not to Thessaly, as was once thought, but towards Macedonia where the best parallels occur at Nea Nikomedeia. The question of the origins of the Karanovo I culture is closely linked to that of its western neighbour the Starčevo culture of the Vardar–Morava valley in Yugoslavia.

The Starčevo Culture in Yugoslav Macedonia

The Vardar and Morava valleys occupy a great fault zone that runs from Thessaloniki to Belgrade and forms a natural route into Europe from the Aegean. This is the homeland of the Starčevo culture,[288] named after a site near Belgrade which as far as we know is the earliest farming culture in the region. Sites were generally situated on the edges of river terraces and show shallow deposits, often only 1 m thick and of only one building level, suggesting short spells of occupation which prevented the formation of mounds. In economic terms this implies greater mobility of the population than was found in the well-established and permanent sites farther south and east, but one would like to have economic data from a number of Starčevo sites. To what extent were the villages permanently occupied and why did they shift so often during this period, which we now know is of considerable duration (*c.* 5400–4300 BC)? What is the reason for the much larger and evidently more permanent settlements of the Vinča culture, which stratigraphically overlies Starčevo? Were they newcomers from the east, as has been suggested, moving from areas like Bulgaria with an expanding population into the sparsely settled territories of the Starčevo culture, the western areas of the Near East?

Somewhat thicker layers of occupation with several periods of building and associated objects occur in Yugoslav Macedonia, for example at Vršnik north of Štip, Zelenikovo near Skopje, Rug Bair near Sveti Nikole, and Anza near Anzabegovo half-way between Titov Veles and Štip. From Anza comes much new information.[289] It is not a mound, though four superposed periods of occupation were established; the top levels (Anza IV) are Early Vinča, III and II are like the Starčevo material from farther north, but the lowest, Anza I, represents something new and ancestral to what followed. Anza I is divided into two phases, IA and IB, dated by a series of C14 tests: 5390±250, 5260±100, 5190±100, 5170±100 for Anza IA, and 5130±100, 5120±100, 5070±320 and 4930±250 for Anza IB. Little is known of the buildings of Anza I, but fallen walls of plano-convex mud bricks occur late in the phase, a feature obviously derived from the south. In Anza II and III vertical posts daubed with clay were used for constructing rectangular houses 8–10 m long and 4 m wide, as at Nea Nikomedeia and in the Karanovo culture. Stone wall enclosures were also found. The earliest settlement was already fully agricultural and with the exception of the horse, all the animals kept – predominantly sheep and goat, but also some cattle, pig and dog – were domestic. Cultivation of wheat, barley and lentils is reported, but the exact varieties are not yet known. The environment is sub-Mediterranean with juniper, oak and elm.

The twenty-eight skeletons found belong to the Mediterranean (or Proto-Mediterranean) race of gracile build and small stature – the maximum height is 163 cm. They have a pronounced dolichocephalic skull and a narrow ellipsoid face. Pot burials of infants occur in Anza I.

The chipped-stone industry employed local chert for sickle blades, scrapers and borers and greenstone for polished axes and

163 Pottery from Anza I: white-on-red pot and decorative motifs, monochrome burnished ware below (after Gimbutas)

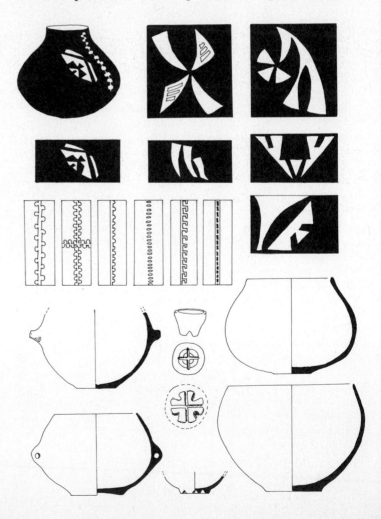

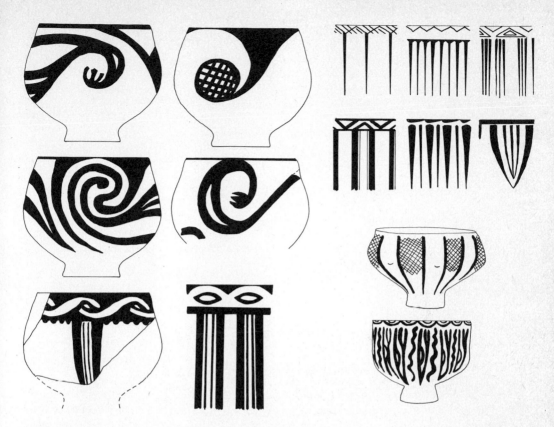

164 Painted pottery from Anza II (top two rows) and Anza III; two pots (bottom right) from Tečic and Starčevo (after Gimbutas and Galovic)

adzes. Obsidian did not apparently reach this far north, but contact with the Aegean was maintained throughout the existence of the site and there was a trade in sea-shells, especially *Spondylus*, used for the manufacture of beads, pendants and bracelets. There were also pendants made of greenstone, finger-rings, flutes and spatulae carved from bone, while seals and figurines are found as early as Anza I. From Anza II there are red-slipped and burnished, seated or standing figurines wearing a belt, and a ritual pit yielded a white marble birth-giving goddess in the form of a frog, as at Nea Nikomedeia, Azmak and Hacılar VI. Phallic stands and cult vessels with heads in bird or animal shapes are also reported.

The pottery is of great interest; in Anza I plain black and red burnished ware with simple bowl or hole-mouth shapes is common and there are miniature vessels on cruciform feet, a feature also found in the Karanovo and Hacılar cultures. Coarse ware is decorated with finger-nail and finger impressions. The fine painted pottery is decorated in white on a red burnished slip with a variety of patterns based on a vertical line with dots on either side; these would seem to derive from imitating stitched leather vessels, or they may represent somewhat stylized flowering plants or ears of corn. The larger motifs, on the other hand, offer some striking parallels to the 'fantastic style' of Hacılar V–II, with which Anza I is contemporary. Recognizable are at least three figures which at Hacılar were identified as a goddess, a bull's head and a rampant leopard. A fragment of a well-modelled human

163

	THESSALY	SERBIA	MACEDONIA	BULGARIA	ANATOLIA
EARLY NEOLITHIC	Late Neolithic	Early Vinča	Anza IV	Karanovo III	Late Chalcolithic II
				—4300—	
	Middle Neolithic	Starčevo III	Anza III black-on-red	Karanovo II	Late Chalcolithic I
			4500		
	Sesklo	Starčevo II	Anza II	black-on-red Karanovo I white-on-red	Dutluca? black-on-red
			—4800—		
	Pre-Sesklo	Starčevo I (monochrome)	Anza I	5050	Hacılar I
		Nea	white-on-red		Hacılar V–II
	Proto-Sesklo	—Nikomedeia—	—5400— First Painted Pottery Cultures	5400 (red-on-white)	Hacılar IX–VI
				—5700—	
	Early Ceramic (monochrome)				
	Aceramic Neolithic 6000?				Kızılkaya? (monochrome)

Table III Chronology of southeastern Europe and Anatolia

hand belonged to a large pot, again a feature familiar from all the Anatolian-Aegean cultures.

The transition from Anza I to II and III occurred without a break but the pottery changed somewhat, with pinched, stabbed and barbotine ware taking the place of nail- and finger-impressed wares. Monochrome ware continues much as before, but in Anza II there is a new thin painted ware with elegant shapes on pedestals or rim bases, decorated in brown or orange with spiral or floral motifs in a very free style. In Anza III the decoration, still in brown on orange, assumes more rigid geometric forms with clusters of vertical lines, cross-hatching, triangles and running spirals on the rim of the vessels. Sometimes these resemble a pair of eyes and the vertical patterns are identified by the excavator with rain. Much of this Anza III pottery shows a decorative style paralleled – fortuitously no doubt – in the decoration of Hacılar I pottery. Even more striking is the anthropomorphic pithos, 92 cm high, showing a female figure painted with red and cream bands and wearing a necklace; though it belongs to Anza IV, which represents a version of the Early Vinča culture, it would seem that this type of pot has an unmistakable west Anatolian origin, while the black burnished and yellow-orange channelled and black-topped vessels point rather to Thrace.

With so little fully published material available, it is obviously difficult to visualize the rather intricate relationships, both geographical and chronological, between the various cultures in the northern Aegean. A tentative scheme is offered in the chronological table above. What becomes immediately evident from such a scheme is how incomplete the material is outside Thessaly; the Aceramic and Early Ceramic (monochrome ware only) are still absent in Macedonia, Serbia and Bulgaria. Theoretically this

164

is of course possible and the first settlers need not have moved into Bulgaria until they already had painted pottery; but this seems unlikely as the earliest Starčevo (I) and its relative, the Criş culture of Romania, apparently arrived before painted pottery had developed. The latter, it seems, never took over impressed or barbotine ornament, the hall-mark of Starčevo and Körös, in the northwestern provinces of the Balkans. This may be a feature connected with basketry, and as we have seen, it frequently characterizes pottery-making in the peripheral areas (Levant, Cilicia, Dalma, Starčevo, the Adriatic and the western Mediterranean in general). With acculturation it usually disappears. It is clearly not, as some have maintained, a characteristic feature of the earliest Mediterranean pottery, for it was not manufactured in the greater part of the Aegean-Anatolian area.

One striking feature of the painted-pottery distribution is that whereas Greece, including Nea Nikomedeia, follows the south Anatolian fashion for red paint on a cream slip, areas farther north prefer white paint on a red slip. It is perhaps no coincidence, therefore, that when dark burnished wares of the Late Neolithic (Greece) or Late Chalcolithic (Anatolia) come to supplant the earlier painted-pottery cultures they again used white paint on black, brown, red or buff pottery. In each case the dark wares came from the north and it is not impossible that the use of white paint was influenced by the difficulty of producing an even, dead-white slip. This was certainly the case in the poorly made Late Chalcolithic wares of Anatolia. The distinction, then, is not necessarily one dictated by taste or the expression of the personality of a culture – even if it tended to develop that way – but may owe its origin to technological deficiency. One should note that white-on-red painted ware occurs in the southern group, in Hacılar VI and especially Hacılar I, across the Aegean in the Sesklo culture, and of course at Nea Nikomedeia which occupied a 'border' position. The use of black paint on red slip is characteristic of Starčevo, but also occurred in the Sofya plain and less frequently in the later Karanovo I culture. Some black-on-red pottery occurs sporadically in Anatolia: in the Uşak region, at Yazir and at Büyük Güllücek, all in the northern zone. It was never common, and none of these occurrences can, as yet, be properly dated.

The first Neolithic settlements in Greece and the Balkans clearly bear the stamp of the Anatolian tradition, and they are not, for example, Syrian, Lebanese or Cypriote. However, they soon developed in their own way as the splendid pottery of the Middle Neolithic, be it 'Urfirnis', Chaeronea, Sesklo, Starčevo, Anza II–III or Karanovo I, abundantly demonstrates. Wherever the evidence is available, we find that these settlers arrived with a fully developed farming economy and soon engaged in trade and industry. With sheep and goat, wheat and barley not native to Greece or the Balkans, the alternative hypothesis of local southeast European domestication of crops and livestock must be abandoned. Still, it is known that the land was not entirely empty, but inhabited here and there by hunters and gatherers of Upper Palaeolithic stock, armed with bows and arrows tipped with transverse trapezoid flints. These are not, as far as is known, a Near Eastern feature and their presence in the early farming sites may perhaps be attributed to an admixture of natives with the newcomers. Farther north in the Balkans archaeologists have noted the absence of contact between the hunters and the settlers, each exploiting different habitats.[263] This may be so, for example, at the sites of the Mesolithic fishermen of the Lepenski Vir culture in the Iron Gates area on the Danube, who seemed to have kept aloof from the Starčevo farmers for a long time.[290] However, one finds it difficult to believe that the entire area from Greece to the east Hungarian plain and from Thrace to the Ukraine was all settled by farmers of Near Eastern stock, without the participation of the descendants of the old hunting populations. Does the thinning out of settlements, which increases in direct proportion to the distance from the Aegean, perhaps indicate an outer zone of more adaptable and acculturated natives, more mobile and less economically efficient than the early colonists?

To those desirous of following up these developments, one can do no better than recommend Ruth Tringham's book *Hunters, fishers and farmers of Eastern Europe, 6000–3000 B C.*

Chapter Ten

Epipalaeolithic and Neolithic in the Southeast Mediterranean

Archaeological discoveries made over the last twenty years in the central Sahara (Tassili n'Ajjer, Algeria; Tadrart Acacus, Libya) and in Egypt are gradually disclosing entirely new vistas of the cultural development of northeast Africa, which may not be entirely irrelevant to the rise of agriculture and stockbreeding in the Near East and its accompanying cultural manifestations. The astounding discoveries of prehistoric art in the central Sahara by H. Lhote and F. Mori and their teams at Tassili and Acacus are clearly related to minor manifestations of the same art at Jebel Uweinat on the Libyan-Egyptian frontier, and in the Egyptian deserts and the Nile valley. The latter, in the absence of excavations which might yield material to date these rock paintings and engravings, were assigned by most Egyptologists to the Predynastic period, i.e. the post-Neolithic Amratian and Gerzean periods, c. 3800–3100 B C, and the first radiocarbon dates obtained in Tassili, ranging from c. 3550 to 2500 B C, seemed to support both a low chronology and theories of Egyptian derivation, at least for the paintings of the cattle-herders, otherwise known as Bovidians or Pastoralists. Admittedly then, these herdsmen were gifted painters, but at a period when Egypt was already developing into an agricultural nation with a superior civilization, soon to become a unified state (c. 3100 B C) and the greatest cultural power in Africa. If one accepts W. Emery's hypothesis that the First Dynasty went back to c. 3400 B C, as seems probable, then the art of the cattle-herders of the central Sahara could be dated to the Late Gerzean, the Archaic period and part of the Old Kingdom, i.e. mainly to the historical period, and the deterioration of climatic conditions that set in towards the end of the Old Kingdom would conveniently explain the end of the great but 'peripheral' art in the Sahara. The preceding pictures attributable to the 'Round-head phase' of hunters would then fall in the Predynastic period, including perhaps the Egyptian Neolithic of the Faiyum and Merimde in Lower Egypt and the Badarian of Upper Egypt, going back, at the earliest to c. 5000 B C. The even earlier engravings of the *Bubalus antiquus* phase, the extinct African wild buffalo, carvings of which are widespread from Morocco to the Fezzan (Libya), would fall in an ill-defined 'Mesolithic'.

This chronology, which seemed plausible enough at the time, has been rudely shattered by the application of radiocarbon dating during excavations at Acacus. A series of dates now shows the Saharan Neolithic (i.e. the Bovidian or Pastoral period) to have started at the end of the seventh millennium B C (6122± 100 Wadi Fozzigiaren, cf. 6160±320 northwest Sahara, Wadi Saoura),[299] whereas the earliest Neolithic date from Egypt (Faiyum) is only 4441±180![304] The beginning of the Neolithic of Cyrenaica is computed at *c.* 5000 BC at Haua Fteah,[298] but these eastern dates are about a millennium or more behind those of Acacus. Now that an Epipalaeolithic culture of hunters and fishermen is known to have preceded the Faiyum Neolithic (with radiocarbon dates ranging from *c.* 6150 to 5190 BC), the central Saharan Neolithic is unlikely to derive from that of Egypt's Faiyum.[304]

Radiocarbon dates of 2700 from the Tassili[296] and 2780±310 from Acacus help to date the onset of climatic deterioration which was to turn the area into a desert,[299] These dates lie some two hundred years before the First Dynasty radiocarbon dates,[294] and thus show that these events took place during the Gerzean period in Egypt, in calendar years sometime during the first half of the fourth millennium BC and thus not as late as the end of the Old Kingdom!

Epipalaeolithic in Egypt

Recent archaeological surveys and excavations in Upper Egypt have yielded abundant evidence for a series of Epipalaeolithic assemblages spread out over a period from *c.* 16000 to 9500 BC and associated with a number of arid and moist climatic phases.[302-4] The remains of the camp sites of these hunters and fishermen have yielded evidence for the local fauna, catfish, hippopotamus, bubal antelope (hartebeest), wild ass, extinct African buffalo, native wild cattle, and Barbary sheep, denizens of the Nile valley, the savannah on either side of the river, or in the case of the Barbary sheep, the Red Sea hills. Freshwater molluscs occur in some cultures.

Microlithic and other larger tool types of various traditions are as characteristic of these cultures as of the Kebaran and the Natufian in the Levant. In some of the later cultures ('Complex G') during the arid climatic phase of the Sahala upper silts dated between 12000 and 10000 BC, very large sites appear which contain many grindstones and sickle blades with a silica gloss. This may reflect the cutting and grinding of some local plant foods, though not the cereals wheat or barley which, being winter rain crops, were not native to Egypt. J. D. Clark has suggested that the adoption of these Asiatic crops in Egypt during the Neolithic in the fifth millennium was retarded by the fact that the Egyptians already had local food plants.[293] Only with irrigation could the Asiatic crops be grown in Egypt and once this was done the older crops gradually disappeared, to reappear only in times of stress and famine. Similarly the late arrival of Asiatic domestic animals, such as sheep and goat, unknown before the Faiyum Neolithic, has been attributed to the abundance of game in Egypt, and the adoption of sheep and goat may well have been for the products these animals provided, milk, wool, etc., rather than meat.

Unfortunately the period from *c.* 9500 to 5000/4500 BC is almost a blank in the Nile valley and it is thought that sites of this period lie below the present-day cultivation. For this reason we cannot follow Egypt's development from the Epipalaeolithic to the Neolithic, and the period which corresponds to the Pre-Pottery Neolithic A and B of Palestine is so far missing. The situation in Lower Egypt is even worse; here only one site, Helwan with Natufian-like tools, has been reported, no other early sites having been investigated, though they probably exist.

The Faiyum Neolithic

In the Faiyum a local late Epipalaeolithic of fishermen and hunters dates from *c.* 6150 to 5200 B C, separated by a gap from the Faiyum Neolithic (earliest date 4441 ± 180), which is thought to be intrusive with its Asiatic crops (emmer, barley, flax) and animals (sheep or goat).[292] Other creatures like cattle are probably local, but they are not definitely domestic. African contacts are clearly present, such as hollow-based arrowheads, gouge-axes, and a blue stone, Amazonite, used for ornaments which came either from as far afield as Egei Zuma, the eastern prong of the Tibesti massif in the Sahara or from the Eastern desert. Straight reaping knives of wood with a row of serrated sickle blades, linen and plain burnished pottery, red-brown or black without any decoration, point to Levantine inspiration though obviously of local manufacture. Architecture is not attested and seems to have consisted of wind-breaks and probably reed huts, but numbers of storage pits, sunk into the ground and lined with straw matting or basketry, have survived. This Faiyum culture and that of a possible related culture at Merimde, still represent the earliest remains of the Neolithic in Egypt. How typical are these sites? Are they really the first Lower Egyptian Neolithic sites or are they marginal settlements, as their location might suggest, of Libyan bedouin? Shall we one day find an earlier and much more representative Neolithic in Lower Egypt? Something more like a Pre-Pottery Neolithic B, which we now know penetrated into Sinai? Stranger things have happened in archaeology and we can only look forward to the results of further exploration.

Rock engravings abound in Egypt, but few of these can be clearly dated. Some, like the ships, are clearly of Gerzean date, others might belong to the Amratian period, similar decoration having been found on the pottery of these periods. Few, if any, rock engravings can be assigned to the Badarian period with any degree of certainty. Recent discoveries of female figures and engravings of wild cattle found on the sandstone cliffs of Gebel Silsileh at the north end of the Kom Ombo plain may be among the oldest,[301] and possibly associated with some of the Epipalaeolithic culture remains from that extraordinarily rich plain.[303]

Rock Engravings and Paintings in the Sahara

Similar engravings in a long series found in the Sahara are generally considered to be the earliest.[295-6] They depict *Bubalus antiquus*, giraffes, antelopes, equids, etc., as well as human figures, some of them masked, e.g. in the Wadi Jerat in Tassili, Auis in Acacus, etc.[299] There is nothing to tell us who the artists were or when they lived; but a hunting and gathering existence is assumed, and the engravings could be Epipalaeolithic. Though there are apparently no paintings as early as this, they characterize the next period, that of the 'Round-headed' figures, otherwise described as the

Archaic. Rather than animals, human figures or anthropomorphic deities, often masked, dominate these paintings, and the scenes in which they appear, frequently associated with animals and often overpainted, evidently tell stories or myths. Many of the rock-shelters give one the impression that they were used as sanctuaries, especially at sites like Sefar, Tanzoumaïtak, Aouanrhet and Jabbaren, in the Tassili massif.

Unfortunately no remains of dwellings of this period have yet been excavated and pottery and arrowheads are not found yet in association with the paintings, although bowmen are shown. Chipped flint or chert axes are the only tools so far reported and they were evidently needed to supply fuel in the Mediterranean environment of this period, when the uplands of Tassili and Acacus carried abundant vegetation and woodland cover, details of which in the form of pollen have been recovered in the next, Bovidian period. Aleppo pine, holm oak, cypress, nettle tree, alder, lime and wild olive are reported and fig trees still grow as the last remnants of a Mediterranean flora. The wall paintings of the rock-shelters show an abundant African fauna with *Bubalus antiquus*, antelopes, giraffe, elephant, rhinoceros, hippopotamus, Barbary sheep (not the Asiatic moufflon), wild cattle, lion, ostrich, snakes and fish. At this stage none of the animals depicted suggest domestication and it is assumed that the people of the 'Round-head' paintings were still essentially hunters, fishermen and food gatherers. Radiocarbon dates for the beginning of a Pottery Neolithic, firmly linked to the later Bovidian style of *c.* 6000 BC, suggest that the 'Round-head' phase had by then run its course, but we have as yet no evidence for when it began.[299] All authorities agree that it was a long period and its beginning may well have coincided with that of the Holocene, now dated around 8300–8000 BC. This would give a range of about two millennia for the art of the 'Round-head' period which comprises a long series of different art styles. The uniqueness of this material should perhaps be emphasized, for with the possible exception of Spain, nowhere else in the ancient world has yielded such a 'museum' of great art of the eighth and seventh millennium BC. There is certainly nothing comparable in the preceramic Neolithic cultures of the Near East, except perhaps in the lower levels at Çatal Hüyük, whose earliest paintings and those of the end of the 'Round-head' period of Tassili and Acacus overlap chronologically.

The tentative chronology of the Tassili paintings of the phase of the 'Round-headed' people, established by H. Lhote and based on overpainting, runs as follows:[295−6]

1 An early phase with small human figures, rather stick-like and with horned or feathered heads, executed in violet ochre (e.g. Sefar, Tin Teferiest), followed by some others, looking like 'little devils' painted in yellow and violet (evolved; Jabbaren).

2 A middle phase of larger 'Round-headed' figures in yellow ochre, outlined in red (e.g. Jabbaren, Tin Teferiest).

3 A mature or 'evolved' phase with larger, more rounded figures and polychrome painting, using yellow, greenish-yellow, light-red ochre with darker-red outlines (e.g. Jabbaren).

4 A 'decadent style' of huge imposing figures up to 6 m in height, more coarsely drawn; the bodies, which are white-filled, are outlined in red, or have a double outline of red and yellow. (Especially at Sefar and Jabbaren.)

5 These are possibly, but not certainly, followed by polychrome paintings in various styles, using red or brown ochres with white details and outlines, and a slatey-blue-grey paint. Among these are some of the finest paintings – masks (Sefar), masked figures in all their finery (Tanzoumaïtak, Sefar), 'negro mask' figures (Aouanrhet, Matalen-Amazar), the 'helmeted figures' from Sefar, the 'judges' from Jabbaren, the 'dancers' from Ti-n-Tazarift, the 'race' from Aouanrhet, the swimming woman from the same place, the masked men and women dancing from Jabbaren and the goddesses, 'Antinea' from Jabbaren and the 'horned goddess' from Aouanrhet. H. Lhote suggests Egyptian influence in these paintings, already foreshadowing the arrival of the Bovidian style of the Neolithic cattle breeders. In view of the early date of these paintings, any suggestion of Egyptian influence is evidently out of the question, as there is nothing in Egypt at this period to compare with them. The suggestion that the paintings of the 'Round-headed' people were the work of a negroid population is clearly not proven, but the possibility that several ethnic elements were present in these regions cannot be ruled out and might well have contributed to the diversity of styles of painting.

Until the Tassili paintings are fully published (there are said to be some 10,000 of them) it is difficult to form an opinion of the full range of scenes represented; many of these are clearly of religious rites and ceremonies and show women with raised arms praying to a giant male god with the mask of an antelope. The god is always associated with animals: *Bubalus antiquus* and antelopes, huge wild cattle, or, in each of three shrines at Sefar, a feline. Headless gods too are found at Sefar, while processions of women bearing baskets (?) on their heads (Jabbaren) or performing dances (Wadi Ekki in Acacus) also occur. Other scenes show groups of men and women, groups with animals, archers, men with tridents, men in a swimming position, or hunting scenes.

In the later polychrome style ceremonial scenes again predominate, progressively increasing in splendour, but the clumsy giant figures disappear, and refinement is now sought instead of imposing presence. Masked figures abound in ritual scenes, also in the Acacus area (Wadi Tamauat), while unusual scenes at Uan Muhaggiag show a boat (?) and what is possibly a burial with two corpses wrapped up in animal skins. Although interpretation is extremely difficult there can be little doubt that elaborate ritual marked the period of the 'Round-headed' peoples, whose economy one assumes was essentially that of hunters and gatherers.

The interest of this Saharan art is considerable in that (together with Spanish Levant art) it seems to form a transition between the Upper Palaeolithic art of France, Spain and Sicily and the art of Egypt in the Chalcolithic and Bronze Ages.

The Saharan Neolithic of the Pastoralists

Considerable changes took place *c.* 6000 B C with the arrival of new peoples with a Neolithic economy, based on domestic cattle, accompanied by dogs. They built domed reed huts of circular or oval plan, the doorway of which was closed by a reed mat, grouped presumably in compounds below the overhanging cliffs in the more open valleys of the Tassili and Acacus highlands. The cattle were kept in the compounds, surrounded by curvilinear stone walls in front of the rock-shelters, as is shown not only in the paintings, but demonstrated by the thick layers of cattle dung. These people have left numerous remains, such as arrowheads, blades and scrapers, polished axes, bone tools, a multitude of querns, grindstones, pounders, suggesting agricultural pursuits, as well as stone palettes and saucers for preparing and using paints made from local ochres. They also went in for pottery on a big scale, mainly hemispherical bowls, decorated with impressed and rouletted decoration, producing an effect probably derived from basket imitation. A number of paintings show garments rather than animal skins and it is possible that cloth was woven from animal hair or plant fibres. Agricultural pursuits are suggested by pictures of women working in the fields, but it is still unknown what plants were grown. Neither the Tassili nor the Acacus areas would have contained much arable land and cattle breeding was probably far more important than agriculture, which may have been limited to horticulture in small plots along the banks of the narrow streams that flowed in the wadis. If, as has been assumed on ethnological parallels, these people were predominantly pastoralists, the uplands may have served as summer quarters, the winters being spent in the savannah and steppes of the lowlands. The dead were buried individually in contracted position below the rock-shelters and perhaps under stone tumuli, which abound in the Tassili area,[295] but none of which have yet been investigated.

The art forms of the cattle-herders, predominantly naturalistic engravings with or without colour (the paintings were first engraved, then filled in with colour), are so different from those of the earlier period that one wonders what had happened to the earlier population. Were they still there when the cattle breeders arrived? If so, were they enslaved or had the earlier population departed, perhaps as the result of a climatic oscillation that temporarily resulted in an arid spell, such as the one that took place at the end of the seventh millennium in the Levant leading to the decline and disappearance of the Pre-Pottery Neolithic B culture? We just do not know. In any case, the study of pollen and animal bones from Uan Muhaggiag shows that from *c.* 5500 B C a humid climate with Mediterranean fauna and flora prevailed as during the period of the 'Round-headed' people, and this was to last for the next two millennia, during which period the pastoralists filled the rock-shelters with thousands of pictures now assigned to two main phases, an early one and a middle one.[299] A late phase can be dated between *c.* 3500 (C14 2800–2700 B C) and *c.* 1500 B C, when a new style with chariots and horses appears in the Late Bronze Age. This phase is thus contemporary with Egypt's

Archaic period, and the Old and Middle Kingdoms, a period in which Libyans were gradually pressing towards Egypt, posing a constant threat of invasion to the inhabitants of the Nile valley. The reason was probably the progressive desiccation of the Sahara.

It is the two earlier phases of the period of the naturalistic paintings, Neolithic in local and Predynastic in Egyptian terms, that concern us here. The spirit of this 'Bovidian' period is altogether different and much of the awe and mystery that surrounds the art of the earlier peoples is gone. There are, however, some exceptions as in the engraved scenes of sexual intercourse in which masked males (deities?) are shown with women on the rocks of Ti-n-lalan in Acacus. Moreover, in the graffiti of animals, there is, or seems to be, a clear continuity with the engravings of the *Bubalus antiquus* phase, a continuity which was much less evident in the somewhat clumsy engravings of the previous period. It is here that we may well be touching on the origins of the naturalistic art of the new-comers, whose art tradition may also go back to this presumably Epipalaeolithic period. In general, however, the art of the cattle-herders is naturalistic rather than ritualistic, homely and colourful. Masks have not altogether disappeared and masked men are seen in several hunting scenes, but there are few paintings in which deities, rather than ordinary men and women, can be discerned. The paintings do not strive after colossal dimensions, the paint, predominantly red and brown ochre, is thinly applied on the sandstone rock; much attention is paid to naturalistic detail, and everyday life. It seems a gentler, less frightening world, in which the peaceful scenes of cattle herding, which form the vast majority of the paintings, are occasionally interrupted by cattle raids leading to fights between bowmen of various groups. Other scenes, no less common, show the hunting of game, such as antelopes, Barbary sheep, hippopotamus (from boats made of reeds), giraffe, ostrich, rhinoceros and baboons. Sometimes dogs are used in the hunt.

There are numerous scenes of a man and woman or two women in conversation, two people in a hut, a woman dragging along an unwilling child, groups of people conversing or dancing, as well as pictures of domestic life, hut plans with pots in a row, people lazing about, doing up their hair, escorting an old female, or having animated conversations (Uan Amil, Acacus). The physical types are richly varied; in the early phase in Acacus, most of the figures wear their hair in a turban which falls forward over their brow, but others show long black and blonde hair, a coiffure *à la Égyptienne* (Uan Amil), whereas at Jabbaren (Tassili) what is referred to as the painting of the 'Peul' girls shows white caps and sleeveless dresses.[296] Some of the men wear conical caps and animal skins or checkered loin-cloths, women sometimes wear striped garments, what looks like short trousers, or nothing at all. A fan-shaped headgear is seen at Jabbaren on a number of small figures and in the overpainting of the 'White Goddess' at Aouanrhet.

If articles of dress and hair-styles are varied, so are the physical types depicted, but in the absence of appreciable quantities of skeletal remains, paintings are a dangerous guide to the identification of racial types. These people are frequently described as

Hamitic-Nilotic Mediterraneans – which means no more than that they are like the later Egyptians, Sudanese, Berber, Peul, etc., i.e. non-Negroid – yet the only skeleton examined, that of a two-year-old child from Uan Muhaggiag, turned out to be of negroid type.[299] It was buried, after evisceration, in an antelope skin, which gave a radiocarbon date of 3455 ± 180. This, our earliest example of mummification, came from the middle levels at this site after an arid interval, which shows up in the pollen profile. By the end of the period bones of the sheep/goat family (not necessarily the Asiatic ones!) appear in larger numbers than those of cattle, a possible sign of climatic deterioration. A date of 2780 ± 310 comes from a layer that covered a fallen block of rock with part of a wall painting of the Middle (or Uan Tabu) phase of the art of the cattle-herders in the Acacus area. In this phase vast herds of cattle are shown together with possible scenes of milking near a hut with a series of pots and with red figures in white caps (Teshuinat II), similar to many of the famous scenes at Jabbaren (Tassili). The change in hair-style in the Acacus, if also applicable to the Tassili area, might help to subdivide the paintings of the pastoral phase there, like the drawing of the cattle's horns – single or none in the early phase, sweeping horns in the middle, and lyre-shaped horns in the late phase (type Ti-n-anneuin and Ti-n-lalan in Acacus).

Another characteristic of the art of the cattle breeders is the rarity of symbols; only negative hands or positive hands with forearms are found.

The art of this period evidently reached a climax in its middle phase with such masterpieces as the polychrome herd from Jabbaren,[295-6] the seated man and woman from Sefar, the 'Peul' girls from Jabbaren, the paintings at Ozaneare, the camp scenes at Jabbaren or the battles of archers at Ti-n-Tazarift and Sefar, to mention but a few. The late phase, though still able to produce impressive paintings, shows increasingly taller figures of herdsmen and cattle with lyre-shaped horns, green-painted herdsmen, ostriches and many giraffes. Paintings of this late phase seem less common than those of earlier phases.

This remarkable culture naturally poses a number of problems, not the least intriguing of which is its origin. As we have already seen, there are still no known Neolithic cultures in Egypt early enough to have influenced such a development, nor does the material from the Sudan at present offer any hope of correlation. It is equally clear that neither the Iberomaurusian nor the Capsian cultures of the Maghrib (Tunisia-Algeria-Morocco)[291] have any obvious connections with the Saharan Neolithic, forming as they do an altogether different entity with other traditions.[297] Yet the Saharan Neolithic, 1500 km south of the Mediterranean, is unlikely to have sprung up as the result of coastal penetration from the Near East, such as the pottery with its rouletted borders and impressed design, not unfamiliar at Mersin or Byblos around 6000 B C, might at first suggest. As yet there is no botanical evidence to show what forms of agriculture were practised, nor is there any evidence for exclusively Asiatic animals such as sheep or goat. Cattle, of course, is native to North Africa, and one would expect its domestication to be a local affair, irrespective of similar and contemporary domestication in Anatolia. Finally, there is little support for the theoretical alternative that the cattle breeders were descended from the previous 'Round-headed' people and thus for a local develop- ment of a Neolithic economy. It is of course possible that at some future date proof of such a development will be found either in Tassili and Acacus or in areas somewhat farther to the east such as the region of Tibesti and Jebel Uweinat, which could have been the home of similar cultures. One might even go so far as to suggest that until we know something about what occurred in the Nile valley between *c.* 9500 and 4500 B C eastern influences cannot be ruled out, but it must be admitted that in the absence of excava- tions this is pure speculation. It would seem hardly credible, though, that the most fertile valley in North Africa, that of the Nile, should not have played some role during the five thousand years that saw so many significant developments among both its eastern and its western neighbours, in the Levant and the central Sahara respectively. Here in my opinion lies the greatest challenge for Egyptian archaeology in the future.

A no less intriguing question posed by these recent discoveries in the central Sahara is the extent to which the culture of these cattle breeders may have contributed to Egyptian ethnogenesis and the relatively sudden rise of Egyptian civilization. The onset of a new arid climatic régime, carbon-dated to *c.* 2780–2700 B C, a few centuries before the First Dynasty, the desertion of many sites in the central Sahara, and the gradual disappearance of the cattle breeders may have involved some migration to the Nile valley. It has long been known that in the western Nile delta Libyan influence was notable. Here was situated the Libyan nome and the Pre- dynastic royal city of Sais had a war goddess, Neit, frequently regarded as Libyan. Her cult was strong during the First Dynasty as the names of several queens, Neithotep and Merneit, testify. Cattle-breeding becomes a feature of the delta from the time of the First Dynasty, but may go back earlier. The shift of political power to Lower Egypt with the foundation of Memphis may have accelerated Libyan contacts. The classical art of the Old Kingdom with its painted low reliefs reminds one of the painted engravings of the cattle-herders not only technically but also in their intense interest in naturalism, everyday life, and serenity, features that seem essentially African rather than Asiatic. Whether these influences are imaginary or real, the dynastic art of Egypt is essentially Egyptian and from the foundation of the United Monarchy, or 'the joining of the two lands' as the Egyptians put it, Egyptian civilization maintained its supremacy for some thirty dynasties, as the ultimate heir of three earlier periods of southeast Mediterranean cultures: that of the Epipalaeolithic carvings of the *Bubalus antiquus* phase, that of the 'Round-head' people, and that of the Neolithic cattle breeders of the Sahara.

The foregoing account of these essentially African manifesta- tions of early cultures, and their art in particular, may seem irrelevant to the major theme of this book, the Neolithic of the Near East, if defined in narrow and modern geographical terms. The development of the Neolithic in Egypt was certainly influenced by Near Eastern developments, as crops, animals and irrigation techniques show; that of the Neolithic of the central Sahara is still a mystery. Yet, even if future research would prove its development to have been independent of the Near East, it offers, especially in the earlier phases of its art, a chronological, if not related parallel, with which to compare and contrast Near Eastern developments.

Chapter Eleven

Conclusions

The period studied in this book ranging over some ten millennia from *c.* 15000 to 5000 B C is concerned with the evolution of man, the hunter and gatherer; man, the trader and farmer; and in some cases man, the city-dweller. In other words it deals with that economically evolutionary progress that Gordon Childe with keen appreciation of its ultimate effect on mankind called the 'Neolithic revolution'. Yet he envisaged a second stage in man's quest for civilization, the 'urban revolution' marked by the foundations of cities. Recent discoveries tend to suggest that these two supposedly successive stages can be reduced to one; there were cities as well as villages in the Neolithic Near East, and what Childe regarded as something new – the urban communities of the third millennium in Sumer or Egypt – were in all probability only later, larger and more elaborate versions of their Neolithic prototypes. A more complex organization had led to the invention of writing, initially an aid to administration, which only gradually became a vehicle for literacy. It was a precious tool for the few who knew how to use it and today still, more than five thousand years later, illiteracy is a world problem. City-dwellers invented writing, but writing did not create civilizations; many flourished quite happily without it. In fact it is remarkable how few attempts were made at writing (they concern Mesopotamia, Egypt, 'Hittite-Hieroglyphic' (Luwian) – the only Indo-European script – Crete, India, China and Central America (Maya)), and *we* still write in borrowed signs. Civilization, then, could exist without writing and Childe's second stage was a restricted phenomenon, useful but not essential to man's cultural progress. Art, thought, ethics, morals, laws, religion, song, dance, epics, language and rituals, all could and can operate without the benefit of writing in many societies, but where they are not recorded we of course know less about them. In such cases the only record may be archaeological, telling us of a conflagration or a volcanic eruption, the desertion of cities or the founding of new ones, the flourishing or decline of the culture, migrations and so forth. Civilization implies living in cities and this took place, as we have seen, long before man ever dreamt about writing. It was not the prerogative of a few select nations.

The first steps towards civilization were taken unwittingly in the far distant past throughout a vast area of geographically and ecologically diverse terrain extending from the deserts of Central Asia and Arabia to the Hungarian plain. Some regions clearly played a primary role, not shared by others, yet sooner or later they all contributed to the emergence of civilization. The natural environment is evidently of paramount importance, especially during the Late Pleistocene period and during the anathermal phases of the Early Holocene affecting as these did the vegetation zones, inhabited by the animals that formed man's food supply. Ecological studies have been carried out in far too few areas to provide us with a coherent account of the conditions in which the early cultures developed. This is one of the chapters that cannot yet be written.

If we know little about the environment, we know less about the men and women who were responsible for the developments which the archaeologist endeavours to piece together from the scanty remains that have survived. It is only in the last few decades that scholars have learned to pay proper attention to plant and animal remains, but how many have realized the potential of anthropological studies, demography and the pathology of the human skeletal remains?

Until it is brought home to the sponsors of archaeological excavations that archaeology is not just concerned with spectacular artifacts (works of art, architecture, pottery or tablets) and the like, but demands full-scale excavation for the purpose of reconstructing environmental and social conditions, the structure of society, settlements, and cemeteries, little can be done in that field. Culture is rarely the concern of governments and archaeology ranks low among the arts in the bureaucratic mind. It is, therefore, not surprising that the archaeological material, as known, varies considerably in both quantity and quality and represents a motley collection from which conclusions can be drawn in several ways.

The ten thousand years of evolution described here can easily be divided into three main periods: the Epipalaeolithic extending from c. 1500 BC to the Pleistocene-Holocene boundary c. 8000 BC; the aceramic or Pre-Pottery cultures of the Early Holocene, c. 8300–6000 BC, and the fully Neolithic cultures with plain or painted pottery, c. 6000–4200 BC. It is only in the third and last period that there are enough durable remains to allow us to form some opinion about the culture of its bearers, and the farther back one goes in the Near East, the scantier are the remains. This is partly the result of the accidents of discovery and partly that of the increasing complexity of cultural inventories as technological competence, combined with trade and industry, enriches the various cultures.

In general economic terms, the first Epipalaeolithic and still Pleistocene phase marks the emergence in certain areas of food conservation by the herding of animals and the collection of grain. New tools are invented to facilitate grain collection, preparation and storage.

Agriculture, i.e. the planting of crops and the breeding of animals, appears at the very beginning of the next phase, soon after 8300 BC. Morphologically domestic sheep occur at Bus Mordeh, cultivated crops outside their natural habitat at Mureybet and Jericho PPNA. During the two thousand years or so of this period there is a steady development of agriculture on one site or another, which is evidently the result of increased contacts brought about by trade.

By the end of this period, *c.* 6000 B C in radiocarbon terms, the agricultural 'revolution' was an established fact and fully agricultural societies began expanding into hitherto marginal territories such as the alluvial plains of Mesopotamia, Transcaucasia and Transcaspia on the one hand, and into southeastern Europe on the other. Some of this contact, as in Crete and Cyprus, definitely went by sea, and in each case it would appear that the newcomers arrived with a fully fledged Neolithic economy. As a consequence hunting declined, except in new marginal territories unfit for agriculture, such as the forested mountains. The next few thousand years saw a consolidation of food production and an increase of population which gradually expanded into all the more favourable agricultural niches of the Near East. In a number of areas, central and southern Mesopotamia, southern Anatolia and Transcaspia, simple irrigation agriculture was introduced which led to improved hybrid crops; bread-wheat and six-row barleys, as well as flax (in Mesopotamia and Khuzistan). Cultural progress went hand in hand with economic efficiency and new arts and crafts flourished, particularly the ceramic industry which produced not only plain and painted pottery but also clay figurines and statuettes. The textile industry thrived as animal skins, the produce of hunting, gave way to woven cloth. In a few advanced highland cultures in Anatolia and Iran metallurgy developed, though its needs were still mainly geared to trinkets. The widespread use of cast copper tools belongs to the real 'Chalcolithic' period, *c.* 4000 B C by C14 dating, *c.* 5000 B C in true calendar years, a description of which falls outside the scope of this book.

The rate of progress can be discerned on the accompanying chronological chart. The Epipalaeolithic developments are very slow and the tempo does not significantly increase until the mid-aceramic period (*c.* 7250 B C by C14). All major areas then show significant advances; the problems of agriculture have been overcome and diffusion takes place. The great expansion, whether through emigration of population surplus or through acculturation, leads to a proliferation of individualistic cultures, each with its own way of making pottery, figurines, and undoubtedly textiles yet linked by the traditional farming equipment which they have in common. While all the evidence points to rapid cultural advancement during the two thousand years of development of this third phase, there are also signs of exhaustion in once creative regions, such as the Zagros and Palestine, which tend to be outstripped by their neighbours and sink into the role of backwaters. This shift in cultural eminence may be responsible for the great delay in the spread of agriculture towards Egypt on the one hand and towards south Iran and the road to India on the other. From the more active northern areas, however, farmers spread into Europe and the western margins of Central Asia.

Towards the end of the period there are clear signs of stress in many territories; the Halaf culture of the northern Fertile Crescent disappears or disintegrates, and in southern Anatolia the inferior Late Chalcolithic cultures cause the old painted traditions to disappear, and stagnation sets in. The stage is thus set for a thoroughly new realignment of cultures in the Chalcolithic period, from which in another two thousand years the first literate civilizations will emerge, but then only in Sumer and Egypt. The calibrated dates show that the Chalcolithic (i.e. the Late Ubaid, Uruk and Jemdet Nasr periods in Mesopotamia and the Egyptian sequence from the Faïyum to the Gerzean) lasted considerably longer than was once assumed. The momentum of the Neolithic was not maintained and as the highland zone gradually sinks into obscurity a new dawn of civilization breaks over the lowlands of the Fertile Crescent.

It is at this point that archaeologists only twenty-five years ago would have started their account of Near Eastern cultures. The developments over the preceding ten thousand years constitute the 'prehistory of Near Eastern Civilization'.

Although archaeological research has made great progress in the last quarter of a century, interpretation has not kept up with discoveries and much of the theory of cultural development seems sadly out of date. The economic sequence – hunting, intensified hunting and gathering, early farming – is, broadly speaking, correct but it is the interpretation of the cultural features associated with these various stages of development that is in need of re-appraisal. To depict all Upper Palaeolithic cultures as consisting wholly of nomads, hunting in small self-sufficient bands, without trade or industry and at best inspired by 'hunting-magic' served by 'cave art', is, to say the least, naive. During the next stage (the old Mesolithic), we are told, man, still nomadic, showed a greater interest in other foods and became acquainted with grain; there were still no villages, and neither trade nor industry. Then followed the 'era of primary village farming efficiency', in other words agriculture had come with the domestication of plants and animals. Out of this rural development the first cities grew in southern Mesopotamia c. 3500 B C and their economy was based on trade and industry, which was not able to develop before agriculture had laid the necessary foundations for urban life. When writing was invented, public buildings appeared, metal and art developed; civilization, a term narrowly applied only to Mesopotamia, Egypt and the Indus valley, had arrived; the rest of the Near East, for a long time to come, remained a cultural backwater. Civilization, it was argued, was impossible without writing, towns and cities were developed from villages, and villages and culture as such were impossible without agriculture.

Simplifications of this kind are misleading, and the time has come to put the record straight. Agriculture did not make man, but man made agriculture. At the centre of all cultural development stands *Homo sapiens*, a fact not missed by Alcaeus when he wrote c. 600 B C: 'Not houses finely roofed nor the stones of walls well built nor canals nor dockyards make the city, but men able to use their opportunity.' Man alone is capable of thought and when he wants a thing he is usually able to find a way of getting it; the crude distinction between self-sufficiency and 'acquisitive' communities is probably imaginary. Barter takes place even at the simplest level, with marriage. There is nobody in the world, however poor, who does not have some food or trinket or service to offer in exchange for something else. To talk about self-sufficiency in archaeology, where only non-perishable remains survive, is clearly absurd. How many sites are actually located near their flint resources, making it reasonably certain that the users owned them and did not obtain this primary material from a neighbouring group? Trade, barter, exchange of goods for other goods or for services rendered must be an inherent feature of all cultures from earliest times onward. Whether this later developed into important trade is irrelevant, for it is not the question of degree that counts but the principle. If trade in its simplest form was present in the very beginning so was the manufacture of goods – whether flint tools or works of art – for not only raw materials form the basis of exchange; services, or the exchange of knowledge, so important for contact, leave no direct archaeological remains, but can only be recognized as influences. Human contacts, exchange of information at all levels, whether accompanied by gifts, trade goods, theft or raids, marriage contracts or slavery, are the essential basis for cultural development. All else stems from this. Archaeology is much concerned with habitations of one form or another and with the permanency or impermanency of occupation. With the exception of tents and shelters that can be moved, most archaeological remains are, fortunately, permanent; it is the movements of population that are in question, and for one reason or another thought to be economically important. The emphasis on impermanency, though economically justifiable, is much less so culturally and there is no essential difference between a base camp, a village or a city – each provides shelter and a territorial base, even if only for part of the year. It is man's home, the place where he feels he belongs, the place he cherishes and where he longs to be buried. J. Perrot's hypothesis that secondary burials are those of people who died away from home, were temporarily buried elsewhere and returned to their homes later, seems wholly satisfactory as an explanation for the beginning of this custom. The large number of Upper Palaeolithic sites, caves, rock-shelters or open settlements, provides a potent argument against the old theory of aimless wandering as a characteristic of the period. The presence of numerous rock sanctuaries in western Europe should have immediately dispelled such ideas; territoriality and circumscribed culture areas were probably not much different from those in later times. Agriculture did not produce permanent settlements, though one cannot deny that it helped to stabilize patterns that were already in the making. Pre-agricultural sites like those of the Natufians, the Kostienki group in the Ukraine, a number of Magdalenian sites in France and Germany, and the Lepenski Vir group were all permanent settlements, even if only seasonally occupied. Many modern village communities in the Mediterranean and the Near East have two sets of habitations, an upper village for the summer, a lower one for the winter. They are none the less permanent. Suberde may have been a summer village for a site in the Konya plain.

Summer and winter occupations differed, as indeed they do today still, and we cannot prove that after the introduction of agriculture sites were occupied all the year round, as is so often assumed. For health reasons alone this might have been inadvisable, both for humans and their beasts. The decay of many cultures, cut off from hills or mountains and forced to stay in such insalubrious places as southern Mesopotamia, Cilicia or the lower Jordan valley, might to advantage be investigated in this light.

In archaeology it is too often size that is used as a criterion for distinction, but one ought to enquire into the economy and cultural achievement of a centre. Was Çatal Hüyük a village, a town or a city? The question is often asked, and can only be answered satisfactorily by enquiring into how it maintained itself, what economic process it generated, what services it provided. It might be useful to define the terms village, town and city by their economic function as has recently been done. 'A city is a settlement that consistently generates its economic growth from its own local economy, whereas towns do not. The occasional export a town may have generated for itself has produced no consistent self-generating growth thereafter. A village is merely a smaller town.' (Jane Jacobs, *The economy of cities*, New York 1970, p. 262). If one adopts these definitions and excludes the immaterial question of size (as one should in any case), then it is perfectly clear that a great number of sites described in this book should be called 'cities'. They are of course the cultural centres, where trade and industry, government and religion were concentrated. The others, towns and villages, are the minor sites. Inadequate excavation, which more often than not hampers interpretation on early Near Eastern sites, deters us from drawing up a list of the sites mentioned in this book and dividing them into cities, towns and villages. With so little known about most of them such attempts are surely premature; nor would such classifications serve any useful purpose, except perhaps in individual cases, where the assessment of economic and cultural status is desirable if only for comparison with later equivalents. Long-lived settlements that generated their own economic growth on the basis of their economy, such as Jericho, Mureybet, Çatal Hüyük, Beidha, Alikosh, Tepe Guran, Tell es-Sawwan, Eridu, Hacılar, Siyalk and Byblos, I would regard as cities. Each of these may be seen as the centre of a city-state, even if it had no dependent towns and villages, for it must have controlled territory, however small, for its economic needs. Patterns of dependence may have grown as populations increased and more land was needed to feed the city population, so that towns and villages may have developed to serve the city's requirements. The very small number of early sites in most areas certainly does not support the idea that cities developed out of overgrown villages; the reverse – surplus city people emigrating into rural (or part rural, part trading) villages – seems far more logical. Indeed, archaeology has shown that cities came into being as early as towns and villages and the first demonstrable signs of the cultivation of plants and the herding of animals emanate not from villages, but from the important primary sites, cities such as those mentioned above. They had developed the necessary drive and incentive for native growth and were familiar with a large variety of wild foods brought in by the hunting and gathering populations who may have exchanged these for raw materials or manufactured goods from the city. This in turn may have led the city-dwellers, thus well supplied, to experiment with growing wild seeds, as at Mureybet and Jericho, and to keep wild livestock on the hoof, which would have encouraged taming and breeding as the more recalcitrant animals were the first to be killed off. Interbreeding and hybridization would have had better chances of success in the fields surrounding the cities than elsewhere. This interpretation of events allows for the creation of the right environment for agricultural development among people above the level of simple hunters and gatherers, and explains the opportunities grasped by the city-dwellers who found that they could grow food which their neighbours could only collect. The resulting economic change is easy to imagine; wild food, unless exotic, did not need to be imported and it became necessary for the villages to barter rarer materials instead. Thus the city changed its imports; such processes are obvious at a place like Çatal Hüyük, which abounds in exotic materials, or on a smaller scale at Beidha, Jericho and Çayönü. As new crafts and techniques developed such places would grow richer and richer, providing more and more work, and thus probably encouraging immigrants from other regions. In order to feed them, more land had to be brought under cultivation and as the population rose accordingly, this presented few difficulties. In this way cities surrounded themselves with villages and towns, some of which may have carried part of the trade and added a few specialities of their own. The process was capable of constant evolution provided men kept the pattern going and adapted themselves to any change in circumstances. Failure to do so spelt stagnation, and stagnating cities can no doubt be found in the archaeological record, if one knows what to look for.

The Neolithic way of life in all its aspects continued into the Chalcolithic and the Bronze Age – indeed much of it is still with us today for it formed the basis on which all later cultures and civilizations have built. As the Neolithic period is wholly pre-literate, serious attention has never been paid to the question of Neolithic languages, which are assumed to have been lost. Has no trace of them survived from this remote period?[305] This is admittedly perilous ground where most archaeologists fear to tread. Yet it is common knowledge that many languages spoken today have known ancestries reaching back some 2000–3000 years; Iranian has existed for at least 3250 years, Chinese for at least 3500, and Greek at least since Early Helladic III, *c.* 2350 BC – a mere 4300 years, whilst Gaelic may be as old as Greek. Pride of place goes to Ancient Egyptian, which is still alive as Coptic after 5500 years – to put it at its minimum. If languages can maintain themselves for thousands of years irrespective of cultural changes, invasions, periods of foreign domination, then we must seriously consider the possibility that this could also have happened in prehistoric times. Many changes of culture were not necessarily accompanied by a corresponding change in language for, like religion, language tends to resist political changes. People identify themselves with language and religion and they tend to preserve these outward signs of their identity through thick and thin. The Caucasian languages at the one end of the Mediterranean and Basque at the other have resisted the Indo-Europeanization of the rest of Europe. In the Near East as well as in the Mediterranean there are remains of earlier languages, usually in the form of topographical and vocabulary words which the newcomers adopted from the earlier inhabitants. All this is common knowledge, but its archaeological implications have not often been spelled out in detail. Let us illustrate this with a few examples. Ancient Egyptian appears fully fledged, complete with both hieroglyphic and cursive hieratic script, at the beginning of Dynasty I, corresponding to a calibrated C14 date of *c.* 3400 B C. Evidently the language is older than this date, but it is known that Old Egyptian contains Semitic grammar but a Hamitic vocabulary. This suggests that these features go back at least to the previous half-millennium of the Gerzean period, when Egypt shows clear signs of having links with Palestine in the Late Chalcolithic period, contacts which were sporadic if not altogether lacking before. If the Semitic structure thus goes back to 4000 B C at the very least, it may be suggested that Semitic languages were then already spoken in the Levant. Pre-Gerzean Egyptian may have been Hamitic like the languages of Egypt's neighbours, Libyans and Nubians. If the Amratian developed out of the Badarian, as is generally suggested, the Badarians may have spoken Hamitic, and with the Badarians we are back in the Neolithic period. If this argument is sound, a Semitic language was spoken in Palestine from *c.* 4000 B C during the Late Chalcolithic period when there were cultural links with Lebanon and Syria (Amuq F). How old are the Semitic languages? The presence of non-Semitic topographic terms in Syria and Lebanon would suggest a pre-Semitic substratum in the Levant. Could it be that the cultural break between Halaf and Ubaid marks the appearance of the first Semitic-speaking peoples in Syria and in Palestine (Proto-Ghassulian and Ghassulian)? This would be hard to prove or disprove, but to me it does not seem inconceivable. It would fit into the pattern of disruption of the old Neolithic cultures *c.* 5000 B C (C14 *c.* 4200 B C), while implying that the entire Neolithic development of the Levant back to the Aceramic and Epipalaeolithic periods was Pre-Semitic. This in turn would mean that the first speakers of Semitic languages could be identified with the pastoralists of the Syrian and north Mesopotamian steppe in the marginal territories south of the area of the Halaf culture. In later periods also it was from this territory that further waves of Semites – Accadians, Amorites, Hebrews and Aramaeans – erupted, before they spread out over the Fertile Crescent, a pattern that was to be repeated by the Arabs from a more southern homeland. In other words, the post-Halaf development of the countries of the Fertile Crescent may owe much to two new ethnic elements: the first Semites in the north and west, and the Sumerians in the south of Mesopotamia.

Samuel Noah Kramer, the eminent Sumerologist, is convinced that the Sumerians were not autochthonous in the lands they occupied in southern Mesopotamia, holding that they came from the Zagros zone to the east or northeast. The first Sumerian texts date from the Late Uruk (Proto-literate B) period, *c.* 3800–3700 B C (calibrated dates) but it is generally assumed that they were present since Middle Uruk, *c.* 4000 B C. If we accept that the red and grey Uruk wares mark the arrival of the Sumerians – an assumption, based on the archaeological evidence, that is not uncontested – this would mean an arrival during Late Ubaid when these wares first make their appearance *c.* 5200–5000 B C (calibrated C14 date from *c.* 4200). Professor Kramer and other Sumerologists have pointed out that there is good evidence in Sumerian for a Pre-Sumerian substratum, which gave the language not only the names of the Twin Rivers, but that of nearly every Sumerian city as well as a number of technical terms. These, I venture to suggest, were derived from the earlier, i.e. the Ubaid population, the Neolithic farmers who first settled on the Mesopotamian alluvium. Pre-Sumerian in our terms would thus be a 'Neolithic' language. If one follows this line of argument back into the distant past, both Sumerian and Pre-Sumerian lead us to the Zagros cultures of the Aceramic and perhaps the Epipalaeolithic period, from which those later cultures are evidently descended.

Our final example is perhaps the best documented one: pre-Greek. In a recent study, *Die wichtigsten konsonantischen Erscheinungen des Vorgriechischen* (The Hague – Paris 1972), E. J. Furnée estimates the number of pre-Greek loan words in Greek to be between five thousand and six thousand. The sources from which these words found their way into Greek comprise the Aegean basin and Asia Minor, and one suspects that the major contribution was made by the pre-Indo-European language of the Minoans of Crete. If, as is now believed, the first Greek-speaking elements entered the Greek mainland in the Early Helladic III period, *c.* 2350 B C (calibrated C14), there would have been a considerable overlap of Greek and pre-Greek in Crete and the Islands for nearly a thousand years, which may account for the formidable amount of loan words the northern 'barbarians' picked up from their more civilized neighbours. Attempts to isolate a number of topographic names ending in -assos and -nthos and ascribe these to an Anatolian Indo-European language such as Luwian or Hittite (Laroche and Palmer, followed by myself) have failed to convince most archaeologists and philologists, as similar names extend to the Balkans and Italy. They would make much better sense as a pre-Indo-European substratum, as F. Schachermeyr was the first to realize. On this assumption pre-Greek should be earlier than the arrival of the Greeks in Early Helladic III, beginning *c.* 2350 B C and also earlier than the arrival of the Indo-European Anatolians during the Troy II period (after 2900 B C in calibrated C14 terms) in Anatolia. It is not known how long the pre-Greek language survived in Anatolia, but this factor must of course be kept in mind in considering the transmission of elements of the older language, as in the case of Minoan. The non-Indo-European character of pre-Greek is well established morphologically and its distribution has been charted from Anatolia (west of the Euphrates) to Greece, the Cyclades, Crete, Thrace and Macedonia – the diaspora of the Anatolian Neolithic, and an area of fairly close cultural contacts right down to the period of the Indo-European invasions or infiltrations during the Early Bronze Age. This may well have been an area of more or less linguistic unity as is suggested by the evidence of pre-Greek, and the cultural development, at least in the more southern parts of the area and especially Crete, shows no decisive breaks that *must* be associated with a change of language since the Neolithic. The basic population of Neolithic southeastern Europe would have consisted of Neolithic farmers, descendants for the most part (the Epipalaeolithic element is probably numerically insignificant) of the Anatolian settlers that brought agriculture to Europe. It is perhaps not surprising that the bulk of pre-Greek words which have survived are concerned with an Anatolian-Aegean environment, its flora and fauna, 'Neolithic' foodstuffs, artifacts and only vague references to metals. Another group of words are pejorative, describing attitudes that were not appreciated (lecherous, boastful, etc.); could they have served to keep alive a native reaction to the invaders? Theoretically at least the survival of a Neolithic language over some three thousand to four thousand years has parallels, and such a possibility cannot be ruled out.

This hypothesis finds further support in the presence of traces of similar substratum in the Balkans, Italy and southern France, areas beyond the Near Eastern Neolithic agricultural diaspora, but early centres of secondary Neolithic cultures, influenced by the Neolithic of Greece, Macedonia and Thrace. We may assume that in these areas local Epipalaeolithic groups picked up the ideas of agriculture from their more advanced eastern neighbours and with it they may well have carried westward a number of technical and environmental terms. To the east also, some of the Caucasian languages contain words similar to those of pre-Greek, and Furnée suggests that a number of pre-Greek words usually explained as Semitic were borrowed by and not from the Semitic. To an archaeologist, then, it would cause no surprise to learn that pre-Greek may have been introduced into southeastern Europe by Anatolian Neolithic farmers and the language of Çatal Hüyük, Hacılar and Can Hasan may have been preserved in Crete well into the Late Bronze Age, late enough in fact to have been recorded, however imperfectly, by the classical Greeks. This is, in my opinion, a phenomenon to which too little attention has hitherto been drawn. Seeing that the earliest farmers in the Near East were descendants of Upper Palaeolithic hunters, as we now know, there may be a substratum of Upper Palaeolithic language and vocabulary in languages such as Ancient Egyptian, Pre-Sumerian, Sumerian, Elamite and pre-Greek, which has not yet been detected. Alternatively, could these languages be those of the Upper Palaeolithic, with Neolithic terms added as innovations?

These conjectures spring logically from our interpretation of man's development from hunter to farmer in the Near East and its underlying continuity. They should not be dismissed as idle speculation.

List of Radiocarbon Dates

List of conventional, uncalibrated radiocarbon dates, calculated with Libby half-life of 5568 years. All dates are B C. Calibrated dates in calendar years, not yet fully established before 4200 C14, are approximately 1000 years earlier in the C14 time range between 4200 and 6500, but full details are not yet available. Published results up to date till December 1974. Dates from charcoal, unless otherwise indicated. Italics indicate averages of consistent dates.

A. Period I. Epipalaeolithic

18500±300 RT 227	Kebara 14, ash layer 26, pre-Kebaran Levanto-Aurignacian
16960±330 I–6865	Rakefet, Kebaran
16300±320 UCLA–1776–C	Nahal Oren, layer IX, Kebaran
14930±340 UCLA–1776–B	Nahal Oren, Kebaran
13850±300 UCLA–1776–A	Nahal Oren, Kebaran
13750±415 GRN–5576	Ain Gev I. Kebaran
12400±280 UCLA–1703 A	Palegawra, Zarzian (bone)
11650±460 UCLA–1714 D	Palegawra, Zarzian (bone)
10050±400 W–179	Shanidar, layer B1. Lower Zarzian
10300±65 Hv. 4074	Senufim cave, Mt Carmel end of Kebaran
9250 *PPS* 37 (1971), 27	Jericho 'Natufian shrine'
8920±300 W–681	Zawi Chemi, lowest building level
8650±300 W–667	Shanidar, layer B1, final Zarzian
8640±140 Lv–607	Mureybet phase I (Natufian), end of
8640±170 Lv–605	Mureybet phase II ⎫
8510±200 Lv–606	Mureybet phase II ⎬ cf. Jericho 'Proto-Neolithic'
8450±150 GAK–807	Ganjdareh E (lowest level)
8260±235	Aq Köprük (Ghar-i-Asp)
9980±168 P–1668	Franchthi cave, Late Palaeolithic
9143±260 P–1520	Franchthi cave, Late Palaeolithic

B. Period II. Early Holocene

8350 *PPS* 37 (1971), 27	Jericho, beginning of Early PPNA, i.e. end of 'Proto-Neolithic tell'
8265±115 P–1217	Mureybet, phase II, level II
8142±118 P–1216	Mureybet, phase II, level I ⎫
8056±96 P–1215	Mureybet, phase II, level I ⎬ end of I, *c.* 8100
8018±115 P–1220	Mureybet, phase I, level X–XI
7954±114 P–1222	Mureybet, phase II, level XVI–XVII. (End of phase II)
7780±140 Lv–604	Mureybet, phase II
7950±200 UCLA–750D	beginning Bus Mordeh phase at Alikosh
7632±89 P–377	Jericho, end of Early PPNA, *c.* 7650 B C, beginning of Late PPNA
7542±122 P–1224	Mureybet, phase II, level XVI
7570±110 GRN–4458	Çayönü
7350 *PPS* 37 (1971), 27	Jericho, end of Late PPNA
7289±196 P–1485	Ganjdareh D

7250±60 GRN–4459	Çayönü
7018±100 P–1484	Ganjdareh
6960±170 Gak–994	Ganjdareh
6938±98 P–1486	Ganjdareh
7100±300 UCLA–1714 F	Asiab (bone) ⎫
6950±100 UCLA–1714 B	Asiab (bone) ⎬ *c.* 6930
6750±100 UCLA–1714 C	Asiab (bone) ⎭
6990±160	Beidha VI, Early PPNB *c.* 7000
6760±160	Beidha VI
6830±200	Beidha IV
6780±160	Beidha IV ⎫
6690±160	Beidha V ⎪
6860±50 GRN–5136	Beidha IV ⎬ Late PPNB with re-used older wood
6690±50 GRN–5063	Beidha VI ⎭
6650 *PPS* 37 (1971), 27	Beidha, end of VI (Early PPNB)
6840±250 Michigan 1609	Çayönü
6620±250 Michigan 1610	Çayönü
6890±210 Shell 1174	Bus Mordeh phase, Alikosh
6700±100	Aq Köprük I (Ghar-i-Mar)
7008±130 P–1240	Aşikli Hüyük
6857±128 P–1238	Aşikli Hüyük
6843±127 P–1241	Aşikli Hüyük
6828±128 P–1245	Aşikli Hüyük
6661±108 P–1239	Aşikli Hüyük
7525±134 P–1665	Franchthi cave, 'Mesolithic'
7348±130 P–1522	Franchthi cave, 'Mesolithic'
7314±144 P–1519	Franchthi cave, 'Mesolithic'
7148±159 P–1398	Franchthi cave, 'Mesolithic'
7084±108 P–1517	Franchthi cave, 'Mesolithic'
6991±117 P–1664	Franchthi cave, 'Mesolithic'
6988±100 P–1518	Franchthi cave, 'Mesolithic'
6792±114 P–1666	Franchthi cave, 'Mesolithic'
6767±110 P–1518A	Franchthi cave, 'Mesolithic'
6239±78 P–1536	Franchthi cave, Late 'Mesolithic'
6072±76 P–1526	Franchthi cave, Late 'Mesolithic'
5947±88 P–1527	Franchthi cave, Late 'Mesolithic'
6650 *PPS* 37 (1971), 27	Beidha V, beginning of Late PPNB
6600±160	Beidha II
6750±180 BM–127	Aceramic Hacılar V
6414±100 P–460	Ras Shamra VC1 (Aceramic)
6192±100 P–459	Ras Shamra VC2 (Aceramic)
6290±100 GRN–4832	Bouqras I
6190±60 GRN–4818	Bouqras I
6010±55 GRN–4819	Bouqras II
5990±60 GRN–4820	Bouqras III
6260±50 GRN–4426	Tell Ramad I
6250±80 GRN–4428	Tell Ramad I
6140±50 GRN–4821	Tell Ramad I
5970±50 GRN–4472	Tell Ramad II

5950±50 GRN–4822	Tell Ramad II
5930±55 GRN–4823	Tell Ramad III (re-used wood?)
6040±140 K–1430	Labwe I
5910±140 K–1428	Labwe I
5900±140 K–1429	Labwe I
6326±300 P–1387	Suberde II (lower)
6299±91 P–1391	Suberde II (lower)
6226±79 P–1388	Suberde II (lower)
6045±76 P–1386	Suberde II (upper)
5957±88 P–1385	Suberde II (upper)
6465±180 Humble O–1816, O–1833	Alikosh phase, Alikosh
6450±200 Shell 1246	Alikosh phase, Alikosh
6290±175 Humble O–1845	Alikosh phase, Alikosh
6150±170 I–1491	Alikosh phase, Alikosh
6450±200 K–	Tepe Guran U (Aceramic)
6575±175 H–551/491	Jarmo
6030±140 UCLA–1714 E	Jarmo (bone)
6000±200 W–652	Jarmo
5850±120 UCLA–1723 A	Jarmo (bone) } *c.* 6050 B C (*PPS* 37 (1971), 27)
5800±250 W–608	Jarmo
5320±200 UCLA–1723 B	Jarmo (bone)
6006±98 P–466	Tepe Sarab S5
c. 5900 UCLA–1714 A	lowest Sarab (bone)
5810±150 K–	Tepe Guran H (end of Sarab phase)
5694±89 P–467	Tepe Sarab S1
5655±96 P–465	Tepe Sarab S4
c. 6200 UCLA–1657 A	Argissa (bone). Aceramic
c. 6000 UCLA–1657 D	Argissa (bone). Aceramic
6100±180 BM–124	Knossos X. Aceramic
5960±140 BM–278	Knossos X. Aceramic
5790±140 BM–436	Knossos X. Aceramic
5844±144 P–1394	Franchthi cave. Aceramic
c. 5650±150. St. 414–416	Khirokitia. Aceramic

C. Period III. Ceramic Neolithic

6240±99 P–779	Çatal Hüyük IX
6015±100 P–782, 1389–72	Çatal Hüyük X
5903±97 P–1367	Çatal Hüyük VIII
5734±90 P–1366	Çatal Hüyük VIII
5867±100 P–770, 797, 1362, 1364	Çatal Hüyük VIB
5700±100 P–769, 772, 781, 1363, 1365, 1375	Çatal Hüyük VIA
5629±86 P–827	Çatal Hüyük VIA (human brain)
5588±89 P–778	Çatal Hüyük VIA (?) (intrusive grain in VII)
5549±93 P–1361	Çatal Hüyük V (hearth fuel)
5690±91 P–776	Çatal Hüyük V
5581±94 P–774	Çatal Hüyük III
5571±77 P–796	Çatal Hüyük II (grain)

5780±	Erbaba (*Science* 171 (1971), 280–2)
5754±81 P–1525	Franchthi cave. Early Neolithic
5620±150 BM–272	Knossos IX. Early Neolithic
5607±91 P–1212	Nea Nikomedeia. Early Neolithic
5830±270 GX–679	Nea Nikomedeia. Early Neolithic
5550±90 GRN–4145	Argissa. Early Ceramic Neolithic
5331±74 P–1203A	Nea Nikomedeia I
5328±86 P–1667	Franchthi cave. Early Neolithic
5820±180 BM–125	Hacılar VII
5590±180 BM–48	Hacılar VI
5399±79 P–313 A	Hacılar VI
5390±250 LJ–2181	Anza Ia

6000±250 W–617	Mersin XXXIII
5736±112 P–458	Ras Shamra VB (Amuq A)
5234±84 P–457	Ras Shamra end of VA (Amuq B)
5410±70 GRN–1544	Byblos, layer 43, middle of Early Neolithic
5620±35 GRN–2660	Tell Halaf ('near altmonochrom' = Amuq A)
5620±250 W–623	Matarrah, bottom level
5570±120 TK–24	Telul et–Talathat XV (Umm Dabaghiyah)
5506±73 P–855	Tell es–Sawwan I
5349±150 P–856	Tell es–Sawwan III (Samarra)
5090±200 W–660	Hassuna V
5077±83 P–548	Arpachiyah TT 8 (Middle Halaf)
4896±182 BM–483	Chogha Mami. Transitional phase (cf. Chogha Sefid)
4515±100 GRN–	Gerikihaciyan (very Late or Post–Halaf)
5510±160 I–1501	Tepe Sabz (doubtful) ⎫ Sabz phase
5250±100 Si–206	Tepe Sabz ⎭
5560±70 Le–631	Shomu Tepe (earliest Transcaucasian Neolithic)
5319±86 P–455	Hajji Firuz VI
4945±83 P–502	Hajji Firuz II
5085±69 P–1244	Yaniktepe P9
4976±80 P–1243	Yaniktepe P5

5370±100 Bln–719	Togolok. Middle Jeitun culture
5197± TUNC 12	Zaghc, pre–Siyalk I
5270±100	Aq Köprük I (Ghar-i-Mar) ceramic Neolithic
5086±100 Le–592	Chagylly Depe. Late Jeitun culture
5050±110 Le–	Chagylly Depe. Late Jeitun culture
4757±438 P–45	(old solid dates) Hotu cave. Siyalk II culture
4623±438 P–36	(old solid dates) Hotu cave. Siyalk II culture
4631±110 Le–159	Tilkin Depe. Anau IB culture
4660±200 Le–	Shulaveri, 'lower levels'
4295±250 Le–	Toire Tepe
3955±300 Le–	Shulaveri, 'upper levels'
4220±200 Si–203	Tepe Sabz, Bayat phase (cf. Ubaid 4)
4110±200 Si–204	Tepe Sabz, Bayat phase

4207±238	Saudi Arabia. Ubaid site 11
4133±84 TUNC 11	Zaghe, Siyalk III, 4–5 culture
4120±160 H–138/123	Warka, Late Ubaid (Ubaid 4)
4036±87 P–503	Dalma
4039±85 P–442	Siyahbid, Dalma culture
4070±140 Le–	Jebel, layer 4 (pottery)

4920±130 K–1432 ⎫	
4900±130 K–1433 ⎬	*c.* 4880 Ard Tlaïli, lower (cf. Amuq C)
4840±130 K–1434 ⎭	
4710±130 K–1431	Ard Tlaïli, upper (cf. Amuq D)
4184±81 P–	Ras Shamra III C

4882±78 P–795 ⎫	
4880±78 P–790 ⎬	*c.* 4821 Can Hasan 2B
4805±80 P–791 ⎬	
4720±76 P–792 ⎭	

5219±131 P–326	Early Hacılar II A
5244±112 P–1399	Franchthi cave, Early Middle Neolithic
5080±130 GR–3502	Elateia, first painted pottery, Middle Neolithic
5050±180 BM–126	Knossos V, Early Neolithic
5037±119 P–315	Early Hacılar I
5390±250 LJ 2181 ⎫	
5260±100 LJ 2330/1 ⎬	*c.* 5250 Anza I A
5190±250 LJ 2332 ⎬	
5170±100 LJ 2337 ⎭	
5130±100 LJ 2339 ⎫	
5120±100 LJ 2342 ⎬	*c.* 5050 Anza I B
5070±320 LJ 2157 ⎬	
4930±250 LJ 2333 ⎭	
5030±80 LJ 2409	Anza II
4950±80 LJ 2405	Anza II
c. 4950 UCLA 1705 A	Anza II (bone)
c. 5000 (*PPS* 37 (1971), 25)	average, beginning of Karanovo I at Tell Azmak
4392±120 Bln–430	end of Karanovo I at Tell Azmak (I,5)
4750±80 UCLA–1705c	Anza III (bone)
4610±120 UCLA–1705b	Anza III (bone)
4615±250 LJ–2185	Anza III (bone)
4300±100 LJ–2339	Anza IV, Early Vinča culture
4250±200 LJ–2411	Anza IV, Early Vinča culture

4741±81 P–1662	Franchthi cave. Transition Middle to Late Neolithic
4696±79 P–1537	Franchthi cave. Middle Neolithic
4206±70 P–1661	Franchthi cave. Late Neolithic
4160±86 P–1630	Franchthi cave. Late Neolithic

4220±74 P–1322	Saliagos (shell). Late Neolithic
4124±79 P–1396	Saliagos (shell). Late Neolithic
4190±150 BM–274	Knossos V
3875±145 Birm. 182	Ayios Epiktitos Vrysi

EGYPT

6400±160 LV–393	El Kab
6150±130 I–4128 ⎫	
6120±115 I–4126 ⎪	
5550±125 I–4130 ⎬	Faiyum. Final Palaeolithic
5190±120 I–4129 ⎭	
4441±180 C–550, 551 ⎫	
4145±250 C–457 ⎪	
3910±115 I–4131 ⎬	Faiyum. Ceramic Neolithic
3860±115 I–4127 ⎭	
4180±110 ⎫	
3580±100 ⎭	Merimde. Neolithic

SAHARA

6122±100 Pisa	Wadi Fozzigiaren (bottom layer)
c. 5950	Wadi Fozzigiaren (upper layer with pottery)
5950±150 WSU–316	Dingul Oasis (plant remains)
5095±175 Geochron	Uan Tabu
4804±175 Geochron	Uan Telocat
4002±120 Pisa	Uan Muhaggiag VIII
3450±150	Meniet el-Hoggar (pollen)
3455±150 Pisa	Uan Muhaggiag (antelope skin of mummy)
c. 3250	Tassili (pollen)
c. 2850	Tassili (pollen)
2780±310 Geochron	Uan Muhaggiag
c. 2700	Tassili (guano)
cf. 2550±110 BM–229	Early Dynasty I (reeds from brick)
2420±50 LJ–1490	Hor Aha, beginning Dynasty I (reeds from brick)

Photographic Acknowledgments

The photographs used for the undermentioned illustrations are reproduced by courtesy of:

J. Cauvin (16); Cyprus Museum, Nicosia (76, 77); Director, Directorate General of Antiquities, Iraq (89); Director, Service des Antiquités, Lebanon (144, 147); Kathleen Kenyon (6, 17); Diana Kirkbride (22); P. Mortensen (36, 37); Joan Oates (93); J. Perrot and the Department of Antiquities, Israel (5, 7); Josephine Powell (69); P. E. L. Smith (32–4).

List of Abbreviations

AAAS	Annales archéologiques arabes de Syrie
ADAJ	Annual of the Department of Antiquities of Jordan
AJA	American Journal of Archaeology
Ath. Mitt.	Athenische Mitteilungen des Deutschen Archäologischen Instituts
BASOR	Bulletin of the American Schools of Oriental Research
BSA	Annual of the British School at Athens
CAH	Cambridge Ancient History
CNRS	Centre National du Recherche Scientifique
God. Nar. Arkh. Mus.	Godišnik na Narodnija arkheologičeski Musej v Plovdiv
IEJ	Israel Exploration Journal
ILN	Illustrated London News
JEOL	Jaarbericht 'Ex Oriente Lux'
JNES	Journal of Near Eastern Studies
LAAA	Liverpool Annals of Archaeology and Anthropology
MIA	Materialy i Issledovanija po Arkheologii SSSR
MUSJ	Mélanges de l'Université Saint-Joseph
OIP	Oriental Institute Publications, Chicago
PEQ	Palestine Exploration Quarterly
PPS	Proceedings of the Prehistoric Society
SAOC	Studies in Ancient Oriental Civilization
Sov. Arkh.	Sovetskaja Arkheologija
ZfA	Zeitschrift für Assyrologie

Bibliography

The purpose of this bibliography in this book is twofold: (a) to refer the reader to the source material and (b) to list existing general works on the subject. References to more detailed bibliographies can be found in all the entries cited.

Chapter One The Levant from the Epipalaeolithic to the End of the Aceramic Period

General

1 ANATI, E. *Palestine before the Hebrews.* London 1963.

2 BRAIDWOOD, R.J. The Early village in South-western Asia. *JNES* 32 (1973), 34–9.

3 HAMBLIN, D.J. *The first cities.* New York 1973 (popular).

4 LEONARD, J.N. *The first farmers.* New York 1973 (popular).

5 PERROT, J. *La Préhistoire Palestinienne* (Supplément au Dictionnaire de la Bible). Paris 1968 (with major bibliography for Palestine).

6 PRAUSNITZ, M.W. *From hunter to farmer and trader.* Jerusalem 1970.

Specific

7 BAR-YOSEF, O. *The Epipalaeolithic cultures of Palestine.* Unpublished Ph.D. thesis, Hebrew University, Jerusalem, 1970.

8 — Prehistoric sites near Ashdod, Israel. *PEQ* (1971), 52–64.

9 BAR-YOSEF, O. and E. TCHERNOV. The Natufian bone industry of ha-Yonim cave. *IEJ* 20 (1970), 141–50.

10 BUTZER, KARL W. Environmental changes in Southwestern Asia and Egypt during terminal Pleistocene and Early Holocene. In *Die Anfänge des Neolithikums vom Orient bis Nord Europa* Vol. I Ed. H. Schwabedissen (in print).

11 — Physical conditions in Eastern Europe, Western Asia and Egypt. *CAH* I, 2, 1970.

12 ÇAMBEL, H. and R.J. BRAIDWOOD. An early farming village in Turkey. *Scientific American* 222 (1970), 50–6.

13 CAUVIN, J. Nouvelles fouilles à Tell Mureybet (Syria): 1971–1972. Rapport préliminaire. *AAAS* XXII (1972), 105–15.

14 — Découverte sur l'Euphrate d'un village natoufien du IX⁰ millénaire av. J.-C. à Mureybet (Syrie). *C. R. Acad. Sc. Paris* 276 (1973) Série D, 1985–7.

15 CONTENSON, H. DE. Sondages à Tell Ramad en 1963. *AAAS* XIV (1964), 109–24.

16 — Seconde campagne à Tell Ramad en 1965. *AAAS* XVI (1966), 167–76.

17 — Troisième campagne à Tell Ramad, en 1966. *AAAS* XVII (1967), 17–24.

18 — Tell Ramad, a village site of Syria of the 7th and 6th millennia BC. *Archaeology* 24 (1971), 278–85.

19 — La station préhistorique de Qornet Rharra près de Seidnaya. *AAAS* XVI (1966), 197–200.

20 — Tell Aswad, fouilles de 1971. *AAAS* XXII (1972), 75–80.

20a — Chronologie absolue de Tell Aswad. *Bull. Soc. Préhist. Française* 70 (1973), 253–6.

21 CONTENSON, H. DE and W. J. VAN LIERE. Premier sondage à Bouqras en 1965. Rapport préliminaire. *AAAS* XVI (1966), 181–92.

22 COPELAND, L. and J. WAECHTER. The stone industries of Abri Bergy, Lebanon. *Bull. Inst. Arch. London* 7 (1967), 15–36.

23 DORNEMANN, R.H. An early village (El Kowm). *Archaeology* 22 (1969), 68–70.

24 FRANCE-LANORD, A. and H. DE CONTENSON. Une pendeloque en cuivre natif de Ramad. *Paléorient* I (1973), 107–15.

25 GARROD, D. *The Natufian culture. The life and economy of a Mesolithic people in the Near East.* London 1957.

26 GARROD, D. and D. M. A. BATE. *The Stone age of Mount Carmel* I. Oxford 1937.

27 GILOT, E. and J. CAUVIN. Datation par le carbone 14 du village Natufien et précéramique de Mureybet, sur l'Euphrate (Syrie).

28 HENRY, D.O. The Natufian site of Rosh Zin. A preliminary report. *PEQ* (1973), 129–40.

29 KENYON, K.M. Excavations at Jericho, 1957–58. *PEQ* (1960), 1–21.

30 — The origins of the Neolithic. *The Advancement of Science* 26 (1969–70), 1–17.

31 KIRKBRIDE, D. A Kebaran rock shelter in Wadi Madamagh. *Man* LVIII (1958), 55–8.

32 — Five seasons at the Pre-Pottery Neolithic village of Beidha in Jordan. *PEQ* (1966), 8–72.

33 — Beidha 1965. *PEQ* (1967), 5–13.

34 — Beidha 1967. *PEQ* (1968), 90–6.

35 — Beidha: Early Neolithic village life south of the Dead Sea. *Antiquity* 42 (1968), 263–74.

36 LIERE, W. VAN and H. DE CONTENSON. A note of five Early Neolithic sites in inland Syria. *AAAS* XIII (1963), 179–209.

37 LOON, M. VAN. The Oriental Institute Excavations at Mureybit, Syria. Preliminary Report on the 1965 Campaign. *JNES* 27 (1968), 265–90.

38 MARKS, A. Prehistoric sites in the Central Negev. *IEJ* 19 (1969), 118–20; *IEJ* 20 (1970), 223–5.

38a NOY, T., A.J. LEGGE and E. S. HIGGS. Excavations at Nahal Oren, Israel. *PPS* 39 (1973), 75–99.

39 PERROT, J. Le Néolithique d'Abu Gosh. *Syria* XXIX (1952), 119–45.

40 — Les deux premières campagnes de fouilles à Munhata. *Syria* XLI (1966), 323–45.

41 — La troisième campagne de fouilles à Munhata. *Syria* XLIII (1966), 49–63.

42 — Le gisement Natoufien de Mallaha (Eynan), Israel. *L'Anthropologie* 70 (1966), 437–83.

43 RONEN, A. New radiocarbon dates from Mount Carmel. *Archaeology* 26 (1973), 60–2.

44 SCHMANDT-BESSERAT, D. The beginnings of the use of clay in Anatolia (in press).

45 STEKELIS, M. and O. Bar-Yosef. Un habitat du Paléolithique superieur à Ein Guev, Israel. *L'Anthropologie* 69 (1965), 176–83.

46 STEKELIS, M. and T. Yizraely. Excavations at Nahal Oren. *IEJ* 13 (1963), 1–12.

47 VITA-FINZI, C. and E. S. HIGGS. Prehistoric economy in the Mount Carmel area of Palestine, site catchment and analysis. *PPS* 36 (1970), 1–37.

48 TELL ABU HUREYRA. Personal communication from the excavator, A. M. T. Moore.

49 WESTERN, C. The ecological interpretation of ancient charcoals from Jericho. *Levant* III (1971), 31–40.

50 WRESCHNER, E. Prehistoric rock-engravings in Nahal ha-Me'arot, Mount Carmel. *IEJ* 21 (1971), 217–18.

Animal and plant remains

51 BRAIDWOOD, R.J. *et al.* Beginnings of village farming communities in southeastern Turkey. *Proc. Nat. Acad. Sci. USA* 68, 6 (1971), 1236–40.

52 CLUTTON-BROCK, J. The primary food animals of the Jericho tell. *Levant* III (1971), 41–55.

53 DUCOS, P. *L'origine des animaux domestiques en Palestine.* Bordeaux 1968.

54 — The Oriental Institute excavations at Mureybit, Syria. Preliminary report on the 1965 campaign. Part V: Les restes de bovides. *JNES* 31 (1972), 295–301.

55 HOPF, M. Plant remains and early farming at Jericho. In *The domestication and exploitation of plants and animals.* Eds. P. Ucko and G. W. Dimbleby. London 1969.

56 LEGGE, A.J. Prehistoric exploitation of the gazelle in Palestine. *Papers in Economic Prehistory.* Ed. E. S. Higgs. Cambridge 1972, 19–24.

57 ZEIST, W. VAN. The Palaeobotany (Mureybit). *JNES* 29 (1970), 167–76.

58 — Palaeobotanical results of the 1970 season at Çayönü. In *Helinium* 3 (1972).

59 — Wild einkorn and barley from Tell Mureybit in Northern Syria. *Acta Bot. Neerl.* 17 (1968), 44–53.

Human remains

60 FEREMBACH, D. Squelettes du Natoufien d'Israel. Etude anthropologique. *L'Anthropologie* 65 (1961), 46–66.

61 — Esquisse d'une histoire raciale de la Palestine du Paléolithique inférieur au Chalcolithique. *Bull. de la Soc. d'Etudes et de Recherches Préhistoriques* 11 (1962), 1–12.

62 — Étude anthropologique des ossements humains de Tell Ramad. *AAAS* XIX (1969), 49–70.

Stone industries

63 CAUVIN, M.-C. L'Industrie natoufienne de Mallaha (Eynan). Note préliminaire. *L'Anthropologie* 70 (1966), 585–94.

63a HOURS, F., L. COPELAND and O. AURENCHE. Les industries paléolithiques du Proche-Orient, essai de corrélation. *L'Anthropologie* 77 (1973), 229–80; 437–96.

64 KIRKBRIDE, D. A brief report on the Pre-Pottery flint cultures of Jericho. *PEQ* (1960), 27–32.

65 MORTENSEN, P. A preliminary study of the chipped stone industry from Beidha. *Acta Archaeologica* 41 (1970), 1–54.

Chapter Two The Zagros Zone: the Development from the Epipalaeolithic to the Neolithic

General

66 BRAIDWOOD, R.J. The Iranian Prehistoric Project. *Iranica Antiqua* I (1961), 3–7.

67 BRAIDWOOD, R.J., B. HOWE, et al. Prehistoric investigations in Iraqi Kurdistan. Chicago 1960.

68 BRAIDWOOD, R.J., B. HOWE and C.A. REED. The Iranian Prehistoric Project. *Science* 133 (1961), 2008–10.

69 SMITH, P.E.L. Iran 9000–4000 BC. The Neolithic. *Expedition* 13 (1971), 6–13.

70 SMITH, P.E.L. and T.C. Young, Jr. The evolution of early agriculture and culture in Greater Mesopotamia; a trial model. In *Population Growth; Anthropological Implications*. Ed. B.B. Spooner. Cambridge, Mass. 1972, 1–59.

71 WRIGHT, G.A. Origins of food production in southwestern Asia. A survey of ideas. *Current Anthropology* 12 (1971), 447–77.

Specific

72 DUPREE, L. Prehistoric archaeological surveys and excavations in Afghanistan, 1959–60, 1961–63. *Science* 146 (1964), 638–40.

73 — Prehistoric research in Afghanistan, 1959–1966. *Trans. American Philosophical Society* 62 (1972), 3–84.

74 HOLE, F. and K.V. FLANNERY. The prehistory of southwestern Iran. A preliminary report. *PPS* 33 (1967), 147–206.

75 HOLE, F., K.V. FLANNERY, J.A. NEELY and H. HELBAEK. *Prehistory and human ecology of the Deh Luran plain*. Ann Arbor 1969.

76 MORTENSEN, P. Excavations at Tepe Guran, Luristan. Early village farming occupation. *Acta Archaeologica* 34 (1964), 110–21.

77 — Seasonal camps and early villages in the Zagros. In *Man, Settlement and Urbanism*. London 1972, 293–7.

78 SMITH, P.E.L. Ganjdareh Tepe. *Iran* VI (1968), 158–60; *Iran* VIII (1970), 78–80; *Iran* X (1972), 165–8.

79 SOLECKI, R.S. Shanidar cave, a late Pleistocene site in N. Iraq. *Report VIth Inqua Congress 1962*. Vol. IV (1964), 413–23.

80 — Prehistory in Shanidar valley, North Iraq. *Science* 139 (1963), 179–93.

81 — A Copper Mineral Pendant from Northern Iraq. *Antiquity* 43 (1969), 311–14.

82 SOLECKI, R.L. Zawi Chemi Shanidar, a post-Pleistocene village site. *Report VIth Inqua Congress 1962*. Vol. IV (1964), 405–12.

Obsidian trade

83 CANN, J.R., J.E. DIXON and C. RENFREW. The characterisation of obsidian. *PPS* 30 (1964), 111ff.

84 RENFREW, C., J.E. DIXON and J.R. CANN. Obsidian and early cultural contacts in the Near East. *PPS* 32 (1966), 30–72.

85 WRIGHT, G.A. and A.A. GORDUS. Distribution and utilisation of obsidian from Lake Van sources between 7500 and 3500 BC. *AJA* 73 (1969), 75–7.

Animal and plant domestication

86 BERGER, R. and R. PROTSCH. The domestication of plants and animals in Europe and the Near East. *Orientalia* 42 (1973), 214–27.

87 BUTZER, K.W. *Environment and Archaeology*. Chicago 1971. 2nd ed. London 1972.

88 HARLAN, J.R. and D. ZOHARY. Distribution of wild wheats and barley. *Science* 153 (1966), 1074–80.

88a OATES, J. The background and the development of early farming communities in Mesopotamia and the Zagros. *PPS* 39 (1973), 147–81.

89 PERKINS, D. JR. The beginnings of animal domestication in the Near East. *AJA* 77 (1973), 279–82.

90 REED, C.A. The pattern of animal domestication in the Prehistoric Near East. In *Domestication and exploitation of plants and Animals*. Eds. P.J. Ucko and G.W. Dimbleby. London 1969, 361–79.

91 ROWTON, M.B. The Woodlands of Ancient Western Asia. *JNES* 26 (1967), 261–77.

92 STRUEVER, S., ed. *Prehistoric Agriculture*. New York 1971.

92a TURNBULL, P.F. and C.A. REED. The fauna for the terminal Pleistocene of Palegawra Cave. *Fieldiana Anthropology* 63 (1974).

93 ZOHARY, M. *Plant life of Palestine – Israel and Jordan*. New York 1962.

Human remains

94 FEREMBACH, D. Le Peuplement du Proche Orient au Chalcolithique et au Bronze Ancien. *IEJ* 9 (1959), 211–19.

95 — Formation et evolution de la brachycephalic au Proche Orient. *Homo* 17 (1966), 160–72.

96 — Etude anthropologique des ossements humains Proto-Néolithiques de Zawi-Chemi Shanidar (Iraq). *Sumer* XXVI (1970), 21–64.

Chapter Three Anatolia and Cyprus

Anatolia

General

97 MELLAART, J. *Earliest civilisations of the Near East*. London 1965.

Specific

98 ANATI, E. Anatolia's earliest Art. *Archaeology* 21 (1968), 22–35.

99 ANGEL, J.L. Early Neolithic skeletons from Çatal Hüyük. Demography and pathology. *Anatolian Studies* XXI (1971), 77–98.

100 BIALOR, P. The chipped stone industry of Çatal Hüyük. *Anatolian Studies* XII (1962), 67–110.

101 BORDAZ, J. The Suberde excavations in Southwest Turkey. An interim report. *Türk Arkeoloji Dergisi* XVII (1969), 43–61.

102 — Erbaba (Beyşehir), 1969. *Anatolian Studies* XX (1970), 7–8.

103 — A preliminary report of the 1969 excavation at Erbaba, a neolithic site near Beyşehir, Turkey. *Türk Arkeoloji Dergisi* XVIII (1970), 59–64.

104 — Current research in the neolithic of South Central Turkey; Suberde, Erbaba and their chronological implications. *AJA* 77 (1973), 282–8.

105 BOSTANCI, E. Y. Researches on the Mediterranean coast of Anatolia: A new Palaeolithic site at Beldibi. *Anatolia* 4 (1959), 129 ff.

106 — The Belbaşı Industry. *Belleten* 26 (1962), 253 ff.

107 — The Mesolithic of Beldibi and Belbaşı. *Antropoloji* 3 (1965), 91–134.

108 BURNHAM, H. Çatal Hüyük; the textiles and twine fabrics. *Anatolian Studies* XV (1965), 169–74.

109 DREW, M., D. PERKINS, JR and P. DALY. Prehistoric domestication of animals. Effects on bone structure. *Science* 171 (1971), 280–2.

110 ESIN, U. and P. BENEDICT. Recent developments in the prehistory of Anatolia. *Current Anthropology* 4 no. 4 (1963), 339–46.

111 FEREMBACH, D. Les hommes du gisement néolithique de Çatal Hüyük. *VII Türk Tarih Kongresi (1970)* 1972, 15–21.

112 — A quoi ressemblait l'Homme néolithique d'Anatolie? *Archaeologia* 17 (1967), 46.

113 — Aperçu sur le peuplement de l'Anatolie et du Moyen Orient au néolithique. *Belleten* 130 (1969), 137–41.

114 FRENCH, D. H. Early pottery sites from Western Anatolia. *Bull. Inst. Arch. London* 5 (1965), 15 ff.

115 — Excavations at Can Hasan, first to sixth preliminary reports in *Anatolian Studies* XII (1962), 27–40; XIII (1963), 29–42; XIV (1964), 125–34; XV (1965), 87–94; XVI (1966), 113–23.

116 FRENCH, D. H., G. C. HILLMAN, S. PAYNE and R. J. PAYNE. Excavations at Can Hasan III, 1969–70. In *Papers in Economic Prehistory*. Ed. E. S. Higgs. Cambridge 1972, 180–90.

117 GARSTANG, J. *Prehistoric Mersin*. Oxford 1953.

118 HELBAEK, H. Textiles from Çatal Hüyük. *Archaeology* 16 (1963), 39–46.

119 — First impressions of the Çatal Hüyük plant husbandry. *Anatolian Studies* XIV (1964), 121–3.

120 — The Plant Husbandry of Hacılar. In *Excavations at Hacılar*. Edinburgh 1970, 189–244.

121 KÖKTEN, K. I. Tarsus-Antalya arasi sahil şeriti üzerinde ve Antalya bölgesinde yapilan tarihöncesi araştirmalari hakkinda. *Türk Arkeoloji Dergisi* VIII (1958), 10 ff.

122 MELLAART, J. Çatal Hüyük West. *Anatolian Studies* XV (1965), 135–56.

123 — *Çatal Hüyük, a Neolithic town in Anatolia*. London 1967.

124 — Excavations at Çatal Hüyük, first to fourth preliminary reports in *Anatolian Studies* XII (1962), 41–65; XIII (1963), 43–103; XIV (1964), 39–119; XVI (1966), 165–91.

125 — *Excavations at Hacılar*. Edinburgh 1970.

126 MORTENSEN, P. The Çatal Hüyük chipped stone industry. Unpublished MSS.

127 NEUNINGER, H., R. PITTIONI and W. SIEGL. Frühkeramikzeitliche Kupfergewinnung in Anatolien. *Archaeologia Austriaca* 35 (1964), 98–110.

128 PAYNE, S. Can Hasan III, The Anatolian aceramic and Greek Neolithic. In *Papers in Economic Prehistory*. Ed. E. S. Higgs. Cambridge 1972, 191–4.

129 PERKINS, D., JR. Fauna of Çatal Hüyük. *Science* 164 (1969), 177–9.

130 PERKINS, D., JR and P. DALY. A hunter's village in neolithic Turkey. *Scientific American* 219 (1968), 96–106.

131 RYDER, M. Report of textiles from Çatal Hüyük. *Anatolian Studies* XV (1965), 175–6.

132 SOLECKI, R. S. Cave-art in Kürtün Ini, a Taurus Mountain site in Turkey. *Man* (1964), 87 ff.

133 TODD, I. A. The obsidian industry of Avla Dağ. *Anatolian Studies* XV (1965), 95 ff.

134 — Aşikli Hüyük, a Protoneolithic site in Anatolia. *Anatolian Studies* XVI (1966), 139–63.

135 — The Neolithic period in Central Anatolia. *Papers of VIIIth International Congress of Pre- and Protohistorical Sciences*. Belgrade 1971.

Cyprus

General

136 CATLING, H. W. The Earliest Settlers in Cyprus. *CAH* I. Cambridge 1970, 542–7.

Specific

137 DIKAIOS, P. *Khirokitia*. Oxford 1953.

138 PELTENBURG, E. J. Interim report on the excavations at Ayios Epiktetos Vrysi in 1969–1971. *Rep. Dept. Ant. Cyprus* 1972, 1–13.

139 STANLEY-PRICE, N. P. A prehistoric survey of the Analiondas region. *Rep. Dept. Ant. Cyprus* 1972, 15–21.

140 WATKINS, T. F. Philia-Drakos site A; pottery, stratigraphy, chronology. *Rep. Dept. Ant. Cyrpus* 1970, 1–9.

141 — Philia. In Cyprus number of *Archaeologia Viva*.

Chapter Four Cultures of the Mesopotamian Lowlands

General

142 MALLOWAN, M. E. L. The development of cities. *CAH* I, 1. Cambridge 1970.

143 PARROT, A. *Archéologie Mesopotamienne* II. Paris 1953.

144 PERKINS, A. The comparative archaeology of Early Mesopotamia. *SAOC* 25 (1957).

145 PORADA, E. The relative chronology of Mesopotamia. In *Chronologies in Old World Archaeology*. Ed. R. Ehrich. Chicago 1965.

Specific

146 ABU ES-SOOF, B. Tell es-Sawwan excavations of the fourth season (spring 1967). Interim report. *Sumer* XXIV (1968), 3–16.

147 al-A'DAMI, K. A. Excavations at Tell es-Sawwan (second season). *Sumer* XXIV (1968) 54–94.

148 BÖKÖNYI, S. The fauna of Umm Dabaghiyah; a preliminary report. *Iraq* XXXV (1973), 9–11.

149 BRAIDWOOD, R. J. *et al.* New Chalcolithic material of Samarra type and its implications. *JNES* 3 (1944), 47–72.

150 — Matarrah. *JNES* 11 (1952), 1–111.

151 BURKHOLDER, G. Ubaid sites and pottery in Saudi Arabia. *Archaeology* 25 (1972), 264–9.

152 DELOUGAZ, P. and H.J. KANTOR. New evidence for the prehistoric and protoliterate culture development of Khuzestan. *Vth International Congress of Iranian Art and Archaeology* 1. Tehran 1972, 14–25.

153 — Chogha Mish. *Iran* XI (1973), 191.

154 FLANNERY, K.V. and J.C. Wheeler. Animal bones from Tell es-Sawwan, Level III (Samarra period). *Sumer* XXIII (1967), 179–82.

155 HELBAEK, H. Traces of plants in the early ceramic site of Umm Dabaghiyah. *Iraq* XXXIV (1972), 17–19.

156 — Early Hassunan vegetable food at Tell es-Sawwan near Samarra. *Sumer* XX (1964), 45–8.

157 — Samarran irrigation agriculture at Choga Mami in Iraq. *Iraq* XXXIV (1972), 35–48.

75 HOLE, F., K.V. FLANNERY, J.A. NEELY and H. HELBACK. *Prehistory and human ecology of the Deh Luran plain*. Ann Arbor 1969.

158 IPPOLITONI, F. The pottery of Tell es-Sawwan, first season. *Mesopotamia* V–VI (1970–71), 105–79.

159 KAPEL, H. *Atlas of stone age cultures of Qatar*. Aarhus 1967.

160 KIRKBRIDE, D. Umm Dabaghiyah, 1971: a preliminary report. *Iraq* XXXIV (1972), 3–19.

161 — Umm Dabaghiyah, 1972. *Iraq* XXXV (1973), 1–7.

162 — Umm Dabaghiyah, 1973. *Iraq* XXXV (1973), 205–9.

162a — Umm Dabaghiyah, 1974. *Iraq* XXXVII (1975).

163 LLOYD, S. and F. SAFAR. Tell Hassuna. *JNES* 4 (1945), 255–89.

164 — Eridu. *Sumer* IV (1948), 115–27.

165 MALLOWAN, M.E.L. Excavations at Tell Chagar Bazar and the archaeological survey of the Khabur region. *Iraq* III (1936).

166 MALLOWAN, M.E.L. and J.C. ROSE. Excavations at Tell Arpachiyah, 1933. *Iraq* II (1935), 1–178.

167 MERPERT, N.Y. and R.M. MUNCHAEV. Yarimtepe. *Sumer* XXV (1969), 125 ff.

168 — Excavations at Yarim Tepe 1970. Second Preliminary report. *Sumer* XXVII (1971), 9–21.

169 — The archaeological research in the Sinjar valley. *Sumer* XXVII (1971), 23–32.

170 — Early agricultural settlements in the Sinjar plain. *Iraq* XXXV (1973), 93–113; 202–3.

171 MESNIL DU BUISSON, H. DU. *Baghouz l'ancien Chorsote*. Leiden 1948.

172 MORTENSEN, P. *Tell Shemshara. The Hassuna Period*. Copenhagen 1970.

173 — A sequence of flint and obsidian tools from Choga Mami. *Iraq* XXXV (1973), 37–53.

174 MUNCHAEV, R.M. and N.Y. MERPERT. New studies of early agricultural settlements in the Sinjar valley. *VIII Congress international des sciences préhistoriques et protohistoriques*. Belgrade 1971.

175 — Sovetskie arheologicheskie issledovania v severo-zapadnom Irake. *Vestnik akademii nauk SSSR* 1 (1970), 105–15.

176 — Rannezemledelcheskie poseleniya sebernoi mesopotamii. *Sov. Arkh.* 3 (1971), 141–69.

177 — Raboti sovetskie arheologov v Irake. *Vestnik akademii nauk SSSR* 1 (1972), 72–8.

178 OATES, J. Ur, Eridu; the prehistory. *Iraq* XXII (1960), 32–50.

179 — The baked clay figurines from Tell es-Sawwan. *Iraq* XXVII (1966), 146–53.

180 — Survey in the region of Mandali and Badra. *Sumer* XXII (1966), 51–60.

181 — Prehistoric investigations near Mandali, Iraq. *Iraq* XXX (1968), 1–20.

182 — Choga Mami 1967–68: A preliminary report. *Iraq* XXXI (1969), 115–52.

183 — A radiocarbon date from Chogha Mami. *Iraq* XXXIV (1972), 49–53.

184 — Prehistoric settlement patterns in Mesopotamia. *Man, Settlement and Urbanism*. London 1972, 299–310.

185 STRONACH, D. The excavations at Ras al Amiya. *Iraq* XXIII (1961), 95–137.

186 VAN DEN BERGHE, L. La nécropole de Hakalan. *Archaeologia* 57 (1973), 49–58.

187 Some results of the third international conference on Asian archaeology in Bahrain, March 1970. *Artibus Asiae* XXXIII (1971), 294–5.

188 WAHIDA, G. The excavations . . . at Tell es-Sawwan, 1966. *Sumer* XXIII (1967), 167–78.

189 EL-WAILLY, F. and B. ABU ES-SOOF. Excavations at Tell es-Sawwan. *Sumer* XXI (1965), 17–32.

190 YASIN, W. Excavations at Tell es-Sawwan, 1969 (6th season). *Sumer* XXVI (1970), 3–11.

Chapter Five The Highland Cultures of Iran

General

191 BOBEK, H. Vegetation. Chapter 8 in *The Cambridge History of Iran, Vol. I. The Land of Iran*. Cambridge 1968, 280–93.

192 DYSON, R.H. Problems in the relative chronology of Iran. *Chronologies in Old World Archaeology*. Ed. E. Ehrich. Chicago 1963.

193 FISHER, W.B., ed. *The Cambridge History of Iran*.

194 HARRISON, J.V. Minerals, Chapter 15 in *The Cambridge History of Iran*, 489–516.

195 McCOWN, D. The comparative stratigraphy of Early Iran. *SAOC* 23 (1941).

196 SMITH, P.E.L. Iran, 9000–4000 BC. The Neolithic. *Expedition* 13 (1971), 6–13.

197 WERTIME, T. Man's first encounter with metallurgy. *Science* 146 (1964), 1257–67.

Zagros

198 GOFF, C.L. Luristan before the Iron Age. *Iran* IX (1971), 131–52.

198a SCHMANDT-BESSERAT, D. The use of clay before pottery in the Zagros. *Expedition* 16 (1974), 11–17.

199 YOUNG, T.C., JR. Survey in Western Iran, 1961. *JNES* 25 (1966), 228–39.

Fars

200 VAN DEN BERGHE, D. Opzoekingen in de Merv Dasht vlakte. *JEOL* 12 (1951–2), 212–14; 13 (1953–4), 400.

Giyan

201 CONTENAU, G. and R. GHIRSHMAN. *Fouilles de Tepe Giyan*. Paris 1935.

Siyalk

202 GHIRSHMAN, R. *Fouilles de Tepe Siyalk* I. Paris 1938.

Tehran Area

203 BOVINGTON, C. and M. MASOUR. *Tehran University Radiocarbon Dates*. (in press)

204 MALEKI, Y. Abstract art and animal motifs among the ceramists of the region of Tehran. *Archaeologia Viva* I (1968), 43–50.

205 NEGAHBAN, E. *Excavations at Tepe Sagzabad and Zage*. Symposium Tehran University, June 1971.

Kerman

206 Caldwell, J. *Investigations at Tal-i-Iblis*. Chicago 1967.

207 LAMBERG-KARLOVSKY, C.C. Excavations at Tepe Yahya, Iran, 1967–69. *American School of Prehistoric Research Bulletin* 27 (1970).

Chapter Six Early Cultures in Transcaucasia and Azerbaijan

General

208 BURNEY, C.A. and D.M. LANG. *The peoples of the hills; Ancient Ararat and Caucasus*. London 1971. Chapter 2 and footnotes.

209 DZHAPARIDZE, O.M. and A.L. DZHAVACH-NISHVILI. *Kultura drevneishogo zemledelichaskogo naseleniya na territorii Grusii*. (Georgian text with Russian resumé.) Tbilisi 1971.

210 KUSHNAREVA, K.H. and T.N. CHUBENISH-VILI. *Drevnie kulturi yughnogo Kavkasa*. Leningrad 1970. Chapter 11.

211 NARIMANOV, I.G. Sur l'agriculture de l'Enéolithique en Azerbaijan. *Sov. Arkh.* 3 (1971), 3–14.

Specific
Shulaveri group

212 CHUBENISHVILI, T.N. and K.H. KUSH-NAREVA. Novie materiali po eneoliti yughnogo Kavkasa. (Georgian text) *Matsne* 6 (1967), 336–62.

213 DZHAPARIDZE, O.M. and A.I. DZHAVACH-NISHVILI. Resultati rabot Kvemo-Kartliiskoi arkheologicheskoi ekspeditii (1965–1966). (Georgian text) *Matsne* 3 (1967), 292–8; 1968, 19–26.

Hajji Firuz

214 DYSON, R.H. A decade in Iran. *Expedition* 11 (1969), 42–3.

215 — Preliminary report on work carried out during 1969. *Bastan Chenassi ve Honar e Iran* 2 (1969), 26.

216 YOUNG, T.C., JR. Sixth and fifth millennium settlements in the Solduz valley, Persia. *ILN* Nov. 3, 1962.

Dalma

217 HAMLIN, C. The 1971 excavations at Seh Gabi, Iran. *Archaeology* 26 (1973), 224–7.

218 YOUNG, T.C., Jr. Dalma painted ware. *Expedition* 5 (1963), 38–9.

Yaniktepe

219 BURNEY, C.A. Excavations at Yanik Tepe, Azerbaijan. *Iraq* XXVI (1964), 55–7.

Soviet Armenia

220 SARDARIAN, S.A. *Primitive Society in Armenia*. Erevan 1967, 327–31.

Kobystan

221 FORMOZOV, A.A. The petroglyphs of Kobystan and their chronology. *Rivista di Scienze preistorichi* XVIII (1963), 91–114.

222 — Ocherki pervobitnomy iskusstvy. *MIA* 165 (1969), 24–59.

Chapter Seven Cultures of the Transcaspian Lowlands

General

223 MASSON, V.M. *Central Asia and the Near East*. (Russian text.) Moscow–Leningrad 1964. (with review in *JNES* 30 (1971), 226 ff.)

224 — Prehistoric settlement patterns in Soviet Central Asia. In *Man, settlement and urbanism*. Eds. P. Ucko, R. Tringham and G.W. Dimbleby. London 1972, 263–77.

225 MASSON, V.M. and V.I, SARIANIDI. *Central Asia. Turkmenia before the Achaemenids*. London 1972. Chapters IV and V, with bibliography.

Specific
Jeitun culture

226 BERDYIEV, O.K. Novii reaskopkii na poselenii Pessedzhik i Chakmakly depe. *Karakumskie Drevnosti* II (1968), 10–17.

227 — Nekatorie resultati izucheniya drevnezemledelcheskii poselenii (on Pessejik wall paintings). *Karakumskie Drevnosti* III (1970), 14–32.

228 KOROBKOVA, G.F. On Chopan, Togolok and Pessejik in *Karakumskie Drevnosti* I (1968), 54–61.

229 MASSON, V.M. *Poselenie Dzheitun*. *MIA* 180, Moscow 1970.

Caspian caves

230 McBURNEY, C.B.M. The cave of Ali Tappeh. *PPS* 34 (1968), 385–413.

231 COON, C.S. *Cave explorations in Iran, 1949*. Philadelphia 1951.

232 — *The Seven caves*. New York 1957.

Namazga I

233 CHLOPIN, I.N. *Eneolit yudnich oblastei Srednei Asii*. Moscow–Leningrad 1963.

Yalangach

234 CHLOPIN, I.N. *Pamyatnika razvitogo eneolita yugo-vostochnoi Turkmenii*. Moscow–Leningrad 1964.

Namazga II

235 MASSON, V.M. *Eneolit yudnich oblastei Srednei Asii*. Moscow–Leningrad 1962. These four

volumes in the series *Arkheologia SSR* contain rich illustrative material.

Late Namazga II and III

236 SARIANIDI, V.I. *Pamyatniki posdnego eneolita yugo-vostochnoi Turkmenii.* Moscow–Leningrad 1965.

Chapter Eight Early Pottery Cultures in the Levant

General

1 ANATI, E. *Palestine before the Hebrews.* London 1963.
237 CAUVIN, J. *Les outillages néolithiques de Byblos et du litoral libanais. Fouilles de Byblos* IV. Paris 1968.
237a — *Religions néolithiques de Syro-Palestine.* Paris 1972.
18 CONTENSON, H. DE. Tell Ramad, a village site of Syria of the 7th and 6th millennia BC. *Archaeology* 24 (1971), 278–85.
238 MOORE, M.T. The Late Neolithic in Palestine. *Levant* V (1973), 36–68.
5 PERROT, J. *La Préhistoire Palestinienne* (Supplément au Dictionnaire de la Bible). Paris 1968.
6 PRAUSNITZ, M.W. *From hunter to farmer and trader.* Jerusalem 1970.

Specific
Lebanon

239 CAUVIN, J. and M.-C. CAUVIN. Des ateliers 'Campigniens' au Liban. In *La Préhistoire; problèmes et tendances.* Ed. *CNRS*, 1968, 103–16.
240 COPELAND, L. Neolithic village sites in the Southern Beqa'a, Lebanon. *MUSJ* XLV (1969), 85–106.
241 DUNAND, M. Rapport préliminaire sur les fouilles de Byblos, 1957–59. *Bulletin du Musée de Beyrouth* 16 (1961), 69 ff.
241a — *Fouilles de Byblos* V. Paris 1973.
242 KIRKBRIDE, D. Early Byblos and the Beqa'a. *MUSJ* XLV (1969), 45–59.
243 PERROT, J. Néolithique du Liban. *MUSJ* XLV (1969), 44 ff.

Amuq

244 BRAIDWOOD, R.J. and L. BRAIDWOOD. *Excavations in the Plain of Antioch. OIP* LXI. Chicago 1959.
245 GARSTANG, J. Excavations at Sakje-geuzi in North Syria. *LAAA* 24 (1937), 132 ff.
246 MAXWELL-HYSLOP, R., *et al.* Archaeological survey of the plain of Jabbul. *PEQ* (1942), 8–20.
247 PERROT, J. (*apud*) M. MELLINK. Archaeology in Asia Minor (Tell Turlu). *AJA* 68 (1964), 156.

Syria

248 CAUVIN, J. and M.-C. CAUVIN. Sondage à Tell Assouad. *AAAS* XXII (1972), 85–96.
249 CAUVIN, M.-C. Problèmes d'emmanchement des faucilles du Proche-Orient; les documents de Tell Assouad (Djezireh, Syrie). *Paléorient* I (1973), 101–6.
250 CONTENSON, H. DE. Poursuite des recherches dans le sondage à l'ouest du Temple de Baal (1955–60). Rapport préliminaire. *Ugaritica* IV. Paris 1962, 477–519.
251 — New correlations between Ras Shamra and Al Amuq. *BASOR* 172 (1963), 35–40.
252 — Découvertes récentes dans la domaine de Néolithique en Syrie. *L'Anthropologie* 70 (1966), 388–91.
253 — Notes on the chronology of the Near Eastern Neolithic. *BASOR* 184 (1966), 2–6.
254 — Contribution à l'étude du Néolithique en Syrie. *MUSJ* XLV (1969), 63–77.
255 — Sondage ouverte sur l'acropole de Ras Shamra. *Syria* XLVII (1970), 1–23.
255a CONTENSON, H. DE. Le niveau Halafien de Ras Shamra. *Syria* XLVX (1973), 13–33.
256 WOOLLEY, C.L. The prehistoric pottery of Carchemish. *Iraq* I (1934), 146–54.

Palestine

257 KAPLAN, J. EIN EL JARBA. Chalcolithic remains in the Plain of Esdraelon. *BASOR* 194 (1969), 2–38.
258 MELLAART, J. The Neolithic site of Ghrubba. *ADAJ* III (1956), 24–33.
259 PERROT, J. Les deux premières campagnes de fouilles à Munhata. *Syria* XLI (1964), 323–45.
260 — La troisième campagne de fouilles à Munhata (1964). *Syria* XLIII (1966), 49–63.
261 — La Préhistoire. (On Munhata) *Bible et Terre Sainte* 93 (1967), 4–16.

Chapter Nine Southeastern Europe: the Aegean and the Southern Balkans

General

261a THEOCHARES, D. *Neolithic Greece.* Athens 1973.
262 TITOV, V.S. *Neolit Grecii.* Moscow 1969.
263 TRINGHAM, R. *Hunters, fishers and farmers of Eastern Europe, 6000–3000 BC.* London 1971 (with rich bibliography).
264 WEINBERG, S. The Stone Age in the Aegean in *CAH* I, Cambridge 1970.

Specific
Greece

265 EVANS, J.D. Excavations in the Neolithic Settlement of Knossos, 1957–60. *BSA* 59 (1964), 132–240.
266 — Neolithic Knossos; the growth of a settlement. *PPS* 37 (1971), 95–117.
267 JACOBSON, T.W. Excavations at Porto Cheli and vicinity. Preliminary Report II; The Franchthi cave, 1967–8. *Hesperia* 38 (1969), 343–81.
268 JARMAN, M.R. and H.N. JARMAN. The fauna and economy of Early Neolithic Knossos. Knossos Neolithic, Part II. *BSA* 63 (1968), 241–61.
269 MILOJČIĆ, V. Ergebnisse der deutschen Ausgrabungen in Thessalien, 1953–1958. *Jahrb. des röm.-germ. Zentralmuseums Mainz* 6 (1959), 1–56.
270 — *Die deutschen Ausgrabungen auf den Argissa – Magula in Thessalien* I. Bonn 1962.
271 RENFREW, J.M. A report on recent finds of

carbonised cereal grains and seeds from Prehistoric Thessaly. *Thessalika* 5 (1966), 21–36.

272 — *Palaeoethnobotany.* London 1972.

273 RODDEN, R.J. Excavations at the Early Neolithic site at Nea Nikomedia, Greek Macedonia.
PPS 28 (1962), 267–88.

274 — A European link with Çatal Hüyük: un-
covering a 7th millennium settlement in Macedonia. Part 1 – Site and pottery. *ILN* April 11.
Part 2 – Burials and the shrine. *ILN* April 18
1964.

275 — An Early Neolithic village in Greece.
Scientific American (1965), 212.

276 THEOCHARES, D.R. *I Avgi tis Thessalikis
Proistorias.* Volos 1967.

277 — Nea Makri. Eine grosse neolithische Siedlung
in der Nähe von Marathon. *Ath. Mitt.* 71 (1956),
1–29.

278 ZEIST, W. VAN and S. BOTTEMA. Plant
husbandry in Early Neolithic Nea Nikomedeia,
Greece. *Acta Bot. Neerl.* 20 (1971), 524–38.

Bulgaria

279 BOEV, P. *Die Rassentypen der Balkanhalbinsel
und der ostägäischen Inselwelt und deren Bedeutung
für die Herkunft ihrer Bevölkerung.* Bulgarian
Academy of Sciences, Sofia 1972.

280 DENNELL, R.W. The interpretation of plant
remains; Bulgarian 1970 excavations. *Papers in
Economic Prehistory.* Ed. E.S. Higgs. Cambridge
1972, 149–59.

281 DETEV, P. La localité préhistorique près du
village de Mouldava. *Praistoricheskotp seliske
pri celo Muldave. God. Nar. Arkh. Muz.* VI
(1968), 9–48.

282 GEORGIEV, G.I. Die Erforschung der neo-
litischen und bronzezeitlichen Siedlungshügel
in Bulgarien. *ZfA* 1 (1967), 139–59.

283 GIMBUTAS, M. The Neolithic cultures of the
Balkan peninsula. In *Aspects of the Balkans.* Ed.
H. Birnbaum. The Hague – Paris 1972, 9–48.

284 — Old Europe *c.* 7000–3500 BC. The earliest
European civilisations before the infiltration of
the Indo-European peoples. *Journal of Indo-
European Studies* 1 (1973), 1–19.

284a — *The Gods and Goddesses of Old Europe, c. 7000–
3500 BC.* London 1974.

285 QUITTA, H. and G. KOHL. Neue Radio-
karbondaten zum Neolithikum und zur frühen
Bronzezeit Südost Europas und der Sovjetunion.
ZfA 3 (1969), 226–8.

286 VAJSOVA, H. Stand der Jungsteinzeitforschung
in Bulgarien. *Slovenska Archeologia* XIV, 1
(1966), 8–11.

287 WATERBOLK, H.T. Working with radiocarbon dates. *PPS* 37 (1971), 15–33.

Yugoslavia

288 GALOVIĆ, R. Die Starčevo kultur in Yugo-
slawien. In *Die Anfänge des Neolithikums vom
Orient bis Nord Europa* II. Cologne 1968.

289 GIMBUTAS, M. Excavations at Anza, Macedonia. *Archaeology* 25 (1972), 112–23.

290 SREJOVIĆ, D. *Lepenski Vir.* London 1971.

Chapter Ten Epipalaeolithic and Neolithic in the Southeast Mediterranean

291 ALIMEN, M.H. and M.-J. STEVE, eds. *Fischer
Weltgeschichte* I, *Vorgeschichte.* 1966. Chapter
D1–3, Africa, 148–99.

292 ARKELL, A.J. and P.J. UCKO. Review of Predynastic development in the Nile Valley. *Current
Anthropology* 6 (1965), 145–65.

292a BARICH, B.E. and F. MORI. Missione paletno-
logica Italiana nel Sahara Libyca. *Origini* IV
(1970), 79–144.

293 CLARK, J.D. A re-examination of the evidence
for agricultural origins in the Nile Valley. *PPS*
37 (1971), 34–79.

294 DERRICOURT, R.M. Radiocarbon chronology
for Egypt and North Africa. *JNES* 30 (1971),
271–92.

295 LAJOUX, J.-D. *The rock paintings of Tassili.*
London 1963.

296 LHOTE, H. *The search for the Tassili frescoes.*
London, 2nd ed., 1973.

297 McBURNEY, C.B.M. *The Stone Age of northern
Africa.* Harmondsworth 1960.

298 — *The Haua Fteah (Cyrenaica) and the Stone Age
of the South-East Mediterranean.* Cambridge 1967.

299 MORI, F. *Tadrart Acacus. Arte rupestre e culture
del Sahara preistorico.* Rome 1965.

299a — Figure umane incisi di tipo ittiomorfo
scoperte nel Tadrart Acacus. *Origini* I (1967),
37–52.

299b — Proposto per uno attribuzione alle fine del
Pleistocene delle incisioni dalla fasi piu antica
dell'arte rupestre Sahariana. *Origini* V (1971),
7–20.

299c — The earliest Saharan rock engravings. *Antiquity* 58 (1974), 87–92.

300 REED, C.A. The Yale University prehistoric
expedition to Nubia, 1962–1965. *Discovery* I
(1966), 16–23.

301 SMITH, P.E.L. Expedition to Kom Ombo.
Archaeology 17 (1964), 209–10.

302 — The Late Palaeolithic of Northeast Africa in
the light of recent research. *American Anthropo-
logist* 68 (1966), 326–55.

303 — New investigations in the late Pleistocene
archaeology of the Kom Ombo Plain (Upper
Egypt). *Quaternaria* IX (1967), 141–52.

304 WENDORF, F., R. SAID and R. SCHILD.
Egyptian Prehistory; some new concepts. *Science*
169 (1970), 1161–71.

Chapter Eleven Conclusions

305 MELLAART, J. Bronze Age and earlier languages
of the Near East; an archaeological view.
Archaeological Theory and Practice. London, 1973,
163–72.